After the Gold Rush

After the Gold Rush

Tarnished Dreams in the Sacramento Valley

DAVID VAUGHT

The Johns Hopkins University Press

Baltimore

Johns Hopkins Paperback edition, 2009
2 4 6 8 9 7 5 3 1

The Johns Hopkins University Press
2715 North Charles Street
Baltimore, Maryland 21218-4363
www.press.jhu.edu

The Library of Congress has catalogued the hardcover edition of this book as follows:
Vaught, David, 1958–
After the Gold Rush : tarnished dreams in the Sacramento Valley /
David Vaught.
p. cm.
Includes bibliographical references and index.
ISBN-13: 978-0-8018-8497-9 (hardcover : alk. paper)
ISBN-10: 0-8018-8497-7 (hardcover : alk. paper)
1. Agriculture—Economic aspects—California—Sacramento Valley—History.
2. Sacramento Valley (Calif.)—History. I. Title. II. Series.
HD1775.C2V38 2006
338.109794′5—dc22
2006017407

A catalog record for this book is available from the British Library.

ISBN 13: 978-0-8018-9257-8
ISBN 10: 0-8018-9257-0

To my mother and in memory of my father

CONTENTS

PART FOUR   THE NEW GENERATION EMERGES

ACKNOWLEDGMENTS

This book would not have happened without the wonderful people at the Yolo County Archives in Woodland, California. Like most repositories of local records, the Yolo County Archives operates on a shoestring. It is open one day a week and only for a few hours at that. When I first walked in the door in June of 2000 not expecting much, Howard Moore, one of the many volunteers who keep the place running, showed me Deed Book L, which contained a detailed hand-drawn map of the Big Ranch on Putah Creek. Wow, I thought, there might be something for me here. The archivist, Mel Russell, a true professional in every sense of the word, agreed a few months later to keep the small reading room open for me every day for two weeks. Seventy-two days later by my count (in two-week trips over the next four years), thanks in no small part to Mel's incredible patience and expertise, my research finally came to an end. On most of those days, volunteer Virginia Isaacs "supervised" me, photocopied countless documents, and kept me going with her wicked sense of humor. When Virginia could not come in, Shipley Walters, *the* historian of Yolo County, stepped in for her. I am most grateful to them as well as to the Friends of the Yolo County Archives, without whom there would be no archives. Thank you all very much.

Other individuals and institutions (in California unless otherwise indicated) also made the research possible. I extend my deep appreciation to the librarians and staffs at the Bancroft Library, University of California, Berkeley; California State Archives, Sacramento; California State Library, Sacramento; California State Railroad Museum, Sacramento; Davis Public Library; Dixon Public Library; the National Archives, College Park, Maryland; the National Archives, Pacific Sierra Region, San Bruno; Placer County Archives, Auburn; Solano County Administrator's Office, Fairfield; Solano County Archives, Fairfield; U.S. Bureau of Land Management, California State Office, Sacramento; and Yolo County Surveyor's

Office, Woodland. Special thanks go to John Skarstad at the Department of Special Collections, University of California Library, Davis; and Pat Johnson at the Sacramento Archives and Museum Collection Center. Generous and greatly appreciated financial support came from the National Endowment for the Humanities, which helped me launch this project with a Fellowship for University Teachers and finish it with a Summer Stipend. And at Texas A&M University, grants from the Program to Enhance Scholarly and Creative Activities, Glasscock Center for Humanities Research, College of Liberal Arts, and Department of History paid for much of my travel and research expenses.

As always, I relied heavily on Michael Magliari, who knows more about California history than anyone I know, to read each chapter critically as they rolled off the printer. My debt to him is incalculable. Don Pisani showed me the ropes at the National Archives, provided good company on a couple of other research trips, shared his vast knowledge of California land policy, and gave invaluable feedback on the manuscript itself. Brian Linn, Linda Kato, Ethel Vaught, and Joe Bax also read the manuscript in full and provided insightful and enthusiastic comments. Joe, a former student of mine, taught me much more than I ever taught him, especially about the wonders of Lexis-Nexis and how to decipher nineteenth-century legal verbiage. Steve Wee, a historian of Putah Creek in his own right, shared with me census records, maps, and other crucial documents. David Brody, my mentor in graduate school, did not read a word of the manuscript this time, but his voice was in my head every time I sat down to write. Others who graciously offered assistance of one kind or another along the way include Quince Adams, Hal Barron, Stuart Graybill, Doug Hurt, Bill Issel, Jeff Kolnick, Joann Larkey, John Lofland, Peter Moyle, Don Palm, David Robertson, Jim Rose, Susan Rugh, and Richard Schwab. I have not at all times followed everyone's advice, but I have always valued it highly.

Bob Brugger, my editor at the Johns Hopkins University Press, deserves special mention. Upon reading rough drafts of the first few chapters, he uttered the words every historian dreads: "You're not writing another dissertation." With his incisive comments at the forefront of my mind, I revamped those chapters, began the next one, and in the process really hit my stride. Kevin Starr, one of my heroes, read the manuscript for the Press and overwhelmed me with his generosity. Many thanks to Ethel Vaught, who drew the maps with patience and precision, and to copyeditor Barbara Lamb, who enhanced the quality of the final product substantially. I wish also to thank the Western History Association for granting permission to reprint material that appeared previously in my article, "After the Gold Rush: Replicating the Rural Midwest in the Sacramento Valley,"

Western Historical Quarterly 34 (Winter 2003): 447–67; and to acknowledge the copyright of the Agricultural History Society for three additional articles: "State of the Art—Rural History, or Why Is There No Rural History of California?" *Agricultural History* 74 (Fall 2000): 759–74; "Putah Creek: Water, Land, Wheat, and Community in the Sacramento Valley in the 1850s," *Agricultural History* 76 (Spring 2002): 326–37; and "A Tale of Three Land Grants on the Northern California Borderlands," *Agricultural History* 78 (Spring 2004): 140–54.

Friends and family sustained me through good times and bad. On the conference circuit, my "ag" buddies—Doug Helms, Doug Hurt, Don Pisani, Bill Rowley, and Fred Williams—and I have more fun than should be allowed. Back in Texas, I am especially grateful to my two most valuable friends, Quince Adams and Chip Dawson. Colleagues Troy Bickham, Daniel Bornstein, Walter Kamphoefner, John Lenihan, and Brian Linn offered their good cheer as well, especially on Friday afternoons. Walter Buenger, friend first and department head second, assisted my endeavors in every way possible and with unfailing enthusiasm. Many thanks also to my sister, Katy, and sister-in-law Linda Kato for their unwavering support. At home, my wife, Ethel, and daughter, Diana, survived my "grumpy" periods. Their love, joy, and laughter mean everything to me. And long before I thought much about history, my parents, Robert and Marilyn, instilled in me a strong work ethic, an appetite for achievement, a fondness for storytelling, and a passion for all things Californian. I dedicate this book to them.

Please note, finally, that I have reserved most of my historiographical remarks for the Essay on Sources at the end of the book. Readers who want to know where this narrative stands in the larger context of American rural history and California studies might want to start there.

After the Gold Rush

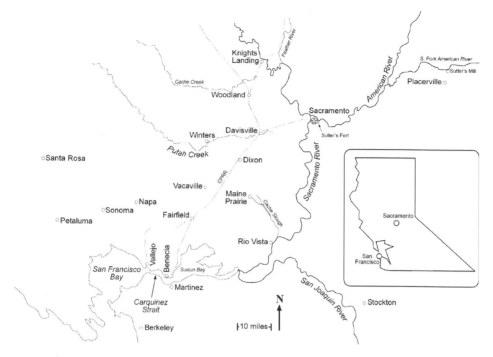

Putah Creek and vicinity, northern California, in the second half of the nineteenth century. Ethel Vaught.

"Glorious"

"My eye was caught with the glimpse of something shining in the bottom of the ditch. . . . I reached my hand down and picked it up; it made my heart thump, for I was certain it was gold. The piece was about half the size and of the shape of a pea. Then I saw another."[1] So recalled James Marshall of that fateful moment of discovery along the south fork of the American River. It could not have happened to a less likely fellow. A carpenter by trade, Marshall had wandered through life in obscurity, haunted by misfortune and his own restlessness. In August 1847, he stumbled upon work as a construction superintendent for a sawmill near the village of Coloma in the foothills of the Sierra Nevada. Marshall's employer, John Sutter, wanted lumber for his own use and to sell to settlers at his New Helvetia colony, the center of trade and communication in the Sacramento Valley, about forty-five miles downstream from the mill site. As the mill neared completion, Marshall noticed that the tailrace needed to be deepened to accommodate the volume of water necessary to turn the wheel. On the morning of January 24, 1848, while inspecting the progress of his crew's work, Marshall spotted the gleam that made his heart thump. His words send shivers down one's spine to this day. The gold rush, the epic adventure that ensued, changed the course of history in countless ways—many familiar, even legendary, others still waiting to be told.[2]

The pea-shaped nuggets, grains, and flakes that Marshall found were known as *placer gold,* from a Spanish word meaning a place near the bank of a stream where alluvial deposits collected. They had been waiting to be found for a long time. Some 200 million years earlier, when the mighty Sierra Nevada thrust through the surface of the earth, long ribbons of molten gold ore flowed up into fissures in the granite rock. Over the centuries, powerful glacial and climatic forces tore loose particles of gold and washed them into rivers, where they lodged on sandbars, behind stones, or in potholes in the banks or in streambeds. Generations of native Californians could not have missed the gold, but they considered it of little value, while Spaniards, Mexicans, and previous Anglos simply missed it altogether. Marshall himself found it by accident. The action of the water running through the dug-out tailrace freed the glittering granules from their hiding. That very process of digging and washing became the method that tens of thousands of argonauts, armed with picks, shovels, and pans, would soon use in their search for gold.

The excitement built slowly at first. Marshall's men did not drop their tools and run off looking for more; instead, they assumed that the discovery was a fluke and went back to work. On January 28, after four days of more shiny findings, Marshall could no longer contain his curiosity. Taking a few samples with him, he rode over to New Helvetia to consult Sutter. Behind a locked door, they conducted several tests that Sutter had found in an article in his copy of *Encyclopaedia Americana*. "I declared this to be gold of the finest quality, of at least 23 carats," Sutter remembered.[3] At that point, Marshall became the first to catch gold fever, scurrying back to Coloma in the rain in the middle of the night to start prospecting at daybreak. More concerned with lumber, Sutter rode over the next day and persuaded the men to finish the mill and to say nothing to outsiders, in exchange for allowing them to dig for gold in their spare time. Even as the news leaked out over the next several months (Sutter himself could not resist gossiping to his friends), it attracted very little attention. Nobody took it particularly seriously. Rumors, legends, and boasts of gold, after all, had fooled many a Californian since the days of Spanish exploration. The one time gold had been found in the mountains north of Los Angeles, in 1842, the deposit was shallow and very limited. Even when the two weekly newspapers in San Francisco mentioned the Sutter mill discovery—the *Californian* on March 15 and the *California Star* ten days later—the response was negligible.

Sam Brannan, an enterprising merchant and real estate speculator, then took matters into his own hands. In early April, Brannan saw the diggings along the American River for himself and calculated that more money might be made from the miners than from the mines. He spent the next several weeks purchasing every article of merchandise he could get his hands on that would be in demand by gold seekers and stockpiled them in his store at New Helvetia. On May 12, he bought enough gold dust to fill a jar and rode down to San Francisco. Parading through town, waving the jar in one hand and his hat in the other, he shouted over and over, "Gold! Gold! Gold from the American River!"[4] The bubble of collective restraint burst. Two weeks later, the previously skeptical *Californian* described both the scene and the spirit: "The whole country from San Francisco to Los Angeles and from the seashore to the base of the Sierra Nevada resounds to the sordid cry of gold, gold!, GOLD! while the field is left half planted, the house half built, and everything neglected but the manufacture of shovels and pick-axes."[5] The paper also announced that it was suspending publication because it's staff, subscribers, and advertisers had all left for the goldfields. Brannan's store, meanwhile, grossed up to $5,000 a day through the summer and fall.

While Californians dropped everything and flocked to the foothills, skepticism prevailed throughout the rest of the country. "Doubts still hovered in the minds of the great mass," wrote one observer. "They could not conceive that such a treasure could have lain there so long undiscovered. The idea seemed to convict them of stupidity."[6] Thomas O. Larkin, among the most prominent Americans in California, sent the *Californian*'s announcement to Secretary of State James Buchanan, but received no response. The *New York Herald* printed a letter from California that predicted a "Peruvian harvest of precious metals."[7] Another letter, in the *Philadelphia North American*, boasted, "Your streams have minnows in them, and ours are paved with gold."[8] Not until President James K. Polk confirmed the strike in his annual message to Congress on December 5, however, did the gold craze spread over the whole country. Polk welcomed the news as a justification of his policies in acquiring the Mexican cession. In evidence, he cited a report from a U.S. Army captain declaring that there was enough gold in California to pay the cost of the Mexican War "a hundred times over."[9] Polk not only released the report to the press, he also placed 230 ounces of American River gold on display at the War Department in Washington, D.C. The president's endorsement, backed by hard evidence, transformed rumor and skepticism into hard news and unrestrained enthusiasm.

Day after day, wave after wave, came the gold seekers, often selling or mortgaging their homes and farms, taking out life savings, or borrowing from friends or family to finance their journey. There were three main routes available to them: around Cape Horn, by way of the Isthmus of Panama, or overland. The most eager took to the sea in the winter of 1849, fearing that all the gold would be gone if they waited until the spring thaw, and most of them took the Panama shortcut, which took at most half as long as the five-to-eight-month, 18,000-nautical-mile journey around the Horn. Either way, seasickness, spoiled food, stagnant water, and months of inactivity took their toll. In the long run, more than twice as many gold seekers came by land as by sea. The two main routes, already established by earlier emigrants, were the California Trail, by way of the Platte River, South Pass, and the Humboldt Sink; and the Santa Fe Trail, from Missouri through the territory newly acquired by conquest from Mexico, with various branches leading to

Los Angeles. The greatest menace to overland travelers was not Indians, as many feared, but a combination of disease (cholera especially), injuries from accidents, and the temptation to rely on a number of useless "emigrant guides." One way or another, more than 40,000 argonauts found their way to California in 1849.

The more that arrived, the greater the mania became. Large city newspapers around the country featured daily articles on gold discoveries, with small-town weeklies often reprinting the most sensational, blurring fantasy and reality in the process. Gold was so abundant, one such story read, "that there is not necessity for washing the earth; $700 per day is the amount by each man."[10] The imagery of the fabled Spanish Empire that captured the imagination of the gold seekers came as much from eastern newspapers as from California itself. References to El Dorado, *La Bonanza*, "the dreams of Cortez and Pizarro," "the Age of Gold," and Ponce de León filled the pages of urban and rural papers across the country.[11] The same papers also published much practical information for budding argonauts, including calls for companies of emigrants to organize, advertisements for products they might need on their journey (especially guns, supposedly needed to fight off the Indians), and, most significantly, personal reports direct from California of hometown success stories. Even the faintest of heart could not resist letters from neighbors describing gold digging along rivers called the American, Feather, Yuba, and Mokelumne, where fortunes of tens of thousands of dollars were just waiting to be made.

Once the hazards of crossing the Great Plains or sailing the open seas were behind them, the argonauts arrived ready to hit the ground running, full to the brim with enthusiasm and optimism. It was a state of mind very hard to articulate, though Stephen J. Field, the future U.S. Supreme Court justice, tried his best three decades later. On his first day in San Francisco in December 1849, after a long, tiresome voyage from New York, Field spent two of the only three dollars he had to his name on the cheapest breakfast he could find. As he strolled through the city, however, his worries vanished. "There was something exhilarating and exciting in the atmosphere which made everyone cheerful and buoyant. . . . Everyone in greeting me said, 'It is a glorious country,' or 'Isn't it a glorious country?' or 'Did you ever see such a glorious country?' or something to that effect. In every case the word 'glorious' was sure to come out. There was something infectious in the use of the word, or rather in the feeling, which made its use natural. I had not been out many hours that morning before I caught the infection; and though I had but a single dollar in my pocket and no business whatever, and did not know where I was to get the next meal, I found myself saying to everybody I met, 'It is a glorious country.'"[12] Field's pronouncement was more than just an expression of exuberance. For a brief but electrifying moment, he and his fellow argonauts found themselves face-to-face with something commensurate with their capacity to dream.

Therein lay the great irony of the gold rush. The more people who "caught the infection," the less likely they were to sustain the "glorious" moment. Success was hardly a sure thing, even in the earliest stages. Most argonauts were rank amateurs—"green-horns," as they often called themselves.[13] They had trouble, for example, deciding whether to stay put and dig deeper at one location or search for even richer diggings. Many, fooled by a prevailing geologic myth, abandoned the riverbeds and climbed higher up into the canyons and gorges, believing that all the gold had washed down from a single source—a fountainhead that, if found, would yield unimaginable riches. Still, by the end of 1848, some 6,000 miners had found $10 million worth of gold. The amount produced tripled in 1849, but the number of miners to share in it grew by a factor of seven. By 1852, the peak year, the output was $80 million and the number of miners exceeded 100,000, with argonauts now migrating from every corner of the globe. Not only did the individual miner's average daily return decline dramatically, but so too did the sheer amount of placer gold in the beds and banks of streams. There were even richer deposits far below the surface in solid rock or deep in the gravelly hillsides, but mining them required sophisticated engineering techniques, heavy equipment, and enormous amounts of capital. "The miners are beginning to discover," commented the *Alta California* late in 1851, "that they are engaged in a science and a profession, and not in a mere adventure."[14] Said one frustrated argonaut more succinctly, "It takes a gold mine to work a gold mine."[15]

The more that reality became apparent, the more the glory of El Dorado faded. Letters from home, stories in newspapers, and entries in diaries increasingly focused on the dark side of life in the mines—exhausting work, wildly inflated prices, overwhelming loneliness, illness and disease, and prevalence of death. "It's an everyday occurrence," wrote one prospector in August 1851, "to see a coffin carried on the shoulders of two men, who are the only mourners and only witnesses of the burial of some stranger whose name they do not know."[16] "Suicides, caused by disappointment," wrote another, "are as numerous as the deaths resulting from natural causes."[17] There was even a desperate kind of humor in the naming of many of the camps—Hell's Delight, Gouge Eye, Devil's Retreat, Murder's Bar, Poverty Hill, and Hangtown. As the prospects for individuals to strike it rich declined and all but disappeared by 1852, depression and disillusionment descended over the picked-over goldfields, where elation and dreams had abounded only a short time before.

Much about the gold rush—from Marshall's discovery, to Brannan's gleeful cry, to the great migration of argonauts, to their ultimate disappointment—has become part of American folklore. Yet, this seminal event still generates considerable excitement and fascination—almost as much today, one might argue from the plethora of sesquicentennial books and essays that have appeared, as during the "days of '49" themselves.[18] While the debate over the meaning, impact, and legacy of these fabled times continues, few question Hubert Howe Bancroft's famous description, itself approaching its sesquicentennial, of the participants themselves—"the toiling farmer, whose mortgage loomed above the growing family, the briefless lawyer, the starving student, the quack, the idler, the harlot, the gambler, the hen-pecked husband, the disgraced, [as well as] many earnest, enterprising, honest men and devoted women."[19]

Farmers stood at the top of Bancroft's list for good reason. In the 1880s, when he wrote, farmers constituted well over half the American population and agriculture had long since passed mining in California in economic importance. We know a fair amount about the farmers-turned-miners who journeyed westward in search of gold, especially from the rich diaries and letters of argonaut William Swain.[20] The great majority of them came via an overland route, fully expecting to return to their farms after plundering California of its treasures, but never actually hit pay dirt. They were predominantly male (more than 90 percent), young (under thirty), and by the end of their stint in the mines had lived a lifetime of adventure. Many, such as Swain, returned home empty-handed, while others, at least in the words of one recent account, "simply vanished into a California landscape once golden and now simply remote."[21]

Such a comment reveals how little we know about the miners-turned-farmers who remained in California. Theirs is a remarkable if obscure story. Far from vanishing into the landscape, these farmers, still in the prime of their lives, helped transform the landscape into one of the most productive agricultural regions in the world. They began by supplying miners in the foothills and residents of San Francisco and Sacramento with much of their grain and beef. As wheat production skyrocketed toward the end of the 1860s, they helped California earn its reputation as "the granary of the world." And as the state's great bonanza wheat era began to wane in the late 1880s, many of them (or their sons) participated in the extraordinary transformation to specialty crops. Throughout, they shared the same point of reference. Like Judge Field, they never forgot that first "glorious" moment in California when anything seemed possible. The sheer excitement, supreme optimism, and high drama of the gold rush both motivated and haunted them for the rest of their lives.

In their efforts to strike it rich in California after the gold rush—to, in effect, recapture and vindicate lost hopes—farmers in the Sacramento Valley tried, early on, to replicate the Midwest, "back home" to the overwhelming majority of them. That meant committing themselves not only to materialistic goals but to community life as well. At mid-century, most American farmers were market participants of varying degrees of enthusiasm, but they still strongly believed in the traditional values of rural life—hard work, mutuality, family, and religion. The gold rush did not turn farmers into capitalists, nor did it undermine their agrarian principles. While their basic values did not change, the pressure to live up to them—to succeed both economically and socially—increased enormously. Having found the rigors of mining too severe and the earnings too meager, they turned to agriculture and rural life with the same intensity of expectation that had brought them to California in the first place. Admitting failure a second time would simply not be an option, even with the ravages of flood and drought, monumental disputes over Mexican land titles, mass confusion over federal and state land policies, and the vagaries of local, national, and world markets that made farming in the Sacramento Valley in the latter half of the nineteenth century an immense challenge.

These distinctive features in the end foiled farmers' attempts to make the West the Midwest but provided other golden opportunities. Indeed, this atmosphere—highly competitive and charged with emotion—unleashed the full spectrum of farmers' energies, from speculation, arrogance, and corruption to persistence, hope, and creativity. The result was a potent combination of entrepreneurial relentlessness and agrarian virtue that created a rural culture unlike any in American history. Farmers—whether cattle, wheat, or fruit, large-scale or small, landowners, squatters, or "swamplanders"—produced with a zeal that often defied belief, but with little regard to the consequences—immediate or long term, economic or environmental. They exhibited the same boomtown mentality in their communities, where, feeling at home almost immediately, they boosted the virtues of their particular regions to the outside world but seldom lived up to their own rhetoric. As in the goldfields, the rare moments of glory were well worth the many disappointments. The risks they were willing to withstand and the degree to which they became engaged in the market blurred the distinction between farmer and gold seeker, entrepreneur and gambler and, in the process, marked a crossing of the Rubicon into the modern age of American agriculture. In that sense, James Marshall's heart-thumping discovery on the south fork of the American River did indeed change the course of history.[22]

The gold rush played out its economic, social, and cultural implications in a number of rural communities in northern California that proliferated in the 1850s and 1860s—not in the standard American fashion of settlers moving westward along a broad front, cultivating the land homestead by homestead, but communities nonetheless. Putah Creek, twenty miles west of John Sutter's New Helvetia in the lower Sacramento Valley, was one such community; it serves as this book's center stage. The miners-turned-farmers who made it one of the richest agricultural districts in the state are the key historical actors. Their dramatic story, in its broadest sense, is an extended commentary on American optimism and hard work—a true-to-life allegory of the American dream amid the harsh realities of life in rural California after the gold rush. Four of the main characters— George Washington Pierce, Champion I. Hutchinson, Jerome C. Davis, and William Montgomery—capture the opening spotlight.

MAKING A SETTLEMENT

Removals

George Washington Pierce and his wife, Eunice, first saw the land along Putah Creek that would be their home for most of the rest of the century (and the family home for generations to come) on February 17, 1854. Permanent settlement was the last thing on their minds that day, however. Not much seemed to be going right for them. They had intended to arrive the day before to begin work as hands on the "Big Ranch," but a torrential downpour that came out of nowhere interrupted their fifteen-mile trek from Sacramento City just as they were crossing the immense tule swamps west of the Sacramento River. "Got stalled in the Tuly [sic] near Grays bend and carried Mrs. Pierce to dry land on my back," George later recalled. That same storm turned Putah Creek, flowing due east out of the coast mountains, from a trickle of a stream into a raging torrent. When the Pierces arrived the next afternoon, by boat for part of the trip across the prairie, Putah Creek had overflowed its banks, submerging a good portion of the Big Ranch under several inches of water. It was an inauspicious beginning to their lives in the lower Sacramento Valley, but rather fitting to their experiences in California to date. Indeed, not much had gone right for the Pierces since they left Kenosha, Wisconsin, two years earlier with grand expectations for the gold rush.[1]

They might well have paused that first day on the Big Ranch to reflect not only on their recent misfortune but also on their lives in general. *Removals*, the word contemporaries often used to describe their migrations, were nothing new to either of them. At the age of eighteen in 1835, Washington (as George was known then) left upstate New York with his parents and brother for Pike Creek (renamed Southport in 1836 and then Kenosha in 1850) on the western shore of Lake Michigan. One of the first fifteen families to make this new settlement their home, the Pierces were revered as "pioneers" almost instantly by those who followed in their footsteps and by scores of local historians ever since. These families were part of the "Western Emigration Company," which, in the lore of Kenosha history, had organized the year before at a dinner party in Hannibal, New York. The dominant theme that night was the West—especially the country beyond the Great Lakes in what was then the Michigan Territory. Its beautiful prairies, productive soil, and remarkable possibilities, many around the dinner table were convinced from talking with travelers, promised a better life than the increasingly crowded and worn-out lands of upstate New York. After raising $8,000 in stock subscriptions, the company appointed an advance party to explore the region, and the first families, "following the lakes" between Buffalo and Chicago, arrived shortly thereafter. Eunice French and her family made the same trip nine years later, though with considerably less fanfare. At the age of fourteen, this was already her second removal, having migrated from Connecticut to Fredonia, New York, seven years earlier.[2]

Removals were a fact of life for Americans during the first half of the nineteenth century. Everything seemed to be expanding—from transportation networks, to markets, to people's horizon of experience. One of the key catalysts was the Erie Canal, whose construction began in 1817, the same year that Washington Pierce was born. This engineering marvel would transform not only the lives of farm families like the Pierces and the Frenches but also the American economy itself. The canal stretched 364 miles from Albany to Buffalo, but of even greater significance, it connected, by extension, the Great Lakes and upper Ohio Valley to the Hudson River, New York City, and the trans-Atlantic world. Western migration had already begun in the late eighteenth century, when settlers eager to escape the increasingly crowded Northeast poured into upstate New York and the Old Northwest. Land was plentiful, but without adequate transportation to eastern cities, farmers produced primarily for themselves and local markets. Geography was their main obstacle. Most of the major rivers in the eastern half of the United States run north-south, but east-west routes were needed to link the growing cities along the Atlantic seaboard to the growing hinterland. With the completion of the canal in 1825, the isolation that had made self-sufficiency a virtue out of necessity for western farmers was gone. The flood of farm products from America's interior soon made New York City the most important commercial center in the nation. It would have been hard to say who was more ecstatic—western farmers or eastern businessmen.[3]

Years later, Pierce would refer to Southport as a "Yankee Settlement."[4] The description was most apt for the town, his family, and his own character. Most of the early settlers descended from seventeenth-century Puritans who had fled Great Britain to colonize much of New England and then, after the Revolutionary War, flocked to upstate New York. They tended to be literate, enterprising, frugal, and competitive. Poverty was their worst enemy, and it was the fear of poverty, induced most often by population growth and land depletion, that kept them in motion. Fear was not the only motivating factor, however; it may have provided the initial push, but the pull of superior opportunities and new adventures, which invariably came from the West, enticed them all the more.[5]

It was typical of the Pierces, therefore, to pride themselves on every triumph, however small, in their early years in Southport. Washington and his father, Jonathan, were among the first to build houses in the new settlement. Jonathan's carpentry skills, in fact, were evident all over town. Washington's brother, Elijah, built the first barn in Kenosha County. Jonathan planned the first religious service, secured itinerant preachers, and helped build and organize the first Presbyterian church. Washington's mother, Electra, took a prominent role in the local temperance society. Washington (and probably Elijah) served in the Fourth Regiment of the Wisconsin militia. The Pierce men participated in township government, helped establish public schools, and promoted commercial development. All three were among the first to file preemption claims and receive patents after U.S. government officials began surveying the region in 1840. And all three kept daily journals and meticulous account books.[6]

Many of these deeds, it is important to note, served traditional as well as newer economic ends. Indeed, though perhaps only a byproduct of their zeal to achieve, the communal impulse in Yankee culture was every bit as strong. Individual accomplishments were highly valued, but especially when they served the community and even more so when they imposed structure on the community. Institution building—church, school, and local government, in particular—gave the Pierces and their peers a sense of stability and, perhaps even more importantly, the confidence to take on the challenges of day-to-day life on the frontier. By all (albeit sketchy) accounts, neither Indian threats, squatter conflicts, catastrophic fires, sheer isolation, nor even the brutal Wisconsin winters discouraged them. Even as the population of Southport surpassed 3,000 in the 1840s, including a significant number of Irish and German immigrants, Yankee institutions remained the foundation of community life. The settlers seemed, in essence, to have one foot in an agrarian past and the other in the modern economic order. What we might see as a contradiction between traditional and capitalist values was in fact what made Jonathan, Electra, Washington, and Elijah pillars of the community.[7]

There is no denying, however, that economic growth was their primary objective, and economic growth had long been identified with wheat. Wheat was the dominant crop in the Mohawk and Hudson river valleys of New York since the late 1780s and throughout much of New England long before that. With production declining from soil exhaustion—50 percent in New England and 25 percent in New York during the decade 1830–40—farm families like the Pierces and Frenches headed west for greener pastures. That decision was reinforced by a number of other considerations. Wheat flourished on the virgin soils of the frontier, its culture was well known and inexpensive, and it required only a limited amount of largely unskilled labor. It was not unusual for a first crop to return a sizeable profit. Moreover, because bread was central to the American and European diets, wheat invariably brought the best market prices of any grain. Wheat was also nonperishable and could be transported at minimal cost to distant markets in oceangoing ships. When the Napoleonic wars disrupted the European supply, a vigorous trans-Atlantic trade developed that made more than a few American merchants and farmers rich. With the possible exception of cotton, no crop in the first half of the nineteenth century was more financially intoxicating.[8]

That was certainly the case in Southport. The land was cleared, plowed, and sown almost as soon as the first settlers stepped off the boat. What attracted the advance party of explorers to this site in the first place was that the depth and width of Pike Creek made an ideal natural harbor. It was not long before several merchants built piers into Lake Michigan for the sole purpose of loading wheat onto eastward-bound sloops. By 1840, farmers from sixty to eighty miles distant were hauling wheat to this busy port, which was already competing with Chicago and Milwaukee for the surplus of the interior regions. Merchants stored the crop in large warehouses during the long winter months until lake navigation could be resumed. The receipts, or "tickets," they issued farmers soon circulated as currency—for paying debts and purchasing groceries, clothing, and even land. The phrase "as good as wheat" became a common expression of the times.[9]

The Pierces took full advantage of Southport's booming economy. Jonathan, Elijah, and Washington owned their own adjoining quarter sections but combined the 480 acres into one farm, sharing livestock and equipment and living together in one home. Employing the latest technology—the Carey plow, the cradle for harvesting, and a 2-horsepower threshing machine—they were producing 15 bushels of wheat per acre and over 500 bushels per year by 1845. Early in 1847, they purchased their first reaper, the harvesting implement that would soon revolutionize wheat production in America. They did not put all their eggs in one basket, however. The men raised hogs and several head of cattle and cultivated corn and hay to feed them, and Electra produced large quantities of dairy products and vegetables—butter and potatoes, in particular—all for local markets. The farm was carefully fenced to separate the fields, pastures, and gardens, and in general the Pierces organized their lives around the cycles of their crops and the needs of their animals. Through most of the 1840s, it made for prosperous times—enough so that by 1845 they were able to attain the most visible sign of wealth on the frontier—hired hands. For most of the rest of the decade, the Pierces employed two permanent workers and at least six harvesters every year.[10]

Prosperity also enabled Washington to consider marriage. Having met Eunice French shortly after her arrival in Southport in the fall of 1844, he wasted little time proposing to her. They married on September 29, 1846. To celebrate, Washington bought his bride a new pair of shoes and, with the help of his father and brother, built the two of them a brick house of their own. Two years later, they celebrated again with the birth of their first son, Henry Albert. By then, Eunice had become a vital contributor to the Pierce farm. She took over the butter and potato production from her aging mother-in-law with such zeal that the family became even less dependent on wheat. Even if the wheat crop failed, Washington calculated, Eunice's efforts would be enough to carry the family through. Wheat remained the family's passion, however. It was a cash crop above all else that the Pierces and their peers wanted. Only a cash crop could satisfy their insatiable appetite for achievement.[11]

All it took to spoil everything was a spell of bad weather. Drought began in 1847, subsided for a year, and then returned with a vengeance in 1849. For three years—through 1851—the rains all but stopped. Rust and various insect attacks soon followed. Wheat transactions—numbers of bushels, wages paid, prices received—filled the pages of Washington's account book through 1848, but disappeared thereafter. Eunice's contribution helped for a while, but the second and third years of the drought made for stubbornly hard times. During the boom, farmers thought nothing of going into debt to extend their purchases of land, implements, and building materials. But once warehouse owners began calling in their debts, the phrase "as good as wheat" lost all meaning. "Wheat growing has proved utterly untrustworthy," bemoaned the editor of the local newspaper. "The wheat crop, our great staple, has proved essentially a failure." The settlement stopped growing, business slowed, and many abandoned their homes and farms—more than a few swept westward to California by the intense excitement of the gold rush in the spring and summer of 1849.[12]

The Pierces stayed put, however. As recognized "pioneers" of the community, they felt a responsibility to lead their neighbors through troubled times. As longtime wheat farmers both in New York and Wisconsin, they knew that bad weather was a fact of life and that conditions were bound to improve. Much more unsettling was young Henry's death in April 1850, just eight months before the birth of Washington and Eunice's second son, George Jr. Immense grief, a new child, and the continuing economic woes of the drought raised Washington's sense of duty to his immediate family. And the sheer temptation of gold—intensified seemingly every day by stories of unimaginable wealth filtering back from California—became increasingly difficult to resist. Here, it seemed, beckoned the biggest opportunity of them all.[13]

Sometime during the winter of 1851–52, Washington made the gut-wrenching decision that confronted so many men of his generation and their families. It was time to go to California. More unusual was Eunice's insistence that she accompany him. While several thousand women participated in the gold rush—some with their husbands, some alone—it was predominantly a male phenomenon. Eunice clearly was just as concerned as her husband about their family's economic and emotional well-being. She may have insisted that the team that worked so well together on the farm should not be broken up—that together they could work a claim that much more profitably and then return home to start anew that much more quickly. She may have insisted more generally that where her husband went, she went. Or, she may simply have been hungry for gold herself. Washington may have resisted at first, but he was no match for his wife's strong will. Once the decision was made, the sense of adventure must have been exhilarating for them both. This would be a removal like no other.[14]

Leaving George Jr. behind with Jonathan, Electra, and Elijah, Washington and Eunice left Kenosha on April 19, 1852. True to character, Washington kept a diary, intent on recording every last detail. For the first month, he made daily entries as his party made its way south and west across northern Illinois, through the Mississippi Valley, and on to the Missouri River. "Splendid cuntry [sic]," he wrote on May 5. "Good prairie and timber." Once on the California Trail heading west, however, Pierce's entries became more irregular and much shorter, eventually stating only the day's destination: June 5, Fort Laramie; June 20, Green River ferry; June 27, Salt Lake. The long, empty distances of the Great Plains, the arid wilderness of the Great Salt Lake Desert (perhaps the most forbidding in all of North America), and "Death's trail," past the Humboldt Sink, drained his earlier enthusiasm, to say the very least. The overland trail may have been the quickest and cheapest route to California's goldfields, but it was an ordeal that tested and often crushed the spirit and enthusiasm of its travelers, male and female alike. Only something as glorious as the gold rush itself could revive them.[15]

The details of the Pierces' lives become even sparser after reaching Placerville, the heart of the Mother Lode, three and a half months after leaving Kenosha. We know only that they arrived on August 4, "tired and dusty," and that they worked the placer mines on nearby Weber Creek for about a year, "with about as good luck as any of them"—which is to say, not much. It could not have taken them too long to realize that surface deposits had been depleted up and down the gold country by the 100,000 or more forty-niners who had gotten there ahead of them. It must also have been difficult for these two devout Presbyterians to tolerate the omnipresent liquor, gambling, prostitution, and general rowdiness. To shelter themselves, they may have tried to make a home, as did many husbands and wives in their predicament. Based on the ample provisions with which they began their overland journey, they appeared to have had enough resources early on to build a cabin and furnish it with a few homey comforts. And there were enough women in the Placerville area for Eunice to have found female companionship.[16]

However they tried to cope, it was not enough. Broke, discouraged, and no doubt exhausted, the Pierces removed once again, from Weber Creek to Sacramento, in the fall of 1853. What they did there is not known, but it is unlikely that they were any more at home in a city that was just as raucous, sinful, and overwhelmingly male as the mining towns were. Harsh realities had surely set in. Washington and Eunice had now been away from Kenosha for a year and a half but had nothing to show for themselves. They had long believed that hard work and right values would be rewarded with success. That faith left them with a profound sense of personal failure. What, they surely asked, must their family have been thinking? After leaving Kenosha with such bright prospects and high expectations, how could they explain their failures to the folks back home? Prolonged periods of introspection must have only made things worse. It is little wonder, therefore, that Washington never mentioned their experiences in the goldfields in his daily journals later on in life, despite his penchant for reminiscing at length. It was at once an experience he could neither forget nor articulate.[17]

Homesick yet too ashamed to return home, the Pierces turned to what they knew best and to familiar faces. Indeed, it was no accident that Putah Creek was their next destination. Farming offered them a comforting familiarity and a chance to redeem themselves and start life afresh—symbolized, perhaps, by George Washington Pierce beginning to identify himself by his first, rather than middle, name. Moreover, Charles Greene was the one who offered them work. Greene was not only the manager of the Big Ranch but also an old acquaintance from Kenosha. So too was his partner, Champion I. Hutchinson, as were at least eight others in the immediate area at the time of the Pierces' arrival. This did not constitute chain migration in the strict sense of the term—just enough personal connections to help ease the pain of isolation. Moreover, wages were astronomically high—$75 a month each and upwards of $4 a day during the harvest season, three to four times the going rate in Wisconsin. The Pierces had long since abandoned their dreams of striking it rich in California but now hoped that in this more congenial setting, they could earn enough money to return home in a year or two with their heads held high.[18]

Champion I. Hutchinson, on the other hand, had no intention of going back, even though he had once been the most revered man in Kenosha. He too was a Yankee, but a different breed from the Pierces and their peers. The degree to which he engaged in the market and the risks that he was willing to withstand set him apart. Hutchinson, simply put, lived to seize the moment, and for such a speculative entrepreneur there was no better moment than the gold rush.

Born in Connecticut in 1815, Hutchinson started a lively business career managing a Georgia textile mill before emigrating to Southport, Wisconsin, in 1841. In less than a year, he built the largest wheat warehouse on the harbor, the longest pier into Lake Michigan, two large state-of-the-art vessels, and the biggest steam mill in the county. He gave liberal advances to farmers storing their crops, owned a large grain farm himself, helped launch the region's first agricultural society, married the daughter of the local Episcopal minister, and played an active role in politics. In 1848 his peers elected him delegate-at-large to the Whig national convention in Philadelphia that nominated Zachary Taylor for president, and Taylor subsequently appointed him U.S. marshal for the district of Wisconsin and gave him a high-ranking administrative position in the Post Office. In the process, Hutchinson earned the sobriquet "General," as high an honor as there was for a man of his ambition.

The drought at the end of the decade, however, brought financial ruin followed by scandal—"the most disgraceful event in the early history of Southport," locals insisted for years. When farmers brought what little grain they had to Hutchinson's warehouse in the fall of 1849, they demanded cash instead of the usual receipts, whose value had greatly diminished. Hutchinson, strapped for cash himself, gave his word that all accounts would be settled when navigation opened up the following spring. But when several vessels full of wheat left the docks on April 6, 1850, no one had been paid. Farmers armed with clubs, pitchforks, and axes stormed the warehouse screaming bloody murder, but too late. Hutchinson had skipped town with the proceeds and was on his way to California.[19]

After an arduous overland journey, Hutchinson arrived in Sacramento on September 1, 1850. The city, his instincts told him, was there for the taking. "Begun by gold," Sacramento had become a major mercantile center in an amazingly short time (supplanting Sutter's New Helvetia in the process) and was just bursting with opportunity.[20] Like Sam Brannan, Hutchinson bypassed the goldfields and set up shop—a two-story building on J Street near the levee along the Sacramento River, with a hotel on the top floor filled with gambling tables and a saloon and a mercantile business below. Both ventures were lucrative but especially the latter, which sold close to $500,000 of goods in its first year of business alone. Hutchinson, true to form, then parlayed his economic gain into political success. In the spring of 1851, he was elected to the city council from the third ward and soon thereafter appointed chairman of the finance committee. One year later, his growing popularity elevated him to the mayoralty. When rumors of his shady past began to surface during the campaign, thirty-three former residents of Kenosha declared their loyalty to "the good General" in a circular published in the *Sacramento Daily Union*, which put the issue to rest. Fire, flooding, and a cholera epidemic marred his one year in office, but he remained popular enough to be elected city comptroller in 1853. Once again, Hutchinson had established himself in the upper echelons of city life.[21]

That was not enough to satisfy him, however. Simply unable to sit still, Hutchinson set out to reestablish himself in agriculture as well. When the opportunity to purchase a huge tract of land on Putah Creek presented itself in October 1851, he jumped at it. It was, Hutchinson thought, the deal of a lifetime— $6,000 for half of Rancho Laguna de Santos Callé, a Mexican land grant of some 48,000 acres (seventy-five square miles, or eleven "Spanish leagues"). To help launch his new enterprise, Hutchinson acquired two associates—William W. Cozzens, a Sacramento merchant with midwestern roots who was largely a silent partner, and fellow Kenoshan Charles Greene, who managed day-to-day affairs. Preparations began for the first crop almost immediately. They chose barley, a traditional "poor man's crop," and planted 800 acres. Barley required a low initial investment and provided a good way to test the fertility of the land. Used primarily as feed for the several hundred thousand draft animals that hauled supplies in the gold country, it also promised a quick and plentiful return. The three partners also ran several dozen head of cattle on the rest of their acreage. A wide-eyed reporter from the *Sacramento Daily Union* called the new venture the "Big Ranch," and the name stuck. It captured not only the size and scale of the operation but also the expectations of its owners and the spirit of the times.[22]

That spirit also accounts for why Hutchinson maintained the loyalty of so many Kenoshans, who only a short time earlier had wanted his head for robbing them blind. Hutchinson was a commanding, if controversial, figure. While his cunning at speculation and political intrigue ultimately made him a villain in Wisconsin, those same traits made him a celebrity in California. Those who defended him during the mayoral campaign and those, like the Pierces, who worked for

him willingly put aside whatever hostility they may have had for the chance to as-
sociate, or to identify, with this rich, powerful, and prestigious man. Especially
for those transplanted Kenoshans whose efforts in the goldfields did not pan out,
Hutchinson provided at least a taste of what it was like to strike it big. Everything
he did was big; everything about him was big.[23]

Jerome C. Davis had already been to California and back when gold fever lured
the young Ohioan westward early in 1849. Very few who made the overland journey once chose to do it again. Far more typical was the gold rusher who wrote
home, "I would swim around Cape Horn on a log before I would cross the Plains
again."[24] Davis, however, never met an adventure he did not like. Before he
turned twenty-one, he was bored with life in Perry County, where he grew up on
the family farm. Said to be the spitting image of his father, Isaac, Davis nonetheless chose not to follow in his footsteps. Efforts to engage in merchandising and
hotel keeping in the town of Somerset did not satisfy him, either.[25]

In 1843, he enlisted in government service and found plenty of excitement
upon joining John C. Frémont's famed topographical survey expedition, which
arrived in California on December 26, 1845. Family recollections and a number
of biographical accounts claim that the following June Davis took part in the
much-celebrated raising of the Bear Flag over Sonoma, then the Mexican head-
quarters for the northern district of Alta California. He also reportedly brought
garrison prisoners to Sutter's Fort, garnered a promotion to officer rank in Frémont's "California Battalion," and served with distinction until U.S. naval forces
formally occupied the capital city of Monterey a month later, thus putting an end
to any thoughts of an independent republic. The lack of corroborating evidence
in military records or any other sources, however, strongly suggest that Davis, like
seemingly every American male in California at the time, later persuaded himself and others to believe that he had participated. (The Bear Flag Revolt was, in
essence, the Woodstock of its time). When his service expired in December 1846,
Davis returned east with military dispatches.[26]

Even more so than most Americans, Davis did not believe the first accounts
of Marshall's discovery in the foothills of the Sierra Nevada; after all, he had not
seen any gold himself in his travels through the region. But when President Polk
confirmed all the rumors in December 1848, Davis could not get back to California fast enough. With his expertise on the overland trail, he had no problem finding a party to accompany him. This time, neither Davis nor subsequent accounts
would have much to say, except that his experience in the goldfields was "brief."
As with Pierce, the sting of failure while others struck it rich hurt much more

than he cared to admit. Tired and discouraged, he wandered into Sacramento with no particular purpose.[27]

Ironically, that was where his luck began to change. By chance, he encountered Joseph B. Chiles, whose reputation as a "trail-blazing pioneer" was second only to Frémont's. (They might also have met before, during Davis's first sojourn to California.) Chiles took a liking to his fellow overland adventurer and, seeing that Davis was down on his luck, proposed a business partnership. They started a dairy in the town of Washington, just across the river from Sacramento in Yolo County, as well as a rope ferry (where the I Street bridge stands today) to capitalize on the many people traveling to the mines. With milk selling for a dollar a quart and with tolls as high as $6 per wagon, gross earnings from the two enterprises soared to as much as $10,000 a month. Meanwhile, Davis took a liking to Chiles's fifteen-year-old daughter, Mary. The courtship cut deeply into his profits. Because the Chiles home was across the American River, Davis had to take two ferries, at a round-trip cost of at least $20, to woo her away from numerous competing suitors. In the end it was well worth it, as Mary, with her father's blessing, agreed to marry him a few months later.[28]

The pendulum of fortune then swung back again early in the winter of 1852, just as Jerome and Mary had managed to build a nice-sized nest egg. The same flood waters that inconvenienced the Pierces their first day in Yolo County destroyed the ferry and, as one observer put it, "washed out to sea" the dairy. Papa Chiles did not let the newlyweds flounder for long, however. A year earlier, he had purchased one league of land (4,426 acres) on Putah Creek, two miles downstream from the Big Ranch and across the tule swamps from Washington. He decided against taking up residence there, however, because "he didn't like the water" in flood-prone Yolo County. Instead, he split his league in two, assigning Jerome and Mary the west half and his other new son-in-law, Gabriel Brown (who had married daughter Fannie) the east, and let both couples run things under his watchful eye.[29]

Having rebelled against farming as a teenager, Davis now had to embrace it to earn the respect of his demanding father-in-law. He was no novice, but he did not feel particularly confident, either. He turned to his own father for help. After an exchange of letters, Isaac Davis and his wife, Rachael, decided to leave Ohio to help their son and daughter-in-law in their new home. They were joined shortly thereafter by Jerome's sister and brother-in-law, Elnora and Joseph Mitchell. Using the lifetime of experience he had gained in the cattle country along the Potomac River in western Maryland and throughout much of the Ohio frontier, Isaac proceeded to launch the Davis stock farm. His instincts told him hogs.

When he and his family removed from Maryland to Ohio in the early years of the century, they brought little else with them but their hogs. Hogs, not cattle, provided the best way to make money quickly, especially when first getting started. Hogs could run free and fend for themselves, as long as their ears were marked and the mark registered with the county, and pork preserved much better than beef. Very quickly, however, the Davis family learned that cattle could defend themselves much better than hogs against Sacramento Valley predators—grizzly bears, in particular—and that the demand for fresh beef was so high that butchers did not have to limit their purchases to only a few cattle each week to avoid spoilage. Best of all, while cattlemen in Ohio regularly drove their herds at least 400 miles for forty days over the Allegheny Mountains to Atlantic markets, Sacramento was but fifteen miles away. Jerome became such a quick study that his father-in-law deeded him the land outright early in 1854. Raising cattle on Putah Creek would be a greater adventure than he had ever imagined.[30]

Twenty-five years before dreams of gold enticed William Montgomery to California, Missouri looked like the promised land to the twenty-three-year-old Kentuckian. Life in the hill country of Logan County on the Tennessee border had long been a struggle. His parents migrated through the Cumberland Gap (probably from Virginia) just before his birth, seeking land and economic independence, but found that the choice locations in the fertile central and Ohio floodplain counties had already been taken by the inrush of immigrants in the last quarter of the eighteenth century. The fact that Kentucky's land system was hopelessly mired in overlapping and dual claims, squatter rivalries, unregistered deeds, and vague boundaries did not help matters. "The same identical tract was frequently shingled over by a dozen claims," wrote the rising young politician Henry Clay in 1822. Rarely able to produce more than a few dozen bushels of corn or much of a hog surplus, the Montgomerys sustained themselves primarily by hunting and fishing. When hog prices plummeted after the Panic of 1819, William, along with thousands of other upland southerners, decided to uproot his wife, Rebecca, and two young boys, Robert and Alexander, and they headed west across the Mississippi River in 1825. Contemporary Missouri boosters were difficult to resist. "The summers here are mild, prolific and healthy; the winters short, keen, and invigorating," wrote one. "The soil of this country can only be objected to an account of its great fertility, which is calculated, perhaps to encourage idleness—for a very inconsiderable part of the time usually devoted to tilling the earth will always insure a competence."[31]

The Montgomerys found conditions in Missouri no better, however. Without sufficient funds to purchase land from the government, much less from speculators, they squatted on public domain in the northwestern portion of Marion County in the northeastern portion of the state—far removed from the rich bottomlands of the Mississippi and Missouri rivers. Even the most enthusiastic of observers described the soil there as "rough, broken, and unproductive." Montgomery hoped, along with many hundreds of other Kentucky immigrants in the county, to take advantage of the state preemption act, which permitted squatters to claim 160 acres of the public domain with the guarantee that, once surveyed, they would have the first right to purchase their lands at the minimum price of $2 per acre. The costs of moving and getting started—clearing and plowing the heavily forested land, buying seed, implements, and hogs, and building a cabin— did not allow them to save any money, however. As a result, between 1825 and 1839, the Montgomerys removed at least three times to nearby Ralls and Shelby counties and back, starting over each time. Once, they might well have settled on a Spanish land grant that covered much of the region, in which case they would have been ejected when a federal board of land commissioners finally resolved the claim in 1833, more than thirty years after Spain had ceded the Louisiana Territory to France. Conflicts with Indians, including the so-called Black Hawk War, a number of crop-killing frosts, and several outbreaks of cholera and small pox also plagued the Montgomerys and other settlers during the 1830s. All along, they continued to sustain themselves by hunting and fishing.[32]

Late in the decade, their hard work and persistence were finally rewarded. On April 1, 1839, William received his first patent from the federal government for eighty acres on the border between Marion and Shelby counties. He also attained the most visible sign of wealth on the Missouri frontier—a slave. Like most farmers in the region, Montgomery needed more labor than his family (now four sons) could provide in order to move from subsistence to commercial agriculture. One slave allowed him to double his corn production, to perhaps twenty acres, as well as to plant a few acres of tobacco or hemp (or both), the staple crops of the region, which were sold to commission merchants in St. Louis and New Orleans. He also, most likely, hired additional slaves during the peak periods of these labor-intensive crops. Slavery in the state was small scale, even in the fertile lands along the Missouri River known as "Little Dixie." In Union Township, where the Montgomerys lived, roughly half the heads of households owned at least one slave, but none more than six. Few, if any, actually considered whether slave labor was more or less profitable than white labor; they assumed slavery to be not only efficient management but also a moral right and a badge of social status. They had, in other words, not left their southern culture behind when migrating to the West.[33]

Montgomery gradually enlarged the size of his farm to 320 acres by 1848, but "hard times" remained the catch phrase for much of the decade. Low commodity prices, additional outbreaks of cholera and small pox, and a string of long, hard winters continued to make life in northeastern Missouri a constant struggle. At some point, Montgomery had to sell his one slave. He probably turned to cattle raising, as did many farmers in the region. In order to earn substantial profits, however, cattlemen had to improve their herds with better feeding and breeding practices, and few in Marion County had the means to do so. That only reinforced the message that confounded Montgomery and other farmers all along: to make money one needed to have money.[34]

That message, in turn, accounted in part for the increasing popularity of horse racing in Palmyra, the largest town in the county. Huge crowds flocked to the track at the county fair in September and other gatherings during the year. The sport had long been popular among the planter class in Kentucky and Virginia, and since the turn of the century had spread throughout most southern and northern states and among all social ranks. For some, the attraction was a love of fine horses, but for most, it was the opportunity to gamble. By mid-century, gambling had become woven into the fabric of everyday life, not only in big cities such as New York and Philadelphia, but in Marion County and other remote regions. Urban and rural Americans alike took to betting on organized activities such as horse racing, as well as on billiards, card games, pigeon shooting, cockfights, the outcome of elections, whether or not someone would survive an illness—on just about anything. The races at Palmyra tantalized Montgomery and his peers with the illusion that their fortunes could be reversed simply by picking the fastest horse on a given day. There was something inherently liberating about this notion. Win or lose, the outcome was clearly defined, unlike the difference between success and failure on their farms year after year.[35]

Then came the gamble of the century, the gold rush. "The desire to go at once to the new El Dorado amounted to a mania," wrote one local observer, "and Marion county caught the infection in its most violent form." Montgomery's oldest son, Robert, joined one of the first companies of emigrants to organize early in 1849. As the year wore on, letters from Marion County gold rushers published in the local newspaper every week dwelled on "sad news": names of "our worthy citizens" reported dead from cholera, gruesome descriptions of the thousands of rotting oxen and mule carcasses on the overland trail, and story after story from discouraged miners ready to call it quits. "My advice to you is, stay where you are," wrote one. Yet, the occasional letter of triumph seemed to trump all the others. "A few days ago a man dug out a chunk of gold which weighed 22 pounds, and gambled it away at monte during the night, and the next day he went to digging again in his hole and found more," wrote one astonished farmer. "If you can," he urged everyone back home, "sell all your property and bring all the money you can." That was precisely what the Montgomerys did. At the age of forty-eight, William and his other three sons, Alexander, William W., and Hugh, joined Robert in El Dorado County in the summer of 1850, leaving behind with neighbors not only Rebecca but also Alexander's new wife, Susan, and their two young children. They knew exactly what they were doing—risking it all for a chance to strike it rich.[36]

As miners, the Montgomerys had just enough success to get by but not enough to keep going. They did not mind the hard work, but they had expected much greater rewards for their efforts. Others, they noticed, seemed to be making more money by selling foodstuffs to miners. Before the end of the year, the Montgomerys decided to give farming a try, no doubt encouraged by the first frost-less winter they had ever experienced. That January, they squatted on 320 acres of unoccupied land where Putah Creek split into two channels before disappearing into the tule swamps, just east of the Spanish league that Chiles had purchased a few months earlier. Much of the tract consisted of "impenetrable thickets of underbrush" (as a federal surveyor would soon describe it), but also several acres of grassland more lush than they had ever seen in Marion County. Whether or not they knew it at the time, their claim lay dangerously close to Rancho Laguna de Santos Callé, whose boundaries remained undetermined. They immediately fell into their familiar routine of clearing the land, farming and stocking it as they went along, and hunting and fishing for subsistence. All that was missing were the wives and children, whom William and Alexander retrieved by the overland route in 1853. They did not bring any slaves but probably would have, had they owned any. The Montgomerys, in short, began their lives along Putah Creek as though they had never left Missouri or, for that matter, Kentucky.[37]

Two married Yankee farmhands too ashamed to return home; their employer, an entrepreneur/politician/farmer/fugitive well trained in the fine art of speculation; an adventurous Ohioan looking, somewhat reluctantly, to make his mark in cattle raising; and a long-struggling family of squatters from Missouri seeking a fresh start—these four profiles illustrate the diversity of experience among the displaced forty-niners who settled along Putah Creek after the gold rush. They were all a long way from home, and home was many places. Putah Creek's population, about 900 by the end of the decade, included many different populations—not only Yankees and upland southerners but also midlanders from Pennsylvania and New Jersey and immigrants from Germany and Great Britain. They brought with them a host of different backgrounds, values, and beliefs, all of which reflected the diversity of experience among rural Americans at the midpoint of the nineteenth century.[38]

This was no undifferentiated mass of humanity, however. All of these emigrants, it should be emphasized, shared the experience of removal, most of them at least twice. The vast majority—80 to 90 percent—identified themselves as "Westerners" (midwesterners in today's parlance) before moving to California.[39] All of them, it is safe to say, could tell a story as compelling as that of Pierce, Hutchinson, Davis, or Montgomery. And for all of them, the gold rush remained the defining experience of their lives. No one at the time, however, knew what to expect next along Putah Creek, nor, for that matter, what had happened before.

CHAPTER TWO

Seduced

Expectations were high when preparations began for the first crop on the Big Ranch in November 1851, just one month after Champion I. Hutchinson had purchased his half-interest in Rancho Laguna de Santos Callé. The land near the creek looked lush and the remaining grassland ideal for livestock. Hutchinson and his two partners, Charles Greene and William Cozzens, proceeded from past experience. The first task at hand was to enclose the land to be cultivated to keep out grazing stock. The available timber along the creek was not strong enough to be cut into planks but could be chopped up to make brush fences. By March, a field of 1,374 acres was ready, 800 of which were plowed. When Hutchinson's buyer, Joseph Haines of Sacramento, rode out to the Big Ranch that June to witness the harvest for himself, he predicted that the huge barley crop, at 4 cents per pound, would bring in no less than $90,000. Yields were simply astounding—fifty-three bushels an acre on average and as high as sixty-six in some locations—four to five times the norm back home in the Midwest. News of these "immense crops," not only on the Big Ranch but also on farms up and down the creek, traveled fast. "The lands of Putah," proclaimed a reporter from the *Sacramento Daily Union*, revealed "the magnificent results of agriculture under the bold and energetic patronage of its farmers."[1]

To Hutchinson and his new neighbors, the results were more than magnificent; they were downright seductive. Putah Creek looked like home to these transplanted midwesterners, only better—much better. It had all the "natural advantages" to which they were accustomed—abundant grasslands for grazing, flatness for easy plowing, and rich riparian forests that provided fencing, housing materials, and the promise of fertile soil—plus no rain during the summer that could damage the harvest, no winter blizzards, no Indian problem, and no shortage of hungry miners and urban residents already accustomed to paying high prices for food. New technology, moreover, just coming on the market allowed farmers to produce on a scale heretofore unimaginable to them. They also seemed to have the place almost entirely to themselves.[2] It looked for all the world as if these farmers had been given a second chance to strike it rich in California.

The natural environment of the Sacramento Valley was indeed exceptionally rich, but much more volatile and much less familiar than it had first appeared to these "Westerners" in the Far West. Bounded on the west by the Coast Range, on the north by the Klamath Mountains, on the east by the southern Cascades and the northern Sierra Nevada, and on the south by the Sacramento–San Joaquin Delta, the valley was essentially one vast floodplain, 150 miles long and 10 to 50 miles wide. (It forms the northern third of California's 400-mile-long Central Valley.) Down its center, the deep-flowing Sacramento River dominated the scene. Fed by the American, Feather, Yuba, and other rivers cascading down from the high Sierra (which boast the nation's deepest snowpack), the Sacramento's normal flow was large—about 5,000 cubic feet per second—but in flood could swell to an astounding 600,000 cubic feet per second. Rarely a winter went by when the river did not pour out of its channel and create a vast inland sea over much of the valley floor. How deep and how disruptive that sea became varied tremendously from winter to winter. During the summer, moreover, the flow seemed positively benign. Mischievous and deceptive, the Sacramento River seemed almost to laugh at humans, as when, for example, it lured Joseph B. Chiles and Jerome C. Davis to build their ferry and dairy one year and then wiped them out the next, using only a fraction of its power.

Three distinctive features characterized the valley floor. Natural levees ten to thirty feet high arose along the riverbanks, built up over the centuries from the heavy silt deposited by the overflows. On the slopes of those levees, riparian vegetation, up to five miles deep, grew so thick and lush that ecologists prefer *jungle* rather than the standard *forest* to describe it. On the lowlands beyond the levees, the overflow left behind sloughs, swamps, and marshes—including "the Tule" (or "the tules"), the dense expanse of large bulrushes, fifteen to twenty feet high and encompassing approximately 100,000 acres, where the Pierces bogged down on their first day in Yolo County. Government surveyors designated those regions "swamp and overflowed"—land that could not be farmed without extensive reclamation. And above the flooded bottomlands stretched the grasslands of the high plains, which were covered with perennial bunchgrasses and, in the spring, sheets of purple and gold wildflowers, but not many trees, save for a scattering of oak and poplar groves. These varied natural communities, replenished each year by the overflows, supported a wealth of life—plants, animals, birds, reptiles, and insects—that was unsurpassed in any region in North America.[3]

Putah Creek, one of three year-round rivers flowing into the valley from the much drier Coast Range, shared many features of the Sacramento River, though in smaller proportions. It originated near Mount Cobb in what became Napa County, wound southeasterly through the Berryessa Valley (now a reservoir), dropped down a steep canyon into the southwest Sacramento Valley (near present-day Winters), and then flowed eastward for about twenty-five miles across its alluvial plain in a channel sixty to seventy feet wide and thirty to forty feet deep. The tule swamps, however, prevented it from reaching the Sacramento River (except through a maze of tiny distributaries), causing the creek to back up into a large sink that was every bit as dense and foreboding as the Tule itself. Putah Creek proved just as deceptive as the Sacramento River. Often bone dry in the summer, it routinely jumped its channel during heavy winter rains—as the Pierces discovered on their way to the Big Ranch.

A rich ecosystem developed over the centuries. Putah Creek's overflow fed a number of sloughs and swamps, including a long, narrow, and deep lake five miles to the north named Laguna Callé by Mexican observers and later renamed Willow Slough by Anglos. A tangled growth one to two miles wide of tall oaks, sycamore, cottonwood, willow, ash, climbing grapevines, wild oats, and bramble bushes lined the banks of both the creek and the slough. Chinook salmon, steelhead trout, sturgeon, beavers, snakes, and turtles populated their waters. Birds of all descriptions—geese, quail, ducks—swept overhead in flocks so thick they could literally darken the sky. And an abundance of animal life—antelope, deer, elk, bear (including grizzly), coyotes, squirrels—roamed its watershed. Unlike the more densely populated areas of Mexican California (the southern coast and the Monterey and San Francisco bay regions), where grasses were depleted and lands eroded by the mid-nineteenth century, much of Putah Creek's natural ecology remained relatively unspoiled.[4]

Perfect, thought the miners-turned-farmers looking to maximize their yields and hunt and fish to their hearts' content. Gold rush emigrants evaluated the land just as they had in the Midwest. They settled at the junction of water, riparian forest, and grassland, where they could exploit each environment to their advantage, and they judged the fertility of the soil by the presence or absence of native vegetation. The first Putah Creek farmers cultivated grain only within a mile or so of the riverbed and often determined where to stop at the point where native plants no longer reached the height of their horses' withers. They also regarded periodic overflows as beneficial to their land—in essence, an inexpensive substitute to artificial irrigation—not yet realizing that severe flooding could literally drown a growing crop in a matter of hours.

While they sensitized themselves to the ecology to some degree (enough to reap the benefits), they were not ecologically sensitive. But then, that had been the case for generations. At every removal point along the way—whether the Midwest, the Upland South, upstate New York, New England, or Europe—Putah Creek farmers and their ancestors helped demolish forests, reduce fertile valleys to wastelands, and eradicate many species of plants and animals. Farm families did not conspire over the centuries to wreak havoc on their natural surroundings, but their Judeo-Christian religious tradition did, in essence, sanction environmental exploitation by stressing that God had devised nature for humankind's sole benefit. With so many natural advantages so readily apparent in the Sacramento Valley, it simply did not occur to Hutchinson and his neighbors to look for or anticipate disadvantages. To them, the "fine jungle of tropical luxuriance," as John Muir later described the bottomlands of the Sacramento Valley, signaled only one thing—a golden opportunity to cultivate grain and raise cattle.[5]

Equally deceptive and seductive as the environment itself was the fact that much of the land along Putah Creek lay largely vacant when these transplanted newcomers arrived. Patwin Indians, Anglo traders and trappers, and Mexican Californians were hardly strangers to the region, but at the time of the gold rush, they were few and far between, numbering fewer than a hundred altogether. That "there was little doing" along Putah Creek, as one observer put it, served only to reinforce the impulse among these new farmers to see what they wanted to see, rather than what others had seen before them—inevitable, perhaps, but much to their detriment nonetheless.[6]

Long before any Europeans saw Putah Creek, the southwestern Sacramento Valley had been home to the Patwin Indians. Their hunter-gatherer culture flourished in the region for more than 1,500 years. They too utilized the land, water, plants, and animals to their advantage, but in a much gentler and more gradual manner. The creek provided the essentials of life, which the Patwin, in turn, managed with considerable skill and resourcefulness. Their well-balanced diet—high in protein and vitamins—consisted of mush made from acorns (which required special processing to remove the tannic acid), tule roots, berries, various greens, fresh fish, and a variety of large and small game and waterfowl. They constructed houses and boats from the tall tule stems, cured animal pelts for blankets and clothing, and hunted and fished with wood, stone, and bone implements. To control underbrush, encourage new growth, and attract game, they burned the grasslands systematically each year. Only the sacred grizzly bear, the Indians' main foraging competitor, was off-limits to native hunters. The Patwin also built their villages on the creek's natural levees, where dry ground was most likely to pre-vail, and when seasonal flooding threatened them even there, they could still es-cape to the coast mountains.

They could not, however, escape a major malaria epidemic brought down from the Pacific Northwest by fur traders and beaver trappers in the early 1830s. For centuries, the Patwin had thrived along Putah Creek without polluting the soil and water, destroying other species, or harming their environment in any no-ticeable way. But in less than a year, mosquitoes carrying "the fever" reduced their population by at least 75 percent. The survivors fled to the mountains. By 1842, wrote one explorer, the region "had no Indian population, but simply signs of an-cient Indian settlements existing all along the creek." Their tragedy was so dev-astating and so complete that the history of Putah Creek can be written from 1850 forward almost as though Indians had never lived there; this is certainly what the first Anglo settlers thought. It took them more than a decade, for example, to ac-cept the spelling *Putah*, the name (phonetically rendered) given to the creek by the Patwin centuries earlier. The new emigrants preferred *Puta*, Spanish for *har-lot*, which often translated to *whore creek* and other derogatory variations.[7]

Though many Anglo traders and trappers died from malaria themselves, many more profited from the riches of the Sacramento Valley. Few if any, how-ever, showed much enthusiasm to plant roots in the area. They complained of rivers "with no good fording places," of vast expanses "destitute of trees," and of land "barren and unproductive, that must forever remain so." It was, summa-rized one, "unfit for advantageous settlement." In the most detailed map of the valley made before the gold rush, Lt. George Derby depicted a virtual wasteland, with annotations such as "plains from 20 to 30 miles wide with but little vegeta-tion or water," "plains overflowed in winter," and "road impassable during rainy season." No one had to tell Derby how quickly conditions could change during a routine winter storm. "We had arrived within half a mile of 'Puta' creek," he re-counted, "when I observed with astonishment and alarm that a strong current was setting down the road, and that the water was deepening around us with ra-pidity. I at once comprehended that the creek had overflowed its banks, and that we were in a dangerous position. I gave the order to the teamster to turn around immediately, but it was too late. The mules sank at once on turning from the road, the wagon was fast blocked in the yielding mud, and the water, as we afterwards found, was gaining on us at the rate of four feet an hour." It is little wonder that so many early visitors warned against settling the region.[8]

There was also an expanding Mexican presence in northern California, though it too was minimal. Expeditions into the Sacramento Valley dated back to the

Spanish colonial period, but their purposes were to evaluate the perceived Indian menace and to search for intruding foreigners—Russian, British, or American— not to encourage settlement. North of the San Francisco Bay, the metropolis was Sonoma, where the last of the Franciscan missions in Alta California had been established in 1824. But even in the 1840s, after Mariano G. Vallejo, commandant general of the northern district of California, had acquired vast landholdings in the area, including Rancho Petaluma (66,000 acres), laid out a town plaza, and built a military post, Sonoma's population was no more than a few hundred. Perhaps the best indication of the limited number of Mexicans in the far reaches of Alta California was that smallpox, which devastated the Indian population in Sonoma and nearby coastal valleys, had little or no effect on the Patwin Indians along Putah Creek, just twenty-five miles or so across the rugged mountains.[9]

The first non-Indian to find Putah Creek inviting came neither from Mexico nor Alta California but from Kentucky. For John Wolfskill and his older brother, William, migration was in the family genes. Their grandfather had fled Germany in 1742 to settle in Pennsylvania, and their father, in search of more fertile land, moved first to North Carolina, then to Tennessee, and again to Madison County, Kentucky, before the end of the century. William and John were born there but did not stay long. In 1807, they emigrated to Boone's Lick, Missouri, where they grew up with members of the Daniel Boone, Kit Carson, and Stephen Cooper families. It was on to Santa Fe in 1822 and then to southern California in 1831. There, William abandoned his wanderings and developed his "Old Adobe" rancho near the Los Angeles River, where, among many celebrated accomplishments, he started the first commercial orange groves in California.

Looking to distance himself from his successful brother, John soon announced that he too wanted his own rancho. Acting on a tip from a traveler, he rode north to explore Putah Creek in the spring of 1840. Delighted with what he found—particularly the lush grasslands, the riparian vegetation, and the pleasantly flowing creek—he headed back to Los Angeles to ask his brother one last favor. John was not a Mexican citizen, but William was, having received his letter of naturalization years earlier, and only Mexican citizens could petition the government for land. John secured his brother's signature and rode back north, this time with horses, oxen, and a small herd of cattle, stopping in Monterey to finish up the paperwork. Technically, it was William's grant, but as far as John was concerned, the land belonged to him.[10]

By Mexican standards, Rancho Rio de los Putos, as Wolfskill called his grant, was small—four square leagues (17,755 acres). He located it carefully on both sides of the creek to control the water and flush against the Coast Range to minimize trespassing. Upon his return in midsummer of 1842, conditions had changed dramatically since the previous spring. The heat was now searing, the land parched, and the creek channel all but empty except for a few scattered pools. Local legend has it that he spent his very first night high up in the fork of a tree after disturbing several grizzly bears, who were seeking refuge from the hot sun in the thick underbrush along the creek. The grizzlies would soon be a menace to his cattle and horses as well.

Determined to make the best of it, Wolfskill built himself a house made of poles and tule rushes (inspired by the now-empty dwellings of a nearby Patwin village), purchased more stock, and began planting a few fruit trees and grapevines. In the grand tradition of the California rancheros, he also began cultivating a reputation for greeting travelers with enthusiasm and hospitality. It was his solitude, however, that he valued the most. He liked to boast that he could go weeks at a time without seeing another human being and that his nearest neighbors were John Marsh, at the foot of Mount Diablo, about forty miles to the south; George Yount, in the Napa Valley, just east of Sonoma; and John Sutter, at the confluence of the American and Sacramento rivers, thirty miles to the east. Though he would not have considered them neighbors, the last remaining group of Indians in the region, led by Chief Solano, resided thirty miles to the southwest in the Suisun Valley.[11]

Much to his dismay, Wolfskill's neighborhood began to get a bit more crowded. With the loss of Texas in 1836, the troubled Mexican republic became desperate to secure its northern frontier. Seeking now to encourage immigration from foreign countries, especially the United States, officials in Monterey began offering huge tracts of land. That was precisely why they were so willing to issue William Wolfskill's absentee grant, why Marsh, Yount, and Sutter secured huge tracts of land themselves, and why two organized companies of settlers began making their way to California in the spring of 1841. The Bidwell-Bartleson party, after a grueling overland ordeal, arrived from Missouri in November, and just days later the Workman-Rowland party reached Los Angeles from New Mexico. Within two years, at least fifty of these emigrants and their families had settled on ranchos in the Sacramento Valley, including four in close proximity to Wolfskill's Rio de los Putos: William Gordon's Rancho Quesesosi on Cache Creek, thirteen miles to the north, Thomas Hardy's Rancho Rio de Jesus Maria, a bit further east, William Knight's Rancho Carmel, further east still on the Sacramento River, and Juan Manuel Vaca and Juan Felipe Peña's Rancho Lihuaytos, on Putah Creek.[12]

The last proved too close for comfort for Wolfskill. Vaca and Peña had been members of the Workman-Rowland party, most of whom settled in southern California. Enticed by stories of the lush cattle feed and inviting climate in the Sacramento Valley, many emanating from Vallejo himself, Vaca and Peña moved on, following the El Camino Real northward. Vaca, a widower, brought his eight children with him, and Peña was accompanied by his wife and six children. Vaca was also Peña's *compadre* (godfather). After building several dwellings and stocking the land with cattle, Vaca and Peña petitioned Vallejo and in January 1843 received a grant of ten square leagues. They named it Lihuaytos, after an old Patwin village on the creek. Its size, shape, and boundaries were only vaguely defined, as was typical of most grants in the wide-open spaces of Alta California. Its *diseño*, or map, identified only the Coast Range, Putah Creek, the Sacramento River, and the estuaries along the Carquinez Strait to the south—not unlike the *diseño* of Rio de los Putos, a fact that did not escape the grantees for very long.

A heated controversy developed. Vaca and Peña coveted the land already occupied by Wolfskill. Closer to the mountains, it had more trees for shelter and a readier source of water. Wolfskill, they complained, allowed his cattle to feed along Putah Creek well beyond his four leagues, all the way to the Tule. In June 1844, Vaca and Peña persuaded Governor Manuel Micheltorena to eject Wolfskill from his tule cabin and to remove his herds of cattle and horses north to Cache Creek. A court in Los Angeles moved quickly to settle the disagreement. As was customary in Mexican law, the goal was not so much to determine a clear winner as to heal whatever social wounds had been opened and to prevent further legislation. With an eye toward compromise, it issued "correcting" grants on August 30, 1845, which upheld Wolfskill's prior claim but insured that Vaca and Peña would have ample access to the creek. The boundaries, however, were only slightly more precise. Lihuaytos, renamed Los Putos, was defined only in relation to Rio de Los Putos—"on the margins of the river adjourning at the east the Rancho of Guillermo Wolfskill." Neither Vaca and Peña nor Wolfskill was particularly thrilled by the ruling, and they would never again be on friendly terms. Indeed, both Vaca and Peña settled as far away from Wolfskill as they could on Los Putos—about seventeen miles south in Laguna Valley, just outside present-day Vacaville.[13]

Their quarrels notwithstanding, Wolfskill and Vaca and Peña shared a similar lifestyle—that of the typical California ranchero. Cattle was the main concern—over 1,000 head roamed each rancho by 1846—and a prosperous trade in hides and tallow made for a strong pastoral economy during much of the decade. Small amounts of garden produce, corn, and wheat were also raised on both ranchos. Wheat cultivation remained very primitive, including the use of wooden plows to break the soil, harvesting by hand, threshing by piling the cut crop in a corral and running horses over it, and winnowing by tossing it up into the wind until the chaff blew away. While Wolfskill remained something of a loner, the Vacas and Peñas loved entertainment—feast days, weddings, baptisms, and especially their annual rodeo and *mantanza* (slaughter), which attracted rancheros throughout northern California. Ranch women garnered considerable respect for the variety of duties they performed, but most of the laborers were Indians. Indeed, this elaborate way of life depended on Indian vaqueros and casual workers, the scattered few who had managed to escape the ravages of disease. No one questioned that the ranchero himself was the master of the estate.[14]

Marcos Vaca, who arrived with his brother Juan Manuel in 1842, was envious and soon wanted his own grant. He built himself an adobe dwelling on the south bank of Putah Creek, where he tended several hundred head of cattle on the plains of Los Putos. By early 1845, after much of the herd had crossed to the uninhabited north side of the creek, Marcos decided that it was time to strike out on his own. "My cattle being used to the place," he later recalled, "I applied for the land." Because he could neither read nor write, Marcos asked Vallejo's personal secretary, Victor Prudon of Sonoma, to prepare the necessary documents for Rancho Laguna de Santos Callé, promising him that "if he could get the grant . . . he might have one half of it." Vallejo gave his formal approval on December 20, 1845, and nine days later, Pio Pico, the last of the Mexican governors, signed off on the grant—or so it was claimed. In fact, Prudon forged all the documents and, in the process, manufactured Rancho Laguna de Santos Callé out of thin air.[15]

The complications that ensued might have become no more than a footnote in the obscure history of these three land grants had not Champion I. Hutchinson purchased Marcos Vaca's half-interest in Rancho Laguna de Santos Callé five years later. In the interim, a series of rapid-fire events occurred that turned the lives of everyone involved upside down. First came the Bear Flag Revolt, in which Prudon was arrested alongside Vallejo, causing considerable damage to both their reputations. The Mexican War soon followed, ending on February 2, 1848, with the signing of the Treaty of Guadalupe Hidalgo, in which Mexico ceded California to the United States. Just nine days earlier, James Marshall had discovered gold at Sutter's Mill. More than 100,000 people from every corner of the globe swarmed the Sierra Nevada foothills, many of whom forded Putah Creek at Wolfskill's crossing on their way from San Francisco. California became a state, governed not by Mexican law, but by a new constitution patterned, often word for word, after those of Iowa and New York. Sacramento, not New Helvetia, became the center of commerce in the valley, full or merchants looking to turn a profit on the miners who floated through. Hutchinson was one of those merchants, and he now intended to see just how much money he could make from the land.[16]

It was not in Hutchinson's nature to consider what might have happened before the gold rush—ecologically, culturally, or otherwise—when he made his purchase. He did not know that during the "Great Flood of 1847," as a few old-timers called it, a man canoed through what became the Big Ranch, "meeting no greater obstructions than the strength of the current," or that four years before that a severe drought had made feed so scarce for cattle that "you could count their ribs at 50 yards."[17] He knew nothing of the legal status of the grant, nor of previous perceptions of the land that conflicted with his own. Whereas Patwin Indians had carefully managed their natural resources and appreciated their dependence on their surroundings, Hutchinson believed he could master the environment through the sheer force of his will. Whereas earlier explorers had emphasized the unpredictable features of the Sacramento Valley, Hutchinson saw unoccupied, unimproved land with virgin soil just waiting to be plowed. And whereas Mexican ranchers cared little about precise boundaries or extensive cultivation of crops, Hutchinson envisioned miles and miles of fences squared off at right angles and enclosing huge fields flowing with wheat and barley. Hutchinson's midwestern neighbors were equally mesmerized by what they saw and experienced, especially after the bumper harvest of 1851, which reinforced everything they assumed to be true.

Success eluded only one of the new landowners on Putah Creek that harvest. Charles De Pendray, a French gold rusher, paid a cool $30,000 for Prudon's half-interest in Rancho Laguna de Santos Callé in March 1850. Like Hutchinson, De Pendray planted a huge barley crop near Willow Slough, but without first enclosing the land. It was only after roaming stock had trampled his fields that the Frenchman realized that the state fence law placed the entire burden of protection upon the grower of crops. Broke and dismayed, De Pendray sold his half-interest to two gold-rush emigrants from the Midwest: Edmund L. Brown, who, along with his son William, settled one and a quarter miles downstream from the Big Ranch, and Joshua Bailey, who remained at Willow Slough. Both Brown and Bailey knew better and fenced their land, using timber from the nearby riparian forests, before planting large crops of barley themselves. So too did Nathaniel Sharp, whose 600-acre farm was one mile below Brown. Between Sharp and the thickets of Putah Sink lay the one square league that Joseph B. Chiles had purchased in December 1850 and soon thereafter divided between his two sons-in-law, Gabriel F. Brown (no relation to neighbor Edmund) and Jerome C. Davis. From the outset, they all raised both barley and cattle, but with differing emphases. While Hutchinson and Charles Greene, for example, considered grain their "principal business," Davis identified himself as a stockman. By the end of 1852, Davis, with the help of his father, had 600 acres "under fence," 2,000 bushels of barley in storage, and 2,000 head of cattle roaming Rancho Laguna de Santos Callé.[18]

They did not roam alone. The claimants considered unenclosed land on the grant to be open pasturage where everyone in the area could graze their stock— as was customary throughout much of the Midwest. California's stock law of 1850, in fact, merely replicated previous statutes from several other frontier states, which themselves dated back to colonial-era Anglo traditions. The advantages were self-evident. Because the range was open, extensive, and unrestricted, stock could roam with very little supervision as long as their owners branded or marked them, registered with the county recorder, and agreed to return strays to their rightful owner. Ranchers were spared the enormous expense of fencing, and best of all, the grass and the wild oats were free.

Range cattle, on the other hand, bred randomly, making it virtually impossible for the more enterprising farmers to improve the quality of their stock. At the time, however, that was of little concern. California's explosive population growth created such a huge demand for beef that even tough, unpalatable meat found a ready market. When herds of "American" cattle (mongrel breeds from the Midwest) were driven overland to California from the Ohio Valley and the Missouri frontier in the wake of the gold rush, stockmen such as Chiles and Davis intentionally crossed them with native "Mexican" herds, preferring quantity over quality. This allowed farmers to take advantage of favorable prices in the cattle market while devoting the rest of their energies to farm making and grain raising.[19]

Hutchinson and Davis, in particular, made sure that this whirlwind of activity along Putah Creek did not go unnoticed. Not averse to promoting themselves, they were, in effect, among the first in a long line of boosters of California agriculture. "If instead of going to the mines where fortune hangs upon the merest chance," Hutchinson exhorted as mayor, "[emigrants] should at once commence the cultivation of the soil, [where] they will find themselves, almost before they are aware of it, in the midst of wealth, comfort, and virtue." It was just that reasoning that prompted both him and Davis to help organize the California State Agricultural Society in 1854. Its objectives, following the model already common in the Midwest, were to disseminate information through its fairs and publications and to bring "stability, security, and independence to the population." Both

Hutchinson and Davis lobbied the state legislature to secure funding for the society, served as its president at least once, won several first-place premiums at society fairs, and clearly reveled in the attention. For the rest of the decade, "visiting committees" from the society reported regularly on the progress of farms up and down the Sacramento Valley—down to the last bushel produced, acre plowed, and farm implement purchased—with mandatory stops at the Big Ranch and the Davis Stock Farm every year.[20]

The zeal with which Hutchinson in particular preached agrarian values seems to reek of hypocrisy; he was hardly what Thomas Jefferson had in mind, after all. But Hutchinson was no hypocrite in the eyes of his contemporaries. He was a booster, to be sure, but his vision of a thriving, agrarian California had tremendous appeal, especially to the disillusioned miners-turned-farmers anxious to redeem themselves in the Sacramento Valley. Even those familiar with his scandalous past were won over by the promise of "wealth, comfort, and virtue." Their farming experience "back home" taught them to embrace both traditional and newer market values—to keep one foot in the agrarian past and the other in the modern economic order—and they were bound and determined to replicate that experience in California. Hutchinson told them exactly what they believed, or wanted to believe, about themselves and their future in the Golden State.[21]

The growing excitement about agriculture stemmed from more than just boosterism; it also reflected the vigorous response among American farmers to market opportunities and their extraordinary faith in new technology, so vigorous and so extraordinary that a veritable revolution was under way. It had already begun in the Midwest in the decade before the gold rush—the Pierces were among its participants in Kenosha—and was then literally carried overland to California. Technological innovation—plows, cultivators, threshers, and especially reapers—broke down production and cultural barriers by mid-century. Farmers no longer had to limit their fields to the amount their families (and hirelings, if they could afford them) could harvest, a development that transformed the way they thought about themselves and their way of life. Breaking the production bottleneck dramatically altered farmers' perception of the marketplace even more, from a corrupting influence in the Jeffersonian tradition to a golden opportunity all its own. Supply, they now believed, created its own demand. Farmers, or so they thought, could not overproduce, and the more they produced the better off they would be. It was that fundamental assumption of the nineteenth century that compelled Putah Creek farmers to operate on such a large scale.[22]

Nowhere did the reaper catch on so quickly as in California. Hutchinson and

Greene fully intended to use several reapers and threshers during their first harvest, in June 1852. The machines they purchased from eastern manufacturers were late in arriving, however, forcing them to cut and gather the grain "the old Spanish way," as Greene later put it, with scythes, horse rakes, and pitchforks. They did manage to find a Sacramento foundry man to build them a two-horse treadmill-powered thresher for $1,400. Fencing, additional machinery, seed (13 cents per pound), and, above all, labor costs were very high as well. Hutchinson and Greene paid the going rate that year—$75 per month for regular hands and $10 per day for harvesters. The gold rush greatly inflated those figures, but the end result was very real to Hutchinson and Greene. That first crop, it turns out, cost them $33,000 to produce—four times what their buyer had advanced them at the beginning of the season, prompting them to seek out several additional lenders. No one else fared much better along Putah Creek, the glowing production statistics notwithstanding. But for Hutchinson and Greene, it would be a total loss. A huge fire in Sacramento on November 2, 1852, burned their entire crop just days after they had hauled and stored it. And two months later, a Sacramento jury found them liable for the $8,000 their buyer had advanced them. With interest on their loans mounting at 5½ percent per month, the owners of the Big Ranch found themselves more than $40,000 in debt by the end of the year.[23]

But no one seemed to panic. One good crop, creditors and debtors alike believed, would surely take care of everything. So Hutchinson, who had no shortage of connections in Sacramento, borrowed more, using the Big Ranch as collateral. Fully equipped with four threshing machines, five reapers (two McCormick and three Hussey), two mowing machines, and a whole host of other tools and implements, Hutchinson and Greene planted 1,200 acres in barley in early 1853. Newspapers from Sacramento and San Francisco sent reporters to observe just before the harvest began that year. "They have machines," wrote one, "which will enable them to cut seventy-five acres per day." "Barley," wrote another, "will be threshed at the rate of six hundred bushels per day." They also marveled at the blacksmith shop that Hutchinson and Greene had established right on the ranch to keep the machinery they purchased in order and to manufacture more when needed. Other ranchers on Putah Creek stood to benefit as well from Hutchinson and Greene's efforts to mechanize, having made arrangements to rent several of the reapers and threshers for a share of their crops.[24]

Disaster then struck. After what had already been a wet winter, an unseasonable storm on June 12 spoiled everything. It did not look like much at first, but it was enough for Putah Creek to spill over its banks and drown much of the crop. The farmers were not just passive victims here. They did not just severely underestimate the power of Putah Creek; they may very well have contributed to it. In less than two years, they had depleted the creek's riparian vegetation to such an extent that, in the words of one reporter, there was "not a tree to be seen." That timber, both the reporter and the farmers believed, had been put to good use for firewood and fences, the latter "improvement" not only keeping out stock but also demonstrating a certain level of achievement and status. They did not realize that riparian forests also greatly reduced the impact of runoff during a flood. Without the dense vegetation, there was nothing to stabilize the riverbank or hold back the sediment-laden overland flow, especially with the ground already so saturated. Every subsequent heavy rain, moreover, would only make things worse. This "extermination of timber," as one observer called it a few years later, forced farmers to look elsewhere for alternate supplies of wood and, more significantly, left them even more vulnerable to the volatile behavior of Putah Creek.[25]

For some, it was time to bail out. William Cozzens, who was also losing a fortune in a mining venture in El Dorado County, gave up his portion of the Big Ranch to Henry Conner, yet another Sacramento speculator, for $6,000, after defaulting on a promissory note. Conner also acquired from Hutchinson and Greene one quarter of their interest in Rancho Laguna de Santos Callé and one quarter of their enclosed 1,374-acre tract for payment on a $10,000 loan. Sharp sold his land to Davis, and Bailey unloaded his to Simon H. Lettner, a German immigrant looking to return to farming after a successful stint in the goldfields. None of the sellers made money, an almost unheard-of phenomenon on the frontier, where newly developed land generally appreciated very rapidly. By the same token, there seemed to be no shortage of buyers or lenders either.[26]

For Hutchinson and Greene, the bad start those first two years served only to spur them on. They spared no expense. In advance of the 1854 season, they replaced their brush fences with much sturdier redwood planks, purchased and shipped from a mill on the Russian River, near the coast. The new fence, which was more secure against any kind of stock, also brought Hutchinson and Greene considerable fame, with newspapers throughout northern California detailing the size of the posts and planks, just how deep it was set in the ground, its total length (12 miles), and how much it cost ("thousands and thousands of dollars"). Hutchinson and Greene also raised their first crop of wheat—600 acres—again with phenomenal success, averaging forty-five bushels per acre. When a reporter from the *Stockton Argus* visited the ranch in June, he found portions of land yielding as high as seventy-five bushels per acre. The crop was harvested by a workforce of fifty, sold to a prominent Sacramento flour miller, and hauled there in September—all without a hitch—and for the first time Hutchinson and Greene made a profit. But they were still deeply in the red. To finance the whole endeavor, they kept borrowing at very high interest rates, so by the end of the year they had thirty-eight different creditors; and yet, the successful harvest could not even cover the interest on their loans, let alone the principal. At the end of the season, they could not even pay their workers, including George and Eunice Pierce. The Big Ranch's total debt now stood at approximately $85,000.[27]

Not a single one of the 38 creditors was a bank. One of the first laws passed by the state of California in 1850 prohibited the incorporation of banking houses, the painful memories of financial ruin during the Panic of 1837 back east still fresh in the minds of most legislators. The law, however, did not prevent private associations, partnerships, or individuals from opening their doors for business. In fact, anyone with confidence in his ability to operate as a banker could hang out his shingle. John Wolfskill, for example, held deposits of gold dust (often stored in champagne bottles) from miners totaling many thousands of dollars. The small fee he charged was well worth it, one customer maintained, to keep "a fellow's money safe." High rates of interest, the absence of usury laws, and the extraordinary crop yields reported seemingly every day in the papers made loaning money to promising farmers very attractive.[28]

Most of Hutchinson and Greene's creditors were small commission houses and mercantile firms that drifted in and out of business themselves. These loans and advances were numerous but small—$100 here, $100 there—suggesting that their purpose was as much to maintain Hutchinson's place among Sacramento's economic elite as to secure funding. When pressed, however, Hutchinson turned to individual lenders with whom he had established strong, personal ties—not only Henry Conner, but also Benjamin Cahoon, an old business acquaintance from Kenosha. Backed by D. O. Mills & Company, a bank in everything but name at the time (Mills would become the state's most important banker), Conner and Cahoon actively sought out opportunities by riding from farm to farm on horseback and assessing their potential. They generously extended credit to those deemed worthy, not only Hutchinson and Greene but most farmers along Putah Creek as well. They were equally attentive for opportunities to collect their debts, but they were willing to wait for their money, in most cases, provided that the borrower kept up interest payments. The process, reflecting long-established practices of farm credit, was often very informal, with promissory notes scribbled on the backs of envelopes or scraps of paper, even though it was not uncommon for tens of thousands of dollars to be riding on a given transaction or account.[29]

Regarding the Big Ranch, everyone involved still believed that one good crop would take care of everything. Hutchinson and Greene's biggest creditor, Angus Frierson, certainly thought so. A large speculator of town lots in Sacramento and surrounding farm lands, Frierson loaned $53,000 to expand operations on the Big Ranch in advance of the 1855 season, with Hutchinson and Greene agreeing to let him hold most of their improved acreage and all of their farm equipment and stock as security. The Big Ranch once again produced a big crop, grossing $40,000, but not nearly enough to pay off the creditors. Moreover, Frierson died unexpectedly in February, and over the course of the year it was revealed that he was deeply in debt himself—not the best news for creditors and workers who were expecting a big payoff from the bumper crop.[30]

Additional costs during the season and the accumulated interest left Hutchinson and Greene well over $100,000 in debt. Still, their belief that one good crop would take care of everything prevailed, and the two men devised an elaborate scheme to keep the Big Ranch afloat. On January 24, 1856, twelve of Sacramento's most prominent lawyers and merchants agreed to advance a total of $30,000— half of which went to Frierson's estate and half "for carrying on farming operations." The agreement further declared that one of the lawyers, Robert C. Clark, would hold all the property, loans, and future proceeds in a trust, from which all debts would be paid. All parties involved, still clearly seduced by the Big Ranch, agreed that "it was a good and safe loan."[31]

But as Clark later recounted, the 1856 crop and the next three as well "all fell short of expectation." Drought was the problem the first two years. Barley and wheat were sowed early in January both years, but little or no rain fell thereafter. Putah Creek fooled farmers once again. Just as many, at considerable expense, had begun to construct levees to contain the high water, the creek all but dried up in the spring of 1857. As a result, grain on the Big Ranch, as reported by the visiting committee from the state agricultural society, "shares the same fate with most others this year: it is light." Even the several tons of hay that Hutchinson and Greene managed to cut that year went up in flames in another warehouse fire in Sacramento. The problem the next two years was not production but a glutted market caused by the state's diminishing population of miners and a nationwide economic downturn. Low prices had dire consequences. In their frustration, Hutchinson and Greene insisted that their buyer, A. W. Hall, hold their 200 tons of barley and 220 tons of wheat until the market recovered, despite steep storage costs. Much to their chagrin, Hall's business failed a short time later, and by the time his affairs were straightened out, prices had dropped considerably more. In the end, the Big Ranch's two big crops cleared just $20,000.[32]

The solution, once again, was to borrow and expand. Hutchinson and Greene (through Clark, their trustee) obtained another $79,000 from several different lenders. Those who wavered at first were easily seduced. Hutchinson had only to drive them out to the Big Ranch for the day to look things over: 3,000 acres of wheat and barley, a substantial orchard and vineyard, 29 plows, 20 harrows, 7 reapers, 3 threshing machines, 4 hay presses, 2 grain drills, 9 revolving horse rakes, 3 dozen hand rakes, 16 wagons, 3 workshops (blacksmith, wagon-maker, and harness-maker), 4 wells, 7 corrals, 1 large dairy house, 300 head of cattle, 75 horses, 35 mules, 100 hogs, and a large assortment of poultry. But as the list of implements and improvements kept getting longer, so too did the list of creditors. Two years later, despite ample rains, a slight upturn in the market, and a decade's worth of big expectations, both Hutchinson and Greene filed for bankruptcy.[33]

Not all farms along Putah Creek met the same fate as the Big Ranch, but they all struggled to varying degrees. Like Hutchinson and Greene, E. L. Brown overextended himself trying to grow hundreds of acres of barley and wheat and by 1854 was more than $25,000 in debt. Brown, however, did not have Hutchinson's connections. Unable to pay off even the interest on his loans, Brown lost a series of lawsuits and watched helplessly as the county sheriff seized his land piece by piece. By 1857, his estate had been reduced to 200 acres.[34] Gabriel Brown managed to hold on to his land a bit longer, but only by renting a large portion of it to Hutchinson and Greene. When the Big Ranch went under, he relinquished his half league to Joseph B. Chiles's nephew, Isaac, for a meager $2,000. Simon Lettner lost money as well, though his ability to keep his name off the mortgage books and courtroom dockets suggests that he was able to hold his head above water. It no doubt helped that his interests lay primarily in stock, which made him far less vulnerable to inclement weather.[35]

That was certainly the case with Jerome C. Davis. Over the course of the decade, Davis continued to replace Spanish cattle, whose value lay in their hides and tallow, with "American" breeds (Durham and Devon, especially) imported from Ohio and Missouri. He also cut hay and planted alfalfa to feed livestock during the dry summer season rather than rely solely on native grasses; grew other grains, fruits, and garden crops to augment his income; used state-of-the-art tools, machinery, and methods; and employed a largely Anglo cowboy workforce. So successful was Davis at "midwesternizing" his ranch that the state agricultural society, in 1858, awarded him "the highest premium for best improved and furnished stock-farm of the first class"—the pinnacle of achievement in his profession.

Success came at a cost, however. To improve the quality of his stock, Davis had to wall off his farm from the open range, which required no less than thirty-three miles of redwood planks and posts costing $700 per mile. Moreover, as demand from the goldfields diminished, Davis felt the pinch every bit as much as his neighbors. His principle buyer, the Empire Market, Sacramento's oldest and largest butcher, paid him $40 a head in 1856 but only $15 four years later, and beef prices on the Sacramento market fell from 8 cents to 3 cents per pound over the same period. He too fell heavily into debt.[36]

What had happened? From a strictly economic standpoint, high production costs at the beginning of the decade and falling prices at the end never gave farmers much of a chance.[37] The volatile climate, Putah Creek's erratic behavior, and flat-out bad luck did not help either. Greed? It cannot be denied that these farmers were speculative entrepreneurs who, after failing as miners (or, in Hutchinson's case, gouging them), took up the two most easily and profitably produced frontier crops with a vengeance.[38] Arrogance? Had they paid even the slightest attention to the natural and human history of the region, they might at least have limited their mistakes and excesses. None of these elements by themselves, however, explains the extraordinary willingness, even exuberance, to take such risks, often poorly calculated ones at that, over and over again.

The sheer power of seduction—to which all humans, by nature, are subject—should not be underestimated here. It played an enormous, perhaps even the key, role. The abundance of natural advantages, huge fenced fields, amazing new technology, gigantic yields, and instant fame—all on the heels of the disillusionment of the gold rush—drove these farmers, blindly it often seemed, to aggressively pursue market opportunities even though the odds were stacked against them. In their quest for material gain, however self-indulgent, they could not have fully anticipated the results. Once again, it all seemed too good to be true—more so than they even knew.

CHAPTER THREE

Farms without Titles

The eagerness to keep pumping money into these establishments was all the more astounding given that title to the land itself was in question. No one truly owned the land. In the midst of all their hard work and mounting debts, farmers on Ranchos Rio de los Putos, Los Putos, and Laguna de Santos Callé found themselves in the position of having to defend their property rights. Under the provisions of the Treaty of Guadalupe Hidalgo and the California Land Act passed by Congress in 1851, claimants (whether Hispanic or non-Hispanic) were required to have their titles confirmed by a three-member California Land Commission. The stakes were all or nothing. Claims made under Mexican rule would either be confirmed to individuals or rejected and become part of the public domain. Both the claimant and the United States could appeal the Land Commission's decision to the appropriate federal district court and then to the U.S. Supreme Court. The mass of litigation that ensued—the Land Commission heard over 800 cases between 1852 and 1856, and the average length of time for a claimant to secure a patent was seventeen years—has become part of the lore of early California history.[1]

John Wolfskill had a relatively easy time of it. Unlike most Hispanic claimants, Wolfskill had a rudimentary knowledge of both Mexican and U.S. law and was able to present a convincing, if not ironclad, case. He had kept all the written documentation from the Mexican government including the original hand-sketched *diseño* of his grant, paid a federal surveyor to draw up a more exact version, secured the testimony of several prominent Californians (including John Bidwell, whose reputation for honesty was unsurpassed in these hearings), and had actually occupied his claim all along. It also helped that his lawyer, Henry Hancock (who was also the federal surveyor), understood that the earlier the case could be presented to the Land Commission, the better its chance of confirmation. With precedent a key factor, Hancock reasoned that fraudulent cases could later disadvantage authentic ones. Wolfskill's claim was filed on May 15, 1852, and while it took seventeen months for Hancock to collect the various documents and depositions, the Land Commission itself took less than a month to confirm the claim, on November 7, 1854. U.S. attorneys appealed the case but only as a matter of procedure. Their appeal was dismissed on March 14, 1857, and Wolfskill received his patent from President James Buchanan shortly thereafter.[2]

Juan Manuel Vaca and Juan Felipe Peña's experience with the Land Commission, in contrast to Wolfskill's, was anything but routine. To present their claim, they hired the prestigious law firm of Jones, Tomkins, and Strode (headed by William Carey Jones), who proceeded much the same way that Hancock had for Wolfskill. Nevertheless, on November 15, 1853, the Land Commission rejected Los Putos. The fact that Peña, for inexplicable reasons, used the name Armijo (his stepfather's name) in the grant documents raised considerable suspicion. Even more importantly, the claimants' lawyers did not have the grant properly surveyed, presumably because of its "floating" nature. Unlike most grants, which specified an amount of land in terms of given boundaries, Los Putos purported to give the grantees ten square leagues of land within an area five or six times that size. "The Commissioners," the opinion stated, "have no power to supply so vital a defect in the Claimants' testimony."

But the lawyers did have the power to conduct a survey. They could have simply made up the boundaries to Vaca's and Peña's liking—just as they had a year earlier with John C. Frémont's famous Mariposa claim, a grant whose floating nature was even more pronounced than that of Los Putos but which was nonetheless confirmed by both the Land Commission and the U.S. Supreme Court. With regard to Los Putos, however, Jones, Tomkins, and Strode—perhaps overconfident, perhaps less committed to Hispanic clients—presented the case badly. Though the California Land Act of 1851 in essence demanded it, few of these grants could be measured with any sort of precision. Even those that did not float, such as Rio de Los Putos, provided only vague approximations of their actual boundaries. It was left to the lawyers to impose or create that precision if they were to make a convincing case.[3]

After learning that lesson the hard way, Vaca and Peña hired John Currey to prosecute their appeal. Currey, a noted Solano County lawyer and future California Supreme Court justice, knew that he had a tough task ahead. The appeal would be presented before Justice Ogden Hoffman, the U.S. District Court judge who earlier had rejected Frémont's claim before being reversed himself by the U.S. Supreme Court. Currey cleared up the confusion over Vaca's name, carefully documented the history of the grant, and then insisted that ten square leagues

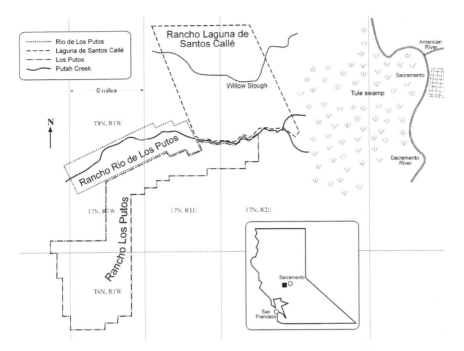

Putah Creek land grants, as surveyed in the 1850s (unofficially, in the case of Laguna de Santos Callé). Based on the patent maps for Rio de los Putos and Los Putos, U.S. Bureau of Land Management, California State Office, Sacramento, and "Map showing the Exterior lines of the Rejected Claims, Laguna de Santos Callé," California Room, California State Library, Sacramento.

could easily be located within the enlarged boundaries to everyone's satisfaction. On July 5, 1855, Hoffman, now in the position of having to anticipate the Supreme Court, reversed the Land Commission's decision, declaring Los Putos "to be a good and valid claim, to the extent of ten square leagues . . . and for no more."[4]

Currey did not offer his services for free, of course. His legal fees amounted to almost 4,500 acres of land—and not just any land. Currey insisted that most of his payment border the south bank of Putah Creek a few miles downstream from Wolfskill's eastern boundary, just opposite the Big Ranch, where the grant's most fertile soil could be found. To insure this, he personally "superintended," as he put it, the official survey of Los Putos, which was conducted by Dewitt C. Cage of the U.S. Surveyor General's Office in 1857. Currey's choice of location created a problem. The confirmed ten leagues had to be surveyed in such a way as to enclose both his claim and the nine square miles located eighteen miles to the southwest that Vaca had deeded to William McDaniel in 1850 on the condition that a city (Vacaville) be named after him. At the same time, the surveyed property had to extend to Wolfskill's grant to the west. The resulting plat, as one observer put it, "was more irregular than the map of Italy." Said another, it "stretched out in a zigzag, crooked, and irregular form" not only to include the desired portions of the grant but also to "catch in their net" several improvements that had been made by squatters. Nonetheless, in rapid succession, the survey was approved, the U.S. Supreme Court affirmed Hoffman's decree, and Vaca and Peña received their patent on June 4, 1858. Over the next several years, a number of lawsuits were filed to challenge the patent, but to no avail.[5]

Meanwhile, Rancho Laguna de Santos Callé generated a much more complicated set of legal issues because, as it turned out, it simply did not exist. A glance at the *diseños* of Rio de los Putos and Los Putos suggests that there was no land left for another grant in 1845. Both ranchos clearly lay on both sides of Putah Creek—"on the margins of the river," as the Los Putos claim read—and together extended from the Coast Range across the valley to the Sacramento River. But that did not prevent Victor Prudon and Marcos Vaca from squeezing in a phantom grant of 48,000 acres on the north bank of Putah Creek. While Vaca sincerely wanted the land for his cattle and for the prestige, Prudon's objective from the outset was to swindle land-hungry Anglos.[6]

As Commandante Mariano Vallejo's chief aid, Prudon knew that the situation was ripe for the taking. Even before the Bear Flag Revolt and subsequent occupation of Monterey in the summer of 1846, he and other officials realized that the end was near for Mexican California. The more Americans settled in the Sacramento Valley (roughly 1,000 by 1845), the more reluctant they were to follow Mexican laws and procedures, much less become Mexican citizens or convert to Catholicism. Not coincidentally, the granting of land greatly accelerated. Of the 700-odd claims that were issued after 1832 by the Mexican government, 115 were so-called midnight, or eleventh-hour, grants, dated 1845 or 1846 and totaling over 2 million acres. Colonization was no longer the objective. Most of the grants went to friends, business associates, and relatives of high-level Mexican officials, including Vallejo himself, in anticipation of the transfer of California to American control. The grantees had every reason to believe that the United States would follow the time-honored practice of respecting and protecting the land titles made under the previous regime and that land values would surely rise.[7]

Others, including Prudon, were not thinking that far in advance; resale was on their minds. The rush to push through claims when there was little or nothing to lose and plenty to gain led to considerable fraud and deceit—forged signatures, antedated documents, and widespread disregard for standard requirements, such as providing *diseños*, establishing residence, and making improvements. The most famous of these late grants was, once again, Frémont's ore-rich Rancho Las Mariposas, which the original grantee, Juan Alvarado, had never even seen, let alone occupied or improved. Another was Rancho Laguna de Santos Callé. When Prudon put the grant up for sale in early 1846, Joseph B. Chiles showed an immediate interest. The land, he later recalled, "was as well adapted to grazing cattle as any in California." Given the volatile political climate at the time, Chiles was suspicious at first, but after making several inquiries, he became satisfied that the grant was legitimate. Prudon had everyone fooled. Just as Chiles and Vaca were about to proceed, negotiations were put on hold by the string of events that transformed California at the end of the 1840s. When the dust settled, Prudon and Vaca had no problem finding buyers. The transplanted midwesterners who purchased large portions of Rancho Laguna de Santos Callé thought they had made a killing. But just who suckered whom would not be determined until the Land Commission convened in San Francisco in 1852.[8]

For Edmund L. Brown, Joshua Bailey, and C. I. Hutchinson, the principal petitioners in the hearing, the answer came soon enough. The evidence emerged, piece by piece, over four years. No *diseño* could be found, although the claimants had a map made to look like one. The various signatures of Governor Pio Pico on the title papers were either traced or forged. The date on which he presumably signed the papers had been a "feast day" between Christmas and New Year's several weeks after the Departmental Assembly had adjourned for the year. High-ranking officials of the Mexican government, from Vallejo to José de los Santos Berryessa, perjured themselves shamelessly. Prudon, who managed to avoid testifying, even offered to "make the title good" for the claimants in 1853 for an additional $10,000. Neither he nor Vaca, needless to say, ever established residence on the grant. Vaca, embarrassed by his role in the matter, spent most of the hearings in far-away Los Angeles. Nor did it help that the claimants' principal lawyer, Volney E. Howard, had earlier been a federal prosecutor—in the Los Putos case, no less. Like many of his peers, he saw how lucrative the other side could be. But Howard too made the wrong choice. When U.S. attorneys argued that the case was "fraudulent in all its parts," the Land Commission strongly concurred.[9]

They knew not the half of it. Though it never came out in the hearings, Rancho Laguna de Santos Callé was not only an out-and-out forgery, it also (had it existed, that is) overlapped with Rancho Los Putos. E. L. Brown had purchased 980 acres of his land on the north bank of Putah Creek not from Vaca and Prudon's Laguna de Santos Callé but from Vaca and Peña's Los Putos on July 7, 1851. Nor could Jerome C. Davis trace the deed to his land back to Laguna de Santos Callé.

His father-in-law, like Brown, had purchased his square league from Vaca and Peña on December 7, 1850. Everyone knew what was happening. The day after Brown's purchase, the owners of the grants filed an agreement at the Yolo County Recorder's Office that tried to reconcile their conflicting boundaries. All previous purchases from Los Putos north of Putah Creek would be recognized as valid, the agreement read, but the rest of the land north of the creek would belong to Laguna de Santos Callé. That the same boundary—Putah Creek—now separated Yolo and Solano counties made the division between the grants that much more legitimate, the claimants believed. Neither Brown nor Davis was going to take any chances, however. Both also secured deeds from the Laguna de Santos Callé grantees and then followed the proceedings of the Land Commission and subsequent appeals very closely. All they needed, both figured, was for one of the two grants to be confirmed.[10] In what was becoming a familiar refrain, it would not be that easy.

The claimants and their assignees on Rancho Laguna de Santos Callé were not the only ones who had a stake in the grant's outcome; large numbers of farmers and ranchers operating on a much smaller scale were also settling within or near its boundaries. Indeed, squatters and "swamplanders," as those who purchased tule land were called, played an equally significant and, in many ways, more lasting role in the making of Putah Creek. Small farms and large estates, the federal manuscript census of agriculture reveals, developed side by side up and down the Sacramento Valley—but with the former being much more numerous and widespread than has generally been acknowledged.[11]

These farmers and ranchers, large and small alike, were mired in a clash of fundamentally irreconcilable legal principles. On the one hand, when California was transferred to the United States by the Treaty of Guadalupe Hidalgo, landowners were guaranteed that their property rights would be "inviolably respected." The fact that 75 percent of the more than 800 Spanish and Mexican grants in California would eventually be confirmed testifies to the sanctity of treaty obligations and private property in American law. On the other hand, preemption—the preferential right of a settler to purchase public land at a modest price—seemed just as compelling. Most of these grants were huge—from one to eleven leagues—empty, and unproductive. For many who came of age on the midwestern frontier during the Jacksonian era, this was monopoly at its worst. For them, land was the foundation of opportunity, freedom, and independence in principle as well as law, as exemplified by the abundance of national and state preemption legislation passed in the 1830s and 1840s. It was inconceivable that, treaty or no treaty, thousands of acres of unsurveyed, unoccupied, and unimproved land could be granted to so few individuals. Only the U.S. government seemed not to be caught up in the heat of the moment. Consumed by the turbulence of the decade leading up to the Civil War, Congress treated California like an "unwanted child." The lack of attention, urgency, and funding given to the adjudication of these grants forced claimants and squatters to take matters into their own hands.[12]

Conflict on Laguna de Santos Callé was minimal, at first. Few squatters found the land desirable. Again, they judged the fertility of the soil just as they had in the Midwest—by the presence or absence of native vegetation, timber in particular. Thus, on Laguna de Santos Callé, only the land within a mile or two of Putah Creek or Willow Slough was deemed fit for cultivation. But that was precisely the land that Davis, Hutchinson, Greene, and the other claimants had already enclosed. The rest of the grant—the vast majority of its 48,000 acres—was open range, deemed fit only for livestock farming and held by the claimants as tenants in common. Squatters also were well aware that, should the grant be confirmed, they would be ejected and lose whatever improvements they had made. Most grants, moreover, were being confirmed, even Frémont's infamous Mariposa rancho, despite grave doubts as to its validity. Even though the claimants now knew that Laguna de Santos Callé was a fraud (Prudon told Hutchinson as much in 1853), they had reason to be confident of their case. Not surprisingly, squatters stayed away. The county assessor found only twenty in the immediate area in 1853, most of them along Putah Creek, either to the west or east of the grant's presumed boundaries, or far out on the prairie, and most of them small stock raisers.[13]

Among these were William Montgomery and Fred Werner, both of whom settled on Putah Creek just east of the Davis ranch in 1852—Montgomery and his family on the north bank, Werner on the south. A native of Germany and a lifelong bachelor, Werner seemed to have little in common with his neighbor from Missouri. But their status as "landless" farmers, passion for hunting, and love of quality stock—fine horses, in particular—created a strong bond between them. The two became known for leading high-stakes grizzly-killing expeditions in the wilds of Putah Sink—high stakes because of the extreme danger involved. Using fresh deer or antelope carcasses as bait, the hunters would wait at great peril in the thickets for the "great monsters" to appear. Even those known to be good shots found themselves tested to the utmost. The powerful beasts did not go down easily and on more than one occasion tore their attacker into pieces. With any luck, however, the hunters would have a wagon load of fresh meat ready for market in Sacramento, where bear jerky was considered a delicacy. After one particularly successful expedition in 1857, Montgomery and Werner pooled their earnings and, along with Davis, purchased three young stallions from an eastern breeder, thereby launching what would become one of the most famous racing stables in northern California. Montgomery and Werner were what many contemporaries called "bona fide" settlers—those who entered the land "in good faith" and with at least the tacit approval of the grant claimants.[14]

Larger numbers of squatters began to move in after the Land Commission struck down Laguna de Santos Callé on January 15, 1856. The claimants could still appeal their case to the U.S. District Court and, if necessary, to the Supreme Court. The mass of conflicting testimony, forged signatures, and shameless perjury from high officials of the Mexican government, however, strongly suggested that the land would sooner or later be declared part of the public domain and subject to preemption. A new U.S. attorney general, who seemed bent on vigorously defending government titles in California, increased the sense of doom hanging over Laguna de Santos Callé.[15] By the summer of 1856, at least 60 new settlers inhabited the region, and by September 18, 1860, when the U.S. District Court rejected the claimants' appeal, more than 130 had started small farms. To many contemporaries (and subsequent historians), these were "intruders," "law-breakers," or worse. They were the ones who gave squatters such a bad name in California, in contrast to the Midwest, where the term was not nearly as derogatory.[16]

A few ejection suits were filed while the case was on appeal. Most notably, George Peck, who purchased several hundred acres of land along Putah Creek from Hutchinson and Greene in 1853, fought squatter Lewis Horton three times in court before the end of the decade and at least once with his fists.[17] These sorts of battles were commonplace in California during the first two decades of statehood. With tensions high, violence could erupt at any time over land conflicts, as it did most conspicuously during the squatter riots in Sacramento in 1850 and on the Suscol claim thirteen years later. On a day-to-day basis, however, life on these land grants was generally more mundane. Conflict did not invariably dominate the relationship between squatters and "owners." Indeed, in Putah Creek, claimants sought more often to accommodate squatters than to fight them.[18]

In part, this was a deliberate strategy devised by the claimants' lawyers. Because no one could deny any longer that Laguna de Santos Callé was a hoax, the appeal had to be made on different grounds. The claimants, their lawyers argued, "ought not to be made to suffer" just because they had been hoodwinked. What had they done wrong, the lawyers asked, other than purchase the land in good faith, make large improvements, and in general "make a settlement" of an area that had previously been unsettled? With that in mind, Hutchinson, Davis, and ten other landholders had the entire grant surveyed, partitioned it among themselves with precise boundaries, sold off portions of the land not already enclosed, rented other parts, and even permitted squatting if agreements were made to vacate or purchase the land should the grant be confirmed.[19]

Claimants also found squatters to be invaluable as laborers. Their obsession with new technology notwithstanding, Hutchinson and Greene still needed fifteen to eighteen hands year-round and at least seventy during the harvest season by the end of the decade. In 1858 and 1859, most—perhaps two-thirds—of their harvesters were local squatters seeking to supplement their farm income. The going wage had dropped considerably since the early 1850s, to $2 per day, but was still an attractive option to small farmers just starting out. Davis, Brown, Lettner, and the other landholders also took advantage of this convenient source of experienced laborers. James T. Lillard, to cite just one example, worked for Davis for ten years while tending to 320 acres of his own on the northern fringes of his employer's stock farm.[20] Accommodation was a small price to pay, Davis and his cohorts believed. Conventional wisdom, after all, still insisted that squatters' land was no good anyway. As late as 1858, federal surveyors identified it as *adobe*— "second rate" and "unfit for cultivation."[21]

Unlike the Hispanic and Anglo rancheros a decade earlier, Putah Creek ranchers rarely employed Indian workers. Given the financial straits in which they found themselves for much of the 1850s, it may seem odd that they chose not to take advantage of this low-wage source of labor. Part of the reason lay in the ever-dwindling numbers of Indians. During the 1850s, the native population in California fell by 80 percent, to about 30,000, and very few of those who survived lived in the lower Sacramento Valley. At the same time, California had the highest ratio of white farm laborers to farmers in the United States. In addition, the proliferation of farm machinery gave employers fewer incentives to hire Indians, who generally were not considered capable or worthy of operating the new technology. Moreover, the mere presence of Indians, let alone putting them to work on their ranches, would have compromised, in the minds of these ranchers, their efforts to create "wealth, comfort, and virtue." There were Anglo farmers in the Sacramento Valley who continued to employ Indian workers after the gold rush— John Bidwell and John Sutter, for example—but the new emigrants preferred the comfort and familiarity of white hired hands and plowboys wherever they were available.[22]

A number of these squatter/laborers on Rancho Laguna de Santos Callé were determined to cultivate the adobe, conventional wisdom notwithstanding. While roughly two-thirds stayed with stock raising, the others turned to wheat and barley, the crops that had served them so well in the Midwest. The land proved to be more fertile than it appeared. The water level was only nine to twelve feet below the surface, and the soil, though considerably harder than the bottomlands, could still be cultivated if plowed after the first heavy rains in November or December. Yields were not spectacular, but twenty bushels per acre were common. In fact, squatters such as Andrew McClory, William Platt, and Silas Woolery found that just about anything that grew back home would also grow on "Putah prairie," as they called it, including apple, peach, and pear trees, grapes, corn, oats, beans, peas, onions, and potatoes.

No one was more stunned by these developments than the county assessor upon making his rounds in the summer of 1858. He found at least sixty "improved" farms on Laguna de Santos Callé where none had existed a year or two earlier, each containing 25 to 125 acres of wheat or barley, newly planted orchards and vineyards, more than a few hogs, turkeys, and chickens, and a horse or two. The amount of "miscellaneous" property the assessor recorded for each farmer— roughly $50 to $500—suggests that they either owned or shared in the purchase of reapers, mowers, plows, and threshers. So unprepared was the assessor for all this that he had to record his findings on blank pages in the back of his roll. Just three years later his report to the State Surveyor-General credited the "fertility and fruitfulness" of Putah Prairie to the "practical experience" of its farmers.[23]

An even greater surprise emerged from the tule swamps between Laguna de Santos Callé and the Sacramento River, which had been judged even more "unfit for cultivation" than the adobe. These "impenetrable thickets" did not deter settlers either, especially those with experience draining swampy prairies in the Midwest.[24] Among the first was William Marden, a New Hampshire native who at the age of twenty-seven had already lived in five different states. In October 1855, Marden removed to what became known as the South Putah district, where the Tule and Putah Sink overlapped to such an extent that it was impossible to say where one swamp began and the other ended. The daunting task of reclaiming the land appeared not to phase Marden, whose reputation for toughness and fortitude had already been well established on the overland trail, where he single-handedly guided a company of forty-niners safely through a particularly difficult journey. For his efforts, he too earned the sobriquet "General," which stayed with him all his life, even after failing in the goldfields of El Dorado County along with most of his fellow argonauts.[25]

Like other swamplanders, Marden found the terms set by the California state legislature irresistible. A settler could purchase a maximum of 320 acres for one dollar per acre with a down payment of just 10 percent and the balance, with no interest, due in five years. If half the land was reclaimed by that time, the state would grant title. Swamplanders chose their locations very carefully. The tule lands were not uniform in composition, but consisted of a maze of sloughs, channels, and the so-called islands they formed. The first purchasers snatched the largest of these islands. Not wanting to waste a single acre, they insisted that the county surveyor include only "dry" land in their official plats. The resulting field notes often resembled those of Mexican land grants—"commencing at a stake standing in the timber about twenty five or thirty feet from a large Cottonwood," as the description of Marden's 320-acre tract began. In all, thirty-five settlers, including Marden, took up the challenge in South Putah in 1855, followed by forty-one in 1856 and another forty-two by the end of the decade.[26]

Most found it a tantalizing experience. Stock raisers, such as Marden, Sessions M. Enos, and Ransom S. Carey, learned that burning off the tule in the fall created lush pastureland the following spring, and grain farmers who undertook the arduous task of clearing and draining the land, such as brothers John C. and Lewis C. Drummond, discovered rich, porous soil. It did not take long for them to realize, however, that the landscape itself changed constantly, some years more dramatically than others. The sloughs and channels that meandered endlessly throughout the region often abruptly altered their course during winter storms. What might be an island one summer, in other words, could very well be under water the following spring. The winters between 1855 and 1860, moreover, were mild by Sacramento Valley standards. The real test for swamplanders would not come until the following decade.[27]

There were other serious problems as well. Swamplanders knew that, like squatters, they too could be ejected if the courts confirmed Rancho Laguna de Santos Callé and included all or part of the tule swamps within its borders. Just where to draw the line between swamp and dry land was not clear either. The federal Swamp Land Act of 1850, which ceded these lands to the state, required U.S. surveyors to decide, but after waiting five years the state legislature authorized its own survey—in effect allowing people to make swampland purchases prior to federal approval. Buyers lived in fear that the swampland they purchased from the state might later be declared federal land. Another problem was the expense of reclamation itself. Small farmers simply could not afford to pay the estimated $960 needed to reclaim 320 acres, let alone what it might cost to maintain the land thereafter. They planted crops and made improvements just like their neighbors out on the prairie, but by the end of 1860 more than 90 percent of them had forfeited their land back to the state. There was nothing in the law that prevented them from trying again—on the same property or somewhere else—and almost half of them, including Marden, Carey, Enos, and the Drummonds, did just that.[28]

Swamplanders and squatters were seduced by the potential riches of the region every bit as much as large landholders. Given a taste of what the Sacramento Valley could produce, they were bound and determined to overcome all obstacles. The gold rush alone did not make them hungry for achievement and profit; they brought their appetites with them from the Midwest. But the gold rush did raise the stakes considerably. Emigrants hoped to get rich in California. Those who fell short of that lofty goal in the goldfields of the Sierra Nevada foothills felt tremendous pressure to succeed in the grain fields and pastures of the Sacramento Valley. The reapers and threshers now at their disposal, moreover, seemed to provide them with yet another golden opportunity. In the blink of an eye, they anglicized (or more specifically, midwesternized) the agricultural economy—farming, ranching, and market relations—to meet their needs in their new home. Few, if any, referred to themselves as *dons,* employed Mexican agricultural practices, or married into Hispanic families. As for Mexican land policy, it only seemed to get in their way.

In their haste to succeed in California, they committed themselves not only to material pursuits but to community life as well. Neither the legal chaos caused by Ranchos Rio de Los Putos, Los Putos, and Laguna de Santos Callé, nor the seductions of farming in the Sacramento Valley, nor the unfulfilled dreams of the gold rush dampened the community sentiments they had brought with them from the Midwest. In the mass of confusion of the 1850s, speculators, farmers, squatters, and swamplanders did, in fact, "make a settlement"—Putah Creek, as they called it as early as 1852. Its highly active economy and "spirited citizenry" made it, in the eyes of a reporter from the *Daily Alta California* of San Francisco in 1860, "the richest cereal district in California" and a community of "splendid success"—even though not one farmer, large or small, held clear title to the land.[29]

CHAPTER FOUR

"A Very Public Place"

A trotting stallion named Rattler died on the ranch of Jerome C. Davis on April 10, 1863. Rattler was no ordinary horse. One of the three purchased by William Montgomery, Fred Werner, and Davis in 1857, Rattler won more races, took more premiums, and earned more in stud fees than any horse in northern California over the course of his illustrious career. His record time of five minutes and twelve seconds in a two-mile heat against "Honest John" at the state fair three years earlier was already the stuff of legends—so much so that the *Sacramento Daily Union* ran Rattler's obituary as its feature news story on April 13. "The death of this fine animal," the paper bemoaned, "will be regretted by turfmen throughout the State."[1]

Rattler's passing was especially regretted by those who cheered him the most—settlers along Putah Creek. The beloved trotting stallion helped put this burgeoning community on the map. Indeed, the celebration of Rattler's life and the mourning of his death reveal how quickly rural life matured in the decade or so after the gold rush and, more precisely, the resolve with which these miners-turned-farmers tried to replicate the Midwest. Rural California, simply put, developed just as "instantly" as urban California.[2] What took a generation or more in Sugar Creek, Illinois, for example, happened all at once in Putah Creek, California—that is, a self-conscious community with many distinctive features evolved well beyond the frontier state. Putah Creek was characterized not by subsistence farming, Indian wars, and kinship bonds, but by market-oriented agriculture, legal battles, and displaced forty-niners.[3] Nonetheless, in just a few years, residents shared strong community sentiments—a specific sense of place, similar patterns of everyday life, common obligations, and a number of public rituals and institutions that pulled men, and eventually women, together as a social unit. Dreams of striking it rich preceded rural settlement in the Sacramento Valley but did not preempt community. The legend of Rattler the trotting stallion could not have evolved otherwise.

At first glance, Putah Creek had neither the look nor the feel of a community. The farms and ranches that developed there seemed isolated from one another, and no nucleated village or town center existed that bound people together—save for Sacramento, which was fifteen miles away and often inaccessible in the winter. The settlers themselves did not find this unusual. In fact, this was typical of rural development in the trans-Appalachian and trans-Mississippi wests. These "open-country settlements" actually fostered a sense of community. The lack of any sort of "downtown" or compactness compelled people to find cooperative means of production, develop creative systems of exchange, intermarry within the area, and join together in any number of other communal patterns.[4] But Putah Creek was different. Open-country communities prospered elsewhere because settlers brought with them a tradition of self-sufficient farming. What kind of community, if any, could be maintained when the number-one concern was profit? Did farmers whose preeminent goal was to compete and accumulate capital even care about community? Was community of any sort even possible where no rational person, it seems in retrospect, should have taken up farming in the first place, given the high costs of production, land controversies, and volatile climate?[5]

The abandonment of self-sufficiency, it turns out, did not mean the abandonment of all traditional values. Nowhere was this more evident than on the open range of Rancho Laguna de Santos Callé. When ranchers, large and small alike, let their stock graze freely on the open pasture, they were following a practice that went back many generations. Only now, they were raising cattle, sheep, and hogs primarily for market, not for subsistence. Nonetheless, the open range still necessitated cooperation, particularly in locating lost and stolen animals.[6]

Three of the first laws passed by the state legislature addressed the issue directly. The first simply required owners to identify their animals with distinctive marks or brands and register them with the county. William Montgomery followed the second to the letter in November 1857, as any of his neighbors would have done. When two "American" steers wandered on to his homestead, he posted (within the ten-day limit) a full written description of their marks and brands, along with a sworn statement that he had made no alterations, at all the nearby ranches and gave a copy to the local justice of the peace. The judge then appointed two of Montgomery's peers, Silas Woolery and Ransom S. Carey, to appraise the animals. For the next twelve months or until they were claimed, Montgomery assumed responsibility for the care of the strays and could be fined if found negligent. When that period expired, he had first option of purchasing the animals, with the proceeds going to the county. The third law concerned outright theft, perhaps the most heinous crime of all on this or any frontier. Grand larceny would be the charge. A stiff fine and jail sentence awaited the perpetrator, but the even greater deterrent was expulsion from the community that worked so diligently to protect itself from rustlers. Everyone benefited, but especially squatters, who could rarely afford to fence in their animals.[7]

Grain farming also fostered a sense of community identity. Although machines were used with increasing frequency, there was still a rhythm to the cycle of production that linked wheat and barley growers together. Great anticipation as well as great anxiety began every year as early as November, when plowing, seeding, and harrowing began. By the late 1850s, the Big Ranch and other large farms commonly used gang plows, which enabled one man and eight horses to turn over more land than fifty men could with single plows. Everyone then held their collective breath for the next few months, hoping that nature would cooperate. If heavy rains did not flood the fields, or if little or no rain did not dry them up, or if a severe hail storm did not damage the standing crop, or if a hot north wind did not sweep down the Sacramento Valley unhindered by forest cover in May or June and knock the heavy ripe kernels off the stock, then the grain would be ready for harvest.

Horse-drawn reapers first cut the stalks close to the ground. They were followed by crews of two or three men who raked the gavels of cut grain together, bound the sheaves, and hauled them to a central location for threshing. In the Midwest, shocking (stacking the bound sheaves upright in the field for drying) preceded threshing, but the dry, hot summer air in the Sacramento Valley cured the grain as it ripened, rendering this stage unnecessary. Another crew of men then fed the stalks into a treadmill thresher, powered by horses walking around the machine in an endless circle, to separate the grain from the straw. Larger farmers who owned their own machines (which cost about $700 in the late 1850s) threshed not only their own crop but also, for a share, crops brought in by squatters and swamplanders. The grain was then loaded onto wagons for the short haul to Sacramento. Farmers both large and small shared an avid interest in the outcome and talked endlessly among themselves about ways to improve the system. They took great pride in Putah Creek's reputation as "the richest cereal district" in the state, which in turn gave them a strong attachment to their new home and a sense of communal feeling.[8]

While no central village or town existed in the region, Putah Creek did assume a certain shape by the end of the 1850s. At the center of both its geography and economy was the ranch of Jerome C. Davis. Most large landholders agreed that accommodation with squatters was best for all concerned, but only Davis saw that there was money to be made from it. All these new farms, he realized, required capital, machinery, and markets. Borrowing $10,000 from Sacramento heiress Anna Tryon in 1856, Davis built a slaughterhouse, a steam flour mill, a dairy, and two large "manufacturing shops." By 1860, virtually every settler within a five-mile radius of the Davis ranch had opened an account, with balances ranging from $5 to $5,000. They sold their stock and produce, obtained advances, and purchased reapers, wagons, harnesses, buggies, and various "sundries" such as salt, gunpowder, rope, and coffee. Prices and interest rates were slightly higher than could be obtained in Sacramento, but the convenient access to market more than made up for it, especially during the winter months, when crossing the Tule was often impossible. Davis then sold the flour, fresh meat, and dairy products not only to Sacramento merchants and hotels but also to landholders in the area with large workforces. The profits he made as middleman more than offset his losses in the declining cattle market. By one contemporary's account, he was the only farmer in Putah Creek not to have lost money during the 1850s. With an estate worth almost $110,000, he was the wealthiest man in the region by 1860.[9]

Several distinct neighborhoods and landmarks also developed around the Davis ranch. Most of the original 170 or so ranches carved out of Ranchos Laguna de Santos Callé and Los Putos by the claimants, squatters, and swamplanders became well known to all inhabitants. In most cases, the land was named after its owner, and those names continued to be recognized long after the owners had passed from the scene—as in, "the road that passes the old Bailey ranch." The same was true for sloughs (Bable's), bends in the creek (Brown's), crossings (Gregory's, Peck's), bridges (Merritt's), and other sites. Smaller ranches were often clumped together in named clusters—Putah Sink, Putah Prairie, Plainfield, Willow Slough, Tremont—some of which offered small service facilities. The Tule House halfway to Sacramento, the Solano House in Tremont south of Putah Creek, and Plainfield Center just north of the Big Ranch, for example, provided residents and travelers small stores, blacksmiths, and saloons. Of those neighborhoods, only Plainfield established any sort of ethnic identity, with the Oestes, Schmeisers, Heinzes, Blanchards, Meyers, and Rooses among the German immigrant families who settled there. And only Tremont belonged to another county, Solano, whose northern boundary was the creek itself. Because the population of Solano County was centered far to the southwest in Vallejo, Benicia, and Suisun City (and later Fairfield), the small number of residents in Tremont, tucked in between Rancho Los Putos and the Tule, identified much more with their neighbors north of the creek in Yolo County. By ordering and naming these and other elements of the landscape, the men and women of Putah Creek were making a cumulative, active record of the place they had come to share.[10]

This evolving community was shaped by more than the forces of economic life and geographic place. By the end of the decade, the Davis ranch had become the center of Putah Creek's economy as well as its social and cultural life. Or, as Davis himself later put it, it became not only a marketplace but also "a very public place." The two were, of course, very much interconnected. It was not unusual, for example, especially in the summer months, for fifteen to twenty squatters and swamplanders to conduct transactions on the same day. This gave them the opportunity to discuss new farming techniques, to boast of their recent improvements, and to bask in their accomplishments in the midst of the large, modern facilities on the famous Davis stock farm. The establishment of a tavern in 1859 suggests that male patrons were making the trip whether hauling crops or not.[11]

Other activities on the ranch reflected the growing presence of women in the area. In the early 1850s, males outnumbered females by more than nine to one. But as miners-turned-farmers felt more comfortable on their homesteads and, more importantly, felt the pinch of labor, they began calling for their families to join them. By 1860, single-male farms were the exception rather than the rule.[12] As a result, evening dances and Sunday morning church services conducted by itinerant preachers were held regularly in Davis's palatial home. The biggest event of the year was the Fourth of July, when families gathered from miles around. In 1856, ceremonies commenced with Davis himself reading the Declaration of Independence, followed by toasts to the governor of California and the president of the United States, political discussions (the Vigilance Committee of San Francisco was a hot topic that year), sack races, apple bobbing, a greased-pole contest, an elegant supper, and dancing that continued well into the night. Given the lack of extensive kin and family networks in the region, these community activities took on special meaning to settlers trying to preserve in the Sacramento Valley what they had valued back home.[13]

They also took on special meaning to the Davises themselves during a particularly painful time in their lives. Jerome and Mary's daughter, Amelia Susanna, was killed in a tragic accident in 1856 at the age of three. While playing a favorite game with her father in his new mill, she accidentally fell from a moving belt and was fatally injured. In one horrifying moment, the symbol of Davis's rise to wealth became the site of his worst nightmare come true. The distraught parents would not have another child. "After this little one was killed," Mary's obituary stated, "none succeeded it in its parents hearts." Making their home "a very public place" may very well have been the Davis's way of compensating for their heart-breaking loss.[14]

Women committed themselves to this new community in other ways as well, both traditional and innovative. With regard to work, women made their presence known in no uncertain terms, as demonstrated by the experiences of Eunice Pierce and Bertha Greene (Charles's wife) on the Big Ranch. Both engaged in traditional women's responsibilities, tending to the garden, raising chickens, making soap, and producing homespun and dairy products. Only in dire emergencies did they assist their husbands in the field. With the dairy, however, the two women took an expanded role, producing not just for home consumption or small surpluses. As early as 1855, they were in charge of the massive dairy operation on the Big Ranch. A writer from the *California Culturist* marveled at the way these "accomplished ladies" managed the herd of 100 milch cows and a small crew of "dairy women," and came to appreciate why "the produce stands so high among consumers in the Sacramento market." As the Big Ranch lost money year after year in wheat and barley, dairy became an increasingly "important item in the receipts of the farm," bringing in $1,000 to $2,000 a month by the end of the decade. Far less is known about the dairy on the Davis ranch, but there is little reason to believe that it operated much differently.[15]

With regard to marriage, there was considerably less activity. Because the vast majority of the few women in the region arrived already married, weddings, perhaps the premier event of the rural social season back home, were few and far between in Putah Creek. Only ten were recorded in the county register before 1861, many of which were held on the Davis ranch. Though no one could have known it at the time, the significance of those weddings would far outweigh their numbers. The marriages of James T. Lillard and Mary Mears in 1853, and of Lewis Drummond and Eliza Reid (a sister of his brother John's wife) five years later, for example, seemed to be random, unconnected events. It would not be long, however, before son Henry Lillard would marry daughter Jennie Drummond, or before other offspring in the two families would marry into other original settler families—a pattern of intermarriage that would bind this community together even more in the coming years.[16]

And with regard to religion—the building of churches, in particular—there was still less activity. On the midwestern frontier, settlers established churches almost immediately, but not in Putah Creek. The reason, once again, seems to have been the lack of strong family and kinship connections. In the Midwest, church congregations first coalesced around kin-related groups that moved into an area together. Groups of interrelated families constituted the core of each church. Near Putah Creek, Baptist/Presbyterian services were held every Sabbath in Silveyville, a stage stop about four miles south of the Big Ranch, though in the sitting room of Elijah Silvey's hotel, not a proper church. Several residents in southern Yolo County, including the Greenes and the Pierces, attended on occasion. On special days it was not unusual for families to make the one-to-two-hour ride to Sacramento. For the most part, however, itinerant preachers, or "circuit riders," had to suffice. For much of the 1850s, Methodist minister Henry B. Sheldon filled that role. His circuit covered most of the Sacramento Valley west of the river and north of Putah Creek. Riding twenty to forty miles a day, he preached three to five times each Sabbath and most weekday evenings as well. Ministers of other denominations followed, but an actual church in the area was not established until late in the 1860s—just about the time, not coincidentally, when families began to intermarry.[17]

While men and women were gradually discovering their common ties and interests, Putah Creek was receiving considerable recognition from outside the community. For much of the 1850s, Putah Creek was as famous as any farming district in northern California, due in large part to the publicity given to the productive exploits of the Big Ranch and the Davis stock farm. During the second half of the decade, the state fair gave numerous others the opportunity to showcase their community. Every fall, usually in late September or early October, Putah Creek residents and thousands of other farm people eagerly descended upon Sacramento (the permanent site of the fair after 1858) to view crop and cattle exhibits, inspect new farm machinery, and sample the many diverse entertainments. The air of excitement was exhilarating, especially for those who vied for the coveted cash premiums. The most celebrated prize-winner from Putah Creek was Rattler, the trotting stallion. Many others participated in a wide array of other competitions—for the best displays of various grains, fruits, vegetables, flowers, and livestock, and for the best leatherwork and embroidery, for example. That fair officials thought it necessary to establish a Committee on Protests to handle disputes reveals just how seriously these contests were taken.

Putah Creek always did well, but in 1859 its reputation soared. That year, C. I. Hutchinson delivered the presidential address, Rattler won several races, and no fewer than twenty Putah Creek men and women entered competitions, with nine taking away premiums. Perhaps the surest signal of Putah Creek's ascension to prominence occurred when an enterprising manufacturer from San Jose sought out Hutchinson to promote a new invention, the steam-powered thresher. No other farm region stirred so much excitement.[18]

Rattler trotting to victory at the California State Fair in 1858. *Transactions of the California State Agricultural Society during the Year 1858* (Sacramento: State Printer, 1859). Department of Special Collections, University of California Library, Davis.

With the increased attention came a greater sense of responsibility to the community, which for the men of Putah Creek was manifested in public rituals of local democracy. Nothing made them feel more at home or simply more important than the activities, procedures, and institutions of township and county government. Most of these were established by the first state legislature of California in 1850 and the state constitution itself, often employing the identical language of lawmakers from the Midwest—Iowa, in particular. Putah Township itself, which engulfed much of Rancho Laguna de Santos Callé and surrounding lands, was established the following year. Residents expected that they would be called upon to serve and serve they did. Though important decisions might be made in Sacramento, San Francisco, and Washington, D.C., Putah Creek residents focused primarily on local issues and placed a premium on local participation—even though none of them had lived in the area for more than a few years.[19]

At the very least, participation meant paying their taxes—which over 90 percent of them did in the 1850s.[20] Property taxes were tricky. No statute stipulated how to assess farms on Mexican land grants whose status before the California Land Commission or an appellate court was pending, or whether farms without titles should be assessed at all. This was also long before any principle of state equalization existed, which meant that taxation could vary from county to county and even within counties. Every November and December after the county assessor had made his rounds, the Board of Supervisors (which doubled as the county's Board of Equalization) faced long lines of farmers waiting to negotiate what they would pay. The board often tried to increase the assessed value of unimproved, or "wild," land on Rancho Laguna de Santos Callé to $2.00 or $3.00 per acre but was almost always talked down to $1.25. The assessed value of improved or enclosed land, however, rose from $3.00 to as high as $10.00 per acre over the course of the decade. All taxes (state, county, school, road, hospital, poll) were levied against property and were collected together at varying rates per $100 of taxable property owned (real, personal, and improvements).

Things could add up very quickly, especially for the large ranches. In 1856, for example, Jerome C. Davis paid almost $225 (on $18,000 of property taxed at $1.25 per $100 of assessed value), and that was after his successful appeal to reduce the value of his land. Four years later, after adding 4,000 acres to his estate and substantially increasing the size of his herds, his tax bill totaled $789 (on $54,440 at $1.45 per $100). Between 1856 and 1863, Davis paid almost $6,000 in taxes into the county coffers. Some land "owners" refused to pay (for example, E. L. Brown in 1856), but again the vast majority consented year in and year out. Delinquent payers faced fines but rarely paid those either, knowing that board members realized it was cheaper to avoid litigation than to try to collect the tax or the fine. Grant claimants may also have feared the possibility that the Land Commission or U.S. District Court would find them unworthy of a patent for not paying their taxes.[21]

Compliance, however, came less from fear of retribution and more from a sense of obligation. Government, the taxpayers of Putah Creek knew from past experience, rested squarely on their shoulders. When called upon, large landholders, squatters, and swamplanders not only paid their taxes but also sat on juries, supervised elections in their own homes, appraised stray animals, and, perhaps most importantly early on, built roads and bridges. The law required every able-bodied adult male to donate five days' labor each year on the roads, and virtually no one refused. To do so would have been to violate a tradition that went as far back as the Middle Ages. Citizens decided where roads would be built by petitioning the Board of Supervisors and determined their quality by the time and energy devoted to their construction.

By 1860, a matrix of roads and bridges connected farmers in the region to the Davis ranch, Sacramento, and other important points. These included roads from Putah Creek to Washington, Cacheville, and Woodland (each served as the county seat at one time or another in the 1850s, with Woodland taking the honor permanently in 1862); a plank road through the Tule to Sacramento, which required considerable repair after every winter; several bridges across Willow Slough and other swampy areas; and another bridge across Putah Creek at the Davis ranch. Farmers worked in local "districts" with their own neighbors on the roads and bridges they used the most, socializing and often sharing meals during breaks. Road building, in short, did not just enhance the community; it was itself a community-building activity.[22]

The centrality of localism was also reflected in the large number of individuals who sought county and township offices. Sixty-seven men from Putah Township ran for judge, sheriff, assessor, coroner, auditor, public administrator, surveyor, treasurer, or recorder between 1855 and 1860. The most important local official was the justice of the peace, whose term lasted just one year. State law limited their jurisdiction to claims of $200 or less, but settlers invariably turned first to their local judge to settle just about any dispute. In six straight elections between 1857 and 1862, voters in Putah Township entrusted the office to George W. Pierce.[23]

Pierce became a local hero of sorts when he sued the administrator of Angus Frierson's estate in the summer of 1856. The Big Ranch's largest creditor never paid Pierce or his wife their wages, which then totaled $1,700. On the advice of the local justice at the time, swamplander William Marden, Pierce filed his complaint in the District Court of Sacramento County and, upon losing there, appealed to the California Supreme Court. At stake was a large sum of money as well as the fate of dozens of Putah Creek workers who shared the Pierces' predicament. The main opposition, it turned out, came from the Big Ranch's long line of creditors, who argued that their loans took precedence over back wages. The court ruled otherwise and awarded Pierce a full settlement—$2,345, including interest. As justice of the peace, Pierce showed no mercy for negligent employers, consistently enforcing his own precedent, as in the case of *Hext v. Hartley* (1858), when he awarded the plaintiff, a former co-worker on the Big Ranch and future neighbor, a $750 settlement.[24]

It was not a coincidence that Judge Pierce, as he would be known for the rest of his life, was a Yankee. Of the sixty-seven men from Putah Township who sought office between 1850 and 1860, at least fifty of them had been born in New England or New York, and most of them had migrated from Yankee settlements in the upper Midwest. In part, this reflects their dominance of the population—42 percent by 1860.[25] It also reemphasizes that this community formed less around ethnicity and religion than around enterprise and expediency. The process of transplanting ethnic and religious values, traditions, and institutions from one community to another required groups of interrelated families, friends, and neighbors to migrate together or in chains. That was the typical pattern of migration *to* the Midwest but not *from* the Midwest. In Putah Creek, the lack of extensive family ties and kinship networks among displaced gold rushers left control of township government up for grabs. Because upland southerners tended to be slow to develop locals institutions (except for churches) and Yankees just the opposite, it is not surprising who seized the initiative.[26]

This is not to say that Putah Creek was a full-fledged Yankee settlement in 1860. One need look no further than at Rattler, the trotting stallion, to make the point. Horse racing was not part of the Yankee heritage. Even as the sport spread northward from Kentucky and Virginia during the first half of the nineteenth century—even, for example, as "Justin Morgan," a product of Vermont, became the most famous horse in America and the progenitor of a long line of fast trotters—Yankees continued to look down on the sport. Horse racing, they believed, was just as vulgar as gambling, drinking, cockfighting, dueling, and other southern vices.[27] In Putah Creek, such sentiments were tempered by community loyalties that found vivid expression in cheering and betting on Rattler. Some transplanted Yankees no doubt retained their disdain for such things, but many adopted Rattler as their own, including Charles Greene and at least six others who paid $100 each to have their mares covered by the famous trotting stallion. Moreover, Jerome C. Davis—a Yankee in spirit if not by birth—owned a one-third interest in him, along with upland southerner William Montgomery and German immigrant Fred Werner—symbolizing, in many ways, a flattening of cultural differences in this post–gold rush farming community.[28]

Nor is this to say that Putah Creek was somehow conflict-free; it would be difficult to imagine a more litigious group of people. They sued each other over every imaginable issue, both serious and trivial, from past-due promissory notes and land disputes worth thousands of dollars to personal slights and insults harmful to no one but the litigants.[29] This was not unique to Putah Creek. It was reminiscent of much of rural America in the nineteenth century, before society came to rely on the state and federal governments to oversee and police economic and social life. People instead tended to turn to the lawsuit as a ready instrument for regulating day-to-day affairs and were quite willing to abide by the decisions of the local judicial system. With so few ethnic or religious institutions, Putah Creek residents placed even greater faith in the law's orderly procedures. A rape case such as *The People v. Solomon Thorn* (1855), for example, might well have been handled more discreetly by the local church in a typical midwestern community. Here, however, jury members, witnesses, attorneys, and the judge himself, all well known to one another, assembled in an open courtroom, heard the graphic details of the case ("he threw me down; pants unbuttoned; hurt me with his thing"), and walked away after a guilty verdict was reached, convinced that justice had been served and a community consensus approximated.[30]

The biggest community conflict of all raged over Rancho Laguna de Santos Callé. Although the hearings before the Land Commission and the Federal District Court pit claimants and their assignees against squatters and, to a lesser degree, swamplanders, in the end that struggle became interwoven in the evolving patterns of community life. Hutchinson, Davis, Brown, Lettner, and other "owners," after all, fought together for more than a decade to establish title of their claims. Their unity never appeared stronger than at a crucial meeting held on the Big Ranch on March 10, 1856, shortly after the Land Commission had declared their grant invalid. Things looked grim. Each of them was already deeply in debt and hoping desperately to get it all back the next harvest, and now it looked as if they all were going to lose everything. Davis, who had as much at stake as anyone, took charge and convinced the others that they had come too far to quit now. They agreed to band together, go forward with the appeal, and share all expenses at a rate proportional to their holdings. Davis and Hutchinson were selected as "agents" for the group and given free reign to "take whatever steps as may be deemed expedient to secure the confirmation of the title." Over the next three years, they would spend more than $10,000 on legal fees and on numerous trips to Sacramento, San Francisco, and Los Angeles in search of new evidence and witnesses who would testify on their behalf. Squatters and swamplanders were less organized but no less committed to saving their farms. Some of them reportedly hired a lawyer of their own to help the federal prosecutors make their case. "When a witness was needed," one observer testified, "they got them" a witness.[31]

Their differences notwithstanding, claimants, squatters, and swamplanders alike shared a common goal that minimized the divisive effects of title disputes: They all wanted Putah Creek to be a great agricultural community worthy of all the booster rhetoric. The featured article in the *Daily Alta California* of San Francisco that declared Putah Creek to be "the richest cereal district in California" maintained that they were well on their way toward achieving that goal. The reporter praised Putah Creek farmers for the "immense amount of capital, care, and hard work they have expended." Despite all their hardships, he continued, "the proprietors, undismayed and persevering, have gone forward together in improving their broad acres." It may have been more accurate to state that they had come together and moved forward precisely *because* of their hardships. Whether fighting in court among themselves or with outsiders or battling the elements year after year, Putah Creek farmers remained convinced that they had struck gold, and they were not going to give up easily.[32]

Perhaps no one demonstrated that resolve more than George and Eunice Pierce. By the end of the decade, Judge Pierce had arguably become the most influential individual in Putah Creek. Working out of his small house on the Big Ranch, he heard almost every dispute that arose and was responsible for either making a decision or sending the case to the proper trial court. Everyone knew him and was acquainted with his idiosyncrasies and biases. Neither a claimant nor a squatter, George's middle position allowed him enough independence to mediate between the two factions. This not only helped account for his local popularity; it also played no small role in preventing the community from becoming hopelessly divided.[33]

George and Eunice had come a long way since that wet winter day in 1854 when they arrived to work for Hutchinson and Greene. Ever ambitious and achievement-oriented, both rose up through the ranks very quickly—she taking charge of the dairy and he becoming Greene's chief assistant, helping him manage ranch operations, from wheat and barley production to raising cattle and hogs. Both were highlighted in the *Alta California* article. George drew praise for the "crack crop" of wheat on the Big Ranch, "which for quality as well as quantity stands unrivalled." The butter, eggs, and chickens raised by his "industrious and amiable wife" impressed the reporter all the more, even if his conception of a typical farm wife caused him to underestimate Eunice's role in management.[34]

Both, moreover, believed they were on the verge of realizing their dream. Despite all the economic and legal problems they witnessed first hand, George and Eunice were still mesmerized by the Big Ranch. Using almost every last dollar of the settlement awarded to him by the state supreme court, George purchased 383 acres of prime land along Putah Creek (roughly one fourth of the original 1,374 acres enclosed by Hutchinson and Greene) on September 29, 1860, having rented it for several months. It was also time, they were now both convinced, to retrieve their nine-year-old son from Wisconsin, who until then had seemed destined to become an orphan of the gold rush. Eunice made the trip in the summer of 1859, not back over the overland route, which she could not face again, but by boat and across the Isthmus of Panama. After a month-long stay with Jonathan, Electra, and Elijah in Kenosha, Eunice returned with George Jr. just about the same time that George received the deed for his property. Less than a year later, their third son, Frank Alonzo, was born. Putah Creek was now their home.[35]

PART TWO

DISASTER AND PERSISTENCE

CHAPTER FIVE

"To Begin Again"

In the winter of 1861–62, a flood of enormous, almost biblical proportions hit the Sacramento Valley. It began in early December, when a series of warm, tropical rains melted several feet of snow that had accumulated in the Sierra Nevada. Rampaging rivers poured out of their channels, filling much of the valley in less than three days. On the morning of December 9, the American River burst though its levee at Thirty-first Street in Sacramento, submerging the city in a "sea of water" by sunset. As the floodwaters were receding, an even fiercer storm hit, on January 10, spreading devastation throughout the valley. Cattle died by the tens of thousands, cities and towns, most notably Sacramento and Marysville, were buried deep in water and mud, farms and ranches were destroyed, and hundreds of people were swept away to their deaths by high waters. "This is a fearful calamity," wrote one newspaper, that only "an Angry God" could have precipitated. To this day, the "double flood" of 1861–62 remains the most massive in the state's history and one of its worst natural disasters.[1]

Putah Creek was hit especially hard. From east to west, the waters of the Sacramento River spread well beyond the Tule and approached the Davis ranch, drowning the region in a torrent twelve miles wide and eight to eleven feet deep. From there to near the west rim of the valley, Putah Creek created a lake so deep and so vast that sloops were seen sailing across it. Putah Sink, where the two overflows overlapped, was completely under water. "There is nothing to indicate the locality of the ranches but a windmill," observed one stunned swamplander. Hundreds of miles of fences, many dozens of farms, and countless stock were wiped out. Like others in the Sacramento Valley, Putah Creek farmers found it difficult to comprehend what had happened. In addition to the sheer suddenness and magnitude of events, they had been lulled into a false sense of security because no serious flooding from either the creek or the river had occurred since 1854—many no doubt crediting their makeshift levees for keeping them dry during the intervening years. But in one fell swoop, as the *Sacramento Daily Union* put it, "all this

"The Climate of California on a Rampage." Sacramento Valley flood refugees, humans and livestock alike, depicted during the flood of February 1878, in a woodcut by Charles Nahl in the *Pacific Rural Press*, March 2, 1878. By all accounts, the flood of 1861–62 was an even greater calamity. Department of Special Collections, University of California Library, Davis.

has been washed away by the relentless flooding, and [the farmers] are left to begin again in the world, if they have the courage to undertake another improvement on the land."[2]

For most Putah Creek settlers, this was at least the third time since their arrival in California that they had been "left to begin again." Failure in the goldfields, the uncertainties of land tenure, the vagaries of the grain market, and now the sheer force of nature tested their resilience to the utmost, as the *Union* well understood. But it took more than courage to begin again. Farmers were no strangers to disaster—ecological, economic, or otherwise—but few had experienced anything like the great flood of 1861–62. Its impact had an influence on their lives almost as powerful as the gold rush itself. The most widespread response at first was simply to act as though it had never happened. Neither stoic nor heroic, many farmers chose, however consciously, to try to put the fury of the flood behind them as quickly as possible; they had come too far to do otherwise. While gloomy prophets in northern California newspapers predicted the demise of agriculture in the Sacramento Valley, farmers plowed forward, head down, convincing themselves that the day of disaster had passed. But nature would neither cooperate nor be tamed, a lesson that farmers never fully learned. The flood, moreover, did not wash away the daunting problems that had confronted them during the previous decade. The struggle to survive, much less prosper, would be mighty indeed—as revealed, with special clarity, in the experiences of George W. Pierce and the fate of the Big Ranch.

Even before the great flood, Pierce knew that his days on the Big Ranch were numbered. While visiting committees and newspaper reporters continued to celebrate "this great grain farm," Champion I. Hutchinson, Charles Greene, and their trustee, Robert C. Clark, sought desperately to dig their way out of a mountain of debt.[3] As early as the fall of 1857, they tried to cut their losses by selling out. From September 18 to the middle of the following January, a front-page advertisement ran in the *Sacramento Daily Union* detailing every last "natural advantage," improvement, implement, and farm animal, and offering "liberal credit." There were no takers, however. The advertisement did not mention Rancho Laguna de Santos Callé, but its presence loomed large. Everyone knew that the Big Ranch might soon become part of the public domain.[4]

One last ray of hope shone on the proprietors when Hutchinson learned in the spring of 1858 that the San Francisco and Marysville Railroad Company planned to grade its line through the west side of the Big Ranch. Promoters wanted to build not only the main route through the Sacramento Valley but also the western link of the proposed transcontinental railroad. Hutchinson, Greene, and Clark, in turn, envisioned a depot sitting squarely on their property that would rescue them from debt. But it was not to be. The company had trouble financing the project and ran out of money in July 1860. Shortly thereafter, the Central Pacific Railroad made Sacramento, not Marysville, the hub of the valley and the western terminus of the transcontinental line, and its connecting line to Vallejo at the north end of the San Francisco Bay bypassed the Big Ranch.[5]

Increasingly, the Big Ranch became the domain of lawyers more than of farmers. Creditors filed no fewer than a dozen lawsuits in three different counties (Yolo, Sacramento, and Placer) against Hutchinson, Greene, or Clark in 1860 and 1861, and numerous others were still pending. In every case, the judge or jury ruled in favor of the plaintiffs and awarded them a full settlement. The defense attorneys' strategy was to stall—to demure and appeal, hoping against hope that the Big Ranch would deliver the one big crop that would save them all.[6] A Sacramento district court judge finally said enough in a case tried in March 1861 and ordered the sheriff to execute attachment proceedings to recover the $998.21 awarded to the plaintiffs. In a well-publicized sale conducted on the Big Ranch on May 13, the sheriff auctioned off reapers, gang plows, wagons, cattle, and other personal property to the highest bidders. The problem was that several other creditors showed up, demanding their fair share of the proceeds.[7] Thus began a legal imbroglio—just what the team of defense attorneys had hoped for to buy some more time. With so many creditors demanding their money, it was not at all clear who should get paid first or in what order.

It was left to the California Supreme Court to decide. Several of these cases were consolidated and heard by a district court judge in Placer County, with Hutchinson, Greene, and Clark, not surprisingly, appealing his decision.[8] This brought them face-to-face with Chief Justice Stephen Field, the former forty-niner whose reputation for favoring the interests of large landowners and speculators (he was both himself) was already well established, two years before he landed a seat on the U.S. Supreme Court, where he would advocate "entrepreneurial liberty" for the next three decades.[9] Field's twenty-nine-page opinion was not what the appellants expected. Though expressed in a scholarly, measured manner, the decision scolded Hutchinson and Greene for their "failed" enterprise and singled out Clark for creating such a mess. The twelve original lenders who put together the trust on January 24, 1856, Field stressed, advanced Clark $15,000 "for carrying on farming operations," but only for the 1856 season. With Hutchinson's encouragement, however, Clark went on a borrowing spree for the next four years trying to recoup his losses. In doing so, he not only exceeded his powers as trustee but also left behind a string of angry, confused creditors.[10]

Field's solution was nothing short of stunning. He decided to divide the creditors into seven "classes," ranking them by the order in which they would be paid, with the twelve original lenders coming first. As many as possible would be paid from a sale of the real property—but not in one piece. The Big Ranch, Field declared, was too big. "Operations could not be carried on without large expenditures of money each year . . . [and] those operations have failed." He then ordered the 3,223 acres of enclosed land to be subdivided "into parcels of not less than 160 acres, nor exceeding 320 acres each," with each lot carefully surveyed and sold, one by one, at public auction. Traditional logic, especially among speculators, long held that a man could never own too much land, but the Big Ranch convinced Justice Field, if only temporarily, that smaller was better.[11]

Field's decision, which came in April 1862, was delayed for four months while the Sacramento Valley dried out from the flood. He may have wished he had waited longer. With the shock of the disaster still reverberating and with Rancho

Laguna de Santos Callé still not fully adjudicated, the situation was ripe for speculation. The responsibility to administer the sale of the Big Ranch lay with the trial court in Placer County, which in July appointed Isaac M. Hubbard of Sacramento commissioner of the proceedings. Hubbard was a man of many hats—engineer, banker, railroad agent, and, most prominently, land speculator. He had already made several thousand dollars from the Big Ranch back in 1854, buying a portion of it from Henry Conner and selling it a month later to Angus Frierson. While his original intentions were not clear when he rode out to the Big Ranch in September to look things over, Hubbard, like so many before him, was seduced by its splendor and decided that he wanted it for himself. An obvious conflict of interest proved to be only a minor hindrance. Sanford E. Herrick, a Sacramento grain dealer, agreed to pretend to buy it for him, in exchange for Hubbard's future business.[12]

The auction for all eleven surveyed lots, ranging in size from 209 to 320 acres, began at noon on November 25 and was held on site. Herrick bought every last lot. He had little competition for the first six furthest away from Putah Creek, paying $3.00 to $5.50 per acre, but for the remaining five along or near the channel, the bidding reached as high as $25.00. The final tally was $23,886 for all 3,223 acres, more than twice the previous year's assessed value. Hubbard gave the money to Herrick, whose name went on the deed of sale. Their secret deal not only kept the Big Ranch big but put it in limbo as well. Neither Hubbard nor Herrick had any interest in farming the land, but both were convinced that the speculative spirit of the times would quickly drive up the price of the land.[13]

Clark, Greene, and Hutchinson managed to wash their hands of the whole sordid affair, even though the proceeds from the sale were not enough to pay even the third class of creditors. Clark quickly capitalized on the notoriety the Big Ranch had given him, becoming one of Sacramento's most sought-after lawyers and, before the end of the decade, an assemblyman, state senator, and county judge of considerable distinction.[14] California's lenient debtor laws, designed to give industrious men the benefit of the doubt, saved Greene and Hutchinson. Promissory notes had a five-year statute of limitation, which meant that it was already too late for many of the creditors. The others were thwarted when Hutchinson and Greene both filed for insolvency in the summer of 1861—Greene in Yolo County, Hutchinson in Sacramento.[15]

In exchange for disclosing all their finances, providing public notice of their intentions to their creditors, and surrendering their estates, Hutchinson and Greene were discharged of all debts and liabilities. Greene also took advantage of a state law that had just been amended. He and his wife, Bertha, filed a declaration of homestead in March 1861—the first married couple to do so in Yolo County—which assured that up to $5,000 of their real and personal property would be exempted from forced sale from any court. This left them with two cows and two mares, a wagon, harness, saddle, and bridle, their household and kitchen furniture, and 960 acres situated just north of the Big Ranch. Hutchinson could have done the same thing, but it was more his nature to pick up and move on. The General emerged in San Francisco a few years later and would soon hit it big in business and politics once again, this time on the West Coast's biggest stage.[16]

In the end Pierce made out better than anyone. He and Greene had kept the Big Ranch running since 1858, sharing the management of grain production and cattle raising. Ever short on cash, Hutchinson and Greene (through Clark, their trustee) made alternative arrangements to pay Pierce's monthly salary of $55: a lease on one undivided fourth of the original 1,374 enclosed acres in May 1859, half the hogs on the Big Ranch (valued at $750) later that October, and a promissory note for $600 the following June, which Pierce used to buy several head of cattle. By that time, he was essentially running his own farm. During the 1860 season, he plowed two fields of thirty-six and twenty acres near the creek, producing twenty-eight tons of wheat in one and thirteen tons of barley in the other. By the terms of his lease, half the proceeds went to Clark. After purchasing the land in September 1860, however, he no longer had to share the fruits of his labor.[17]

With Eunice and George Jr. back from Kenosha, a new baby, and a farm of his own for the first time since leaving Wisconsin, George was more determined than ever as the 1861 season approached. Never one to play it safe, he set out to find a new buyer for his grain—preferably one from outside Sacramento with no previous ties to the Big Ranch. Twenty miles north of Putah Creek on the Sacramento River, the town of Knights Landing had become a well-established shipping point for farmers in the vicinity. The Eagle Steam Flouring Mill, Yolo County's largest manufacturer, had been grinding wheat and barley at competitive prices at this small ferry crossing since 1856. The roads from Putah Creek to Knights Landing, however, were not as well maintained as those to Sacramento, and there was very little merchant activity to entice farmers from further away. Pierce might have tried it anyway had there not been one other alternative to consider.[18]

Twenty miles south of Putah Creek at the head of Cache Slough, the port of Maine Prairie had just opened. The longest of several finger-like tidal channels extending northward into the interior from the Sacramento River delta, Cache Slough was wide and deep enough for large sailing vessels and shallow-draft steamers to navigate the sixteen miles to its tip. Joseph C. Merrithew had the fore-sight not only to launch a grain-shipping business in what seemed to be the middle of nowhere (the land for miles around was too swampy to farm) but also to contract with several Pacific Coast lumber mills to cater to one of the biggest needs of prospective customers. Merrithew, who liked to be addressed as "Captain," was one of several new grain dealers and warehouse owners in northern California who was being financed by an enterprising San Francisco shipping broker named Isaac Friedlander. Some of Merrithew's wheat would be sold in the city to the Eureka Flour Mills (where Friedlander was a major partner), but most of it would be exported to Great Britain or Australia through a complex system of trade that Friedlander and several British merchants had just started to build.[19]

In the spring of 1861, Pierce visited Captain Merrithew's landing on Cache Slough and liked what he saw. He signed an agreement that would make him one of the first farmers—perhaps the first from Yolo County—to ship his grain out of Maine Prairie. For two months—mid-September to mid-November 1861—Pierce hauled twenty-one tons of wheat and ten tons of barley to Merrithew's warehouse, making fifteen two-day round trips. He received an even better price than he had anticipated, as Merrithew already had competition on Cache Slough from another new firm, H. G. Deck & Company. On each return trip, he brought back with him 100 to 300 feet of redwood lumber and various building materials. The land Pierce purchased from the Big Ranch was only partially fenced, and he also intended to replace the small worker's hut where he and his family were living. This was his chance, Pierce realized, to finally build a proper home for Eunice, George Jr., and Frank. He did not realize, in all likelihood, that he had just participated in the early stages of a major shift in the California wheat trade. From that point on, most of his wheat would no longer feed miners in the foothills or city people in Sacramento or San Francisco, but bread eaters many thousands of miles away in the United Kingdom. Not even Friedlander foresaw that California was on the verge of becoming, as one observer later put it, "one of the world's great feeders."[20]

Less than a month after Pierce had brought home his last load of redwood planks, the great flood commenced. On the morning of December 9, Putah Creek began to rise rapidly, and by the middle of the day it was spilling over its banks with a vengeance. It must have been evident early on that this was no ordinary overflow. The details are sketchy, but Pierce's first concern was no doubt for his wife and two children. He secured their safety, perhaps by taking them to the Wolfskill ranch, where high ground near the base of the coast mountains provided several families shelter. As for their personal property and farm improvements, however, the flood resulted in a near total loss. Cattle, furniture, fencing, and all that unused lumber were either swept downstream or demolished by the severity of the storm—so much so that by the time the second wave of the flood hit a month later, there was virtually no more damage to be done.[21]

The thirty-one tons of grain that Pierce had stored for shipment in Merrithew's warehouse were lost as well; Cache Slough's long, deep channel made it particularly susceptible to flooding. In a matter of hours, the entire port of Maine Prairie, which was thought to have been built on high ground, was twelve feet under water, as was the surrounding countryside for miles in every direction. "Not a vestige was left where once stood the town," wrote one reporter in disbelief. The townspeople themselves survived only by rushing aboard Merrithew's grain sloop, which was carried several miles away by the swift current and remained adrift for three full days before there was any appreciable decline in the depth of the water. All 140,000 sacks of grain (roughly 7,000 tons) stored in Merrithew's and Deck's warehouses were destroyed, though the remains of a few were found later as far as fifteen miles away. The total cost for the two dealers was over $25,000, not including the grain, "the loss of which," stressed the *Solano Herald*, "falls upon the farmers who had stored it."[22]

The flood spread shock, fear, and devastation, but not defeat—certainly not among the San Francisco and British merchants who had inaugurated the wheat trade, and most certainly not in Isaac Friedlander. Exactly how much the flood cost Friedlander is not known, but however many thousands of dollars it was did not diminish his restless energy. Financial setbacks were part of the game, as he already knew from having made and lost a fortune in the flour business the previous decade. The key was to bounce back ahead of the competition, and no one was more confident or prepared than Friedlander. He knew that British millers prized the hard, dry, and unusually white wheat produced in the Sacramento Valley; his network of grain dealers and warehouse owners remained in place; he still had considerable credit at his disposal; and he had already chartered several ships for the next crop. And the next crop, Friedlander shrewdly anticipated, was going to be huge because floodwaters, no matter how damaging their immediate impact, also delivered fertilizer by depositing layers of fresh soil on the land. From his office in San Francisco, far removed from the damage and destruction, Friedlander viewed the great flood as a great opportunity.[23]

Such a view was ruthless, to be sure, and one befitting the relentless speculator that Friedlander had become. But it was also farsighted and, for most everyone involved, constructive. Without Friedlander's instincts and the services he provided as middleman—his willingness to gamble and especially his business credit—the grain trade in the Sacramento Valley, in all likelihood, would not have recovered from the flood so quickly, if at all. The rebirth of Maine Prairie typified his influence. Almost before the water had subsided, both Merrithew and Deck were up and running again, rebuilding their warehouses on stilts several feet above the now calm waters of Cache Slough.[24] Their optimism was remarkable, given what they had just experienced, but rather blind as well. No stilts of any height would have saved them from ruin during the flood, but with their attentions now focused on the promise of the immediate future, Merrithew and Deck, out of both economic and psychological necessity, could not allow themselves to succumb to the horrors of the immediate past.

Pierce responded in much the same way. He spent the rest of January rounding up his surviving stock, most of February reseeding his crop, and much of the rest of the year almost as though nothing had happened. In fact, in the aftermath of the devastating flood, Pierce actually accelerated his efforts to put down roots in Putah Creek. The demise of the Big Ranch had given him the opportunity of a lifetime, which he was not going to squander, come hell or high water. The latter he had already experienced, and the former would come soon enough.

Pierce's first priority was his grain crop. With a sizeable advance from Merrithew, he planted 50 acres in wheat but only 4 in barley. Friedlander had put out the word to his network that his buyers wanted wheat and only wheat, and in his agreement with Merrithew, Pierce promised to deliver just that. The emphasis on wheat involved several additional expenses. The immediate problem for Pierce was how to keep his stock from trampling his fields with all his fencing demolished. Fortunately, Sacramento businessman Drury Melone, who now owned the old E. L. Brown 980-acre tract a mile and a half downstream, agreed to keep and guard Pierce's cattle and hogs in exchange for half their market value over the next two years.[25] Pierce also had to purchase sacks for his wheat that would hold roughly 100 pounds each. Wheat in sacks, Friedlander and other shippers had found, withstood the long, rough voyage to England much better than in bulk. Putah Creek farmers had always used sacks for the convenience of hauling their crops on wagons to Sacramento, but those were found to be too light and perishable for use on oceangoing ships. Pierce's agreement with Merrithew stipulated that he use much heavier "stout twilled" sacks, which cost as much as 30 cents apiece, two and a half times more than the old ones.[26] And with the local labor supply dispersed in the aftermath of the flood, Pierce hired an itinerant harvesting crew from the northern end of the county to cut and thresh his wheat at more than twice the cost of the previous season.[27]

At the time, it all seemed well worth it. Under the circumstances, just about any crop would have done wonders for Pierce's state of mind. But as Friedlander had predicted, the 1862 harvest proved exceptionally heavy—"the largest," declared the *Knights Landing News*, "ever raised in Yolo County." Pierce himself produced almost forty tons, almost double the previous year's output. Though his margin of profit cannot be calculated with precision, it was enough for him to repurchase all the lumber he lost in the flood, buy $156 of furniture (one sofa, four chairs, and one marble center table) from a Sacramento merchant, and start a small peach orchard and grape vineyard. From his experience in Kenosha, Pierce knew the value of diversifying, and in the wake of the flood, he was intent on securing as many sources of income as he could. To protect his new improvements and possessions, he paid two Chinese laborers—among the first employed in Yolo County—to construct a levee on Putah Creek. Only a few feet high and about a quarter mile long, this mound of dirt had as much chance at preventing flood damage as the stilts under Merrithew's and Deck's warehouses, yet it provided Pierce the same sort of comfort. Whom he hired and what he paid them (less than a dollar a day each for two month's work), though largely unnoticed at the time, would become major issues in Putah Creek and throughout rural California for years to come.[28]

Just as Pierce seemed to have blocked the flood out of his mind, he had to contend with another mammoth ecological disaster of the opposite nature, drought—the most severe and prolonged to ever hit the state. For close to three years, from the fall of 1862 to the winter of 1864–65, the rains failed. Like most farmers in the Sacramento Valley, Pierce managed to produce a small crop in 1863, but the following year virtually no wheat was harvested at all. Pierce waited and waited for the first rain so he could begin plowing, but it never came. Others who did manage to seed their fields watched in horror as acre after acre of grain never formed a head. "A scorching wind, like a blast from a blowtorch, blew down from the north," recalled a Willow Slough resident of one fateful day. "The [wheat], then about eighteen inches high, shriveled to dust before our eyes." Maine Prairie shippers, who had handled an estimated 25,000 tons of wheat in 1862, received only one load in 1864. So severe was the crop loss in the Sacramento Valley that Californians had to import wheat from Chile to make their bread. Drought, wrote a particularly keen observer in the *Overland Monthly*, had become "the great terror of the farmer"—so much so that, as with the preceding flood, a short-term memory became the farmer's best asset. "He goes on with his work," the same observer concluded, "with as cheery a faith as if droughts were never known."[29]

For the Pierces, the suffering endured during these back-to-back ecological disasters was intensified when young Frank, just three years old, died, on September 10, 1863. Though the grieving parents did not disclose the cause of death in the notice they placed in the *Daily Alta California*, Frank had apparently been ill for some time, commanding all his mother's attention. Eunice, in fact, had not resumed her dairy work since returning from Wisconsin. George submerged himself in the day-to-day work of the farm and in local affairs to ease his pain. He served, for example, as public administrator for Putah Township from 1865 to 1869. He also was instrumental in building Stevenson's Bridge, which, by crossing Putah Creek a half mile upstream from his ranch, greatly benefited those farmers in Yolo County who hauled their wheat to Maine Prairie. Eunice, in contrast, felt compelled to leave the farm and withdraw from the community on occasion. In October 1864, she purchased a lot for $250 in Woodland, where she kept a small house for herself for years to come. Twelve miles due north of the Pierce Ranch, Woodland was just far enough away to allow Eunice to escape her troubled past and ongoing depression. Her retreat was highly unusual for the times, but Eunice had always been her own woman. George may not have liked it—he called her absences "calls," as in "Mrs. Pierce made a call" to Woodland—but abided by her wishes.[30]

The Pierces received some measure of relief when it finally started to rain again in December 1864. With most of his cattle and about half his hogs having perished during the drought, Pierce turned headlong to wheat—a choice made by farmers up and down the Sacramento Valley. He rode down to Maine Prairie early in January and was once again received enthusiastically—this time by John Utter, Captain Merrithew's new partner and warehouse manager. Utter and Merrithew were again financed by Friedlander, who was determined to rebuild the wheat trade as quickly as possible. Pierce did his part, planting almost eighty acres and producing sixty-two tons in 1865, and nearly matching that output again in 1866.[31]

In the latter season, Pierce experimented with the latest in harvesting technology—the Haines' header—and found it much to his liking. The header consisted of a twelve-foot-long revolving sickle mounted on wheels and pushed through the fields by four or five horses. Unlike the reaper, which cut the grain stalks close to the ground, this machine, as its name implies, aimed higher, just a few inches below the head (or kernel). The cut heads fell onto a four-foot-wide canvas draper, which conveyed them upwards through a spout and into a slant-bed wagon driven alongside. Once filled, the wagon carried the grain to a central pile for threshing. The header not only worked faster and more efficiently than the reaper, it also eliminated the costs and labor of binding and raking. The seven-man crew Pierce hired—"the headers," as he called them—finished the job in just five days. As for the decapitated stalks left standing in the field, all Pierce had to do was "put the hogs" on them.[32]

With two good crops, a reliable shipper, a new machine, and a normal cycle of rain, Pierce seemed to have finally reached a level of comfort and stability similar to what he had achieved twenty years earlier in Wisconsin. He now also had the same number of permanent hands—two—one of whom, James C. Campbell, became a close friend. Eunice began to show signs of her old self as well, especially after Hudson Fox and his wife, Cyrena, two dear friends from Kenosha, moved to Putah Creek in the summer of 1866, perhaps at George's urging. The Pierces, the Foxes, and the Greenes "took dinner" together frequently and on occasion made shopping trips to Sacramento or Woodland. That fall, when Eunice resumed her butter and egg production, everything finally seemed back to normal.[33]

But a new series of floods then struck the Sacramento Valley, wreaking havoc once again. The first of them, in the last days of December 1866, jolted the memory of many a farmer along Putah Creek, washing away levees, fences, and roads with a ferocity reminiscent of the great flood five years earlier. Jerome C. Davis and William Montgomery barely escaped with their lives. In attempting to ford the creek on horseback just as the heavy rain began, both fell into the surging water and were carried half a mile downstream before being rescued. Several hours later, floodwaters spread at least two miles on both sides of the creek. From February to May, storm after storm pounded northern California, prompting Putah Creek to explode over its banks repeatedly, each time threatening lives and property. For weeks on end, the only way to get to Sacramento was by boat, as the Pierces found when George required emergency dental work that April.[34]

All things considered, the Pierces survived better than most. With the ground "very very wet" through the end of February, as Pierce noted several times in his journal, plowing and seeding commenced much later than usual, and the high water in May nearly ruined the harvest. But unlike many of his neighbors further downstream, Pierce managed to produce a good crop, selling it this time to Deck & Co., which had just constructed a new warehouse on Cache Slough. Its "height and strength," promised the proprietor, will "hold it secure from damage by any overflow." At the conclusion of the harvest, Pierce celebrated his good fortune by taking George Jr. to Sacramento to have a father-son portrait taken by a professional photographer and then spent many days repairing his flood-damaged fences and levees. Plowing and seeding for the next crop began on November 24, right on schedule.[35]

Deck and Pierce seemed to have tempted fate. On December 22, 1867, Putah

Creek began to rise yet again. "Overflow in the evening," wrote Pierce. "Water the highest ever known." That observation was shared by numerous longtime observers, though in fact the flood was not as severe as in 1862. Nonetheless, one vast sheet of water covered much of the Sacramento Valley through the end of January. Twelve inches of rain fell during the last ten days of December alone. Putah Creek jumped its banks and spread across the surrounding farmland as much as a foot deep. A fierce wind—again, said many, like no one had seen before—overturned trees, blew off roofs, and leveled buildings. All of Pierce's earlier repairs and plowing went for naught, needless to say, and much of the crop he had stored in Maine Prairie was destroyed. The force of the waves and current of Cache Slough made a mockery of Deck's earlier assurances, battering the town's buildings—even those elevated above the high-water mark of 1862—and causing many thousands of dollars in damage. When a snowstorm of all things (a once-every-quarter-century event) left three and a half inches on the ground for several days at the end of January, Putah Creek residents had to be wondering just what would come next.[36]

It was now depressingly clear to them, however, that floods and droughts were not flukes of nature. The day of disaster was not over, as Pierce had tried so hard to persuade himself, but would return again and again. This grave realization prompted grave reflection. The most logical response to such a harsh reality, one might think, would be to leave; surely there had to be a better place to live and farm than on the floor of a valley that was buried under water so much of the time. That was an option that, judging by his subsequent actions, seems not to have occurred to Pierce. Putah Creek had given him and his family considerable grief but also considerable opportunity. To quit now, moreover, would be to admit failure, a fear that Pierce had carried with him since the gold rush. The key issue for him was not whether to stay or go but to find a way to take advantage of this volatile environment. Debilitating floods and droughts were part of life in the Sacramento Valley, he now fully acknowledged, but when favorable conditions presented themselves, there was no better place to grow wheat. Pierce knew from experience that a bumper crop would likely follow the flood, giving him a chance to make up for previous losses. But he could only cultivate so much wheat on his 383 acres, so he needed to expand in order to seize the moment. It just so happened that all the land he needed was right next door on the Big Ranch, which neither a plow nor a reaper had touched since 1862.

Indeed, the scheme that Hubbard and Herrick had concocted five years earlier never materialized. All hopes of easy money dried up during the drought. By the end of 1864, Hubbard and Herrick had nothing to show for their secret agreement except a $600 debt to the county in back taxes. Neither of them sat still, however. In 1863, Hubbard started a company to build a toll road over the Sierra Nevada at the infamous Donner Pass. When that risky venture failed in less than a year, one of the creditors, Lester Robinson, sued Hubbard and won a judgment in district court for $9,617. Herrick, who was still acting as Hubbard's secret trustee for the Big Ranch, came to the rescue again. He pretended to loan Hubbard the money in May 1864, and Hubbard, in turn, pretended to deed him the Big Ranch as security for the indebtedness. Robinson, who knew a shell game when he saw one, sued both Hubbard and Herrick for conspiring to hide Hubbard's real assets from his creditors and won again in the spring of 1867. The judge intended to place a lien on the Big Ranch, but his hands were tied. Herrick's name was now not only on the deed but also on a patent issued by the federal government. Undeterred, Robinson took his case to the U.S. Circuit Court in San Francisco, where, one by one, the facts of this sordid affair were exposed. It seemed, finally, that the jig was up for Hubbard and Herrick.[37]

But the Big Ranch worked its magic once again. During the harvest of 1867, Hubbard and Herrick drove George Mowe out to Putah Creek to look over the Big Ranch. Unlike surrounding farms, which were buzzing with activity, the Big Ranch lay vacant, except for the cattle and hogs that roamed its 3,223 acres. It had essentially reverted back to the open range while the litigants battled it out in court. Mowe, yet another of Hubbard's many creditors, could barely contain himself. Here was the legendary Big Ranch, which he had heard so much about, just waiting to be cultivated. Envisioning acre after acre of wheat flowing in the spring breeze, Mowe agreed to front the money to pay off Robinson, provided that Hubbard and Herrick plant a crop for the coming season and deed him the land to secure the loan.[38]

The timing could not have been better, not only for Hubbard and Herrick but for Pierce as well. Though it is not clear just who contacted whom early in the spring of 1868, Pierce and Herrick reached an agreement to revive wheat cultivation on the Big Ranch. Pierce leased the land for two seasons for $6,000, with half the rent due November 1, 1868, and the other half exactly one year later—the installments timed to anticipate the end of large harvests. The lease also stipulated that Pierce should haul the wheat to Deck's warehouse in Maine Prairie, which had already been rebuilt. Deck and his new partner, Harry Wilcox, agreed to pay half of all expenses, including rent, seed, sacks, labor, and shipping, in exchange for half the proceeds. Pierce was careful to keep separate accounts for his own 125-acre field and the 237 acres he planted on the Big Ranch along Putah

Creek. While his own workers harvested and threshed his wheat, he hired an itinerant crew for the Big Ranch at $4.75 per acre. It was a spectacular harvest, yielding 277 tons and, at 1.45 cents per pound, grossing $8,000. But by the time Pierce paid Herrick, Deck, the workers, and various other expenses, he cleared only $269 from the Big Ranch and about half that from his own land.[39]

Determined to cut costs and increase profits, Pierce expanded operations even more in 1869. He plowed over 300 acres on the Big Ranch, purchased his own header, hired his own workers, and cut Deck and Wilcox out of the lease. He also sublet another 400 acres to James Campbell for a quarter share of the crop. For the second straight season, Pierce had a successful harvest, producing over 350 tons from the Big Ranch field and another 80 from his own. This time when he made his payment to Herrick on November 1, he still had almost $1,800 in his pocket—including $300 from the vineyard he had planted years earlier, which was now in full bearing. Pierce sold his grapes to Fred Werner, who, from a distillery in his basement, produced 14,000 gallons of what he called "black burgundy" that year. Though deemed "too strong to be fit for general consumption" by a local critic, Werner's wine making provided farmers such as Pierce a welcome source of additional income.[40]

While the $1,500 he made from his wheat was a considerable sum to Pierce, it was not a margin of profit that excited Hubbard, Mowe, or Herrick, who decided not to renew the lease. Instead, they offered Pierce the 367 acres he had cultivated on the Big Ranch for $35 per acre ($12,846.74)—three and a half times its assessed value. Mowe agreed to finance the purchase through the Capital Savings Bank, which had just incorporated in Sacramento County in February 1869 under a new state law. Mowe himself sat on its board of directors. The terms of the loan were no more favorable to Pierce than the price: a $3,000 down payment followed by four annual payments of $2,500 with interest compounded monthly at 12 percent per year. Moreover, the bank would hold the deed until the entire balance was paid—not only for the 367 acres in question but the 383 acres Pierce had already purchased back in 1860.[41]

Nonetheless, Pierce jumped at the deal. The annual payments were no more than what he had paid Herrick each of the previous two years, and in five years the land would be his. It was an enormous risk but one he felt he had to take. Pierce was no Hubbard or Herrick, but he had come to realize that in order to make it in the volatile environment of the Sacramento Valley, he had to act boldly. Wherever farmers pursued market opportunities, they were, by the very nature of their enterprise, gambling. Every year they rolled the dice on the weather, on the yield of their crop, and on the price they would get for it; that much Pierce had learned in Kenosha. But along Putah Creek, farmers also had to anticipate natural disasters that could destroy a crop at any time and force them to begin again—as would happen two years later with yet another drought, and three years after that with another flood, and seven more times (three droughts, four floods) before the end of the century. The key, Pierce believed, was to produce enough in good years to offset the bad. With that in mind, he set his sights on acquiring his own big ranch. Brimming with confidence, he went to Sacramento to sign the loan papers on May 31, 1870. In his mind, he had finally struck gold.[42]

Much of that confidence grew from the previous season, when Pierce sold his large crop to a new shipper in a new town. Deck & Co. folded prior to the 1869 harvest, as did the other firms on Cache Slough. Maine Prairie, declared a local newspaper that summer, "has been a place of great importance for the grain regions of Solano and Yolo counties. It is now dead."[43] The last flood had been devastating, but shippers expected to rebuild as they had before. This time, however, they did not have the backing of Friedlander, who left Cache Slough shippers high and dry for a new network of agents along the newly constructed California Pacific Railroad. The Cal-P, as it was called from the start, ran fifty-five miles from Vallejo to Sacramento, with a branch line heading up the valley to Marysville. "The whole route," the *Solano Press* declared, "passes through astonishingly fertile grain country." The junction for the Marysville road and an adjoining town site were built on the north bank of Putah Creek. For several days before the first train arrived at this junction on August 24, 1868, there were 3,000 tons of grain piled up along the track awaiting transportation, all of which had been purchased by William Dresbach—"Friedlander's man," as he was already known. Dresbach gave liberal advances to farmers and charged just $3.50 per ton to ship their wheat to Vallejo, nearly 50 percent less than his competitors in Maine Prairie.[44]

Dresbach named the new town Davisville, for it was built on the site of the famous Davis stock farm. Davis's house became the town's first hotel and one of his small farm buildings, the first barber shop.[45] Davis himself, however, was nowhere to be found, having fled his creditors two years earlier. His failure is central to understanding the complex origins of the town that still bears his name.

CHAPTER SIX

Favorite Son

Jerome C. Davis owned one of the finest ranches in the Sacramento Valley in 1860. To this day, the data recorded by the federal census taker that June jump out from the page. The prize-winning stock farm consisted of 7,000 acres of land with a cash value of $70,000. Davis's machinery and implements were worth almost $5,000. He owned 169 horses, 9 mules, 550 milk cows, 934 other cattle, 898 sheep, and 114 hogs, for a total value in livestock of $29,087 (not including another $3,120 in the value of animals slaughtered). During the year ending June 1, 1860, he raised 2,000 bushels of wheat, 10,000 pounds of wool, 200 bushels of barley, and 300 tons of hay, while producing 520 pounds of butter and 1,500 pounds of cheese. The value of his orchard products totaled $2,500. He also owned and operated a flouring mill in which he invested $10,000. It ground 20,000 bushels of wheat and corn valued at $18,000 and employed five hands, each of whom earned a salary of $50 a month. The mill, located on the ranch, was powered by steam and turned out 4,445 barrels of fine and superfine flour valued at almost $25,000. Even the census taker, who visited 144 farms in Putah Township alone that month, must have been impressed. Davis's peers certainly were; they elected him president of the California State Agricultural Society for the year 1861.[1]

Just two months after the census taker had departed, however, it appeared that Davis might lose everything. Throughout most of the 1850s, the dubious status of Rancho Laguna de Santos Callé cast a shadow on his many accomplishments. The darkest day came on September 18, 1860, when Judge Ogden Hoffman of the U.S. District Court upheld the California Land Commission's earlier decision not to confirm the grant. "It is impossible to contemplate without disgust the series of perjuries which compose the record," wrote Hoffman, conveying the substance and tone of his eighteen-page opinion in one sentence. Hoffman showed no mercy to the claimants, dismissing out of hand their argument that they had purchased the land in good faith and paid taxes on it for several years. It appeared certain that landholders on Rancho Laguna de Santos Callé would now face the consequences stipulated in the California Land Act of 1851: "All lands, the claims to which have been rejected . . . shall be deemed, held, and considered as part of the public domain of the United States." That was precisely what happened to the claims made on Rancho Ulpinos in Solano County, a grant that Hoffman had rejected two years earlier for many of the same reasons.[2]

Davis was not about to give up, however. Angry and determined, he took his cause to anyone who would listen, including lawyers, top-level officials in the U.S. General Land Office, and members of the U.S. Congress. It took almost a decade, but on January 7, 1869, he received his patent from President Andrew Johnson. Along the way, his efforts helped persuade Congress to adopt legislation in 1866 that permitted buyers of defective or fraudulent claims to retain possession of their land. Davis never reaped the benefits, however. By the time he received his patent, he neither owned nor operated his ranch but was merely acting on behalf of the California Pacific Railroad. The more headway Davis made in the halls of Congress toward settling his claim, the more his problems on the ranch mounted. Such was the irony of fate for Putah Creek's favorite son.

Hoffman's decision affected all the Laguna de Santos Callé claimants—everyone, that is, who had purchased land either directly from the grantees (Marcos Vaca and Victor Prudon) or their assignees. Davis and his father, Isaac Davis, Champion I. Hutchinson, Charles Greene, Simon Lettner, Isaac S. Chiles, Drury Melone, William Keithley, Richard Hext, and George W. Pierce all stood to lose their land and improvements. No one seemed particularly worried, however. Pierce actually purchased his 383 acres of the grant eleven days *after* the district court decision, so sure was he that these matters would eventually be resolved. It was simply inconceivable to Pierce and his neighbors that the federal government, law or no law, would seize their extensive, well-improved holdings. They still had one appeal left, to the U.S. Supreme Court. Surely, they reasoned, the highest court in the land would protect their property rights and investments. Most of the claimants looked to Jerome C. Davis for guidance and had full confidence that he would pull them through, though that responsibility fell to him in part by default. Davis and Hutchinson had acted as agents for the group during the land commission and district court proceedings, but the co-owner of the Big Ranch, now on the verge of bankruptcy, had all but dropped out of the picture.[3]

The only skeptic among the claimants was Davis himself, who nonetheless agreed to act as their representative. The Supreme Court, he feared, was not likely to reverse Hoffman's decision. The claimants' lawyers seemed to have exhausted every last argument during the district court hearings and not one of them recommended pursuing the case further. In the three previous years, the Supreme Court had turned back twenty-five appeals by grantees on California land claims, many of them far less questionable than Rancho Laguna de Santos Callé. The lawyers informed Davis that he did not have to decide on whether or not to file an appeal until Hoffman issued his formal decree, which might not be for some time. At least a dozen California land cases were already on the docket of the Supreme Court, whose decisions Hoffman would want to hear, and Hoffman's own schedule was packed full. In no hurry himself and under no pressure from the claimants, Hoffman waited until July 31, 1863. In the meantime, Davis, who had no intention of making an appeal, would not have to tip his hand for almost two years. That gave him plenty of time to consider other options. If the courts could not provide the claimants any satisfaction, he gradually came to realize, perhaps it was time to look for a legislative solution.[4]

While the claimants pondered their next move, news of Hoffman's decision sparked a small-scale land rush on Rancho Laguna de Santos Callé. Hoffman's harsh words—which were printed for all to read on the front page of the *Sacramento Daily Union* on September 21, 1860—seemed to leave no doubt as to the status of the land. At least 75 squatters raced onto the tract, put up shacks, and marked out their boundaries, believing that it was only a matter of time before the federal government opened the grant's 48,000 acres to preemption. They stayed clear only where sturdy redwood-plank fencing made it difficult to enter the land. For the time being, that kept the property of most of the claimants free of trespassers, but not the smaller, less-improved farms settled by the previous wave of squatters, who relied on cheaper ditch or brush fences. Indeed, land disputes on Rancho Laguna de Santos Callé were much likelier to occur between old and new squatters than between new settlers and grantees.[5]

One particularly violent incident occurred less than a month after Hoffman's decision. Jacob and Catherine Ryherd, upon hearing of Rancho Laguna de Santos Callé's failure, left Sacramento to pursue their dream of owning their own farm. Early in October, they found a site to their liking just north of Willow Slough and started building a small cabin. "The land is on the open plain," Catherine recalled. "Did not see any other persons about." Nor were there any fences or crops to indicate that Hiram P. Merritt, a gold-rush immigrant from Indiana, had claimed the land three years earlier. Little by little, Merritt made improvements at the opposite end of his 160 acres, hoping for the opportunity to preempt the tract. On the afternoon of October 13, Merritt, along with his brother and four neighbors, discovered a pile of lumber on the far reaches of his land and immediately began loading it onto his wagon to cart away. At that moment, Ryherd emerged and demanded that the group vacate his land immediately. When they refused, he pulled a copy of the federal Preemption Act of 1841 from his back pocket and began reading it to them. Not amused, Merritt screamed back, "God damned your little heart, I will kill you if you do not leave here." When Ryherd kept reading, Merritt took out his pistol and fired a shot in the air. A series of shots were exchanged, one of them killing Ryherd instantly. In the well-publicized trial of "the Willow Slough murder," the judge could not determine who had fired the fatal bullet and dismissed the case. Merritt became a hero among his peers for defending his claim and eventually became one of the most successful farmers in Yolo County.[6]

As the status of Rancho Laguna de Santos Callé remained in limbo, tensions also began to mount among the claimants themselves, especially over the western boundary of Davis's property. The controversy stemmed from the dismantling of the E. L. Brown ranch, just upstream from Davis, the previous decade. At least eight creditors, including Davis, attained portions of the Brown ranch in attachment proceedings. Because the land had not been surveyed, those portions could only be measured in fractions of the whole. In 1854, for example, the county sheriff deeded John Morrison a one-quarter interest in Brown's 980-acre tract as payment for a long overdue promissory note, which Morrison proceeded to sell in equal parts to three other speculators. By the end of the decade, the original tract had been divided into so many bits and pieces that no one really knew who owned what or where. Drury Melone, an enterprising young cattle dealer from Sacramento, began buying up the land tract by tract and by 1861 had pieced together an up-and-coming stock farm. By then, the boundary between Melone's ranch and Davis's ranch was anyone's guess. When Melone built a fence where he thought it was located, Davis protested that he was at least half a mile too far east. By chance, the two adversaries literally bumped into each other that year at the state fair, where Davis was presiding as president of the California State Agricultural Society. After exchanging heated words, Davis raised his cane and Melone drew his pistol before several fairgoers separated the two. Though they parted ways without further incident, the conflict over their border remained unsettled.[7]

Meanwhile, another controversy arose that at first seemed to have little to do with Rancho Laguna de Santos Calle. It concerned a petition for a new road and bridge. Residents of Putah Township who wanted to travel either east to Sacramento or west to Wolfskill's crossing (and on to Vacaville and Benicia) had one road available to them. Built before the gold rush, it ran parallel to Putah Creek about two miles to the north. The petitioners cited two problems with the old road, the first of which revealed a growing awareness of their environment. The old road ran through the region's lowlands, where the gradual slope of Putah Creek's natural levee reached its nadir. In the rainy season, even when the creek did not overflow, muddy conditions made the road "entirely impassable" much of the time. The proposed road ran on higher ground closer to the creek, where rain and overflow drained much more quickly. The second problem was that the old road no longer went where many farmers wanted to go. At a fork about two miles northeast of Davis's homestead, a branch turned south, crossed Putah Creek on a public bridge, and continued on through Tremont. From that fork westward, however, no bridge crossed Putah Creek until the old road itself reached Wolfskill's crossing, a distance of thirteen miles. Farmers who wanted to haul their crops south to Maine Prairie, therefore, often had to travel six or seven miles east or west just to cross the creek. The petitioners proposed to build a bridge at about the half-way point (Andrew and George Stevenson's ranch on the Solano side) to give farmers in the region more direct access to the new port. Conspicuously absent from the long list of signatures was that of Jerome C. Davis, who was already losing business to Cache Slough merchants and vowed to oppose the new road and "Stevenson's bridge." Fellow grant claimants Greene, Hext, and Pierce, however, strongly advocated their construction and in fact led the petition drive. Hearings before the Board of Supervisors were set to start in January 1862.[8]

The great flood that winter, followed by three years of drought, delayed those hearings indefinitely. Everyone concerned now had more pressing problems, especially Davis. Having watched beef prices fall steadily the previous four years, Davis had hoped to increase his volume in 1862 to compensate for his dwindling margin of profit. Instead, almost half of his livestock drowned or starved that winter. Like other cattlemen in Yolo County, the only money Davis made for several months came from skinning the rotting carcasses scattered about his ranch. Unable to pay several past-due promissory notes, his ranch hands, or his taxes—obligations totaling $40,000—Davis turned to his father-in-law for help. Joseph B. Chiles, who had weathered the storm much better on his ranch in Napa County, agreed to assume the payment of Davis's debts in exchange for all his remaining livestock. No exchange took place, however. The transaction was meant only to hide, for a year or so, Davis's personal property from his creditors and the county assessor. With supply greatly diminished throughout the Sacramento Valley, both Davis and Chiles were banking on high prices and a revived livestock market to turn their fortunes around. Instead, the drought caused a near-total collapse. So few cattle survived on the parched grasslands that, for the time being, beef all but vanished from the diet of Sacramento Valley residents. Nine out of ten stock raisers in Yolo County, one contemporary source reported, went bankrupt. When the Empire Market in Sacramento, Davis's best customer for over ten years, closed its account in April 1863, the famed stock farm on Putah Creek appeared headed toward failure as well.[9]

On top of everything else, Davis now had a squatter problem. The flood not only decimated his herds, it also washed away significant portions of his fencing. In the spring of 1862, at least fourteen land-seekers saw that as an opening and staked out claims on the northern reaches of his ranch. Four of them—Abraham Barnes, Abraham Lewis, Lorenz Heinz, and James Cole—were former hands on the Davis ranch, while another—William Platt—was a salaried employee in his flouring mill. For Davis, the presence of squatters may have been the biggest indignity of all. Protected by his fences and his reputation, he had managed, until now, to avoid trespassers. But the extensive newspaper coverage given to the rejection of the grant and to the Willow Slough murder made it abundantly clear to prospective preemption claimants that even Jerome C. Davis had no legal right to stop them. That he had invested heavily in the land and developed it into a prize-winning ranch was immaterial to them.[10]

The solution to Davis's land problems nearly fell into his lap. In June 1862, Representatives Timothy Phelps and Aaron Sargent introduced a bill in Congress to "quiet land titles" in California. As long as they had acted in good faith and had actually settled upon and improved their property, purchasers of invalidated Mexican grants would be allowed to "preempt" their portions of the grants and acquire title to them at the standard legal minimum of $1.25 an acre—without regard to the standard legal maximum of 160 acres. In the ensuing discussion on the floor of the House, Phelps and Sargent focused not on Rancho Laguna de Santos Callé but on Mariano G. Vallejo's Rancho Suscol, in Solano and Napa counties. Still, the two grants had much in common: the original Mexican grantees had sold their titles and, over time, ownership had dispersed among a small group of large landholders who made extensive improvements and faithfully paid their taxes, only to have their titles undermined when the original grants were rejected (Suscol, by the U.S. Supreme Court). While Laguna de Santos Callé generated controversy locally, Suscol became a cause célèbre throughout northern California. It was positively huge—84,000 acres that engulfed the cities of Vallejo and Benicia as well as the U.S. naval shipyard at Mare Island. Its principal claimant, John B. Frisbie, was not only Vallejo's son-in-law but also one of the most notorious speculators in the state, and many of the other landholders were prominent San Francisco businessmen. Though Frisbie and his associates exerted considerable influence over Phelps and Sargent, the bill was not restricted to the claimants of Rancho Suscol; it applied to all grantees statewide. While several congressmen expressed sympathy for the "honest grant-holders" in California, many more objected on principle to conceding them preemption rights in excess of the traditional 160-acre limit. By a vote of eighty to forty, they tabled the bill.[11]

Davis followed the Suscol controversy closely. Though disheartened by the outcome of the Phelps and Sargent bill, he did not have to wait long for his hopes to be revived. Early in 1863, Frisbee persuaded Sargent to try again, and this time the bill passed easily. It contained the same measures and language as the previous one, except this version applied only to landholders within the boundaries of Rancho Suscol. Burdened by the far more pressing problems of the Civil War and weary of California's troublesome land issues, members of both houses approved the Suscol bill without discussion. Davis was ecstatic. He may well have been among the thousand people who attended a huge barbecue thrown by Frisbie to celebrate the victory. If Frisbie could win special legislation for the Suscol grantees with so little opposition, Davis figured, then he ought to be able to secure the same privileges for the claimants of Rancho Laguna de Santos Callé. That summer, Davis, with his wife, Mary, left Putah Creek for Washington, D.C., determined to do just that. Little did they know they would never return as permanent residents.[12]

Davis was not without experience in these matters. As president of the state agricultural society, he had lobbied the legislature for increased funding, a new pavilion for the state fair, and a new agricultural college. One of the society's stronger advocates in the state assembly was John Conness, a gold-rush immigrant from New York, merchant, and politician of great ambition. He ran for governor as a Douglas Democrat in 1861 and lost to Republican Leland Stanford, but was then elected to the U.S. Senate as a Union Democrat in 1863, arriving in Washington just a few months before Davis. In their encounters in Sacramento over the years, Davis and Conness had become acquaintances—perhaps even friends. Davis needed a friend in Washington and Conness wanted to make a name for himself in the Senate. It greatly helped both men that Conness had been appointed to the Committee on Public Lands, which, among its many charges, was responsible for finding legislative remedies to private land disputes involving land grants from other governments.[13]

Before meeting with Conness, however, Davis had a more immediate problem to address. "Through some error or mistake," the U.S. surveyor general later admitted, federal authorities in California on August 15, 1862, declared much of Rancho Laguna de Santos Callé public land, subject to entry or sale. They were "somehow under the impression" that the grant claimants had "acquiesced to the decision" of the U.S. District Court. This was not the first time the surveyor general's office had bungled, nor would it be the last. In the fall of 1857, President James Buchanan, faced with alarming deficits following the financial panic earlier that year, ordered the sale of 11 million acres of public land in California. Although "lands covered by foreign titles" were exempted from the president's proclamation, the surveyor general mistakenly included the six townships engulfing Rancho Laguna de Santos Callé, suspending them only after the error was discovered several months later. The survey of August 15, 1862, inadvertently released those lands into the public domain. When Davis carefully explained that "the title to the Grant is still in the courts undetermined," the surveyor general withdrew the land from entry and placed it back under suspension, on September 1, 1863.[14]

Having averted a potential disaster, Davis turned his attention to settling his claim. Conness, in the meantime, was causing quite a stir in his first year in Washington over a statutory treason case in California. When Justice Ogden Hoffman overturned the conviction of a Confederate sympathizer in San Francisco on a technicality, Conness led a highly publicized drive to remove the district court judge from the bench. While unsuccessful in his stated goal, the junior senator managed to get his name in Washington and California newspapers several months running. Davis, of course, had no love for Hoffman, either. When he and Conness met in the fall of 1864 to discuss Rancho Laguna de Santos Callé, they saw eye to eye almost immediately. Conness would help Davis keep his land, while Davis would give Conness an opportunity to advance his cause in the Committee on Public Lands, once again at Hoffman's expense.[15]

On Conness's advice, Davis issued a memorial to Congress, detailing the "great hardships" he had endured as a result of Hoffman's ruling and asking for the passage of a law that would permit him to act as a preemptor and purchase clear title to his land from the federal government at $1.25 per acre. The memorial, issued on March 24, 1864, did not mention the other claimants on Rancho Laguna de Santos Callé. Since his arrival in Washington, Davis had changed his mind about representing all the others. The boundary dispute with Melone, the road controversy with Greene, Hext, and Pierce, the squatter problems, and the strain of his failing ranch had taken their toll. In addition, in January, Davis ran out of money. To continue his stay in Washington, he sold much of his remaining personal property—from farm implements to blacksmith tools to furniture—at an auction conducted by the proprietors of the Empire Market. He also tried to lease the cropland on his ranch but, in the midst of the drought, found no takers. Increasingly bitter over the course of events back home, Davis now cared only about saving himself.[16]

Conness knew, however, that the bill had a much better chance of passing if applied to all the claimants, just as it had in the Suscol Act. Indeed, the phraseology in the Santos Callé Act, as it came to be known, was essentially the same as its predecessor, with the exception of one word in particular. On the advice of the Committee on Public Lands, Conness carefully omitted *preemption*, not wanting to draw attention to such a sensitive issue. Once in motion, the Santos Callé bill met almost no opposition. On June 29, 1864, the Committee on Public Lands gave the bill its stamp of approval, both houses subsequently passed it without amendment, and, on July 2, "An Act to quiet Titles to Lands within the Rancho Laguna de Santos Callé" became law. The only glitch came when a reluctant senator tried to postpone discussion. Conness immediately insisted that the bill was "of great importance to the people of California," kept the issue on the table, and, a short time later, presided over its passage. Meanwhile, during the same legislative session, the claimants on at least four other grants in northern California also rode the coattails of Suscol, including those on Rancho Ulpinos, which Hoffman had cited four years earlier when he rejected Rancho Laguna de Santos Callé. None of them, however, could have been more jubilant than Jerome C. Davis.[17]

When the news reached the other nine claimants back home, their first reaction was probably more of relief than jubilation, especially after not hearing from Davis for months on end. In any case, all they had to do now was file their applications at the district branch of the U.S. General Land Office (GLO) in Marysville within twelve months, pay the $1.25-per-acre fee, and get on with their lives. Nothing had been that easy for them in California up to that time, however, and the final stage of securing their patents would not be, either. A month later, after the Conness bill became law, each claimant received a copy of "Rancho Laguna de Santos Callé—Instructions," sent by the Commissioner of the GLO in Washington, D.C., to the register and receiver in Marysville. Two years earlier, Congress had approved legislation to "reduce the expenses of the survey" and pass them on to the individual settler—in this case the applicants under the Santos Callé Act. Each was required, at his own cost, to survey his property "within the range" of the rectangular township and section lines already in place. Patents, in other words, would not be issued to irregularly shaped entries measured in metes and bounds. But the claimants' boundaries, in place long before the subdivisional surveys, could not be measured in any other way. Baffled by this new development, Davis turned for help to the man with more nerve and guile than anyone else he knew—Champion I. Hutchinson.[18]

From San Francisco, the General devised a brilliant scheme. The claimants simply redistributed the land among themselves so as to conform their claims to the section lines, making sure as best they could that no one gave away more land than he received. Pierce, for example, deeded Hext 101.13 acres on his west boundary, but picked up 109.67 on his east side from S. E. Herrick, now the recognized owner of the Big Ranch. The plan had the added benefit of forcing Davis and Melone to finally solve their boundary dispute. The claimants entered the deeds —eleven in all—at the county recorder's office in Woodland, paid a U.S. deputy surveyor to make all the official plats, and one by one filed their finished applications in Marysville in June 1865. But they never actually moved—physically, that is—their old boundaries; it would have cost thousands of dollars just to tear down and put up new fences. The surveys in the U.S. patent books consisted of nice, neat, squared-off rectangles overlaying the township grids, but the claimants remained in their old, asymmetrical ranches. There was nothing in the law that said it could not be done, Hutchinson insisted, and, as it turned out, he was right.[19]

Once the claimants had filed their applications, the rest of the process went smoothly—for everyone, that is, except Davis. The register and receiver in Marysville verified that each claim was "bona fide"—that ownership could be traced back directly to the original grantees or their assigns, that the claimants possessed the tract at the date of the Santos Callé Act (July 2, 1864), and that no one contested their holdings. The other claimants, protected from trespassers by each other's fences, Putah Creek, or the Tule, encountered no "adverse claims." However, all fourteen squatters who entered Davis's land across his unprotected northern boundary filed their own applications in Marysville, claiming 160-acre lots by preemption. On Hutchinson's advice, Davis had remained in Washington after the passage of the Santos Callé Act as a contact, but he returned with his wife in December 1865 to defend his claim before the Marysville authorities. Generally, when two legitimate claims conflicted, priority went to the one filed first. In this instance, however, that seemingly straightforward logic gave squatters no chance. The register and receiver ruled that Davis's claim dated to the Santos Callé Act of July 2, 1864, not when he filed his application, while a preemption or homestead claim dated "from the day of its presentation at this office." Because preemptors, by law, could not file declaratory statements until the status of the grant was determined, squatter claims were, in effect, inadmissible. Once that became clear after the first hearing, on December 28, 1865, the other thirteen "conflicting claimants" did not bother to argue their cases.[20]

All that remained for the ten grantees was the paperwork. The authorities in Marysville sent the files to the GLO in Washington, D.C., where officials checked, processed, and copied them. Once approved, the commissioner of the GLO sent word back to the district land office, which then notified the claimants, who then returned to Marysville with full payment in hand. When the receipts reached Washington, the commissioner reviewed the files one last time, drew up the patents, and forwarded them to the president of the United States for his signature. The commissioner and his staff labeled documents in these files "Santos Callé Special," and for the patents themselves used the standard form for pre-emption entries, with "Laguna de Santos Callé Act July 2, 1864" scribbled in the margin. Pierce received his first, on December 6, 1866, and the others followed one by one over the next few months.[21]

Davis waited patiently, realizing that the size of his tract and its irregular boundaries might delay the process. On March 1, 1867, he finally received notification from the commissioner that his file was in order and that he had three months to make his payment. At $1.25 per acre, he needed almost $10,000 for his 7,566.94 acres. Six years of one financial crisis after another left Davis with almost nothing, but he still had his prized possessions—his horses. On May 9, at a well-publicized auction held on the ranch, he sold all seventy-five, including forty colts sired by Rattler. The proprietors from the Empire Meat Market, Fred Werner, and three other former business associates participated as well, selling stock and farm implements and lending the proceeds to Davis. That was enough for him to purchase a federal title to his land eight days later at the receiver's office in Marysville. When a letter arrived from the GLO later that July, Davis no doubt thought that his patent had finally arrived. Instead, it was the commissioner informing him that his "Santos Callé Special" had been canceled. Almost 3,000 acres that Davis had claimed for private entry, the commissioner explained, had also been claimed by the State of California as swamp and overflowed land. A final decision would be made pending further investigation.[22]

Davis was fit to be tied. Even Herrick, who had never actually purchased his land, had his patent by now. Moreover, Davis realized that he was caught in the middle of a dispute over one of the few land issues in California of little concern to him. For more than fifteen years, the state and federal governments could not agree on the definition or selection of swamp and overflowed land. The 2,900.82 acres in question, on the northern half of the Davis ranch, was a case in point. The land straddled the muddy old road that Pierce, Greene, and others had petitioned to replace in 1861. There, overflow from Putah Creek to the south as well as from Willow Slough to the north made for especially swampy conditions—tule even grew in several sections. Much of the land dried off by midsummer—too late to plant wheat or barley but sufficient for a spontaneous crop of grass. While state authorities in these situations invariably cried swampland, federal officials said not swampy enough—or, as the commissioner of the GLO put it in 1859, not "really and truly" swampy. Each also accused the other of surveying at whatever time of year fit their argument. As a stockman desirous of grasslands, especially that late in the season, Davis had no intention of reclaiming this portion of his property, but that did not remove him from the controversy. Without him even asking, a state engineer appointed by the newly created Board of Swampland Commissioners declared the land swamp and overflowed in the fall of 1861. State legislators had come to realize that reclamation on a piecemeal, local, and individual basis did not work in the Sacramento Valley. Earlier that year, they adopted a more centralized policy, which began with a systematic, county-by-county survey of the state's swampland—not a single acre of which was recognized by the federal government.[23]

Consumed by his quest to settle his claim, Davis gave the issue little thought. He may even have welcomed the swamp designation. It gave him the opportunity, should the Santos Callé Act not pass, to purchase at least some of the land, and it also saved him a few dollars in property taxes. He did not anticipate, however, that the U.S. surveyor general of California would be one of his "conflicting claimants"—for all 2,900.82 acres—when he defended his claim in Marysville in December 1865. Unsure how to proceed, the register and receiver stated only that "the question whether said lands are Swamp and Overflowed lands, the property of the State of California, or whether they are public Lands of the United States remains undecided." Three months later, however, they informed Davis that "the state would not contest the swamp portion." With that assurance, Davis included the land in his patent application and paid $1.25 an acre for it on May 16, 1867.[24]

Once again, Davis's timing could not have been worse. The registrar and receiver in Marysville spoke too soon, and Davis paid too late. In the interim, on July 23, 1866, Congress passed "An Act to Quiet Land Titles in California," whereby, after fifteen years of wrangling, the federal government surrendered to the state. Among its many provisions, the act formally approved all the state's previous swampland selections. All the U.S. surveyor general of California had to do was submit formal "lists" and maps of the state's swampland to the commissioner of the GLO for his certification. The act also extended the Suscol and San-

tos Callé precedents to all persons in the state who had purchased and settled portions of Mexican rancho grants later ruled invalid. Not surprisingly, it was Davis's
old friend, John Conness, who introduced the bill in the Senate. He and Representative John Bidwell persuaded their fellow legislators, ever weary of California
land issues, to pass it with minimal opposition. After his success with the Santos
Callé Act, Conness staked his career on defending land titles in California and regarded the 1866 bill as his crowning achievement. The Conness Act, as it quickly
became known, did not do Davis any favors, however. When his patent application, including receipt of payment, reached the GLO in July 1867, already sitting
on the commissioner's desk was "List No. 6 of Swamp and Overflowed Lands,
Marysville District," which consisted entirely of Davis's 2,900.82 acres.[25]

Back to Washington went Davis in August 1867, convinced that the best way
to resolve problems with the federal government was in person. He was anxious
to leave anyway. Since returning from Washington at the end of 1865, he and his
wife had lived in Sacramento, away from the gloom and doom of his ranch. The
mill, the dairy, the slaughterhouse, the cattle, and now even his beloved Rattler
colts were gone. Technically, he did not even own the land any more. Fearful that
his many creditors would seize it to settle past-due promissory notes, Davis transferred the title to his ranch to his father on March 3, 1866. What had once been
the economic and social center of Putah Creek was now a source of embarrassment for him. He felt increasingly estranged from those who had frequented his
ranch only a short time earlier—especially his fellow grantees on Rancho Laguna
de Santos Callé, who wanted nothing to do with him after learning that he had
abandoned them in Washington. Perhaps most tellingly, when Pierce, Hext,
Greene, and others re-petitioned the Board of Supervisors to build Stevenson's
bridge across Putah Creek in the spring of 1867, Davis raised not even a hint of
opposition.[26]

He might have considered selling the ranch to an outsider, but without a patent
knew it would be very difficult to find a viable buyer. Instead, a buyer found him.
As early as 1865, the promoters of the California Pacific Railroad Company saw
the Davis ranch as an ideal location to build a junction for their Marysville branch.
Geographically, it was two miles removed from the forbidding tule swamps west
of Sacramento, a straight shot southwest to Vallejo, and just across Putah Creek,
rendering a second bridge for the Marysville line unnecessary. Economically, the
site lay in the heart of a region long known for its prodigious grain production.
That promised the company heavy traffic for its routes, an opportunity to cultivate a crop of its own, and a chance to develop a prosperous town around the depot. One of the promoters, John B. Frisbie, who knew Davis from their Suscol-

Santos Callé connection, aggressively pursued a deal. Neither Davis's creditors nor his patent problems frightened this skillful and experienced speculator. On June 24, 1867, they reached an agreement. The Cal-P would purchase Davis's ranch, less the swamp and overflowed portion, for $80,000—$2,000 down, $6,000 due November 1, 1867, $22,000 due the following November, followed by five payments of $10,000 at yearly intervals through November 1, 1873. Davis's father would serve as the front man for the sale, with the entire transaction hinging on Davis securing his patent.[27]

A month before the agreement, Davis sent his patent application to Washington for all 7,566.94 acres of his land. Even with the sale to the railroad, he still expected to retain the 2,900.82 acres of swamp and overflowed land. A month after the agreement came the bad news that the U.S. surveyor general of California had submitted List No. 6 to the commissioner of the GLO. While in Washington, Davis discovered that the same reasoning that had worked for him earlier against squatters now worked against him. Because the survey conducted by the Board of Swampland Commissioners in 1861 predated the Santos Callé Act of 1864, the state was "entitled to priority." The commissioner saw no choice but to approve List No. 6 on July 21, 1868, and to refund the purchase money. Davis then turned his attention to the southern portion of his land, but only to fulfill his obligation to Frisbie and the other promoters. He had pursued this patent for almost two decades—four years before the land commission, another four years in district court, and the better part of seven years in Washington. When he finally received his "Santos Callé Special" on January 7, 1869, he had little to show for his efforts but debt, grief, and frustration.[28]

Meanwhile, construction of the Cal-P began in Vallejo in April 1868 and was moving rapidly toward Putah Creek ahead of schedule. Wanting the town in place before the railroad arrived, the promoters—Frisbie, William F. Roelofson, Dewitt C. Haskin, James M. Ryder, and DeWitt C. Rice—moved quickly, patent or no patent, in the spring and summer of 1868. They started a land company "for the ostensible purpose of building a town," secured a partial release of their mortgage from Isaac Davis for a 200-acre town site only a few hundred yards from what was already known as "the old Davis homestead," drew up a detailed plat consisting of a four-by-eight block grid surrounding the depot, and began selling fifty-by-forty-foot lots priced at $150 apiece. By the time the first train arrived on August 24, the fledgling town contained two hotels, a post office, dry goods, drug, and clothing stores, several saloons, one restaurant, a livery stable, a grain warehouse, and blacksmith, wagon-making, carpenter, and furniture shops—"everything of that kind a town should have," the new local newspaper boasted. There was talk of naming it "Veranda City," but when grain merchant William Dresbach suggested "Davis Town" or "Davisville," most everyone agreed—not so much to honor the man but, as one newspaper reporter put it, to link what had once been "a place of great expectations" to this "city in embryo."[29]

For years thereafter, Jerome Davis rode the Cal-P frequently, taking advantage of the lifetime pass Frisbie had included in the deal for his ranch. Though rarely departing at Davisville, he could not have resisted looking out the window as the train left the depot for Vallejo. Immediately to the right of the tracks was a building that conjured up a mix of emotions. The sign on it read, "Davis flouring mill," though the faded lettering was just barely perceptible. Though it had been many years since Davis had witnessed his daughter's fatal fall there, the pain must still have stung. He also must have felt, if only briefly, a strong sense of pride mixed with deep disappointment. During the heyday of the Davis stock farm, the mill had been a place of bustling activity and a symbol of the success that this rebellious adventurer from Ohio had attained. Since then, however, the building had become, in the words of another passenger, "a poor, forlorn looking shed." To look at it was to stare face-to-face at his own failure.[30]

Davis, too, had become but a pale shadow of his former self. He saw very little of the proceeds from the sale of his ranch. His father, ever mindful of sheltering his son from his creditors, changed his will on May 14, 1868, leaving most of his estate to Jerome's sister, Elnora. Isaac intended to use the railroad money to help his son get back on his feet again but never had the chance, dying unexpectedly on October 22, 1869. After several ugly and unsuccessful courtroom battles with his sister, Jerome finally quit fighting. Along with his wife, he lived the remainder of his life in Sacramento in relative obscurity and died in 1881 with less than $2,000 to his name. Not one of the numerous county and regional histories published in the late nineteenth or early twentieth centuries devoted a biographical entry to him or, for that matter, to Champion I. Hutchinson. The two most prominent figures in Putah Creek in the 1850s now had little or nothing to do with the community at this new and crucial stage of its development.[31]

CHAPTER SEVEN

Prominent Citizens

Given the natural disasters, mass of confusion over land titles, complicated and often contradictory federal and state land policies, and economic chaos, the chances of *anyone* persevering through the first two decades of settlement in Putah Creek seemed remote. Yet, fully 35 percent of those who paid property taxes in 1858—grantees, speculators, squatters, and swamplanders alike—eventually received land patents and remained residents at least through 1870. One out of five (or their sons) stayed through the end of the century. Those who persisted, moreover, came almost exclusively from the ranks of George W. Pierce and William Montgomery, not Champion I. Hutchinson and Jerome C. Davis—those who first settled on small-scale farms, not big ranches.[1] At a time when a high degree of geographic mobility and extensive population turnover characterized midwestern and northeastern rural Americans and their communities, the persistence rate in Putah Creek can only be described as remarkable. It matched, and in many cases exceeded, levels in much older, more established rural communities in Wisconsin, Kansas, Iowa, Illinois, Ohio, and Vermont.[2]

Persistence did not necessarily imply success and satisfaction any more than mobility indicated failure and discontent. Earlier in the century on the Ohio frontier, for example, where newly developed land appreciated rapidly, farmers tended to move not from necessity but for the opportunity to take their capital gains and invest in other lands.[3] In Putah Creek, however, such opportunities were few and far between. The persisters—most of them displaced forty-niners—sought stability of residence as much as economic gain. Unlike Davis and Hutchinson, they received little, if any, attention from visiting committees of the California State Agricultural Society or local newspapers. They were the ones, however, who provided tangible evidence that the adobe and tule lands could be cultivated, who emerged as leaders and innovators, and who were recognized by their peers (and later by county and regional histories) as "prominent citizens."[4] A tour through

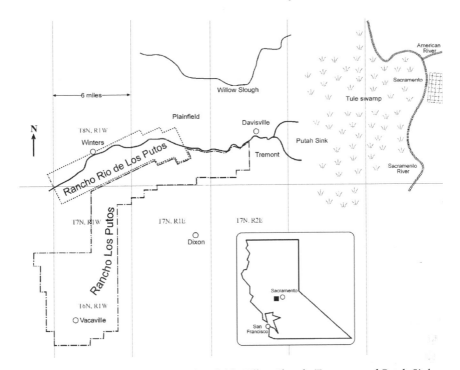

Location of Putah Creek districts—Plainfield, Willow Slough, Tremont, and Putah Sink. Based on *The Illustrated Atlas and History of Yolo County* (San Francisco: De Pue & Co., 1879) and *Historical Atlas Map of Solano County, California* (San Francisco: Thompson & West, 1878).

the region's several districts—Plainfield, Willow Slough, Tremont, and Putah Sink—reveals their struggles and triumphs.

In Plainfield, the southwest portion of Putah Township, squatters followed the controversy surrounding Rancho Laguna de Santos Callé every bit as closely as the claimants themselves and, from their perspective, with just as much at stake. Andrew McClory, for example, had been waiting for a resolution since 1853, when he and his family settled a 320-acre tract strategically located, or so they hoped, on unclaimed land between Rancho Rio de los Putos and Rancho Laguna de Santos Callé. Over the years, the McClorys made modest improvements and, by 1861, raised cattle and hogs valued at about $500. When they spotted a survey party at work in August 1862, their long wait appeared over. Only later, in what must have seemed a cruel hoax, did they learn that federal officials had bungled by calling for the survey prematurely. Not until after the Santos Callé Act passed on July 2, 1864, did they finally get the opportunity to file for preemption. By then, however, the drought had killed off three-fourths of their stock, leaving them unable to afford the $400 purchase cost.[5]

County surveyor Amos Mathews then informed McClory of another, less well known, option. He could buy the land from the state for only 20 percent down and one year's interest in advance, with the remainder to be paid over five years at an annual interest rate of 10 percent. The state, Mathews explained, authorized such sales under the so-called 500,000-acre grant, which California, like all new states, received from the federal government for funding internal improvements under Section 8 of the Preemption Act of 1841. He also proposed to lend McClory $500 for the initial payment, processing fees, and a few head of cattle. McClory jumped at the offer, perhaps without even reading the fine print. He agreed to pay off the loan in one year with interest at 2 percent per month and, moreover, to secure it with the land itself. Like many county surveyors, Mathews had learned that he could augment his salary not only with the six-dollar finder's fee he received from the state but by taking advantage of squatters longing to own their land.[6]

McClory received a "certificate of purchase," but only after undergoing an extraordinarily cumbersome process. Like any prospective purchaser of state lands, McClory first had to file an affidavit with the county recorder in Woodland swearing that he had no claim to other lands. He then had to track down Mathews to survey the proposed site. While Mathews sent copies of his field notes to the surveyor general of California in Sacramento, McClory went back to Woodland to file additional copies with the county recorder and make his first payment to the county treasurer. A copy of the receipt then had to be delivered back to the county recorder so that it could be registered. The county treasurer then sent his copy of the receipt to the state surveyor general and a copy of the certificate of purchase to the state treasurer in Sacramento. Meanwhile, the surveyor general forwarded the receipt with his signature to the state treasurer for his certification, and the state treasurer then returned it to the county treasurer to be filed. If documents were lost or misplaced at any step of the way—not an unlikely prospect—the whole process had to be repeated, all at the applicant's expense. The surveyor general himself estimated that the procedure typically cost the purchaser from $50 to $150 and dubbed the entire system "manifestly wrong" for its inefficiency. State land laws and their administration were so complicated that a number of "settler's guides" were published, including one twenty-four-page, tiny-print version that was so incomprehensible that it seemed to mock the whole process rather than lend assistance.[7]

When his loan matured a year later, in 1865, McClory could not pay even the interest, let alone the principal. In greater danger than ever before of losing his claim, he knew he had to act quickly. First, he paid Mathews by borrowing the money from his older brother, John, in San Francisco, signing over his certificate of purchase as security. Second, like many stock farmers in the aftermath of the drought, McClory turned to wheat to try to get back on his feet. Though planting a crop required far less capital than replacing his cattle, he still had to borrow $200 for seed and implements, which Mathews, once again, was happy to oblige. Neither strategy worked. In January 1867, John died without leaving a will. McClory's other brother, Thomas, whom he had not seen in years, suddenly appeared, insisting that he had as much right to the estate—including the certificate of purchase—as Andrew. A bitter battle in probate court ended only when Thomas died in 1870, with rumors of foul play flying about Yolo County. Two months after John's death, heavy rains drowned Andrew's crop, forcing him to borrow still more—this time from William Dresbach. McClory finally received his state patent on February 3, 1871, but only after accruing over $3,000 of debt. At the time, however, he thought it was well worth it.[8]

Even greater confusion reigned one mile east of McClory over a single 160-acre plot—the northeast quarter of section 10 (Township 8 North, Range 1 East). Gottfried Schmeiser, one of several German immigrants in the area, first settled there in 1856. When he moved three years later to Sacramento, Joshua Palmer and John Markely, both hands on the Big Ranch, squatted on opposite ends of the still-unsurveyed tract, each making modest improvements. When federal authorities appeared to open the township to preemption in August 1862, Palmer and Markely quickly filed declaratory statements within five days of each other, not realizing they were competing for the same quarter section or that the survey itself would soon be suspended. Unfortunately, news of the former preceded the latter by about a week. Each accused the other of trespassing, and after a heated exchange of words, Markely hit Palmer over the head with a board. In all likelihood, he did not mean to kill him, but fearing repercussions he tried to make it look like a dragging accident by tying one end of a rope around Palmer's neck and the other around a horse's head. In the justice court of George W. Pierce, thirteen Plainfield residents testified that Markely had sufficient motive to murder Palmer, but on appeal, a jury of peers from elsewhere in Yolo County found him innocent.[9]

Meanwhile, Schmeiser returned and filed his own declaratory statement shortly after the real survey had been made in the summer of 1864. For the next several years, he split his time between Plainfield and Sacramento, where he co-owned a machinist shop. In his absence, three new squatters—Frank Slocum, Richard Thomas, and Charles Derman—moved in, each claiming forty acres of the quarter section. All three challenged Schmeiser's entry on the grounds that he neither inhabited nor improved the land and was thus unqualified to pre-empt it. The commissioner of the U.S. General Land Office agreed and canceled Schmeiser's entry at the same time that Schmeiser took all three adverse claim-ants to court and had them evicted. Schmeiser could not file another claim on the same tract, but nothing prevented him from preempting the adjacent quarter sec-tion, where Jacob Oeste, his partner in Sacramento, had taken up residence early in 1868. Oeste applied for Schmeiser's quarter section while Schmeiser applied for Oeste's quarter section, and both received patents in 1872 without a hitch. As if to seal the deal, Schmeiser married Oeste's daughter Sophie on November 30, 1868. Oeste became the seventh individual to claim the same 160 acres in less than a decade. He and his descendants, in contrast, retained ownership of the quarter section for the next hundred years, as did their neighbors, the Schmeisers.[10]

Just to the northeast of Schmeiser and Oeste, Charles E. Greene had problems of his own. The terms of Greene's insolvency settlement in 1861 left him with a homestead of 960 acres, all of it sitting squarely on Rancho Laguna de Santos Callé, and little else. So fearful was he that the grant would be declared invalid that when federal authorities jumped the gun on the township survey in August 1862, he filed a declaratory statement of his own, hoping to retain at least some of the land. At the Santos Callé hearings in Marysville in December 1865, the State Land Office denied him one-third of his claim—the 320 acres constituting the south half of section 36 (Township 9 North, Range 1 East). Under a federal act of 1853, sections 16 and 36 of every township were "school lands" reserved to the state to fund public education—except when those sections were "claimed under foreign grant or title." The register and receiver at Marysville argued that because Rancho Laguna de Santos Callé had not actually been confirmed, section 36 be-longed to the state. Greene appealed the decision and, to be safe, also proceeded through the maze of requirements to purchase the land from the state. When the commissioner of the General Land Office granted his appeal, in effect giving him back the 320 acres, Greene withdrew his application for school land and instead filed for another 320 acres of so-called seminary land, made available through an obscure grant of seventy-two sections from the federal government to the state for building a university. When all was said and done, Greene had patents for 1,280 acres by November 1867, just six years after having declared bankruptcy.[11]

Securing his land revived Greene's self-confidence. By the end of the decade, a county directory declared his ranch to be "the best improved in this section"—on land that Greene himself would have considered unfit for cultivation just a short time earlier. For several years after his insolvency, he lived in a small wood-frame house and seemed resigned to raising his ten head of cattle, eight horses, and four dozen hogs. He could not help but notice, however, that squatters all around him on Rancho Laguna de Santos Callé were growing wheat quite profitably on adobe soil just like his. The drought, which killed off much of his stock, convinced him that it was time for a change. After his land problems had been resolved, Greene hired Charles Tinkham—squatter, wheat farmer, and former Big Ranch employee—to transform operations on his ranch. The results were astonishing. By 1870, Greene measured his yearly output of wheat in hundreds of tons and lived in a magnificent two-story mansion that was the talk of the county. "Twelve years ago," the same directory concluded, "the plains here were bare of aught [and] no signs of improvement or progressive life were visible. . . . Now, that portion of the county commonly designated as 'Plainfield' is second to none in its productiveness."[12]

Just to the south of Schmeiser and Oeste, Francis E. Russell made a name for himself as well. A French-Canadian from Quebec, Russell was swept away in 1850 by the westward tide of emigration to California's goldfields, where, like so many others, he eventually became discouraged and turned to farming. Upon hearing that the California Land Commission had rejected Rancho Los Putos in November 1853, Russell squatted on a 200-acre plot near Vacaville, hoping for the chance to preempt it. For the next five years, he raised several dozen head of cattle and earned extra cash in the summer harvesting grain for Edward McGary, owner of a large ranch nearby. He also started a family, marrying Lucy Ogburn in 1856 and a year later witnessing the birth of their first child. They were forced to uproot, however, when the U.S. Supreme Court confirmed the grant in 1858.

That seemingly ominous decision turned out to be Russell's big break. McGary had just purchased several lots totaling 2,316 acres of prime grazing land from John Wolfskill, who began subdividing Rancho Rio de Los Putos shortly after receiving his patent in 1858. Not wanting to relocate himself, McGary offered Russell Lot #1—397 acres along the eastern boundary of the grant—in exchange for managing his 250 head of cattle. Sensing that this was his chance, Russell turned Lot #1 into a stock and grain farm valued at almost $4,000 in less than two years. Though he too suffered the ravages of flood and drought in the 1860s, he did not share the patent worries of his neighbors. When McGary sold the remaining lots in 1866, Russell felt free to enlarge his own farm, which he did by taking advantage of the 500,000-acre grant to purchase an additional 277 acres from the state. The spacious two-story Victorian house that he built in 1868 for his family—now four children with three more to come—still stands.[13]

McClory, Oeste, Schmeiser, Greene, Russell, and other Plainfield residents manifested their persistence not only in attaining their patents, weathering the volatile climate, and improving their farms under such harsh and uncertain conditions but also in participating in the day-to-day activities of local government. Throughout the turbulent 1860s, they continued to pay their taxes, sit on juries, supervise elections in their own homes, run for public office, and build roads and bridges—including the controversial Stevenson's bridge across Putah Creek in 1867. They also accepted responsibility for what the *Sacramento Daily Union* deemed "the rising generation of California" by organizing an institution new to the region—the public school district.[14]

Indeed, Russell's growing family was a sign of the times in Putah Creek. In a community begun by displaced gold rushers, children were few and far between in the first decade of settlement. Of the 900 residents in Putah and upper Tremont townships in 1860, fewer than forty were of school age (six to fifteen years old). Even as the population became sufficiently large and dense to support public schools, there were not enough children to fill them. The closest schools for children in Putah Creek were in Washington, just across the river from Sacramento, or Silveyville, in Solano County. By the early 1860s, however, more children—most of them born in California—began to come of age. The first district to reach critical mass was Plainfield. In June 1861, McClory, Schmeiser, Greene, Russell, and two dozen other residents petitioned the Board of Supervisors to form a school district, and the following fall their children attended Plainfield Schoolhouse, a small one-room building just north of Greene's ranch. Six years later, Plainfield Schoolhouse could no longer accommodate all the children in the district, and residents taxed themselves to build the Fairfield School on the northern boundary of the Russell ranch. The growing commitment to public education reflected not only a demographic change—more women, more marriages, and more children—but also a sense of belonging among residents in the district after so many years of struggle.[15]

With more marriages came another phenomenon new to the region—divorce. On October 19, 1868, Caroline Weimer Heinz filed proceedings against her husband, Lorenz Heinz, in district court. No one from Putah Township had attempted to "dissolve the bonds of matrimony" before. In her complaint, Caroline cited a series of abuses that began the day they married in Yolo County in 1862. Her husband repeatedly beat and whipped her even during her two pregnancies, compelled her to perform "laborious farm labor," including feeding stock and harvesting grain, publicly accused her of being unfaithful on numerous occasions, and threatened to kill her for exposing his own infidelities. She asked the court for $500 to defray legal expenses, half the couple's real estate for herself and her children, and $10,000 for child support. Lorenz denied every charge, accused her of beating the children, secured the testimony of a former hand who admitted to "screwing" his wife at least six times after she had seduced him, and insisted that with a net worth of only $3,000, he could not hope to meet her demands anyway. The judge's decision was made easy when the defendant's star witness, under cross-examination, confessed that he had been paid several hundred dollars for his testimony. Caroline received roughly half of her monetary demands but full satisfaction for the divorce.[16]

Heinz v. Heinz, though just one case, offers a glimpse into popular attitudes about marriage and morality. Though Lorenz and Caroline were both German immigrants, they perceived her role quite differently—in large part because he had immigrated to America only recently for the gold rush, while she had lived in Illinois since childhood. He still strongly believed in the rigid family traditions that he had known as a young adult in Germany, where women were expected to be subservient to their husbands both on the farm and in the home. She, in contrast, understood marriage more as a partnership, in which women were exempt from heavy work and from much of the oppressive behavior that her parents and grandparents had accepted as normal. California law, based in part on Spanish common law, favored her ideal of companionate marriage over his patriarchal prerogative. Physical abuse, desertion, drunkenness, and infidelity were the principal grounds for divorce under an 1851 statute precisely because husbands and wives increasingly placed a premium on mutual deference, respect, kindness, and love. Two decades of case law served only to strengthen those beliefs, with "mental cruelty" becoming every bit as egregious as physical assault. Indeed, when Lorenz falsely accused Caroline of adultery, he committed, in the words of one appellate judge, "the grossest act of cruelty which can be perpetuated against an innocent female."[17]

The fact that Lorenz fell considerably short of the companionate ideal may not have been the product of old world patriarchy alone. His lawyer, while denying all Caroline's accusations, nonetheless hinted that "an almost uninterrupted series of disasters" may have triggered his client's violence. As a squatter on Rancho Laguna de Santos Callé just west of the Greene ranch, Lorenz experienced the same harsh and uncertain conditions that confronted his Plainfield peers. Only in the past year had he secured his patent and made a sizeable profit on his wheat crop.

Saddled by debt and beset by risk for most of his married life, he may well have resorted to wife-beating to vent his frustrations. If so, it seems highly unlikely that he was the only farmer in Putah Creek to have done so.

Why then, the question becomes, were there not more divorces? Part of the answer was that, the companionate ideal notwithstanding, divorce as a legal remedy was frowned upon by community mores. Caroline took an enormous risk going public with the lurid details of her marriage. Had she lost, she would have opened herself not only to considerable humiliation and embarrassment but also to the wrath of her infuriated husband. Breaking her marriage represented a direct challenge to mid-nineteenth-century morality. Neither she nor her neighbors could have known that it also marked the beginning of a "divorce crisis" in Putah Creek that would last for the rest of the century.[18]

By the mid-1860s, the Willow Slough district, on the other side of Putah Township, had become known as the most unpredictable region in the area. The landscape could literally change on a year-to-year, even month-to-month basis, because it was subject to overflow from four different sources: the Sacramento River to the east, Cache Creek to the north, Putah Creek to the south, and Willow Slough itself. A given tract of land could be inundated for the entire year (as in 1862), much of the year (1867), for only a month or so (1861), or not all (1863 and 1864). The land itself, as a result, was less flat—full of subtle dips and rises and with more than a few sizeable depressions and temporary drainage channels. When cattle roamed much of the unsurveyed land in the 1850s, these natural variations went largely unnoticed, but as wheat began to take over, quarter section by quarter section, controversy became almost inevitable and, on occasion, even bizarre—as illustrated by two high-profile lawsuits.[19]

The first case resembled the dispute over the Schmeiser tract, in that there were two legitimate claimants for the same plot of land, but with a swampy twist. Like so many squatters, Ephraim Cone waited for years for the decision on Rancho Laguna de Santos Callé. When it came in the summer of 1864, he was one of the first to file a declaratory statement (on Dec. 1, 1864), receive a certificate of purchase (May 4, 1868), and, after waiting patiently, secure a patent from the U.S. government (May 2, 1870) for the southeast quarter of section 24 (Township 9 North, Range 2 East). He knew his land was near the Tule just to the east, but it never occurred to him that it might actually be swampland. Since his arrival in 1858, after all, he had harvested a crop every season but two—the very wet years of 1862 and 1867. Cone not only followed the letter of the law with regard to his land but also made modest improvements, paid his taxes, served on at least one jury, and donated several days' labor to county road work. He was, in short, a model preemptor.[20]

Imagine his surprise, then, when his neighbor to the west, John Hynes, marched up to him in July 1868 with a patent from the state of California for *his* land. Several months earlier, while filling out forms for his own quarter section at the county recorder's office in Woodland, Hynes had noticed that Cone's land was listed as swampland and available. Back in 1861, when the newly created Board of Swampland Commissioners undertook its statewide survey, the engineer included the southeast quarter of section 24 just inside the segregation line—apparently without informing Cone. When the Conness Act of July 1866 then made that line official, Hynes, or anyone else for that matter, was free to file a claim with the state. When Cone sued Hynes, both presented airtight cases. The jury could not reach a verdict, and the judge threw his hands up in the air as well. Cone then consulted officials at the Marysville land office, who proceeded to obtain authorization from the commissioner of the General Land Office (GLO) to shift the segregation line over so as to split the quarter section in half—the dry west side going to Cone, the wet east side to Hynes. Neither party took exception to the ruling, but neither could have been too pleased.[21]

Cone v. Hynes demonstrates not only the level of absurdity that swampland disputes could reach but also, in a roundabout way, the increasing influence of prominent citizens in local affairs. The state engineer who drew the first segregation line in 1861 had an impossible task. The GLO required "permanent lines" that conformed "exactly to the sections" on a "quarter quarter" (forty-acre) basis. "Each one of such quarter quarters as may contain more swamp than dry land is to be allotted as swamp; and each one on which the greater part of dry land is, of course, to be returned for disposal as other public lands." But how was the surveyor to make such a determination when the line between swamp and dry was neither permanent nor exact? His instructions were to "procure testimony" from "long-time residents" knowledgeable about the region in question. If anyone knew which lands were in fact "unfit for cultivation without necessary drains and levees to reclaim them," the reasoning went, it had to be the old-timers in the area.

In this instance, the surveyor, on November 6, 1861, consulted James T. Lillard, E. L. Brown, W. W. Brown, Joshua B. Tufts, I. S. Chiles, and G. F. Browder—all "long-time residents" by California standards, but none more capable than anyone else of meeting the commissioner's specifications. Who knows where they might have drawn the line just a month later, when the "flood of the century" hit? Nonetheless, their having been called upon to make such an important decision enhanced their stature within the community. All six remained in Putah Creek for the rest of their lives, while neither Cone nor Hynes stayed longer than five years after the trial. Persistence, responsibility, and respectability, this case suggests, went hand in hand, though not always to everyone's satisfaction.[22]

The second case was quirkier still. Edward Connor was among the first wave of squatters who settled on Rancho Laguna de Santos Callé in the late 1850s. He claimed 160 acres just north of Willow Slough (and west of the Cone-Hynes disputed tract). Over the years, as he gradually made improvements, he discovered that during a heavy rain, surface water from the north drained through a shallow depression on his land into Willow Slough. In 1863, while planting wheat for the first time, he constructed a makeshift embankment along his northern boundary to protect his growing crops from the flow. At the time, no one occupied the land to the north. Connor continued to strengthen and enlarge the barrier so that by 1868 a dam, 4 feet high and 500 yards long, was in place. That same year, Samuel Ogburn claimed the quarter section on the other side and began his own wheat farm. Over the next three years, both Connor and Ogburn filed for preemption, received their patents in short order, and produced good crops. When "heavy and copious rains fell" in December 1871, however, the dammed-up run-off submerged 80 acres of Ogburn's land and drowned most of his crop.[23]

Ogburn received little sympathy at first when he sued Connor for damages. The district court judge insisted that Connor had every right to protect his land from the flow of surface water by any means necessary. He based his ruling not so much on previous case law, which he acknowledged was ambiguous, but on the fact that the defendant had constructed the embankment "long before the plaintiff purchased his land from the Government, or had settled thereon." Ogburn appealed the decision to the state supreme court, which reversed the judgment, on the basis that the "rule generally prevailing in this country" prohibited Connor from obstructing the "natural flow of the water," before or after his neighbor's arrival. The argument that persistence deserved reward, the court emphasized, was "not sound."[24]

Ogburn prevailed in the end, but he had already sold the land and left the county. Upon dismantling the dam, Connor, on the other hand, discovered that the "natural flow" had changed its course. Overflow from Willow Slough, particularly during the 1867 floods, as well as his own plowing over the years, had essentially flattened the depression on his property that caused the problem in the first place. With the controversy behind him, Connor went on to become one of

Willow Slough's prominent citizens, cultivating wheat and serving the community until his death in 1890. When all was said and done, persistence did have its reward.[25]

Not so in the Tremont district, at least not for Juan Manuel Vaca, Juan Felipe Peña, and their descendants. Although the U.S. Supreme Court confirmed Rancho Los Putos in 1857, the grantees remained mired in legal turmoil with squatters, speculators, and lawyers. Before long, only a small portion of the grant remained in the Peña family and little or none in the hands of the Vacas. Ironically, the rapid decline of these two once-prominent families strongly influenced who became prominent citizens in Tremont, even on land between the grant and Putah Sink (about half the district) that Vaca and Peña had never owned.

Well before Vaca and Peña received their patent in 1858, both dons made every effort to pass the lands of Los Putos on to their surviving children—nine in Vaca's case, six in Peña's. Between 1851 and 1855, Vaca signed deeds that effectively divided his half-interest in the grant into nine equal shares, and Peña followed suit shortly thereafter. Because the land had not yet been surveyed or even divided between the two grantees, only interests, or "portions," could be conveyed. The deeds, therefore, did not specify location except that the land, in most cases, "be situated on Putah Creek." When Vaca died on May 15, 1858, he went to his grave believing that Los Putos was intact and that he had provided well for his family. Peña lived five years longer only to see a much bleaker picture.[26]

Vaca, Peña, and their children were not the only ones to covet the fertile bottomlands south of Putah Creek. So too did John Currey, their attorney during the district court hearings, who received 4,500 acres for his fees between 1855 and 1857. So too did several squatters—among them Bartlett Guthrie, Dwight Cooley, George Foster, and Joshua B. Tufts—who contested the boundaries of the grant, all of them unsuccessfully. So too did the fee-hungry lawyers who defended the grantees, both first and second generation, and gladly accepted payment in land. And so too did the speculators who preyed on the Vaca and Peña families' ignorance of the law and market conditions to buy and sell their portions at enormous profits.[27]

Of the many who participated in this feeding frenzy, a Solano County attorney named Henry Hartley stood out above the rest. In May 1859, he received 10 percent of the Vaca children's collective interest in Los Putos for successfully defending their property against squatters. Before the end of the year, he persuaded five of the Vacas to sell him their portions for one dollar an acre by intimating that additional suits would eventually drain their assets. He also purchased large tracts from other lawyers involved in the grant's litigation, including several hundred acres from both Currey and the firm of Jones, Tomkins, and Strode. By 1860, Hartley owned at least 15,000 prime acres along Putah Creek, but not for long.

Over the next two years, he sold most of it back to the same squatters he had denied earlier—including Guthrie, Coolie, Foster, and Tufts—for as much as $17 an acre, two to three times the going rate for comparable land on the other side of the creek. Tufts, for example, bought 500 fertile acres across from the Davis stock farm in 1855 for $850 (from either Hartley himself or another speculator), only to see the land included just inside the boundaries of Los Putos two years later. On May 10, 1860, Hartley sold it back to him for $8,500. If Tufts or any other purchaser could not afford full payment, Hartley gladly financed the transaction at the customary high rate of interest. As for the land that did not sell, most of it he leased back to members of the Vaca and Peña families. As speculators liked to say, Hartley made a killing.[28]

The ramifications of Hartley's exploits extended beyond the indignities suffered by the once proud owners of Rancho Los Putos. While the Vacas and Peñas gained very little from their patent, those who purchased their land through Hartley and other speculators reaped the benefits. They sidestepped the cumbersome process of buying government land and did not have to worry about ensuing title conflicts, though many enlarged their holdings by preempting adjacent quarter sections or purchasing state land through the 500,000-acre grant. Much of the land east of the Los Putos boundary and south of Putah Creek—about half of it swampland—sold quarter section by quarter section, with purchasers receiving their patents not long thereafter.[29] The disparity in property values from one side of the creek to the other soon spread to this area as well, with land throughout the upper Tremont district consistently worth 20 to 30 percent more over the course of the decade. Consequently, while several Tremont landowners purchased holdings in Putah Township, Tufts remained the only Yolo County resident to buy land south of the creek for years to come.[30] Those who paid the price for Tremont land, moreover, tended to keep it. From 1860 to 1870, Tremont maintained a persistence rate approaching an astounding 50 percent.[31]

Tufts, Guthrie, Coolie, Foster, and other persisters also became, almost by default, the district's prominent citizens. During the turbulent 1860s, they persevered through flood and drought and led the transition from stock raising to wheat farming in Tremont.[32] They also played key roles in township government—with Tufts and Guthrie being particularly active—and tried their best to represent Tremont's interests in the far-away county seat of Fairfield. It was simply too easy, however, for the Solano County Board of Supervisors to turn a deaf ear to their complaints, especially during the tax season. Indeed, Tremont farmers were well aware that their assessment rate was consistently higher than their neighbors' in Yolo County, where there were no cities comparable to Vallejo, Benicia, or Fairfield. The double burden of high taxes and neglect was most noticeable, perhaps, in the district's roads, which were notoriously bad. Residents looked with envy to the other side of the creek, wishing aloud year after year for Yolo County to annex their community, but to no avail. In the 1870s, in fact, it would prove more difficult to move political boundaries than to move the creek itself.[33]

Socially, however, Putah Creek posed no barriers whatsoever. Indeed, with the decline of the Davis stock farm in the 1860s, the Solano House, just across the creek and a quarter-mile upstream, became the social center of the region, hosting balls, festivals, holiday celebrations, and political meetings. Tufts was the chief proprietor of this stage stop, which in 1862 consisted of a hotel, livery stable, blacksmith shop, general store, and post office. From 1862 to 1868, William Dresbach served as postmaster and also ran the store. Though possessing but a limited command of English, he earned a reputation among Putah Creek farmers as "a gentleman of superior business attainments and social qualities." Most knew him simply as "Solano Bill."

By the end of 1865, that reputation caught the attention of Isaac Friedlander, who had already begun organizing his new network of shippers and agents along the soon-to-be-constructed California Pacific Railroad. Friedlander's strategy was to recruit well-established country merchants and teach them the tricks of the trade—and if they happened to be of German descent, all the better. Dresbach fit the job description to a tee. In November, Friedlander fronted him $8,000 to purchase the Solano House, where he polished his business skills and further enhanced his reputation. Two years later, Dresbach launched his grain store in the new town of Davisville, sold the Solano House for a tidy profit, and proceeded to run his former establishment into the ground in less than a year's time. The education of Solano Bill, now "Friedlander's man," had only just begun.[34]

The three most memorable events held at the Solano House occurred within two weeks of each other early in April 1865. The first took place when the transcontinental telegraph, completed just two-and-a-half years earlier, brought news of the fall of Richmond to the Sacramento Valley. The second followed just days later, when word of General Robert E. Lee's surrender at Appomattox reached California. On both occasions, Putah Creek residents gathered from miles around for impromptu celebrations at Tuft's hotel, where they sang patriotic songs, rang bells, carried torches, and waved flags well into the night. Many also attended the festivities held in Sacramento the next day, which one newspaper called "the grandest spontaneous outpouring of patriotism ever witnessed." The third came on April 15, four days after Abraham Lincoln's assassination, when the shocked and grief-stricken community mourned the president's passing on the day of his funeral in Washington, D.C.[35]

Though isolated from the field of battle, Putah Creek farmers were intimately involved in the Civil War. Emotionally, most still had family and friends back east whose lives were more directly and immediately affected by wartime disruptions. Politically, most brought their sectional prejudices, party affiliations, and loyalties to their states of origin with them and voted accordingly in California. Elections and trends in party politics in Putah Creek in the 1860s mirrored those of the Sacramento Valley and the state as a whole. Roughly 60 percent of the local voters were Democrats, but they found themselves deeply divided over the issues of slavery, secession, and the right of a state to manage its own affairs. As a result, Democrats in Putah Township and throughout Yolo County split their vote in half between Steven A. Douglas and John C. Breckinridge in the 1860 presidential election, and again the following year between John Conness and John R. McConnell in the race for governor. On both occasions, the Democratic schism enabled the Republicans—Abraham Lincoln and Leland Stanford, respectively—to emerge victorious with only a slight plurality. For much of the rest of the decade, Douglas Democrats in California cooperated with the Republicans and together, by shrewdly calling themselves the Union party, managed to brand the former Breckinridge Democrats as disloyal.[36]

Putah Sink was by far the most contested district. Pockets of Confederate support existed throughout the region, but only in Putah Sink did southerners constitute anywhere near a majority of the population. Of the district's forty-five farmers in the 1860s, twenty-one came from south of the Mason-Dixon line, but only two from states that had joined the Confederacy. The nineteen from Missouri, Kentucky, and Maryland were probably just as split over secession as their counterparts back home and no less secure in the Union fold, particularly over the issue of slavery. In all likelihood, very few of them attended the three Solano House gatherings in April 1865. Not only were they in no mood to celebrate or pay homage to the fallen president; they knew to avoid situations in which they were likely to become too outspoken.[37]

William Montgomery and his sons were a case in point. They worked behind the scenes in the county Democratic party in support of secession candidates

Breckinridge and McConnell, only to realize that their efforts had helped elect two hated Republicans. Moreover, in a community whose vocal Confederate sympathizers were such a small minority, the Montgomerys found that it paid to keep a low profile, especially in local matters. Belligerence, for example, would not have gotten them the public road they requested from the county in August 1860 or the reduction in their property taxes a few years later. While not fire-eaters, the Montgomerys certainly did not abandon their southern identity. When Alexander's wife, Susan, gave birth to the couple's sixth and seventh children in the middle of the Civil War, they named the daughter Minnie Jeff Davis Montgomery and the son Lee Jackson Montgomery.[38]

The politics of the Civil War indirectly impacted the most pressing, vexing, and long-term problem confronting Putah Sink farmers—swampland reclamation. Even before the great flood of 1862, William Marden, Ransom S. Carey, the Drummond brothers, and numerous other swamplanders came to realize that Putah Sink and the surrounding tule lands would never be reclaimed if left in the hands of each individual farmer, as legislation in the 1850s intended. As they had witnessed over and over again, even small-scale floods simply overwhelmed the levees and ditches that most property owners could afford to erect. Plans to "drain the Tule" in a more systematic, centralized fashion abounded in the late 1850s, all of them rejected on principle by a state legislature dominated by Democrats, the party of laissez faire, individual initiative, and small, local government. For the many Putah Sink farmers who were Democrats, the irony was that it took the Republican ascendancy of 1861, with its emphasis on order, system, and government planning, to force the action.[39]

One of the first laws passed by the new legislature created the Board of Swampland Commissioners, the first in a long line of independent public agencies in California charged with managing the state's natural resources. Legislators and the five members of the board recognized that to be effective, flood control works had to be aligned not with property ownership but with natural drainage patterns—which in the Sacramento Valley often meant entire basins encompassing more than 100,000 acres. They did not fully recognize, however, the enormity of what lay ahead of them. Simply surveying the state's swampland would create endless frustration and mountains of litigation—as Jerome C. Davis and Ephraim Cone, among hundreds of others—would soon discover. Controlling the floodwaters of the Sacramento Valley, moreover, would prove to be far beyond their means and expertise.[40]

The key to the law was a new legal entity, ambitious in scope and ingenious in innovation, called the swampland district. Upon receiving a petition from one-third of the landowners in any geographic region "susceptible of one mode or system of reclamation," the state board proceeded to establish the district, which was designed essentially to pay for itself. Drawing on the money held in the "swamp land fund" created from the sales of swamp and overflowed land in the district, the board hired engineers and workers to construct a single system of levees, canals, and drainage ditches to protect all the land in common. "In no case," the law stipulated, "shall an account be certified, or a warrant drawn, in payment for the reclamation of a particular district, for a greater sum than has been paid into the Swamp Land Fund for the district." That clause, designed to impose fiscal responsibility, handcuffed the board from the outset. The one-dollar-per-acre selling price did not produce nearly enough money, especially when a substantial part of the swamplands remained unsold. Any hopes that landowners would contribute more in any of the twenty-eight districts scattered throughout northern California by the end of 1861 were wiped out by the great flood that winter. The following spring, the board secured remedial legislation, in which the county boards of supervisors were authorized to levy reclamation taxes on those districts in which one-third of the landowners supported such action. All but one district, however, ran out of money and ceased operations far short of completing their planned works.[41]

Only District 18, which embraced 164,318 acres west of the Sacramento River in Yolo County (the Yolo Basin, as it came to be called) accomplished most of its objectives.[42] Plans for the district included a twenty-five-mile drainage canal running north-south through the middle of the Tule from Knights Landing to Cache Slough, complete with laterals that tapped the sinks of Cache and Putah creeks and a continuous levee along the Sacramento River, seventy-eight miles long. "It is believed," wrote the chief engineer of the project, "that if the waters of these two creeks are prevented from accumulating in the Tule that it can be so thoroughly drained as to make the best grass land in the State." Farmers who had already cleared small portions of their own knew that to be true firsthand. They eagerly submitted to a special reclamation tax that nearly doubled their existing swampland fund, to over $25,000. By the summer of 1865, the main canal and levee were in place and detailed plans for the two laterals were ready to proceed, with almost $7,000 left in the district's account. The board trumpeted the success of District 18 in its annual reports and in northern California newspapers, hoping that others would follow its example.[43]

The flood of 1867–68 exposed these best-laid plans as folly. The Sacramento River, flowing at 50 to 100 times its normal capacity, breached the levee in dozens of places, the largest of which lay directly across from its confluence with the

American River. A rampaging Putah Creek washed away the branch canal still under construction—the very canal designed to carry its floodwaters around the farms of Putah Sink and redeposit them out of harm's way. As for the main canal itself, the thirty-foot-wide, nine-foot-deep ditch lay submerged under a vast inland sea ten to fifteen feet deep. The engineers were dumfounded. Their bold project, a seemingly foolproof plan for reclaiming the Tule, proved utterly powerless against the forces of nature. In a rare moment of humility, one finally admitted, "The average rainfall of the country is doubtless greater than formerly believed. . . . By observation, I am forced to the conclusion that the system of reclamation adopted for this district is insufficient."[44]

Seen in historical perspective, the engineer's overconfidence, shock, and ignorance—all shared in abundance by farmers and legislators—provoke more empathy than criticism. District 18, not to mention the valley-wide flood-control system envisioned by the board, was simply too big a task and way beyond what was remotely possible at the time. Indeed, generations would pass before engineers would develop the knowledge, expertise, and technology to tame (but never conquer) the Sacramento River and its tributaries. Yet, almost before the water had receded, engineers and farmers were back at it with a collective exuberance that was exceeded only by their collective amnesia. Legislators, on the other hand, absolved themselves and the state of the burden of reclamation with two new laws. The first, passed on March 22, 1866, abolished the Board of Swampland Commissioners and turned their job over to the county governments, while the second, two years later, placed the responsibility of swampland management squarely back on the shoulders of the swamplanders themselves.[45]

In Putah Sink, Ransom S. Carey emerged as the key figure during these developments. A gold-rush migrant from Clay County, Missouri, Carey, after struggling in the mines of El Dorado County, began raising cattle about two miles northeast of the Montgomery ranch in 1852. By 1860, he had become Putah Sink's most successful stockman, owning 4,000 acres of mostly unimproved land (320 of his own, the rest purchased from frustrated swamplanders), 1,500 head of cattle, 120 hogs, and a prosperous dairy. Alexander Montgomery later named his tenth child after his ambitious neighbor. When the great flood and subsequent drought decimated his herd, Carey took it personally. Determined to rebuild his ranch and protect it from future inundation, he regularly attended District 18 meetings, learning the basics of levee building and dredging and contributing his own knowledge of Putah Sink's complicated geography. Engineers relied heavily on his input when planning the branch canal. When the Yolo County Board of Supervisors assumed control of District 18 in accordance with the March 1866 law, Carey dominated its meetings even more. The new law placed the county surveyor in charge of supervising all reclamation projects, but Carey was not about to leave the fate of his ranch in the hands of someone who, in his mind, had never had anything more serious to do than survey straight lines. By the fall of 1866, Carey had not only restocked his ranch with over 1,200 cattle; he had also seized control of the construction of the Putah Sink lateral.[46]

When the heavy rains the following winter flooded his ranch and washed away the canal, Carey was beside himself. Unable and unwilling to comprehend the scale and scope of the disaster, he became all the more convinced that more canals and more levees, properly built and situated, would remedy the situation. Others in the Sacramento Valley shared his consuming obsession, most notably Will S. Green of Colusa County, himself a Kentucky-born gold-rush migrant and self-taught engineer. After consulting with Carey and other like-minded swamplanders, Green, who had just been elected to the state assembly, sponsored a bill that changed the face of the state's swampland system.[47]

Its underlying premise maintained that only those with the most at stake—the swamplanders themselves—had the desire and the will to do the job right. Green had no intention of reverting to the practice of the 1850s, when individuals reclaimed their land 320 acres at a time. Indeed, the 1868 law (the Green Act, as it came to be called) instead allowed individuals to buy as much swampland as they could afford at one dollar an acre, provided that title to the property be withheld until the land was adjudged to be reclaimed. The act retained the idea of the "district," in that any group of landholders could create one of their own and tax themselves when "half or more" gave their approval. But no public authority—commission, board of supervisors, or otherwise—could intervene in the affairs of the district at any time for any reason. Moreover, if the owners of a given district could prove that the land had been cultivated for three years, they would receive a full refund on their purchase price. Incentive had always been part of swampland policy, but now the carrot at the end of the stick was larger and more tantalizing than ever. Greene's fellow legislators, delighted to be relieved of the responsibility for reclamation, approved the bill unanimously.[48]

When the Green Act went into effect late in May 1868, swamplanders and prospective swamplanders lined up outside the Yolo County courthouse in Woodland to file their applications. At the front of the line, metaphorically and perhaps literally as well, stood R. S. Carey, William Marden, the Drummond brothers, the Montgomerys, and other prominent citizens of Putah Sink. They had persisted through removals, rough times in the goldfields, two major floods, a three-year drought, and almost two decades of economic uncertainty, and now they had the opportunity to purchase as much land as they wanted for one dollar an acre. Most could only afford a few hundred acres, but Carey more than doubled his already large holdings, to 10,000 acres. In less than a year, virtually every acre of swampland in Putah Sink, much of it deemed fit only for grizzly bears just a few years earlier, passed into private hands. Carey had already made known his plan for reclaiming the region, and the others had full confidence in his expertise. Their dreams of striking it rich, as vivid as ever, could not be realized otherwise.[49]

The impetus behind these revived dreams was the same in Putah Sink as it was in Plainfield, Willow Slough, and Tremont. "Wheat mania" had taken hold. Even a committed stockman like Carey knew that wheat was the wave of the future. The decade's three natural disasters had greatly reduced the number of men engaged in the cattle industry in Yolo and Solano counties. This enabled opposing forces to push through the legislature the first of the state's so-called no-fence laws. Owners of trespassing cattle were now liable for damages to growing crops "whether the land [was] enclosed by a lawful fence or not." That heavy new burden, along with the overwhelming evidence that the adobe and the tules could be cultivated and that the region had finally been thoroughly surveyed, prompted preemptors, homesteaders, swamplanders, and speculators alike to swarm over the remaining public land. "Where one year ago not a house could be seen," reported the *Yolo County Democrat* late in 1867, "nearly every acre of land is now taken up and under proper cultivation."[50]

So began one of the most extraordinary episodes in American agricultural history—California's bonanza wheat era. By coincidence, California produced three straight bumper crops after the drought broke in 1865, at the same time that Great Britain and other European nations suffered dangerously deficient harvests. Enterprising grain merchants in San Francisco and Liverpool, including the already legendary Isaac Friedlander, exploited the opportunity to the fullest, as did farmers in Putah Creek. As production skyrocketed between 1866 and 1869, farm incomes more than tripled and land values rose to as much as $20 per acre. This dramatic turn of events confirmed the prevailing belief among these farmers that demand would inevitably outpace production. Developments over the next decade would call that assumption into question, but for the time being, farmers believed they had finally struck gold.[51]

PART THREE

THE SECOND GOLD RUSH

CHAPTER EIGHT

"As Good As Wheat"

William Dresbach's general store buzzed with activity throughout the summer of 1869. The twenty-sixth of June was a particularly busy day. Needing cash to pay harvest expenses and to begin settling the year's accounts, George W. Pierce, Charles E. Greene, James C. Campbell, Francis E. Russell, Bartlett Guthrie, and R. S. Carey all hauled in their first wheat of the season. While workers unloaded the 125-pound sacks (nearly 3,000 total) from the long line of wagons into Dresbach's huge warehouse, these six prominent citizens gathered out front for a lively conversation. Though disappointed with the $1.50 per cental (hundredweight) that Dresbach offered them, they were encouraged that the price had gone up 10 cents from the previous week. That was a sign, they told each other, that as the year wore on, the market for the rest of their crop would reach the $1.75 to $2.25 range to which they had become accustomed.[1]

"Big crops and high prices," they believed, "were the order of the day. The large surplus from the previous season that accounted for the current glut was temporary, they assumed. There would always be markets, and profitable ones, for all that they would raise. "The high price brought by California wheat in Liverpool," Greene had insisted a few months earlier, "is an assurance that it will always find sale, however full the market may be stocked." They counseled one another to hold on to as much of their wheat as they could; with the impending war in Europe and a lighter crop in California predicted for the year, prices were sure to rebound. Their unbridled optimism stemmed not only from their newfound expertise in world affairs, which they gleaned from conversations among themselves, from the local newspapers, and from their own direct participation in the emerging global economy. They took immense pride in the knowledge that the wheat they grew on their farms moved in greater volume over greater distances than any product ever before in human history.[2]

As the conversation moved to more local matters, the tone and substance remained equally high-minded. How their community had "advanced in prosperity," they boasted. Dresbach's store now offered them a full line of high-quality goods, from tools and implements, to expensive fabrics and ready-made clothing, to imported spices and plugs of the finest tobacco. Olive Street in Davisville had become the center of a thriving business district, which catered to the needs of farm families, townspeople, and visitors. Three churches and a public school-house were either under construction or in various stages of planning. Three fraternal organizations offered men new means of fellowship and conviviality. Balls, dances, and "base ball matches" were held seemingly every week. The town would soon have its own newspaper to keep readers abreast of "local intelligence and improvements" (though it would last only a few months), and an ambitious canal project promised to reroute the volatile waters of Putah Creek away from the town, reclaim thousands of acres of swampland, and enhance the "air of business and prosperity" about the region.[3]

They owed it all to wheat, and they knew it. Putah Creek farmers resurrected the old proverb "as good as wheat"—the same spine-tingling phrase that had captured the imagination of Pierce and his fellow Kenoshans in the 1840s. Wheat, they preached, "was as good and even better than money." It was better, even, than gold.[4]

"Farming new land at two cents a pound for wheat is about as good an enterprise as a man can go into," wrote an early chronicler of California agriculture. Putah Creek farmers agreed wholeheartedly. From 1867 to 1877, they received that magical price more often than not.[5] So profitable was wheat during this time that farmers rarely concerned themselves with calculating the exact cost of production, though $1.50 per cental was widely perceived as the price they needed to break even. All they knew for sure was that the two-dollar benchmark allowed them not only to cover the expenses of producing their crop but also to clear their mortgage debts, pay their taxes, buy supplies, and still have something left over for themselves and their families. Wheat, they insisted, "*ought* to command $2.00 per cental." After two decades of struggle, they firmly believed that they were entitled.[6]

On the basis of the ingenuity they continued to display in their fields, their presumptions seemed justified. Farmers in Putah Creek well understood that the sensational yields they had witnessed during the 1850s could not be sustained indefinitely. They feared soil deterioration every bit as much as bad weather and high interest rates. By the early 1870s, most had adopted the practice of summer-fallowing as "the surest remedy." Pierce employed the most common approach. He divided his wheat acreage into two fields of roughly equal size. Every year after fall plowing, he let one of the fields lie idle for the winter as well as the next spring and summer, before sowing the land the following fall—carefully harrowing periodically to keep the surface clean, loose, and free of weeds. In effect, Pierce used two years of rain to grow one crop on "the summerfallow," as he called the plowed but unseeded section. This allowed him, by means of the increased yield, to raise as much wheat from half of his land every other year as he could had he planted all of his land every year—and with half the cost of plowing, seeding, and harvesting. Summer-fallowing, above all, gave the land a rest on alternate years, which enabled Pierce and his neighbors to cultivate wheat year after year without a rapid decrease in yield. They gradually learned that changing seed periodically had the same desired effect, as did burning off the stubble in the fields after the harvest, which added potash to the soil. In this regard, most Putah Creek farmers demonstrated a keen environmental consciousness in their quest to increase production and maximize profits.[7]

Tenants, however, did not have the luxury of summer-fallowing—especially those who rented portions of the old Davis ranch now owned by the five promoters of the California Pacific Railroad (the "proprietors of Davisville," as they called themselves). Intent on reaping the benefits of wheat mania, John B. Frisbie, William F. Roelofson, Dewitt C. Haskin, James M. Ryder, and Dewitt C. Rice hired Dresbach at the end of 1867 as their "land agent" for their 4,000 fertile acres along Putah Creek. Over the next eight years, Dresbach rented the land (excluding the 200-acre town site) in parcels of 300 to 500 acres to at least fifteen different tenants. The terms of the leases and their effect on the productivity of the land accounted for the high turnover. William Wristen, Napoleon Miner, John and Burlin Cecil, and other tenants all agreed to produce a crop of wheat at their own expense for two-thirds of the proceeds, with the remaining third going to the five proprietors, less Dresbach's fee. Each lease could be renewed at the end of the season at the request of both parties. Renters, who found it difficult to turn a profit under these terms, had no incentive whatsoever to summer-fallow and every incentive to seed every last acre of land. By 1875, after retired Cal-P president John P. Jackson purchased four-fifths of the land (excluding Rice's interest), yields declined dramatically—as much as 75 percent, from more than fifty to fewer than twenty bushels per acre. When Jackson put the property up for sale, Wristen, Miner, and the Cecil brothers went heavily into debt to purchase their sections, believing they could revive the land's fertility. Ten years later, however, the once-rich soil remained, in the words of the county assessor, "of poor quality."[8]

Soil exhaustion was not the only problem that confronted farmers. The sharp rise in production after 1867 also precipitated an outbreak of smut, a fungus whose spores could literally turn a berry of wheat into a ball of black dust. To guard against this "parasite," as Pierce called it, farmers washed the seed in a solution of "bluestone" (copper sulfate). A twenty-minute soak in hot water containing two to four ounces of this antiseptic for every bushel of seed, followed by a dip in freshly slaked lime, proved to be such an effective remedy that smut all but disappeared in the Sacramento Valley by the end of the 1870s.[9] More wheat also attracted more predators. During the winter, flocks of geese descended from out of nowhere to peck away at the freshly seeded fields with such frequency that farmers often had to hire patrols of "goose herders" to shoot them or frighten them away. Stalk-chewing squirrels and gophers became such menaces that local merchants mixed and sold various "acid poisons" to help farmers keep their populations in check. "The rodent that eats it," one advertisement read, "never lives to get into his hole." When such measures failed, the county board of supervisors often established cash bounties—10 cents per gopher scalp in 1873, for example. A spirited competition ensued that year that remained close until December 10, when Nathan Grayson of Plainfield brought in 1,693 scalps, prompting the local newspaper to crown him the "gopher king" of Yolo County.[10]

The greatest terror of the farmer remained drought, which returned to the Sacramento Valley with a vengeance during the winter of 1870–71. Past experience prompted farmers to fear the worst in advance of every season. "We suspicion Providence and expect a dry year," one wrote. "We read it in the heavens, in the lapse of time, in the various phenomena of nature, and in the particular antics of the animal kingdom—anything to borrow trouble and make our minds as miserable as the nature of the case will possibly admit." Beginning in November 1870, their anxiety increased with each passing day of no appreciable precipitation. "No sines [sic] of rain," Pierce wrote repeatedly in his journal. "Everything is as dry as a powder horn. . . . Most farmers have stopped sowing. . . . The grain is past redemption." On April 3, he and his peers admitted defeat. "We have given up all hopes of raising a crop this year." "The wheat," echoed the *Yolo Weekly Mail* in May, "will be a total failure."[11]

Their worst-fears-come-true notwithstanding, farmers were much better prepared this time around. The natural disasters of the 1860s had taught them the value of diversifying, and those lessons quite literally bore fruit in 1871. Without missing a beat, farm families such as the Pierces refocused their energies on producing butter, eggs, soap, candles, pickles, wool, pork, deciduous fruits, and grapes. Instead of cutting, threshing, and hauling wheat that summer and fall, the Pierces made sausage (at least 500 pounds), canned pears, plums, peaches, cherries, and apples, and packed grapes. The well and windmill that George had constructed two years earlier came in quite handy for irrigating his small orchard and twenty-five-acre vineyard. He and Eunice peddled their products to merchants not only in Davisville but also in Woodland, Sacramento, Silveyville, and Vacaville. Farmers, they found, actually paid too much attention to their vineyards that fall. "Too many grapes," George wrote on October 6. "The winerys [sic] are all overrun with them." When the rains returned that November, farmers commenced plowing with both a great sense of relief and a surge of confidence, knowing that they could survive such an ordeal.[12]

Still, with the vast increase in wheat production, Putah Creek farmers had other fears, such as the possibility of labor shortage. "Will harvest hands be scarce in this county?" local newspapers asked before most every season, noting in one instance that a thousand "able-bodied men" were needed. Such fears, however, rarely materialized in the 1870s. While wheat production quadrupled in Yolo County between 1867 and 1875, only twice as many workers were needed to harvest the expanded crop. The reason was that mechanization increasingly dominated the harvests. More and improved headers and threshers significantly decreased the number of men needed to harvest an acre of wheat. Nor was the supply of labor much of a problem. By 1870, Putah Creek's 210 wheat farms, ranging from 40 to 1,400 acres, required 300 to 350 harvesters. As in the 1850s, some of them, though perhaps just 10 percent, were small farmers themselves who joined work crews on neighboring farms upon finishing their own harvests. Another 20 percent were full-time hands such as Luke Rogers, who worked on the Pierce ranch for ten consecutive years. The rest, often recruited by the full-time hands, were casual laborers primarily from Sacramento and smaller valley towns. They were not migratory, in the twentieth-century sense of moving from crop to crop, but tended to work in small groups that returned year after year to the same four or five ranches. From 1868 to 1875, for example, Pierce, Greene, Richard and Thomas Hext, James Campbell, and Hugh M. La Rue (who purchased Drury Melone's ranch in 1866) shared the same core group of harvesters.[13]

The most significant advance in farm machinery in the 1870s, and the implement with the greatest impact on farm labor, was the steam thresher, or "separator," as it was often called. Although its practicality had been demonstrated at the California State Fair in 1859, it took almost a decade for engineers to minimize the fire hazard posed by the hot, spark-spitting machine. The typical unit could thresh 1,200 sacks a day—six times as many as its horse-powered predecessor with the same size crew. Putah Creek farmers, long fascinated with new technology, quickly became enamored of steam power. In addition to its speed and efficiency, the separator eliminated all worries of wearing out horses or shutting down operations entirely to change teams. The imposing straw-burning engine, with its locomotive-type boiler and smokestack, symbolized in no uncertain terms farmers' determination and capacity to, as one put it, "keep up with the times." At $1,700 to $2,000, however, few could afford one for themselves. The six or seven farmers in Putah Creek who purchased steam threshers at considerable risk (before their full value became known) each made a lucrative investment.[14]

Perhaps the most innovative farmer was Bartlett Guthrie of Tremont. Guthrie realized that threshing, which had always been a separate stage of production, would now become even more specialized. When he first set up his separator in 1873, he threshed not only his own crop but also all the wheat that his neighbors hauled to his ranch. Charging 12 cents per 100 pounds, Guthrie found that he could clear about $100 a day. The problem was that after about three weeks, his amazing but immobile separator ran out of wheat to thresh. Realizing he had barely tapped the potential of his new machine, he made his entire operation portable and took it on the road the following year. Placing the steam engine, thresher, and even the bunkhouse (which he labeled the "Palace Hotel") on wheels, Guthrie and his eighteen-man crew drove from ranch to ranch offering their services. That farmers from Pierce and Greene to Campbell and Russell maintained this arrangement for years thereafter suggests their high degree of satisfaction.[15]

The enthusiasm among farmers for steam power and other new technology was not shared by the threshers and harvesters themselves. It was the money, pure and simple, that lured them back year after year. The going rate for harvesters and threshers—$2 a day plus board for the former, $3 plus board for the latter—was, in many cases, twice what they made the rest of the year. Harvesters and threshers kept careful track of their own time and did not hesitate to take their employers to court if they felt they had been shorted—as when William Francis sued R. S. Carey for $299 in 1870. Wages were high because the work itself was exhausting, unpleasant, and very dangerous. Sunstroke, which debilitated many a Sacramento Valley resident every summer, was especially prevalent among workers who toiled twelve to fourteen hours a day with little or no shade. When swarms of black gnats infested the region, as they did almost every June, laborers in the wheat fields wore flour sacks over their heads, gloves tied over their shirt sleeves, and pant legs tied to boot tops, compounding the effects of the intense summer heat. Every season, newspapers reported workers being maimed or even killed by slipping under wagon wheels, stumbling into pulleys, impaling themselves on pitchforks, or simply standing too near an exploding steam engine. Nor was it uncommon for thresher feeders to place their hands a little too far in-

side the cylinder opening and make contact with the separator teeth. They could
lose an arm, a hand, or a finger, or they could be pulled entirely into the machine
and spit out the other end in a bloody pulp along with the threshed grain. Farmers' often-expressed, though largely unfounded, concerns about labor shortage
might very well have stemmed from the perils of the work itself, which they feared
would drive away even the most loyal employees.[16]

Conspicuously absent from the wheat fields of Putah Creek were Chinese laborers. By the early 1870s, farmers regularly hired them to build levees, plant fruit
trees, and prune vineyards. They worked in disciplined gangs that contractors recruited and supervised, making them easy to hire and manage, and the ubiqui-
tous one-dollar-a-day wage that prevailed for much of the late nineteenth century
was already firmly in place. Chinese cooks, laundrymen, domestic servants, and
vegetable peddlers had also become familiar figures in the region. When pressed
on "the Chinese question," Putah Creek farmers invariably fanned the flames of
racial fear and hatred in California by denouncing "the Heathen Chinee," ob-
jecting to "the mingling of the two races," and declaring the aliens "a curse to this
fair land." Nonetheless, they could not resist the advantages of Chinese workers,
except when it came to wheat. Farmers did not discharge their white harvesters
and threshers and replace them with Chinese. There is no evidence that they ever
tried or that it even occurred to them. To have done so would have been an enormous risk. The inflamed rhetoric of the times notwithstanding, Chinese immigrants were tolerated in the Sacramento Valley as long as they toiled in occupa-
tions not coveted by whites. Farmers, who already walked a fine line by hiring
small numbers of Chinese orchard and vineyard workers, would clearly have
crossed it had they put hundreds of them in the wheat fields. And even had they
tried, there were not enough Chinese in the region to drive white workers out of
the market. Nor, like the Indians before them, were the Chinese deemed capable
of operating the new technology or worthy of participating in such an important
endeavor as the wheat harvest. As long as wheat remained the cash crop, these
racial preferences remained intact.[17]

While farmers in the late 1860s and early 1870s had no real reason to fear a
shortage of labor, but did anyway, they rarely worried about the wheat market, but
probably should have. Next to rain, the most popular topic of conversation among
farmers was the price of wheat in Liverpool. Beginning in the fall of 1868, they
had direct access to market quotations in the United Kingdom via the telegraph
in Dresbach's store or the back pages of the *Sacramento Daily Union*. After every
harvest, the question of when to sell became all-consuming. There was never a
shortage of advice available. When prices were low—that is, below the magical

$2-per-cental figure—farmers invariably heeded the call to "hold for something better." There were a few "naysayers" who told farmers they were foolish not to accept the prevailing price if it allowed them at least to break even. One maintained that wheat stored in sacks in granaries dried out much faster than farmers realized—to the extent that their crop could lose fully one-fourth of its weight in a month or two. Another pointed out that storage costs and interest on outstanding loans "eats up profits"—again, much more than farmers realized. Yet, even those farmers heavily in debt, which is to say the vast majority of them, preferred to hold their breath and wait for the market to turn in their favor.[18]

Much to their delight, that strategy actually worked every year between 1867 and 1873, when rates for wheat in the San Francisco market averaged a little over $2.00 per cental and reached as high as $2.80. Putah Creek farmers received 25 to 30 cents less than the prices quoted by San Francisco merchants in order to cover shipping, storage, and handling costs as well as the buyer's (Dresbach's) profit margin. As long as they got their $2.00, however, they rarely complained. Farmers knew that events overseas, 15,000 miles away, impacted the price of their wheat. They cheered when the Franco-Prussian war began in the fall of 1870, rooting openly for "a severe and protracted struggle," just as they welcomed the news of drought in western Europe that same year. But they also believed that their own actions—holding out for better prices year after year, in particular—strongly influenced the wheat market. They would learn, in due time, that their ability to impact the Liverpool price was more an illusion than a reality. For now, however, as long as "big crops and high prices" prevailed, they had little reason to believe otherwise.[19]

Pierce's experience during the 1873 season was classic, in this regard. Although a strong north wind in April and again in May threatened to ruin his crop, the end result—255 tons—was "very very good," he wrote in his journal. On Tuesday, August 12, Pierce rode over to Dresbach's store in Davisville to see how the market was doing. "Offered $1.70 for wheat," he recalled that evening. "Did not take it." Two days later, he went back to see that the price had risen to $1.75. "Did not take it," he wrote again. It rose to $1.82½ on Friday and to $1.87½ the following Tuesday, but Pierce felt he could do better. On Friday, August 22, the price finally reached $2.00, but Pierce still held out for more. It cost him. By the following Wednesday, Dresbach offered only $1.90. When the price climbed back to $1.92½ the next day, Pierce grabbed it. It was his first $10,000 harvest.[20]

Just three weeks later, after hauling the wheat to Dresbach's warehouse, paying several hundred dollars in bills, and buying a new header for himself and a new buggy for the family, Pierce purchased another 448 acres of the Big Ranch

(Lots 9 and 11 along his west boundary) at $30 per acre. The Pierce ranch, now totaling 1,192 acres, quickly became the talk of the township. The prestige of becoming one of Putah Creek's largest landholders came at enormous risk, however. Although Pierce still owed several thousand dollars on his previous mortgage to the Capital Savings Bank, he jumped at the opportunity to take out another—this one for $10,000, payable in three equal installments over the next three years. Many of Pierce's neighbors also rushed into debt to buy more land and better equipment. And why not? A second gold rush had hit the Sacramento Valley. Unlike the first one, however, farmers in Putah Creek found themselves in the right place at the right time, in control, or so they thought, of their own destiny, and ready to strike pay dirt. Things were looking "very very good," indeed.[21]

By 1873, Pierce and other Putah Creek farmers were making the short trip to Davisville with increasing frequency, and not just to check prices or to haul their wheat to Dresbach's. The 500-odd townspeople, the stores and saloons, the hotels and restaurants, and the railroad itself generated excitement, anticipation, and a fierce, often bloated, sense of civic pride. One particularly enthusiastic farmer predicted that "at some future day [Davisville] will be numbered with the cities of the world." Though it never, of course, became "a second New York," Davisville's boomtown prosperity, however modest or fleeting, complemented the boom mentality among the region's farmers. Each drove the other, in many respects—so much so that by the mid-1870s, no one spoke any longer of the "Putah Creek" community but only of Davisville and "the great grain lands surrounding it."[22]

The strong ties between town and countryside would no doubt have evolved over time, but Dresbach left nothing to chance. The only grain purchaser in Davisville, he knew that farmers nevertheless had alternatives—in Woodland, in Dixon (another new railroad town nine miles to the southwest in Solano County), and in Sacramento.[23] Like Jerome C. Davis before him, Dresbach made his presence known in the community to secure his customers' loyalty. He hosted "social balls" on New Year's Eve, the Fourth of July, and other evenings throughout the year; donated $100 to help finance the building of the first house of worship in Davisville, the First Presbyterian Church, and became one of its principal benefactors thereafter; organized the Democratic Club of Putah Township in advance of the party's national convention in 1868; helped establish a town hall association; and led at least six drives to petition the Board of Supervisors for new or improved roads—all of which, of course, led straight to Davisville.[24] Dresbach's immense stock of merchandise, both general and exotic, equaled that of any house in the lower Sacramento Valley, save for much larger establishments in the city of Sacramento itself. And most importantly, he paid farmers cash for their wheat, often on the same day it was shipped, and gave them sizeable advances as long as their credit remained good. Through his efforts, Dresbach established a reputation for "liberality and enterprise," as one newspaper put. His "princely business" shipped 20,000 to 30,000 tons of wheat a year between 1868 and 1873, save the drought year of 1871. Virtually every farmer within an eight-to-ten-mile radius relied on him for their economic well-being.[25]

Dresbach was not the only merchant in Davisville, however. With wheat "as good and even better than money," numerous other entrepreneurs invested heavily in the new town. Second only to Dresbach in the eyes of farmers was Isaac Steele. A squatter on Rancho Laguna de Santos Callé in the late 1850s and a successful merchant in Sacramento the following decade, Steele moved back to Davisville in 1868 and established a large lumberyard along the tracks. Business boomed. Farmers no longer had to make the long trip to Maine Prairie or Sacramento to purchase this scarce and valuable commodity. When Pierce, for example, needed to repair a fence or build a new barn, he now simply "went to Davisville [to get] a load of lumber." Catering to the needs of his customers, Steele sold them a reported 2.5 million feet of lumber in 1874 alone. Three other early settlers in Putah Creek also launched new enterprises. James T. Lillard leased the Yolo House, a "first-class hotel" with a large, elegant barroom for dances, meetings, and other gatherings. William Marden opened Davisville's first butcher shop and later became a hotel keeper himself, a hardware merchant, and postmaster. And E. L. Brown, still trying to recover from his farming debacle on Putah Creek in the 1850s, ran a saloon on Olive Street, one of nine in Davisville in the early 1870s. Two livery stables, a drug store, two doctors and a dentist, two shoe shops, a paint store, a steam mill, and a host of other small businesses all served to make farmers' lives considerably easier.[26]

Davisville greatly improved farmers' social lives as well. During the first two decades of settlement, Putah Creek families were able to satisfy their religious, educational, and leisure needs, but only by traveling to nearby towns or forming their own makeshift organizations. Virtually overnight, Davisville became their focal point of activity. Indeed, the rapidity with which residents created new institutions reveals just how starved they were for a social center of their own. The region's prominent citizens, not surprisingly, took charge.[27]

They turned first to their spiritual interests. Charles Greene, now widely regarded as the elder statesman of Putah Creek, along with Pierce, Marden, Joseph B. Tufts, and Dresbach, was instrumental in establishing the Davisville Presbyterian

Church in the spring of 1869. Services were held in a local blacksmith shop until the proprietors of Davisville donated several town lots to church trustees on November 12, 1870. Shortly thereafter, the congregation raised its new church building with such care and diligence that the structure remains intact today. A smaller but equally determined congregation led by Bartlett Guthrie organized a Methodist Episcopal Church in 1874, sparing no cost. Travelers from throughout northern California came to admire the edifice's beautiful seventy-five-foot tapering spire, built for no less than $3,000. And Catholics, an even smaller group, constructed their own church (St. James), which the renowned Archbishop Joseph S. Alemany of San Francisco dedicated on Christmas Day 1875.[28]

The Davisville School had a much tougher time getting started, in large part because prominent citizens had already organized their own rural school districts in the outlying regions. It was left to William Wristen, Napoleon Miner, the Cecil brothers, several other tenants on the old Davis ranch, and a few townspeople to petition the Board of Supervisors in September 1868 for their own school. Classes commenced later that fall in a small building across from Steele's lumberyard, where, as one resident observed, "there were more scholars than room in the house." Not much changed the following year when the school moved to the backroom of a grocery store down the street. Finally, in June 1870, the five proprietors of Davisville came to the rescue again, donating two lots for a permanent and more suitable location. The school trustees, Wristen, Miner, and the Cecil brothers among them, then raised the funds needed to build a substantial two-story schoolhouse, which served the community for the rest of the century.[29]

While prominent citizens were establishing new churches, many of the same men, though with some reluctance at first, joined one of Davisville's three new fraternal societies—Yolo Lodge, No. 169, Independent Order of Odd Fellows; Athens Lodge, No. 228, Free and Accepted Masons; and Siskiyou Tribe, No. 19, Improved Order of Red Men. Lodges of this sort had been rare in farm communities in the Sacramento Valley but proliferated rapidly in many of the new railroad towns in the late 1860s and early 1870s. In Davisville, the Odd Fellows were the first to organize and proved to be the most popular and lasting of the three orders. Brethren from Woodland, Sacramento, Vacaville, Vallejo, and San Francisco—some 150 in all—gathered together with a hundred local residents at the Yolo House on April 12, 1870, for founding ceremonies—a gala procession, followed by a public installation of officers, a "bountiful supper," and a grand ball. Never before on the west coast, the local newspaper declared, had "so many of the high dignitaries of the Lodge [met] together"—and all for only twelve charter members, eleven of whom were town merchants.

The sole farmer was George W. Pierce. To become a member, Pierce had to withdraw from the Woodland lodge, which he had joined two years earlier but, because of the distance, had attended only rarely. He had no previous history with the Odd Fellows in Wisconsin or New York, but he and his wife might very well have received aid in the fall of 1853 from the large Sacramento association (the state's first), whose main purpose was to assist distressed gold rushers. Or, he may simply have longed for the friendship, harmony, and mutuality that Odd Fellowship offered. Pierce quickly assumed a prominent position in Davisville's lodge. He hosted the order's first picnic on his ranch, served as its first "Noble Grand" during the year 1871, helped lay the cornerstone of a new meeting hall on Olive Street in 1876, and recruited most of the forty to fifty farmers who had joined by the end of the decade. In a speech to his fellow lodge members on February 8, 1872, Pierce, upon accepting the prestigious "Past Grand jewel," employed the words *peace, love, joy, generosity, warmth, duty,* and *pride* repeatedly and with special emphasis—suggesting that these values were still fragile twenty years after the gold rush. He and his brethren, ironically, may have splintered the community more than they brought it together. The five-dollar initiation fee from every new member and the steep annual dues used to finance the hall, buy regalia, and pay for charities and benefits insured that only substantial farmers and successful merchants could become Odd Fellows.[30]

Other diversions emerged as well that were far less exclusive. Horse racing, Putah Creek's favorite pastime for two decades, became that much more popular when a group of entrepreneurs led by William Montgomery built their own track on the outskirts of town, just east of the railway depot. Beginning in 1875, Davisville held an annual pigeon-shooting tournament, which attracted contestants from as far away as San Francisco and Virginia City, Nevada. In 1877, 200 "shooting sportsmen," participating in teams from various localities, competed for the championship, with Davisville taking home the trophy and cash prize—though it hardly seemed a fair contest given that local farmers dominated the panel of judges. Billiard matches, sponsored by local saloons, also captured the attention of local residents. "There are more good billiardists [here]," boasted one newspaper, "than any town of its size in the State."[31]

The most popular sport of all, however, proved to be baseball ("base ball"), which, like horse racing, also arrived in California during the gold rush. Informal games were played on local ranches as early as the late 1850s between peak periods of the production cycle and in Sacramento at the state fair and on other special occasions. But when the Cincinnati Red Stockings, the country's first openly professional team, barnstormed their way through Davisville in the fall of 1869, baseball quickly became a local obsession. Playing their home games in the middle of the racetrack, the Davisville "Haymakers"—mostly farmers' sons, as the name implies—competed against teams from throughout the lower Sacramento Valley, often for purses of $100 or more. When playing their chief rival, the Dixon Silver Stars, free-for-alls often broke out, both on the field and in the stands, in close games such as the 62 to 54 contest in May 1885, when the Haymakers won both the match and the fight. For players and spectators alike, baseball grew into something more than an afternoon at the "ballfield." Citizens found another, perhaps even stronger, way of identifying with their new town.[32]

The railroad itself enhanced farmers' lives and expanded their horizons. Most obviously, shipping their wheat became cheaper and more convenient. Just as importantly, however, the outside world became much more accessible. At first, farmers were so enamored of the train that they often rode to Vallejo or Marysville and back just for the fun of it, gladly paying the round-trip "excursion fare" of $1.50. Gradually, however, they learned to take better advantage of this new mode of transportation. It was now possible to go to Sacramento almost any time of the year (save during a flood) for shopping or business. San Francisco, once a very distant place, was now only three-to-four hours away. The Pierces made the trip to both cities several times a year, often for pleasure alone. "Went to the Cliff House to see the sights, the seals, etc.," wrote George in May 1872. Other trips took them to Yosemite and Big Trees in the Sierra Nevada mountains and, later, to Pacific Grove on the Monterey peninsula. George Jr. began attending the new state university in Berkeley in 1871, in part because the railroad made it feasible. And perhaps most significantly, the railroad allowed visitors from around the country to travel to the Sacramento Valley, many for the first time, including Pierce's brother, Elijah, Eunice's sister Anne and brother Charles, and a number of old friends from Kenosha, all of whom they thought they would never see again. It became commonplace, moreover, for farmers from miles around to crowd around the depot to catch a glimpse of the many famous people whose trains stopped in Davisville, if only for a moment—as when Ulysses S. Grant passed through town in the fall of 1879.[33]

For all its advantages, the railroad also brought considerable controversy. As a major junction in the Sacramento Valley, Davisville was the site of many injurious, even deadly, collisions. Early on, families of the victims often filed lawsuits against the California Pacific Railroad, but they rarely prevailed, which frustrated the community no end. "Someone is to blame, and ought to be punished," remarked one exasperated "sufferer" after a particularly gruesome accident in 1872. The Cal-P seemed to get away with murder on other occasions as well. When the company laid down its tracks through eight acres of Robert Armstrong's property in Tremont in 1868, it neglected, by some administrative oversight, to secure his prior consent. Armstrong sued for both the cost of the land and $1,200 in damages but received only the former. Even when trains ran over farm animals in front of eyewitnesses, the Cal-P was rarely found liable. The company hired the finest lawyers from San Francisco, and in one instance, it did not help that the plaintiff's attorney arrived in court intoxicated. The main reason that the Cal-P got off so often, however, was that, upon its incorporation, the railroad became the leading taxpayer in both Yolo and Solano counties, pumping almost $200,000 a year into both their treasuries. Judges and district attorneys in both counties simply found it imprudent to bite the hand that fed them.[34]

Drunkenness, as the incident in court suggested, also became more of a problem—at least, more of a perceived problem. Davisville, with its nine saloons, now served as the region's drinking center. While these establishments catered primarily to construction workers and farm laborers in their off hours, more than a few farmers took a drink while in town. Early on, residents complained more about the effects of drinking than about drinking itself. "If a day passes without a knock-down or two, or somebody being shot or stabbed, a screw is thought to be loose in the social order of [Davisville]," wrote one newspaper reporter. That the number of criminal trials in Putah Township increased almost tenfold between 1867 and 1875 seemed to confirm this observation and the town's reputation as "Bloody Davisville."[35]

As long as drinking remained relatively dispersed and behind closed doors, efforts to curb it were few and far between, and even with the sudden concentration of saloons, the main impetus for reform came initially from outside the community. By 1871, Davisville had become a regular stop for temperance lecturers from Woodland, Sacramento, and San Francisco touring northern California on the railroad. Their message was powerful, especially to women, who, as one lecturer preached, "suffered the most from the effects of intemperance." Reform moved slowly, however. In June 1874, citizens voted down a "local option" measure on the question of whether or not licenses should be granted for the sale of liquor. Two years later another such measure to close the doors of Davisville saloons on Sunday narrowly passed, but only after all businesses had agreed to observe the Sabbath (baseball was still allowed, however). By the end of the decade, small chapters of the Sons of Temperance and the Independent Order of Good Templars were holding picnics and rallies and bringing in more speakers, but they had not, as yet, come close to achieving their goal of shutting down the saloons, even though the area was overwhelmingly Protestant.[36]

The Pierces help explain why. Both George and Eunice heard the Reverend Strong of Sacramento preach in Davisville on the evils of drink on February 28, 1871. For Eunice, the lecture was an awakening. She became an active member in the local temperance movement, riding from ranch to ranch trying to persuade her neighbors to pass the two local-option measures and rallying members of the First Presbyterian Church to the cause. George, though still a devout Presbyterian and not a drinker himself, remained cautious. It was more difficult for him to remove himself from liquor; he purchased it for his workers (no doubt on their demand), sold his grapes to wineries, and faithfully attended Odd Fellow meetings and balls where the booze flowed freely. Given Eunice's strong will and forceful personality, a spirited conversation or two on the subject no doubt took place in the Pierce household. In the end, of course, only George had the vote.[37]

Spirited conversations were taking place between husbands and wives in households throughout the region—and not just about temperance. Davisville and the railroad expanded the horizons of women every bit as much as men. When rural women traveled, with or without their husbands, to Sacramento, San Francisco, or even just to Davisville, they could not have helped but imagine different lives for themselves, especially if they were being mistreated at home. Their increasing unwillingness to tolerate abusive behavior from their husbands revealed itself in the rising divorce rate of Putah Township in the 1870s. While only one case (*Heinz v. Heinz*) went on the books prior to the coming of the railroad, twelve were filed the following decade. These small numbers, such as they were, in part simply reflected rising marriage rates, which tripled over the same period. Nor did they constitute a "divorce crisis," as one newspaper opined in 1876. They did signify, however, slowly changing perceptions of marriage and slowly expanding opportunities for women—as demonstrated by two cases that husbands and wives talked about for years to come.[38]

Magdaline Glockler filed proceedings against her husband, Charles Glockler, on April 21, 1872, on the grounds of desertion and adultery. The couple married in 1862 and had six children over the next ten years. They began their lives together as squatters on Rancho Laguna de Santos Callé before purchasing 640 acres of the old Davis ranch in October 1870, borrowing $12,000 from the Odd Fellows Savings Bank in Sacramento. Less than a year later, however, Charles ran off with the family nanny to "parts unknown," leaving Magdaline alone with the children and with no means to pay the mortgage and no resources to run the farm. Athough the law required a period of two years before charges of desertion or neglect could be considered, the judge went ahead and awarded Magdaline everything she asked for and more—the divorce, custody of the children, all the couple's real and personal property, and substantial alimony. The problem was that Charles was nowhere to be found. Undeterred, Magdaline sold the land (along with the mortgage), the furniture, and the farm implements, and hopped on a train to San Francisco, taking all her children but the oldest. What she did there is not known, but given the boldness she displayed in escaping Putah Creek to start afresh, one might assume that she got along just fine.[39]

For sheer boldness, no one could match Caroline Greiner, the former Caroline Heinz, who found herself in divorce court once again in 1879. Just months after her successful suit in 1869, Caroline married Jacob Greiner, another German immigrant who treated her only marginally better than had her first husband. Unlike her first marriage, however, her second proved to be economically prosperous. Riding the wave of the wheat boom, the Greiners turned their modest Plainfield farm into an estate worth at least $30,000. After several years of enduring Jacob's physical and emotional abuse, Caroline decided to take him for everything he was worth. She waited patiently, gathered evidence, and secured witnesses who would testify against him.

Filing suit was only the beginning. Just when it appeared that she was about to win her case, Caroline accused Jacob of understating the couple's net worth to defraud her of a proper settlement. Over the years, she told the judge behind closed doors, Jacob had made several loans, totaling $10,000, that he had not disclosed. Jacob maintained that the money financed several wheat transactions. Much to his astonishment, his wife then presented several documents and depositions proving that he had transferred every last dollar to his illegitimate daughter, a nineteen-year-old living under an assumed name in Cache Creek. She then dropped her suit, knowing that Jacob's little secret was worth more to her than any amount the judge might award. She and Jacob stayed married, keeping the terms of their arrangement to themselves. It was clear to anyone who cared to notice, however, that Caroline's fortunes improved dramatically shortly thereafter. Title to all but a few acres of the property were put in her name. Caroline continued to live in the main house, but Jacob moved into the worker's bunkhouse behind the barn. She took over the management of the farm, and he worked as her foreman. Both became objects of local scuttlebutt, but for once the wife reaped the benefits while the husband incurred the humiliation.[40]

Meanwhile, R. S. Carey was waging his own personal battle—not with his wife or his neighbors but with Putah Creek itself. By 1870, he owned, courtesy of the Green Act, over 10,000 acres of swamp and overflowed land—none of which would amount to much unless he could contain the creek's raging winter waters.

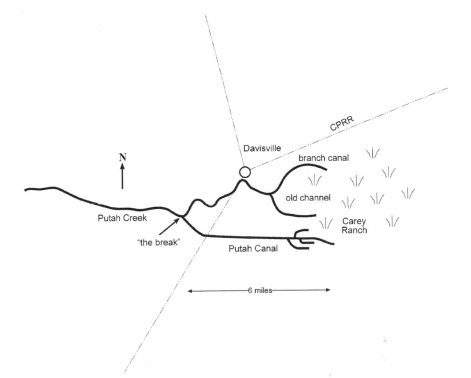

Putah Creek reclamation, 1870s. Based primarily on maps and information in
S. H. Cowell v. Lydia T. Armstrong (1930), California State Supreme Court, no. 4341
(SAC), California State Archives, Sacramento, and Yolo County, "Board of Supervisors,
Swampland District No. 18, Supervisor's Record, 1866–1873," Yolo County Archives,
Woodland.

The wheat boom raised the stakes even higher. If he could protect even a small
portion of his empire and plant it in wheat, Carey stood to be a very wealthy man.
His fellow swamplanders and, eventually, many landowners further upstream
also came to believe that controlling Putah Creek was every bit as important as
controlling the wheat market if they were going to strike it rich in the Sacramento
Valley.

With that motivation, and with the 1867–68 flood still fresh in their minds,
farmers in Swampland District 18 doubled their efforts to reclaim Putah Sink.
Employing gangs of Chinese laborers, they not only rebuilt the branch canal that
had washed away; they dug it deeper and wider and actually made it *the* creek by
raising a levee across the mouth of the old channel and redirecting the flow. That,
along with at least ten miles of levees along the tule line on the east side of the

sink, created approximately 3,000 acres of new farmland, half of which belonged to Carey and the rest to the Montgomerys, Drummonds, and half a dozen other swamplanders. Carey considered this engineering triumph to be his and his alone, and not without good reason. When the district's swampland fund dried up toward the end of 1869, he contributed several thousand dollars of his own money to finish the job. The first crop of wheat in 1870 seemed to make it all worthwhile. Everyone knew that the reclaimed swampland would be fertile, but the reported sixty to seventy bushels per acre exceeded all expectations. The drought the following year brought these new devotees of wheat back to earth a bit, but the dry conditions also reinforced, in their minds, the effectiveness of their levees and canals.[41]

This time, just one storm was all it took to burst their bubble. Twelve inches fell in four days in December 1871, almost half the total rainfall for the season. Though nothing compared to the floods of the 1860s, the deluge was enough for Putah Creek to rise eighteen feet and "fill the Sink," as one newspaper put it. Gathering force in the coastal mountains to the west and roaring across the prairie, a raging torrent rushed toward the man-made barrier standing in its way across the "old" channel. Rather than veering northeastwardly into the branch canal, the creek, on the morning of December 17, slammed into the levee, burst through, and "spread out" over the freshly plowed land, "playing havoc" with the farms that stood in its way. Putah Sink, the paper continued, "is, to use an expressive phrase, afloat." Just what expressive phrases Carey must have uttered that day, one can only imagine. Judging from his subsequent actions, his vendetta reached Ahab-like proportions, with Putah Creek becoming his great white whale.[42]

Indeed, Carey did not give up, even for a moment. Just two days after Putah Creek drowned his wheat fields, he resumed his offensive with a plan that dwarfed all previous ones in scope and ambition. Another break in the levee five miles upstream inspired him. Putah Creek flowed across the valley floor without any sharp meanders until it reached the boundary between Pierce's property (the old Big Ranch) and La Rue's (the old Brown and Melone ranches). At that point, it veered roughly forty-five degrees to the southeast for half a mile before making a full right-angled turn northward. In flood, the creek often spilled over at both bends, prompting landowners, funded by District 18, to construct two huge levees. Though neither contained the floodwaters of 1867, the rebuilt versions held on December 17, 1871. On December 19, however, the creek exploded through the second levee with such a roar that it woke Pierce out of his sleep two miles away. The full force of the creek then maintained its southeasterly course for half a mile before running up against the railroad, where it spread along the banks of the tracks for miles in both directions. Eventually, a crevasse opened up, through which a narrow stream of water began flowing straight eastward down an old farm road right along the section lines. It ran across the Tremont district, and all the way to the Tule, six miles from "the break," as locals called the breech in the levee for years to come. Carey surveyed the situation intently. Putah Creek, he believed, had just provided him with a blueprint for a new and more efficient flood-control system.[43]

When Carey soon thereafter proposed excavating a canal from the break to the Tule, many of his neighbors supported the idea enthusiastically. William Montgomery and most other Putah Sink farmers, whose ranches were two feet under water at the time, did not need much encouragement. If successful, the proposed canal would steer future floodwaters of the creek to the far southern reaches of the sink, past their farms, and out of harm's way. For Tremont farmers as well, any possibility of controlling the overflow was worth a try. Those whose land would border the canal were also pleased that it would run along the section lines and thus not burden any one of them excessively. Several Davisville merchants, who watched their town be inundated for the first time, very much liked the idea of rerouting the creek one-and-a-half miles to the south. And a number of farmers upstream from the break observed that they too might benefit. When the levee broke early that fateful morning, "the water," Pierce wrote, "did not raise anymore" in front of his ranch. By straightening out the creek's channel, the proposed canal, he hoped, would have the same effect. It would eliminate a major pressure point, prevent the creek from backing up, and thus reduce the chance of overflow. Constructing a six-mile canal would not be simple, its advocates knew, but that too appealed to their unbridled optimism and entrepreneurial spirit.[44]

The problem—the initial problem—was how to pay for it. No one knew what such a project might cost, only that it would be much more than the $14,000 it had taken to build the earlier branch canal and levees. And because District 18 had been drained of all its funds, they would have to start from scratch. Carey's first inclination was to organize a new swampland district, and on February 7, 1872, he presented a petition to the Yolo County Board of Supervisors to do just that. The board's collective hands were tied, however. While the vast majority of the farmers who would benefit from this project resided in Yolo County, the proposed canal itself lay south of the creek, almost entirely in Solano County. Neither the new swampland law of 1866 nor the Green Act of 1868 accounted for such a scenario. Who would authorize it, who would pay for it, and who would even survey it? When the bewildered board members postponed consideration of such questions, Carey turned to Frank S. Freeman, his state assemblyman, who recommended legislative action.[45]

Carey and Freeman moved quickly—Carey because he wanted construction to begin as soon as possible, and Freeman because Carey was among the biggest taxpayers in the county. In less than a month, they drafted "An Act to provide for the protection from overflow by Putah Creek of certain lands in the Counties of Yolo and Solano." In the process of trying to please each other, Carey and Freeman made promises that neither could keep. In particular, Carey assured Freeman that landowners in the proposed "Yolo and Solano Canal District" would overwhelmingly approve the bill's provisions, while Freeman insisted that nothing in the bill was unconstitutional. Freeman introduced it at the tail end of the legislative session, persuaded his fellow lawmakers to suspend most of the rules of deliberation, and presided over its passage on April 1—all in the course of just four days.[46]

Had they simply created a new swampland district across the two counties with the usual provisions—especially the "half or more" approval clause—the canal act might have flowed smoothly. Instead, the new law created almost as much disruption as the flooding itself. It was bad enough that the rectangular-shaped district encompassed much too large an area—approximately 50,000 acres starting well west of the Pierce ranch and extending well east of Carey's and covering five to six miles both north and south of Putah Creek. Landowners on the outer portions of the district—perhaps a quarter to a third of the total—stood to benefit far less from the canal than the canal would from their tax dollars. Worse yet, no landowner would get a say in the matter. The law simply imposed the district upon them. It gave a three-member board of trustees (two appointed by Yolo County's board of supervisors and one by Solano's) full power to "levy assessments . . . anytime they deem necessary," to rule on appeals, and to bring suit in the name of the district against delinquent taxpayers—"the same power," the law proclaimed, "as is possessed by County Courts."[47]

Opposition to the district emerged slowly, but when the Yolo board appointed Carey as one of the trustees on April 22 (the other was H. M. La Rue), cries of "inquisition" and "swindle" began to fill the air. On May 4, some 150 landowners met in Davisville to band together against the law. They found it "odious and oppressive," especially the implied power of the trustees to seize their farms if they refused to pay what they were told. "Had the Act been entitled 'An Act to confer the property of all parties within a radius of ten miles to the Trustees of said Land District,' the meaning would have been plain and explicit," declared Justice of the Peace James O'Neal. Many in the crowd—L. C. Drummond and Bartlett Guthrie,

among them—very much wanted the canal, but not on these terms. When someone made known that just a few days earlier Carey had been spotted at the meeting held by the Solano board to appoint its trustee, talk changed to action. Pledg-
ing to "use all honorable means at our command to prevent any of the provisions
of said act from going into effect," they adopted their own code of bylaws, elected
officers, and subscribed "several thousand dollars to fight the infamous bill in the
several Courts of the State."[48]

Unbeknownst to the angry farmers, the Solano board had already sealed the
fate of the law by refusing to appoint a trustee. Never particularly attentive to
affairs in "the extreme northeastern portion of the county," board members could
not have been happy to be called to a special meeting on April 30, with just this
one item on the agenda. They took all of ten minutes to denounce the canal act.
Already burdened with several other swampland districts in their jurisdiction,
they did not want to take on another one. When they discovered that the canal
would serve farmers primarily in Yolo County, that the Solano board would appoint only one of the trustees, and that the law itself was undoubtedly unconstitutional, they declared it a "gigantic fraud" and dared its supporters to take legal
action. When Carey tried to convince them otherwise, he quickly found that he
had nowhere near the pull that he had in his home county. Though the law would
not officially be repealed for another two years, Carey knew that day that it was a
dead letter.[49]

Furious but all the more determined, Carey called his own meeting. Most of
the attendees were Putah Sink and Tremont farmers—the ones most vulnerable
to floods. If the Solano board and a few wayward farmers insisted on being ob-
stinate, Carey told them, then they would simply have to build the canal themselves. Exactly how much they subscribed to the cause that day was not disclosed,
but it was enough, apparently, to get started. Exactly how this informal group
financed the canal thereafter remains even more of a mystery. No records have
survived, if indeed any were kept. The available evidence suggests, however, that
whenever funds were tight, Carey stepped in to make up the difference. He had
already invested too much of his money and too much of himself to do otherwise.
Carey's detractors could have taken him to court to stop the project but chose instead to take a wait-and-see attitude. Few were against the canal; they just did not
want to pay for it. And no one wanted to stop the annual overflows that replenished their fields; they just wanted to control them.[50]

Construction began that summer. The first step was to block the break to prevent the creek's floodwaters from interfering with work on the new channel. Hop-

ing to make a stronger barrier, they built a bulkhead with boards and lumber and reinforced it with earthwork. Work on the canal was then divided into segments, with the adjacent landowners themselves serving as "contractors." Starting at the break and heading eastward, the owner on each side of the section line agreed to remove a 100-foot strip of ground to a depth of six feet, thus making a 200-foot-wide channel—the widest, to date, of any canal built in the Sacramento Valley. Contractors did most of this work with horse teams pulling slip scrapers (similar to those used in the construction of the Erie Canal). They then employed Chinese laborers to raise levees with the earth from the dug-out channel. The heavy, tedious work progressed slowly but surely over the next two years, with few interruptions or problems.[51]

The calm before the storm ended on December 30, 1873. That evening, Putah Creek ripped through the bulkhead into the Tremont district. This time, it did not back up at the railroad but instead rushed under the trellis built by the Cal-P the previous year and down the unfinished canal, "taking out fences and everything as it went," recalled one eyewitness. "Everything" included a good portion of the levees and much of the heavy excavation equipment. Worse yet, the floodwaters deposited thick layers of sediment and debris in the channel, literally washing away several months work. Frustrated but not discouraged, farmers built a bigger bulkhead across the break and resumed the scraping. The same cycle of events occurred again the following winter, in January 1875, and then again one year later, in November 1876. The rebuilt (and still bigger) bulkhead held for the next two years before being obliterated in January 1878 by "a torrent that roared by like the Amazon," as one exasperated farmer put it. The canal levees, wrote a newspaper reporter, were "destroyed on both sides, the channel was filled with sand, and farms for miles were entirely under water." The work resumed, only to be wiped out once again by heavy rains the following year.[52]

The sequence repeated itself, though not always every year or with such force, for the rest of the century and beyond. In the end, Putah Creek—not Carey, not the boards of supervisors, not other farmers—decided where it wanted to go. The more often the creek burst through the break, the more the new channel gradually deepened. By 1880, the two channels were more or less the same depth, which allowed Putah Creek to flow "naturally" in either direction. By the turn of the century, the new channel, observed one farmer, "has to be half full before it goes into the old channel." Recalled another, "Nothing had to be done to turn the water out of the old channel and into the new. It turned itself out." It is little wonder, then, why mapmakers since 1878 could not reach a consensus on what to call the new channel—some labeling it a "ditch" or a "canal," others insisting on "South Fork

Putah Creek" or simply "Putah Creek." Part natural and part man-made, the new channel proved just as confounding as the old.[53]

The doggedness of Carey and the other farmers seems, on the surface, difficult to fathom. In hindsight, their obsession with the canal, given their inability to control the creek's floodwaters long enough to complete it, appears no more rational than their insistence that when it came to their wheat, supply created its own demand. Yet, without the new channel and without the $2-per-cental just price, they knew that there would be no sustained second "gold rush." By the mid-1870s, consequently, building and rebuilding the new channel became part of their day-to-day lives—something they talked about in front of Dresbach's store, along with the weather, the price of wheat in Liverpool, steam power, I.O.O.F picnics, baseball games, and railroad excursions. The topic of conversation that perplexed farmers the most, perhaps, was Putah Creek itself, which, they gradually came to realize, could make them or break them—or both. Farmers depended on the creek's annual overflows to deposit fresh soil on their land and to provide, in essence, a cost-free form of irrigation. But they also knew that the "fickle stream," with little warning, could drown thousands of acres of growing crops. "It is both a builder and a destroyer," remarked one perceptive farmer.[54]

That statement reveals the extent to which wheat dominated their lives. Indeed, no one had even thought about diverting the waters of Putak Creek when cattle ranching was their main concern. Just how central the grain had become was captured by an editorial in the *Sacramento Daily Union* in 1876: "The whole [region] seems to stagnate when there comes a poor harvest. No kind of business prospers, and each man looks blank discouragement in his neighbor's face. But let there be sun and rain enough and at last a fine crop, and then what a change! A magical life awakens smiles and bright looks cheer the heart of the stranger, field hands trudge in from everywhere with the dust of travel on their feet, mowing machines flash in the sun, the thousand implements of farm labor set to work, the housewife sings in the kitchen, the daughter promises herself a long coveted piano, dry goods stores send for new goods, the streets are busy with brisk trade, clients seek their lawyers, patients their physicians, debts are paid, friendships formed and everybody is happy."[55] Too happy, it turned out.

CHAPTER NINE

"A Devil's Opportunity"

The *Sacramento Daily Union* editorial only scratched the surface. Indeed, the second gold rush made many people happy. The wheat boom that began in 1867 gave rise to an extensive export trade, which for the next two decades would play a central role in California's economic growth—its internal development as well as its commercial relations with the rest of the world. Most obviously, the wheat trade was instrumental in bringing huge tracts of virgin land under cultivation, causing many hundreds of miles of railroads to be built, and facilitating the growth of towns and interior marketing arrangements. It greatly stimulated not only manufacturing, particularly of farm implements and grain sacks, but also flour milling, banking, the lumber trade, shipbuilding, and the construction of storage and loading facilities including, in one notable case, an experimental grain elevator. In conjunction with the huge export trade in wheat, imports increased dramatically in the 1870s and 1880s, coal in particular. Ships sailing into San Francisco Bay for grain cargoes usually carried coal as ballast. The abundant supply met the fuel needs of railroads, river and ocean steamers, forges and foundries, waterworks and gasworks, and steam engines used in farm work, all at prices ranging from just $6 to $8 a ton. Trade expanded, capital accumulated, transportation and manufacturing accelerated, and economic relations with the outside world flourished—all because of wheat.[1]

No one was happier that wheat had replaced gold as the chief stimulus of the state's economy than Isaac Friedlander. By 1869, farmers, merchants, and newspapermen alike had dubbed Friedlander the "Grain King" of California, employing the hyperbole characteristic of the times. This particular crowning involved little exaggeration, however. Friedlander's ever-growing network of agents among local warehouse owners and grain dealers in the state's wheat districts, his extensive contacts abroad, his dominance of the supply of inbound shipping to San Francisco, his unlimited credit, his daring personality, and his sheer presence (six foot seven, he weighed 300 pounds, wore a stovepipe hat, and had a long, craggy, hawklike face) made him not only a titan of commerce but a veritable celebrity as well. "Bold and aggressive in business, honorable in his dealings, kind and generous in personal relations, everybody liked him," wrote one contemporary. Even a spokesman for the San Francisco Produce Exchange, which formed in 1867 to challenge Friedlander's reign, later admitted that for more than ten years the King "held the entire field undisputed by a rival." From 1867 to 1876, an estimated three-fourths of all the grain exported from California passed through Friedlander's hands, a fact that gave him, understandably, a rather proprietary feeling about his position in the marketplace. When someone described the effort under way in the early 1870s to strengthen the authority of the Produce Exchange, Friedlander allegedly slammed his fist on a counter in his office and proclaimed, "Here is the Produce Exchange, right here."[2]

And if Friedlander was happy, then William Dresbach was happy. Though Dresbach & Co. conducted thousands of transactions every year, often for thousands of dollars at a time, cash flow posed little problem for "the Davisville Grain King." All he had to do was send a wire to Friedlander's office at the corner of Sansome and California streets in San Francisco and within a day or two he would have whatever he needed to cover his accounts—$10,000 on July 10, 1869 and $14,000 on July 28 and $12,000 on August 25, to cite three typical examples. Widely known as "everyone's favorite business man in Davisville," Dresbach not only purchased grain, sold merchandise, and took an active interest in community affairs; he also provided threshing and hauling services for those who desired them, issued crop mortgages to financially strapped farmers, and in general, in the words of one local, "assisted very materially in building up the town and its business interest." By 1873, his company's assets totaled over $300,000— enough for him to build "the handsomest residence in town," a nine-room, two-story, $13,000 Victorian mansion "with all the modern improvements."[3]

Things were going splendidly for Dresbach, Friedlander, and most farmers, yet they all asked the same question: How can I do even better? The possibilities seemed endless, even as clear signs to the contrary were beginning to emerge. Everyone was determined to mine the second gold rush for all it was worth and for as long as it lasted, but no one—not even the great Grain King and his protégé— could escape the perils of the wheat trade. For the remainder of the so-called terrible seventies, in fact, much of what wheat men touched turned to stone. Seemingly every promising situation that presented itself turned out to be, in the words of a contemporary chronicler, not a golden, but "a devil's opportunity."

Yet, wheat lost little of its luster. "Those of our farmers who have held on," editorialized the *Yolo County Democrat*, "remain intent on striking it rich."[4]

The first such opportunity involved what one local newspaper optimistically and, as it turned out, prematurely called "A New Era in the Grain Trade." As early as the summer of 1868, Friedlander, Dresbach, and other grain merchants recognized the gross inefficiency of the prevailing system of shipping. In order to transport northern California wheat to Liverpool, the grain, bound by farmers in 125-pound sacks, had to be loaded onto freight cars at Davisville and other interior depots, unloaded into warehouses on the wharves of south Vallejo (the terminus of the California Pacific Railroad), loaded again into schooners for the twenty-five-mile trip across the bay to San Francisco, unloaded again for storage there, and then loaded one last time into oceangoing vessels. Some of the warehouses in San Francisco, moreover, stood back from the water's edge, which meant unloading the bags from boats onto drays, hauling them to the storage spaces, and unloading them yet again. Each transfer was effected by hand (on workers' shoulders, to be more precise) and, depending on the size of the cargo, could take several days. Total costs, including labor, maintenance of facilities, and the sacks themselves amounted to at least $1,000 per ton, one shipper estimated. As wheat production boomed, the problem only got worse.[5]

The obstacles seemed ominous, but a better model already existed for Friedlander and his cohorts. Two thousand miles away, under the "Chicago plan," merchants shipped wheat much more cheaply and efficiently. A decade earlier, they had come to realize that wheat had special properties—its "flowing qualities" and nonperishability, in particular—that lent themselves to mechanical methods of handling. The invention of the grain elevator allowed merchants to take full advantage of those attributes. These multistoried warehouses were capable of holding hundreds of thousands of bushels, but even more importantly, grain could be moved into the building on steam-powered conveyor belts, transferred to the top in large buckets, weighed on large hopper scales, dropped into bins, and discharged into waiting ships or railroad cars simply by opening a spout and letting gravity do the work. They could easily be attended by two or three people, as opposed to the dozens or hundreds it took to handle the grain by hand. The key to this process of modernization, in addition to constructing the new facilities, was the wheat had to be moved in bulk, rather than in sacks, to move up an elevator's conveyor belts. In the Great Lakes region in the 1850s and 1860s, farmers adapted with relative ease.[6]

Surely, thought Friedlander and the owners of the California Pacific Railroad, the same could be accomplished in California. An elevator, strategically located in Vallejo, held great possibilities for them. It would enable the railroad, Cal-P president D. C. Rice hoped, to "drain all the agricultural region north of San Francisco, Suisun, and San Pablo bays" and eliminate much of the competition from water transportation companies. Friedlander envisioned turning the deep-water port of Vallejo into his own personal grain mart, with Liverpool-bound ships bypassing the San Francisco harbor and thus avoiding the costly haulage, transfer, and port charges altogether. Farmers would not be difficult to convince, both Rice and Friedlander thought, since for some time they had been complaining about the price of grain sacks. Both also intended, eventually, to broaden their base of speculative activity. Once elevators had been installed up and down the Sacramento Valley, they would implement the next phase of the "Chicago plan"—"futures" trading. Indeed, their ultimate objective was to establish a west coast counterpart to the Chicago Board of Trade, through which they could gamble on the direction of future price movements.[7]

First things first, however. In April 1868, Friedlander and the Cal-P joined forces to launch the Vallejo Elevator, a joint-stock company with a starting capital of $500,000. Construction began in December and the building opened for business in June 1869, just in time for the harvest. It stood on more than 900 piles driven ten to fifteen feet into the ground ("to secure the elevator against the danger of careening over from earthquake vibrations"), had a storage capacity of 10,000 tons of wheat, and could lift and weigh up to 75 tons per hour. Towering over the Vallejo harbor, it also became an instant tourist attraction for both the fine view it offered of the north bay and its intrinsic interest as a prime example of Yankee ingenuity. "Of belting," tour guides told visitors, "there are 3,150 feet. The main driving belt is 226 feet long and 20 inches in width, and runs from a 6-foot pulley on the engine to a 10-foot pulley on the main line of shafting in the top of the building. There are 3,150 feet of belting in service: 226 feet, five-ply, 20 inches wide; 1,200 feet, four-ply, 20 inches wide; 132 feet, four-ply, 18 inches wide; 127 feet, four-ply, 16 inches wide; and 258 feet, four-ply, 8 inches wide. The aggregate total of lineal feet of timber and lumber, used and employed in erecting the elevator, figures up 1,076,000 feet, exclusive of 35,000 lineal feet of piles, used in construction of the building." While all the technical verbiage made little sense, most visitors could not help but marvel at the spectacle before them.[8]

While Friedlander and Rice called it "an experiment," neither anticipated much opposition to the elevator. But as construction neared completion, those with a stake in preserving the old method began voicing their objections. Thousands of warehouse and dock workers rightly saw the elevator as a threat to their livelihood. Members of the San Francisco Produce Exchange and other rivals of Friedlander insisted that the elevator and bulk handling simply would not work for California. Crossing the equator twice on the rough seas on the way to England, grain shipped in bulk would "sweat" in the tropics, "intermix" the bad with the good, and endanger the safety of the vessel by constantly shifting and "resettling," as one exporter explained. Those cargoes that reached their destination, he concluded, would invariably bring a lower price. "Our wheat," concurred one Yolo County farmer, "goes to Liverpool in such a good condition now that it outsells the wheat of any other country. Why change?" Most farmers, moreover, were reluctant to abandon sacks, which they had become accustomed to using over the last two decades. How else, one asked, "would they collect the wheat as it fell from the threshing machine?" Farmers, he made clear, wanted cheaper sacks, not no sacks at all.[9]

Friedlander led a spirited campaign to dispel the fears and rumors. Farmers, he stressed, would simply use bins, rather than sacks, to collect their threshed grain—a change that would be easy to implement and be, in the long run, much more convenient and cheaper. Similarly, wheat would not just be thrown into the ship haphazardly; it would be loaded into large bins "so that from leakage or any other sea accident, the whole cargo will be much more secure than by shipment in sacks." His competitors, Friedlander claimed, were spreading "lies and falsehoods" about the elevator system for fear of losing whatever small portion of the grain trade they controlled. A "ring" existed, he maintained, "that is made up of the bag men, the commission merchants, the warehouse men, the stevedores, and the city of San Francisco, all of whom are interested in keeping in vogue the old mode of shipments, because they make money out of the farmer by the operation."[10]

Friedlander knew that actions spoke louder than words. Farmers, in particular, wanted to see the system work for themselves before making any dramatic changes. With that in mind, Friedlander sent three ships, fully loaded with "sackless" grain, out the Golden Gate—one bound for Liverpool, another for China, and the other for Australia. After all three cargoes had reached their ports "in first rate order" in the winter of 1869–70, Friedlander boasted, "It has been demonstrated by actual experiment that there is no difficulty or additional risk incurred by this mode of shipment." Sacramento Valley newspapers publicized Friedlander's "triumph," stressing that it demonstrated what wheat men elsewhere already knew. "The bulk method of shipment has been in vogue on the Erie canal certainly for twenty years," stated the *Yolo County Democrat*, "and for the last ten to twelve years many vessels each season have taken bulk cargoes of wheat from

Chicago and other lake ports down the lakes, through the Welland canal, the St. Lawrence river, and thence across the Atlantic to Europe." Were California farmers, the newspaper insinuated, "less industrious" than their counterparts in the Midwest?[11]

Having long regarded themselves as being on the cutting edge of wheat culture and technology, many Sacramento Valley wheat farmers no doubt took offense at such remarks. They remained far from convinced, however, that the Vallejo Elevator Company served their best interests. Trial runs at home, it turns out, were not as successful as those on the high seas. Reluctance to change was so great, at first, that Friedlander had to actively recruit farmers to, as he put it, "try out the machinery—give it a public trial." One of the first "volunteers" was William Wristen, one of the Cal-P's original tenants on the old Davis ranch and now a landowner himself. Dresbach persuaded Wristen to step forward when the elevator opened in the summer of 1869. Wristen gave Dresbach his permission to ship, in bulk, eighty-two tons of his wheat to Vallejo, where, he was told, it would be stored until he gave the go-ahead to sell it. But when Friedlander needed "sackless" wheat to fill his three ships that summer, he took Wristen's without permission, paying him (through Dresbach) the current market rate of $1.55 per 100 pounds. A few months later, while Friedlander was celebrating the success of his shipping experiment, Wristen sued both him and Dresbach, claiming that he would not have sold the wheat until the price climbed back to $2.00, which it did in June 1870. Friedlander and Dresbach settled out of court with Wristen, but that did not stop numerous other "test farmers" from complaining, including at least ten other Dresbach patrons, most of whom received similar compensation.[12]

In the end, only one opinion mattered, and it was one that Friedlander could not sway. The responsibility for underwriting marine insurance for the California wheat trade belonged, almost exclusively, to British companies. Despite the success of Friedlander's shipping experiment and despite his impassioned pleas, not one firm would agree to insure his grain in bulk, even though they routinely handled Liverpool-bound wheat from Chicago. The difference, they maintained, was that the latter route did not pass through the tropics, where bulk wheat would be subjected to climatic extremes that could potentially ruin the hard, dry quality of the California product that British and Irish millers so prized. When Friedlander turned to American insurance men, they told him what he already knew: buyers on the English grain exchanges would not purchase cargoes unless they were insured with what were termed "standard British companies."[13]

Just like that, the "new era in the grain trade" was over before it ever really started. For two years, the Vallejo elevator was used only to store grain (in sacks, no less), much to Friedlander's embarrassment. And then, to add insult to injury, the building careened over and collapsed in September 1872, not from an earthquake, but from warehousemen, working by hand, trying to stuff some 80,000 sacks of wheat into its elevated bins. A Vallejo newspaper reported that "the crash could be heard for at least two miles," but Friedlander felt its symbolic reverberations all the way from San Francisco. No one would try this particular experiment again until well after the turn of the twentieth century.[14]

Friedlander did not take defeat lying down. He was bound and determined not only to recover the profits from the now defunct elevator company, which he had already entered into his mental ledger, but to show everyone who was still king. If he could not eliminate sacks, Friedlander figured, then he would use his vast influence to corner the market on this lucrative source of income for himself. In the spring of 1872, he seized control of the "bag ring" that he had chastised just a few months earlier, staged a shortage, and established an artificially high price of 21 cents apiece, more than double what farmers paid in 1870. The harvests of 1872 and 1873 were both plentiful and profitable for farmers in the Sacramento Valley, but the inflated cost of grain sacks severely cut into their earnings—at roughly $4 per ton, or 15 percent of the farmer's total crop value, by one estimate. Even the most arbitrary broker would not have deliberately sought to destroy those who provided him with wheat, but farmers reacted as though Friedlander had turned on each and every one of them personally. "The enormous expense of bagging our wheat," one wrote, "is an attack by Friedlander on our prosperity." In just a few months' time, the "Great Sack Swindle" turned the Grain King from a venerable titan of commerce, in farmers' eyes, into an oppressive tyrant.[15]

In Davisville, Dresbach took the brunt of farmers' frustrations. The sack controversy made them realize that "Friedlander's man" could be both friend and foe. Farmers were the ones who absorbed the full impact of skyrocketing sack prices, not Dresbach, who shielded himself by passing along the added expense to them. More generally, they began to realize that, while farmers' incomes ebbed and flowed with shipping and production costs and the vagaries of climate and weather, Dresbach seemed to make his usual profits in bad years as well as good. From this perspective, "everyone's favorite business man in Davisville" became, at once, everyone's dreaded *middleman*, a term that was just coming into use in the area. Dresbach's palatial mansion provoked farmers' ambivalence. Every time they passed by it, they saw the prosperity and, indeed, the glamor of their enterprise, but also a display of wealth that symbolized the uneven balance of power between producers and middlemen. In the same manner, they could throw Dresbach a surprise birthday party one day and denounce him for his "unsavory business practices" the next.[16]

Most aggrieved were those most deeply in Dresbach's debt—Andrew McClory, for example. Still trying to recover from his longstanding title troubles, McClory sued Dresbach in August 1872 for the added cost of the sacks. Dresbach, in turn, filed a countersuit to collect $3,674 on outstanding promissory notes. Farmers from miles around waited anxiously for the verdict. But McClory, most of them probably already sensed, had no legal leg to stand on; he had not paid any more for his sacks than any of Dresbach's other customers. Unable to pay even the interest ($1\frac{1}{2}$ percent per month) on his loans, McClory suffered the added humiliation of having the county sheriff, in accordance with the judge's writ of attachment, seize every last grain of wheat he had harvested that summer—1,839 sacks in all. A week later, however, the sheriff returned the wheat, when McClory secured two sureties—Charles Greene and George W. Pierce—who agreed to assume the debt.[17]

Greene and Pierce had known McClory since the early 1850s, but this was more than just two farmers helping out an old friend. The growing controversy over the price of sacks exposed tensions that had been largely submerged for some time, especially among the persisters who had survived the turmoil of the 1850s and 1860s. Farmers such as Greene, Pierce, and even the much-troubled McClory seemed now to have it all—new machines that allowed them to sow and harvest enormous amounts of wheat, and fortuitous increases in exports that offset the usual, if not inevitable, consequences of overproduction. The grain sack crisis, however, made them realize how much the entire operation hinged on the efforts of Dresbach, Friedlander, and other providers of transport and warehousing services to move and market their crops. This dependence left many of them feeling vulnerable to the market power wielded by the wheat kings and resentful about their relative helplessness. It also reminded them that much of their success came on borrowed money. Both Greene and Pierce had rushed into debt to buy more land and better farm equipment—much to their benefit at the time. To pay off their mortgages in a timely manner, however, they had little choice but to sell to Dresbach and Friedlander on their terms. Rescuing McClory from Dresbach's clutches gave them a small measure of relief from this festering source of frustration.[18]

A few other farmers had already begun seeking wider-ranging solutions. Influenced by the modest success of a scattered movement in the Midwest, several "farmers' clubs" in California answered a call to organize in December 1871, including one in Woodland. "We have Jockey Clubs, Social Clubs, Bachelor Clubs, and many others, but the Farmers' Club that is customary in the older States is hardly known in California," one enthusiast stated. "It is none to soon," pleaded another, "to be forming plans . . . to improve our own condition and prospects." For the most part, however, the promise of "mental, social, and economic improvement" fell on deaf ears in the region's thriving rural communities. The Woodland club never had more than eighteen members, and the four or five who actually attended meetings spent most of their time bemoaning "the lack of interest which seems to prevent the farmers of the county in uniting with those who initiated the movement." When a meeting was called to organize a farmers' club for Davisville in March 1872, no one attended, and when the state's thirty clubs assembled as the Farmers' Union in April 1873 in their first and only convention, they discovered that total membership, after all their efforts, stood at just 780.[19]

The convention was not without consequence, however. W. H. Baxter of Napa, a promoter for another burgeoning organization, the National Grange of the Patrons of Husbandry, received permission to address the assembly. He caused quite a sensation. Among his more appealing arguments in favor of the Grange were the secrecy of its meetings, its tight organization, and the pecuniary benefits that it had already won for farmers in the Mississippi Valley. Baxter shrewdly spent most of his time, however, on the "sack question." Recounting Friedlander's swindle in excruciating detail and reminding his audience over and over just how much sacks currently cost, Baxter whipped the crowd into a frenzy that no farmers' club had ever witnessed before. All in attendance became instant recruiters, carrying Baxter's message back to their communities. The results were nothing short of astounding. By mid-July, just three months later, thirty-three Granges had emerged, some of them with memberships of more than 100, and plans for "unity of action" were well under way. By October, the new State Grange of California reported 104 local organizations, the vast majority in the northern wheat-growing counties, with a total enrollment of 3,168 members.[20]

Among the charter Granges were one in Woodland and another in Davisville. The organizers of the latter (and its first officers) were none other than Charles Greene, George Pierce, and Andrew McClory—all of them still fuming over the sudden rise in the price of grain sacks. "To break those prices," Greene insisted at the first meeting on September 23, 1873, "the farmer must take matters into his own hands." Though the Davisville Grange started with only fifteen members, it did not take long for Greene's message to spread. Four months later, membership stood at fifty, and by the spring more than 100 farmers from Putah and Tremont townships belonged. In March, an eleven-member delegation, led by

Greene and Pierce, traveled to Friedlander's office in San Francisco and demanded cheaper sacks. The Grain King, always one step ahead, had already set in motion plans for a reduction to quiet the mounting dissent. Still, when prices fell to 12½ cents a month later, Master Greene announced with great pride and confidence that "Granger manipulations" had brought down the "Sack ring."[21]

The increasingly strident hyperbole of Greene and other Grange leaders notwithstanding, the "agrarian revolt" in the Sacramento Valley was, from the outset, a rather tame movement. Few of these farmers (the overwhelming majority were grain growers) faced impending ruin, as the rhetoric of state leaders often implied, and fewer still suffered from the isolation, cruel winters, and hunger for social activity that compelled farm people by the thousands in the Midwest and on the Great Plains to flock to the Grange. The fraternal ceremonies, dances, picnics, and lectures that made the movement so popular back east were already available in Davisville and other Sacramento Valley communities. In fact, after their "victory" in the "sack wars," Grangers such as Greene and Pierce, though brimming with confidence, were not sure what to do next, the latter being more concerned with his impending purchase of 448 acres of the Big Ranch than fighting additional battles.[22]

But with state leaders imploring members to take advantage of their newfound strength in numbers and "become their own middlemen," Davisville Grangers gradually came to believe that Dresbach could and should be sacked. If farmers could obtain lower prices for grain bags, the thinking went, why should they accept any excessive deductions from their gross returns—storage fees, transportation costs, or otherwise? Why curtail their profits at all? "The farmer is *entitled* to a larger share of the returns of our exported wheat," one leader declared in typical fashion, "but only if the will to act so moves him." Anticipating a large harvest, seduced by their own success, and spurred into action by a rising crescendo of rhetoric, Greene, Pierce, R. S. Carey, James C. Campbell, F. E. Russell, and W. D. Wristen organized the Davisville Grangers Warehousing Association on May 16, 1874. They incorporated their new venture with a capital stock of $50,000 and subscribed an additional $19,000 of their own to build a warehouse just up the tracks from Dresbach's. Their purpose could not have been clearer: "to buy, sell, store, and ship merchandise on commission or otherwise and to make advances or loans on merchandise or other security." They intended to beat Dresbach at his own game.[23]

But what of Friedlander? It was one thing to "become one's own merchant" in one's own town, but quite another to supplant the Grain King himself. The sudden and spectacular growth of the movement notwithstanding, the Grangers, individually or collectively, did not possess Friedlander's instincts, capital, contacts, or experience. Realizing this, however reluctantly, the executive committee of the state Grange resolved not to eliminate the middleman but to replace Friedlander with a middleman of their own. After a series of interviews, they selected a New York shipping house, E. E. Morgan's Sons, to be their "central Business Agent." It seemed a perfect fit. The Morgan company, established in 1811, had long been active in shipping between New York and Liverpool, was fully prepared to shift most of its resources to the California market, had already obtained assurance of ample credit from the British-financed London and San Francisco Bank to do just that, and best of all, had no previous ties to Friedlander. It was widely believed, moreover, that in A. F. Walcott, the firm's new San Francisco-based representative, Morgan's Sons had a rising star—"one of the shrewdest and most competent business men on this coast."[24]

But Walcott was no Friedlander. Hoping to reap the benefits of the bountiful harvest, the Grangers and Morgan's Sons rushed into an agreement in the summer of 1874 without fully understanding the nuances of the west-coast trade. Walcott would charter the vessels and handle the business details for the farmers (at reduced fees) and the executive committee would recommend to all members that they ship their grain via the new "Granger fleet." In a clause that seemed of little significance at the time, Walcott's firm, in contrast to Friedlander's normal practice, would consign wheat "for the account of" individual Grangers, meaning that the cargoes would remain the property of the farmers until sold in Britain, with payment to them delayed. Walcott proceeded to charter eighty ships (three times as many as the company had ever attempted in New York) to transport the wheat that he anticipated the individual Grangers would ask him to handle. To secure those vessels, however, Walcott had to bid directly against Friedlander and, in the process, found himself forced to pay much-higher-than-usual oceanic freight rates. Basing his calculations on the previous year's market, when wheat in San Francisco had sold from $1.90 to $2.30 per cental in August and September, he expected to cover his costs—now approaching $1 million—with little difficulty.[25]

When his ships began to arrive in late August, however, California wheat commanded only $1.50 to $1.65—the result, primarily, of a large surplus in Europe. The glut took Friedlander by surprise as well, but the Grain King quickly realized that he could use the slow market to "freeze out his competitor," as one newspaper put it. He not only continued to purchase farmers' wheat outright, which most of them preferred, but also engaged Walcott in another bidding war, offering 5 to 10 cents more per cental than the Liverpool price throughout August and September. Farmers across the state began asking themselves why they should assume the uncertainties of shipping to England when better prices could be had in San Francisco. "If this is the 'light' to which you refer," one frustrated new Granger complained, "then give us Friedlander's darkness and oppression."

By mid-October, Walcott had dispatched only seventeen cargoes of wheat for the Grangers, which left him half a million dollars in the red on shipping costs alone. The accumulating debts were too much for the London and San Francisco Bank, whose agents could see for themselves, from their offices on Montgomery Street, Walcott's five dozen empty Granger ships anchored in the bay. Walcott's chief lender withdrew its support from the venture and attached Morgan's Sons for $165,000, about half the debt due them. With interest accruing at 1 percent per month, and with much of the state's wheat already shipped through Friedlander, Walcott knew that he was running out of options. On October 17, Morgan's Sons declared bankruptcy. Though in retrospect there appeared to be plenty of warning signs, news of the firm's failure hit the Grange "like a thunderbolt in a clear sky," one self-proclaimed "victim of misplaced confidence" recalled. Just seven days earlier, at their second annual convention, state leaders had "heartily endorsed" their shipping agent without a single dissenting vote. Now, even the most optimistic of them felt utterly helpless—"able to grow a crop, but not how to dispose of it," as one put it.[26]

The conditions of the original agreement—in particular, that farmers shipped in their own names—seemed to dictate that the full force of "the Great Disaster" would fall mainly upon Morgan's Sons. But the fallout proved to be long and complicated for those unfortunate farmers—107 in all—whose wheat made it on board one of the seventeen ships from the Granger fleet that set sail out the Golden Gate before October 17. In large part, these were farmers who could afford to wait for their payment until their wheat had been sold in England and who were the most dedicated to the Granger cause. They too could have taken Friedlander's higher price and more expedient terms but believed that to make the Grange work, they had to set an example for the rest of their brethren to follow. They entrusted their crops to Walcott without reservation and still believed that once their grain reached Liverpool, they would receive the payment coming to them even though Walcott's firm had failed. Among them were six from Davisville—Greene, Pierce, Carey, Campbell, Russell, and Wristen—who had just finished constructing their new warehouse a few days before the crash.[27]

On October 20, the six Davisville Grangers called upon Walcott in San Francisco to confirm the status of their wheat—all 20,857 sacks on board the *Pride of the Port*, by then ten days en route to Liverpool. Instead of reassurance, they received startling news that Walcott had, until then, kept to himself. Two days before Morgan's Sons went under, the floundering firm had assigned all 2.7 million pounds of the Davisville wheat to a rival San Francisco shipping company, Daniel Meyer & Co., as security on a promissory note for $75,000. That in itself was not a problem, thought Greene and the others; they would simply get their money from Meyer, instead. It would not be that easy, however. At issue was just what Walcott had actually transferred to Meyer—the right to consign the wheat or the wheat itself. Morgan's Sons did not own the grain, of course, but held it as the commercial factors assigned to sell it on behalf of the growers when the *Pride of Port* reached Liverpool. Meyer's bill of lading, however, explicitly stated that the cargo belonged to Morgan's Sons and not to anyone else. Walcott and Meyer had actually made a verbal agreement to share costs and profits, but after a heated argument over terms, Meyer tore up Walcott's original note and proceeded on his own. With Morgan's Sons insolvent, the wheat already on its way, and Liverpool agents paying 4 cents a pound, Meyer figured he had not only covered his loan but had walked off with an additional $25,000 to $30,000.[28]

But the worldly San Francisco shipper underestimated the shaken but determined Davisville farmers. It took Greene all of three days to file a lawsuit against Meyer, on behalf of himself and the others, in the District Court of the City and County of San Francisco. None of the six plaintiffs was particularly worried, as the facts of the case seemed cut-and-dried to them and, even more importantly, to their creditors as well. Pierce, for example, had little difficulty securing an open-ended extension from the Capital Savings Bank on his mortgage payment on October 28, as well as a loan for $1,000 from the Bank of Woodland to cover his taxes and other expenses two months later. Unfortunately for Pierce and his fellow plaintiffs, their Grange brethren back in Davisville did not rally to their cause. At a meeting the first week of November, local members were assessed $5 each to help sustain the loss and pay for legal fees, but very few answered the call. Greene, Pierce, Carey, Campbell, Russell, and Wristen expressed surprisingly little animosity toward their neighbors, despite being left in the lurch. They knew, along with one blunt observer, that they had "nibbled the tempting bait . . . bit, and then swallowed it all hook, line, bob, and sinker." More embarrassed than angry, they sought to win their suit, plant their next crop, and get the incident behind them.[29]

Litigation over the case dragged on for four years, however. *Greene v. Meyer,* being the first suit filed, became a test case for the other 101 northern California Grangers who also found themselves scrambling to collect on their wheat from Morgan's Sons, whose debts to them totaled $679,000. The District Court judge, in full agreement with Greene's attorneys, awarded the Davisville Grangers every last penny they demanded in April 1875. Meyer not only appealed but had written documentation—bills of lading, invoices, and insurance policies—indicating that the wheat in question had been "lawfully converted to his own use," making him a "bona fide purchaser." When the California Supreme Court ruled on his appeal in January 1877, the three justices delivered separate opinions—two concurring with Meyer, one with Greene—none of them worded with much conviction. The only thing for certain, one of the justices admitted, was that someone was going to go home aggrieved. They granted Meyer a rehearing, but in the District Court of Yolo County, where a jury quickly ruled in favor of the locals. With attorneys' fees taking one full third of the $37,000 settlement, however, not even the winners had much to celebrate. And because the Greene case was not decided convincingly, a number of other Grangers had to sue on their own, many without resolution until 1880 or later.[30]

As for the Davisville Grange itself, the Morgan's Sons fiasco delivered "a death blow," as one disgruntled member recalled a few years later. The November meeting in 1874, two weeks after the firm's failure, was the last one ever held in Davisville. The new warehouse, still awaiting its first sack of wheat, remained largely empty for the next ten years, as though haunted by the "great Granger blunder." Having challenged Friedlander's rule with such brazenness the year before, the routed Grangers now stood at his mercy. Because of the inflated prices he had offered in competition with Walcott, Friedlander had also lost a lot of money in 1874. But that sacrifice was only temporary. Once he regained his monopoly, Friedlander knew, he could get even on his terms. But the Grain King did not gouge his subjects. He charged higher than usual freight rates over the next three years to recoup his losses but was too shrewd a businessman to "squeeze the farmers" so hard as to inhibit their ability to produce, as many had feared he would. In fact, with abundant harvests and a favorable European market in 1875 and 1876, farmers and middlemen worked together and returned to their prosperous ways, as though the Granger debacle had never happened.[31]

Reflecting the upbeat mood that accompanied these good times and good relations, the Davisville brass band formed in January 1877. Made up mostly of sons of pioneer farmers, including coronet players George Pierce Jr., William Russell, and John Carey, the band sometimes performed formal concerts in town but more often responded to requests to play for specific individuals on special occasions. Their first "serenade" went to William Dresbach on his birthday, a "grand party," attended by dozens of farmers, townspeople, their families, and Friedlander himself. Widely known with fondness, once again, as "great grain kings,"

Dresbach and his mentor basked in the community's admiration that day. Both, however, were already in the process of testing their subjects' loyalty once again—for one last time.[32]

Even before the Granger challenge, Friedlander was looking to both deepen and broaden his empire. The best way to increase exports and tighten his grip on the trade, he came to believe as early as 1870, was to extend his operations to the buying and developing of new farm lands. Spurred into action by the speculator-friendly state and federal laws of the late 1860s, he and fellow San Franciscan William S. Chapman joined forces in a mad scramble for acreage in the San Joaquin Valley, which was just being opened up to farm settlement by the construction of the Southern Pacific Railroad. Once thought too dry (or along the San Joaquin River, too swampy) for grain farming, the southern half of California's Central Valley could be highly productive if properly irrigated, investors gradually learned. Buying and selling at a frenzied pace—mostly agricultural college scrip land in Fresno County—Friedlander and Chapman controlled hundreds of thousands of acres by the mid-1870s and launched several ambitious irrigation projects to water them, at times operating within the law, at times not. One enthusiastic commentator referred to Friedlander not as a king but as a "Field Marshall in California's army of speculators" who has "brains, sagacity, generosity, honor."[33]

Such adulation, in the midst of mounting Granger denunciations, stemmed in part from the reputation Friedlander had earned in San Francisco high society. Indeed, the Grain King owed his success as much to his social skills as to his business acumen. He lived in the city's fashionable Rincon Hill district, where he hobnobbed with such men of prominence as Leland Stanford and William Ralston. From Stanford, Friedlander received favors that only such a powerful railroad executive and politician could provide, and through Ralston, he gained access to the considerable credit of the Bank of California. Friedlander also served on the first Board of Regents of the University of California, held a leading position in the city's Jewish community and temple, and made the society columns in city newspapers on a regular basis. The new building for his offices on Sansome Street, constructed in 1875 and said to be among the most elegant on the Pacific Coast, symbolized his ascent and would bear his name until 1920.[34]

At the top of his game and, indeed, seemingly the world, Friedlander suddenly lost it all in one fell swoop in 1877, three years after reestablishing his rule. Perhaps overburdened by his mounting business interests, perhaps overconfident from beating the odds year after year in such an unpredictable market, Friedlander, like many of his competitors before him, fell victim to unforeseen consequences and his own bad judgment. His troubles began when his storied network of local agents failed him that winter, causing him to overestimate the upcoming crop. Though it rained through December, drought set in at the start of the new year, reducing yields in the Sacramento Valley by as much as three-quarters over the previous season. As luck would have it, Friedlander's contacts abroad let him down as well, causing him to underestimate the overseas crop. Bad weather early on in Great Britain and the war raging between Russia and Turkey seemed destined to cut off some of the largest and most available sources of supply across the Atlantic. Much to Friedlander's chagrin, however, England and Scotland enjoyed abundant, if late, harvests, and Russia ended up exporting more wheat that year than ever before. As a result, prices in San Francisco, despite the domestic shortage, hovered around the disappointing low figure of $1.60 per cental for most of the season.

Meanwhile, Friedlander's market power also declined because of his inability to sustain his near monopoly over shipping. With communication now virtually instantaneous via the increasingly reliable transoceanic telegraph, and with the availability of large numbers of so-called tramp vessels (ships not operating on fixed schedules or specific routes but waiting nearby to pick up cargo whenever they could), British buyers were reluctant to place orders with Friedlander several months in advance of delivery. It was now almost always cheaper and much less risky simply to wait until the last minute to choose a carrier. More generally, the world price slump that began in 1873, but had yet to have much impact on the Pacific coast trade, hit hard in 1877. Indeed, this was a bad year for all shippers in California for the first time since the great drought of the mid 1860s. The end result was that the wheat trade not only escaped Friedlander's dominance; it toyed with him and humbled him. Having chartered many more ships than he could fill or sell, he piled up liabilities of more than $800,000. With the market that year all but lost, he had no choice but to declare bankruptcy, stunning wheat men at home and around the world.[35]

But the Grain King was not quite finished. Ever resilient, he persuaded his creditors to allow him to continue his grain operations on a much-reduced scale. By early the following summer, he was back to his old tricks, acting as a commission merchant for twenty charters filled with wheat. With most of those ships on their way to Britain, Friedlander suffered a massive heart attack on July 11, 1878, and died at the age of fifty-five. Among the pallbearers at his funeral were Stanford, Chapman, and several of his fiercest competitors—none of whom doubted that Friedlander could have regained his fortune had time allowed. His estate, including more than $2 million invested in various landholdings, was in such disarray that it took several years for attorneys to liquidate enough of it to pay 10 cents on the dollar to creditors. Though his son, T. Cary Friedlander, would eventually serve as secretary of the San Francisco Produce Exchange, from the mid-1880s until after the turn of the century, he never, as one newspaper put it, "inherited his father's glory."[36]

"WHO IS GRAIN KING NOW?" headlined the *San Francisco Post*, asking the question on everyone's lips. The early front-runner was William Dresbach. Following in the footsteps of his mentor, Dresbach had also been expanding operations over the course of the decade—so much so that the *Post* claimed that "he now controls more of the harvest than any other man in the State." Dresbach certainly saw himself as the heir apparent and made it known to the press that he fully intended to claim Friedlander's mantle. But his brave boasts were hardly justified by his accumulating debts and legal entanglements, which he had kept to himself until this point. Like many before and after Friedlander's empire came crashing down, Dresbach proved to be only a pretender to the throne.[37]

He began small. Between 1873 and 1875, Dresbach purchased at least 3,000 acres in Yolo and Solano counties and leased them in small plots (300 to 500 acres) to young farmers eager to cash in on the wheat boom. He also aggressively went after the business of already-established farmers heretofore outside his domain by opening up another store and warehouse in the new town of Winters, thirteen miles up Putah Creek from Davisville, near the old Wolfskill ranch. Every step of the way, however, Dresbach encountered fierce competition, much of it Friedlander's doing. Over roughly the same period, the Grain King expanded his interior network by establishing new agents at nearby Dixon, Merritt's Station, Woodland, Winters, and Knight's Landing, severely cramping Dresbach's style in the process. Extensions of the California Pacific Railroad northward through Woodland and Knight's Landing and of the Vaca Valley Railroad through Winters also cut into Dresbach's volume of trade by giving farmers easier access to these other merchants. If he was going to survive, let alone expand, Dresbach knew he had to make a bold move.[38]

And bold it was. Early in January 1875, Dresbach called on Hugh Glenn to discuss a contract to handle his forthcoming wheat crop. "Dr. Glenn," as he preferred, was no ordinary farmer. The gold rush had lured him to California from Missouri, where he obtained a medical education, and for a brief time in the early 1850s, he and his family settled on prairie land north of Putah Creek, near the Davis ranch. After several profitable ventures in the cattle trade, Glenn began putting together an extraordinary block of land in Colusa County (bordering Yolo to the north) in 1865. Most of it was adobe, but Glenn had learned from the experiences of squatters (including his own) that the hard soil could be purchased cheaply and cultivated profitably. By the time he met with Dresbach, the Glenn ranch had grown to an astounding 45,000 acres, extending north-south along the west side of the Sacramento River, five miles deep and sixteen miles long, and centered on the river town of Jacinto. Popular journals and newspapers portrayed Dr. Glenn as a legend in his own time. One called his spread "the largest purely grain growing ranch on the American continent," while another referred to Glenn as simply "the world's greatest wheat grower."[39]

Dresbach gave Glenn a deal he could not refuse. The ordinary freight from Jacinto to San Francisco was slow and expensive. Steamers making several trips over several weeks brought the immense crop—averaging 10,000 tons in the early 1870s—down the river and across the bay for $5.00 a ton. Dresbach offered $3.50, using freight trains to carry the cargo to tidewater, from Knights Landing to Vallejo, whence it sailed directly out the Golden Gate. With a crop of 12,000 tons in 1875 and 18,000 the following year, Glenn saved roughly $45,000 on the deal. Dresbach, on the other hand, fell deeply in debt, borrowing some $400,000 over the two years to finance the venture. About a quarter of it came from Friedlander and another quarter from a number of northern California banks. The rest, he hoped, would come from hundreds, perhaps thousands, of farmers and tenants in Colusa, Butte, and Tehama counties in the northern Sacramento Valley in the form of crop mortgages. To get Glenn's 45,000 acres of wheat, Dresbach intended to develop many times that much land in 500-acre tracts. In exchange for furnishing the new farmers with the means to cultivate their wheat, he accepted their growing crops as collateral—at 1¼ percent per month interest. With big crops and high prices prevailing in 1875 and 1876, Dresbach figured to cover his loans and begin raking in profits by 1877, or 1878 at the latest. He was "not afraid of the future of the wheat market," observed the *Colusa Sun*. Indeed, he was banking on it.[40]

Dresbach's high-stakes gamble proved to be the most devilish opportunity of the decade. The 1877 drought-ridden season brought small crops, low prices, and Friedlander's failure. Dresbach lost another $750,000, not to mention his principal backer, but not his nerve. He borrowed another half-million dollars and set his sights on the 1878 harvest, confident that eventually he could fully recover. The heavy rains that began on January 15 dampened his spirits, and the flooding that followed swept away any hopes he had of pulling this grand scheme off. The Sacramento River and its tributaries began spilling their banks and breaking through levees in early February, once again transforming much of the valley into an inland sea. One newspaper called it "the flood of the century"—the havoc it caused apparently blurring all memories of the previous three decades. "The water," the same paper reported after one especially bad day, "was rushing madly everywhere, waves beat against houses and through fences, women screamed, children cried, dogs howled, cattle lowed, and men leaped fearlessly into the tide and nobly struggled to rescue women and children from the danger." Much of the wheat crop drowned, rendering all Dresbach's crop mortgages virtually worthless.[41]

By early November, Dresbach owed interest on more than $1.5 million. Trying desperately to stay afloat, he turned to his one last hope, Hugh Glenn, and asked him for a no-strings-attached loan of $100,000. The doctor, who knew a sinking ship when he saw one, politely said no, having already made arrangements to charter vessels to ship his upcoming crop on his own. Glenn did agree later that month, however, to accept a "deed" from Dresbach for "all my property and estate, real, personal, and mixed . . . for the benefit and satisfaction of all my creditors." Shortly thereafter, on February 3, 1879, Dresbach filed for bankruptcy in the Yolo County Court. Several of his creditors contested his petition, arguing that the deed to Glenn was a "pretended trust" designed only to hide Dresbach's assets—which it most certainly was. Nothing in the law, however, prohibited such a practice, as bankruptcy statutes still heavily favored debtors. After a long and hard-fought trial, Dresbach was admitted to insolvency in January 1880, with the judge discharging him from all his debts, both individual and company. One disgruntled creditor appealed the case to the California Supreme Court, but to no avail.[42]

By the time that judgment was handed down in February 1883, Dresbach had already resurrected himself. In 1879, right in the middle of his bankruptcy trial, he sold his Davisville mansion and fled to San Francisco. The Produce Exchange, which had become the dominant grain-trading force on the west coast in Friedlander's absence, welcomed him with open arms. Taking advantage of his numerous contacts, knowledge of the trade, and many years of experience, Dresbach became one of the city's leading brokers in less than a year, and in 1883 he purchased an even bigger mansion on Union Street. There he remained until his death in 1901, never once returning to the Sacramento Valley. On the floor of the Exchange, Dresbach took one speculative flyer after another, including an audacious but unsuccessful attempt to corner the market in 1887. When his large, unoccupied store in Davisville burned to the ground on September 7, 1880, about a dozen farmers—Pierce, Greene, and Russell among them—gathered at the site the next day, as they had so many times before during the previous two decades. The conversation no doubt turned to memories of old Solano Bill, who in all likelihood knew nothing of the incident himself.[43]

And so the pattern continued. The big wheeler-dealers—from Champion I. Hutchinson and Jerome C. Davis to Dresbach and Friedlander—exerted a commanding presence during their respective reigns, but they tended to come and go, in some cases on to bigger and better things, in others into obscurity. They were, in essence, rural robber barons, extracting great riches from the Sacramento Valley, often without regard to the consequences, before eventually overextending or miscalculating (or both) and finding themselves on the verge of ruin. Yet, like the Rockefellers and the Goulds (on a much smaller scale), they were indispensable to the economic development of the region. The farmers who depended on them were generally less bold, less decisive, and seemingly more vulnerable to the hazards of their enterprise. They were the ones, however, who were much more likely to persist—at a rate, 43 percent, even higher than during the previous decade—and they were the ones who continued to place their hopes in wheat. To do otherwise would have been to admit the fallacy of a second gold rush.[44]

For farmers in Davisville, dreams of striking it rich fluctuated in the 1870s with production, prices, and their own futile efforts to oust Friedlander and Dresbach. The twin catastrophes of drought and flood in 1877 and 1878 were especially discouraging, not only for the scanty yields those seasons produced also but for conjuring up memories of disasters past. The flood in particular drowned farm animals, destroyed roads and bridges, cut through levees, and left in its wake property damage (individual and county) along Putah Creek estimated at $600,000. Though "left at the mercy of the waves" that winter, farmers looked forward to the "abundant crops on the naturally-fertilized soil" that typically followed a flood year. "Like a cloud with a silver lining," maintained one particularly optimistic observer, "this disastrous flood will deposit sediments rich for wheat culture."[45]

But as Pierce recounted in his diary, the much-anticipated crop of 1879 was "attacked by the scourge of rust" throughout much of the region. Many farmers had heard of the fungus that left reddish or brownish spots on the stems of their plants, but no one understood why, after thirty years of cultivation, it had just now begun to appear in abundance, how it spread, or what to do about it. Most resorted to the recommended solution of the time—cut the crop for hay as soon as possible to try to recover at least some of one's investment. Those farmers whose crop managed to escape the infestation fell victim to yet another blight when a dreaded north wind swept down the valley during the last two weeks of June, shriveling the ripe grain and knocking the kernels off the stalks. "Three years in a row of suffering," wrote one Yolo County farmer, "is more than one can take."[46]

Pierce certainly thought so. Like most of his neighbors, Pierce flourished in

1875 and 1876, producing $13,000 harvests both years. But when he settled with Dresbach at the end of the next two seasons, he barely broke even, clearing only $84.97 after the drought and just $11.53 following the flood. The next year was a little better—he netted $1,127.39 in 1879—but that was not nearly enough to pay the $1,400 in interest and the $5,000 in principal that the Sacramento Savings Bank was demanding on his mortgage. Dresbach's insolvency, ironically, gave Pierce a bit of breathing room. The two firms that began competing for his business in 1879—Eppinger & Co. in Dixon and Bullard and Pearce in Davisville—eagerly advanced him the money, though Pierce had to put up his land as collateral. To pay his taxes and other expenses, he rented out Eunice's retreat in Woodland (getting several months in advance), and sold every pound of butter, chicken feed, and fruit that she produced. So exasperated were the Pierces by the end of the year that they contemplated getting out altogether; they began asking real estate agents about putting the ranch on the market.[47]

Farmers and townspeople alike in Davisville shared the Pierce's disillusionment. The booster-driven expectations for rapid growth at the beginning of the decade—even the more subdued ones—had not materialized. "This burg is sadly neglected," wrote one correspondent in 1879, remarking on how little the town had changed. Its population had not grown, nor had that of either Putah or Tremont townships. There were still three churches, one school, roughly the same number of businesses, three fraternal societies, and one baseball team. Two efforts to start a town newspaper had failed and the hotels and saloons changed hands often. More than half the original town lots remained unsold, and another eighty-five added by developer John P. Jackson along Putah Creek in 1871 could be had for one-tenth their original value by the end of the decade. No one spoke of Davisville as a boomtown anymore, but as "a small, quiet village" at best. They were quietly fearful of what lay in store in the future.[48]

Their spirits improved immensely with the turn of the decade. Conditions in the spring of 1880 were made to order for good crops—no floods, no drought, no ill-timed north winds, no disease, and few pests. Davisville farmers looked forward to a bountiful harvest and this time were not disappointed. Many grew more wheat in 1880 than they ever had before, including Pierce, who produced 428 tons. California farmers, in fact, set a record with a yield of 1.6 million tons. "The crop was so large we were unable to move it," recalled a member of the Produce Exchange, "and nearly half of it was carried over into the following year." Few farmers, however, expressed much concern over how such an abundance might affect the market. Nothing seemed to have alerted them to the possibility that their fundamental assumption—that they could not overproduce—might somehow be fallacious. Even the rock-bottom prices that they received that year—$1.30 to $1.40 per cental—did not seem to faze them. Pierce, for example, never did put his ranch on the market, declaring in his diary that everything was progressing "verry [sic] nicely."[49]

Wheat was not the only thing on Pierce's mind that year. For the first time, he began reminiscing at some length about key moments in his life in his diary, where previously he had confined himself to brief, often cryptic, remarks on the weather, farm business, and day-to-day occurrences. His bouts of nostalgia began on April 19, when, after noting the pleasant spring rains, he suddenly added, "Twenty eight years ago to day Mrs. Pierce and Self left Kenosha Wisconsin to come to California by land." The next day, this time before getting to the weather, he wrote, "Forty five years ago to day I left Homer Courtland Co N. Y. to go to the west and landed at Chicago. On foot . . . started for Pike Creek Wisconsin now Kenosha and arrived there the eight day of July 1835." And so he continued—not every day, but whenever the mood struck him. Many of Pierce's neighbors along Putah Creek, it turns out, also felt the need to look back. After thirty years of settlement, this first generation of farmers seemed finally to pause, look around, and take stock of what they had accomplished. What they remembered, as well as what they let slip away, suggests that they were struggling to keep their dreams alive more than they cared to admit.[50]

CHAPTER TEN

Looking Back

William Montgomery died on the morning of May 7, 1877, at the ripe age of seventy-four. One of the older gold rushers when he came to California, Montgomery nonetheless managed to live another full quarter-century on the land where he first squatted in 1851. For years, his age made him the target of many a good-natured ribbing. When, for example, he delivered the Declaration of Independence at the Davisville Fourth of July celebration in 1874, one attendee quipped that "his white locks and reverential appearance carried us on the wings of imagination to the days of seventeen hundred and seventy-six (though we don't quite believe he was born at that time!)." He was known to all, simply, as "Uncle Billy." On May 9, hundreds of mourners, on very short notice, attended the funeral—a gathering larger than anyone could remember.[1]

On paper, Uncle Billy seemed to die a rather inauspicious death. Life in Putah Sink had taken its toll. The floods, droughts, title conflicts, and market swings over the years left Montgomery with more debts than assets. His estate consisted of 510 acres assessed at just under $5,000, along with personal property valued at $2,100, but he owed over $12,000 to banks and individual lenders. In his will, made just two weeks before his death, Montgomery bequeathed 160 acres to his wife, Rebecca, and the remainder of his real property in parcels of equal size to his five children, knowing full well that "the payment of my lawful debts" would come first. Fearful of losing the entire estate to creditors, Montgomery's youngest son, William W., and his closest friend and the executor of his will, R. S. Carey, devised an ingenious plan. At the executor's auction, held on the ranch on August 18, William aggressively outbid everyone in attendance, including several speculators from Sacramento, for his father's possessions. He paid twice the value of the land and purchased, at similarly inflated prices, much of the personal property, including his father's prized horses. William did not have that kind of cash, but Carey did. He loaned William all that he needed in exchange for a mortgage on the land. This not only allowed William to pay off the creditors and keep the land in the family but also let Rebecca keep the quarter section that her husband had left her for the remainder of her life. Many of Montgomery's neighbors, including William Marden and Napoleon Miner, also helped out in this manner by outbidding the outsiders for a number of items.[2]

With Montgomery's estate in such disarray, why did Davisville families turn out en masse for this struggling farmer's funeral? Most obviously, Montgomery was both revered as a prominent citizen and beloved as everyone's uncle. Republicans and Democrats, Yankees and southerners, and wheat farmers and stockmen alike respected and admired their longtime neighbor. But when they kidded Uncle Billy in the waning years of his life, there was more than a tinge of anxiety in their voices. Montgomery's death signified the beginning of the end of the pioneer generation of Putah Creek. Unlike the more established communities in the Midwest from which most of them had migrated, Putah Creek had very few old people and therefore very few deaths (aside from accidents, childhood disease, and the like)—so, like Montgomery, many were unprepared for the often complex process of inheritance. The impending generational change, like death itself, crept up on them almost as if they had been caught unawares—that is, until Montgomery's funeral. On that solemn occasion, they mourned the passing of an old friend, but they also came face-to-face with their own lives, dreams, and failures, as well as their own mortality. The resulting impulse to look back manifested itself in three distinct ways—private recollections, published expressions, and public testimonies.[3]

While they had never been close friends, few in the community had known Montgomery longer than George and Eunice Pierce. They, along with George Jr., were among the first to arrive at the memorial service and among the last to leave. What they were thinking that day cannot be determined with certainty. In his diary that evening, George, in characteristic fashion, wrote only, "Attended 'Uncle Billy' Montgomery's funeral—large attendance." None of the three could have been feeling particularly good about themselves, however. For George Sr., the pressures of producing a crop, securing a good price for it, and paying the mortgage seemed to mount with each passing year. The tensions within the Pierce household, moreover, ran even deeper than George Sr.'s account books revealed. Indeed, the economic and environmental turmoil of the decade greatly impacted not only the Pierce ranch but the Pierce family as well.[4]

After years of struggling to adjust to her new surroundings on Putah Creek, Eunice Pierce had managed to make a good life for herself—not an easy life, but a good one. Her long hours of labor remained crucial to the family economy. In years when the crop failed, the money she made producing dairy and wool products, eggs, and vegetables not only sustained the family but often kept the Pierce ranch afloat. She also took a keen interest in public and church affairs, earning a reputation in the community as "a woman of more than ordinary mentality . . . who always exerted a cheering influence on those with whom she came into contact." Eunice, in fact, became quite the entertainer. It was not unusual for her to invite neighbors over for supper and to spend the night two or even three times a week, prompting George, on occasion, to bemoan his lack of privacy. "Mrs. Brown, Mrs. Ainsworth, Kate Greene, and Kate Hutchinson came on a visit today and played cards until nearly 1 am," he wrote one day. "Visitors finally went home this evening," he added the next, noticeably relieved. And when neighbors were sick, they often called on Eunice to sit with them. While she had no medical training, they greatly valued her patience and bedside manner. Eunice began to feel "quite sick" herself, George noted as early as 1879. Her complaints of fever and arthritic discomfort signaled the early symptoms of the rheumatism ("the rheumates," George called it) that would render her bedridden for days, and later weeks, at a time for the rest of her life.[5]

As was typical of parents in contemporary Yankee families, both Eunice and George derived their greatest source of personal satisfaction from their son's success. Yankee mothers tended to bear only two or three children, to give them "a better chance," even at the cost of shrinking the family labor pool. Because two of the three Pierce children died in infancy, the pressure to succeed fell squarely on the shoulders of George Jr. His parents did everything they could to help him establish himself, knowing that their efforts might well cause their son to leave the farm and the community one day. Education, they knew, was key. With districts in Putah Township being too new for their liking, George and Eunice sent George Jr. to the best school in the county in Woodland during his teenage years. Then, when the new state university in Berkeley opened its doors in 1868, George and Eunice saw their chance to secure their son's future. For four years, he studied civil engineering, thoroughly enjoying everything that college life offered, while returning home in the summers to work on the ranch. So formative an experience were his years in Berkeley that for the rest of his life he rarely missed a charter day ceremony or an important football game. Upon concluding his course work in 1875, he earned the distinction of being the "pioneer graduate" of the University of California from the Sacramento Valley. His parents and his community could not have been prouder when he announced his intention to further his education in law school.[6]

Then, on June 9, 1875, while preparing for the harvest, George Sr. took a bad fall. "I was thrown from a wagon . . . and badly hurt," he wrote seven years later. "Have not got over it yet nor I never will it is much likely." With a bumper crop still in the ground, George Jr. was called home early from Berkeley to take charge of the farm. He would never resume his studies. On more than one occasion in subsequent years, George Jr. hoped to go back to law school, but every year his father's chronically sore hips and knees thwarted his plans. By 1882, with the ranch still heavily in debt and with the added burden of his mother's declining health, he abandoned hope of a professional career and resigned himself to remaining at home to help his father manage the farm. The disappointment was keen for everyone involved, though neither parents nor son expressed their feelings openly. George Jr., in fact, threw his energies into his work on the farm and made it known that he intended to make the Pierce ranch the pride of the county.[7]

Every so often, however, tensions within the Pierce family surfaced. One evening in October 1879, for example, George Jr. rode to Davisville with his mother to go to church, or so he told his father. Instead, as George Sr. recounted the next day, he "attended the drunkun [sic] Band and let his mother sit on the steps at the church an hour after church was out waiting for him." George Jr. could not have devised a more rebellious act. In one fell swoop, he lied to his father, used church to cover it up, got drunk, and abandoned his mother (who caught a "severe cold" that night)—all in the wake of three consecutive bad harvests that had everyone wondering if the farm could survive. George Sr. was furious, but directed his rage toward "the drunken Band" rather than address the underlying causes. What had once been a great source of pride for the family became, in one evening, a lightning rod for the family's frustrations. For about a month, George Jr. continued to assert his independence by attending band practice, but shortly thereafter capitulated to his father's demands and quit—not only the band, but the coronet itself and the defiant trips to Davisville. Already twenty-nine years old, George Jr. would not fully emerge from his father's shadow for almost another decade, a scenario that no one—father, mother, or son—had ever envisioned, much less desired.[8]

This, then, was the context in which George Sr. began looking back on his life, late at night in the privacy of his diary. Worried sick about the ranch, his wife's health, and his son's lost career; shaken by Montgomery's death; and disappointed that his own dreams of striking it rich in California were still, after thirty years, far from fulfilled, George turned to his own memories for comfort. Even when composing his personal thoughts, he remained in perfect character. His jottings were generally brief, orderly, systematic, and void of emotion. On certain days, he wrote about important events in his life, word for word, year after year, in an almost commemorative manner. However repetitive, fragmented, and incomplete, the personal narrative that George created over the last ten years of his life offers an especially deep entry into his troubles and desires.

Most prominent among his reminiscences was the day he married Eunice. Even before he began looking back on other matters, George rarely failed to note his wedding anniversary on September 29. Entries were formal, reading more like announcements than expressions of emotion, but on rare occasions, as in 1874, he added a touch of romance: "Geo. W. Pierce and Eunice French was [sic] married Twenty eight years ago today. I love her as much as ever. She has been a great comfort to me." As the family's economic and personal troubles mounted, George's sentiments became more poignant, if still a bit stiff. "Thirty five years ago today," he wrote in 1881, "I was married to Eunice French. It was the best act of my life. She has been a grate [sic] comfort to me and Stood by me through thick and thin." Every indication suggests that Eunice shared George's feelings and that the two developed a lifelong friendship over the years. Though she valued her solitude, sought close friendships with other women outside the home, and focused most of her attention on nurturing her son, Eunice did "stand by" George, as was typical in Yankee households. That they had shared the same dreams and disappointments—from their days in Kenosha, to their search for gold in California, to their lives along Putah Creek—tightened that bond all the more.[9]

In much the same manner, George also began, in 1880, to reminisce about his various removals. Again, like clockwork, he wrote about them on the same day, year after year, using nearly the exact same words. At first, he focused on two days in particular—when he left New York for Kenosha and when he and Eunice left Kenosha for California. Over time, he added to his life's itinerary. In 1882, the standard entry for February 16 became, "Mrs. Pierce and Self come to Putah Creek Twenty-eight years ago to night and commenced work on the Big Ranch the next day—$150 per month." A year later he began noting that "we arrived in Plaserville [sic] the 4 of August [after] 3 months and 14 days across the plains." The details then began to flow more freely. "Forty nine years ago to day," he wrote on April 20, 1884, "I left Homer, Courtland County New York, to go to Illinois. Went with team to Syracuse and from there to Buffalo on the Canal, from Buffalo to Dunkirk on foot. From there to Monroe Michigan on a little old Steamer called the Peacock—come very near going under." And on July 8, 1886: "Fifty one years ago today I arrived in Kenosha then Pike Creek. There was [sic] only about 6 or 8 folks there at the time. . . . I helped build the second house in the place. It was built of logs near where Baird's Brick yard was for several years."[10]

Gradually, George made entries on more personal matters, but unlike the more routine memories, he rarely repeated them in subsequent years. "Mrs. Bennett, Mrs. Greene's mother, died to day at Woodland aged about 77," he wrote on July 21, 1885. "She was the first Lady that we saw on the creek 19 February 1854." The next year, on April 15, he stated rather abruptly, "Thirty Six years ago today Henry Albert died—our only [first] son." And just one year before his own death in 1890, George recorded his first and last remark about his gold-mining days: "Had about as good luck as any of them. There was a big rush for California in that year." Interestingly, there were no entries about the death of his third son, Frank Alonzo. Nor was there any mention of the early days on the Big Ranch, his years as Justice of the Peace, the floods and droughts that he managed to survive, the Odd Fellows lodge, or the Granger fiasco. George Jr. himself never found his way into his father's recorded memories. Save for the days when he arrived in Placerville and Putah Creek, George confined his reminiscing to life before California.[11]

Indeed, when writing in his diary, George divided his life into two distinct periods—before the gold rush and after, with a particularly conspicuous void marking his and Eunice's year and a half in the mines on Weber Creek. Struggling to comprehend what had gone wrong in recent years, he tried to reaffirm his self-worth by remembering, over and over again, a time when there seemed to be a much stronger correlation between hard work, right values, and success. The sad part was that, despite what he seemed to think of himself, George was by no means a failure. In many ways, in fact, his life was a classic tale of American optimism. Time and time again, he fought through adversity, battled the elements, and came out ahead. Yet, despite all that he and his family had accomplished along Putah Creek, George never achieved the lofty goals that he and Eunice had set for themselves in California. They never, in his mind, relived that glorious moment when anything seemed possible—whether during the first gold rush or the second.

One of his last dreams, more modest in scope, also failed to come true. On July 8, 1884, after recounting, in the usual manner, his arrival in Kenosha, George declared, "I intend to be there again the 8th day of July 1885, which will make fifty years." Homesick and wanting to bring his life full circle, he imagined finally returning to Kenosha in triumph. That year the Pierce ranch produced, as George put it, "verry nice wheat—the best we have raised in years," but it sold for just $1.20 per cental. There were several more funerals to attend, and George himself often felt "quite Sick." When July 8 came again, he recalled his arrival in Wisconsin, but mentioned nothing about the promise he had made to himself a year earlier. He did not return to Kenosha in the remaining five years of his life, nor did he even allow himself to entertain the idea in his diary again.[12]

While the Pierces looked back on their lives within the confines of the family, others took advantage of an opportunity to reminisce much more openly. It came in January 1879, when a sales force from De Pue and Company, a San Francisco-based publishing firm, began scouring the countryside in Yolo County. Farmers were accustomed to traveling salesmen coming to their doors to peddle bibles, encyclopedias, and patent medicines, but these particular "canvassers" pitched an especially intriguing product—advanced subscriptions to a proposed volume entitled *The Illustrated Atlas and History of Yolo County*.[13]

Each salesman carried a copy of a similar work on San Mateo County, which De Pue had just helped publish. Nineteen inches from top to bottom, fourteen inches wide, and beautifully bound, this grand volume, "suitable for any parlor or library," contained property-ownership maps, lithographic illustrations of local scenes, a history of both the county and the state, and biographical sketches of all subscribers. For the base rate of $9, farmers were told, De Pue could put in their hands an even more impressive atlas of Yolo County, complete with their names engraved on the map and a short paragraph on their life histories. A number of tantalizing options were also available, including more extensive biographies at $2\frac{1}{2}$ cents per word and portraits and illustrations from $100 to $250. Those interested in full, two-page, bird's-eye-view lithographs of their farms paid two to three times more. The savvy salesmen appealed not only to the vanity of potential patrons but also to their pride of ownership, their standing in the community, and especially their role in the region's "pioneer times." "Make haste to furnish [us] all the facts you know about the past or present condition of your particular neighborhood," farmers were encouraged, "because such facts will be put in a permanent form and preserved forever in the new history."[14]

If all else failed, these roving marketers had one more trick up their sleeves that few could resist. They could make explicit what some potential patrons probably already knew: everyone else was doing it. Indeed, during the early 1870s, the illustrated atlas became a full-fledged, mass-market novelty item across much of rural America, though the genre had just begun to take hold in California. So many county atlases—upwards of 5,000 titles, by one estimate—were being produced that salesmen could tell Yolo County residents that to not subscribe sent a disturbing message: your community had not yet come of age. Only a mature, prosperous citizenry, after all, could afford such lavish documentation. The logic

was circular but effective. In less than three months, door-to-door solicitations secured almost 400 subscriptions, including 96 requests for longer biographies,
portraits, and illustrations—more than enough for De Pue and Company to begin production.[15]

In early April, the subscription agents hit the road again, each of them accompanied, this time, by a "viewer" (lithographic sketcher), a biography editor,
and a portrait canvasser. They returned to the homes of patrons to begin their
work and along the way continued to solicit subscriptions, anticipating that their
conspicuous presence would persuade others. The mapmakers, in turn, headed
to the county courthouse to study land and tax records and to consult the Board
of Supervisors. But they too, eventually, rode over all parts of the county to sketch
in their own direct observations of roads, churches, schools, town sites, and other
geographical features as well as to run rough drafts of their work past the property owners themselves. And while the sketching, biography taking, mapping,
and checking proceeded, Frank T. Gilbert, a former officer in the Union army and
now the official historian for De Pue and Company, pursued his own extensive
research, both in official records and by conducting lengthy interviews with
longtime residents—those, as he put it, with deep "footprints in the past." Their
input, executives at De Pue and Company knew, was key to the success of the project. It was their personalized accounts of important events, individual achieve-
ments, and civic accomplishments that sold copies.[16]

As such, *The Illustrated Atlas and History of Yolo County* provides a revealing
glimpse into the collective memory of its contributors. Though often lavish, incomplete, and not entirely accurate, the biographies, lithographs, and oral histories recorded what subscribers did and, by omission and implication, did not
want to "leave behind for posterity." The timing of this ambitious undertaking
makes these reminiscences all the more illuminating. Put together just as many
patrons were beginning to look back at their lives, the De Pue historical atlas
sheds considerable light on this difficult period of generational transition.[17]

Residents of Putah Township were among the most enthusiastic participants
in the county, with roughly fifty of them among the charter subscribers. The six
who purchased lithographs—L. C. Drummond, H. P. Merritt, Jacob Guysi, H. H.
Knuppe, William Bullard, Phineas S. Chiles—got their money's worth. De Pue's
talented pool of viewers projected images of success and material abundance.
Even Drummond's rather modest home ranch appears to be a picture of prosperity. Though not as grand as many of the others, the house itself, sturdy and
well maintained, left little doubt that its owner was a man of character. Even the
sheds and barn look to be in perfect shape, and the redwood fences, squared off

at right angles and disappearing out of the field of view, enclose what seems to be yet another bumper crop. The unsuspecting reader would never have guessed that Drummond, like the other farmers in the region, had just endured three straight bad harvests. Yet, such lithographic images should not be dismissed as sheer whimsy or exaggeration; numerous studies have revealed a surprising fidelity between the artist's rendition and the real thing, save for a few embellishments.[18]

The intent and accuracy of these illustrations becomes clearer in the two spectacular images—one on top of the other across two pages—of "the old Chiles ranch." Phineas Chiles spared no expense. He bought the entire package—the two lithographs, an extended biography, and a full-page family portrait—for what must have been at least $1,000. Phineas was the nephew of "trail-blazing pioneer" Joseph B. Chiles and brother of Isaac S. Chiles, who back in 1854 had purchased the land from Gabriel Brown, one of Joseph's two sons-in-law (the other being Jerome C. Davis). When Isaac died in 1863, Phineas was summoned from Missouri to manage the 1,760-acre estate, and he eventually married his brother's widow. No salesman had to tell Phineas that the Chiles ranch merited special attention. The top lithograph of the farm and residence resembled Drummond's, though on a much grander scale. Against the backdrop of the coast mountains (whose horizon is easily recognizable today), the town of Davisville, and two locomotives departing from the depot, the detailed drawing of the ranch exudes order, neatness, and comfort. As Du Pue's biography editor put it, "it needs no description. . . . The view offered gives a better knowledge of its appearance than could be given by us with a pen." It must have looked positively real to Chiles and his neighbors. The bottom lithograph of the stockyards was equally striking, as the illustrator depicted the cattle, horses, hogs, and sheep with stunning clarity, except that the animals appear oversized, perhaps to emphasize their importance. In fact, no one would know from the two views that over half the acreage on the ranch was devoted to wheat. Phineas was determined, both here and in his biography, to link the great Chiles name first and foremost to stock, to emphasize the family's Missouri roots and, perhaps, to distance the ranch's reputation from wheat's recent decline.[19]

As with the lithographs, the biographies are at once rich in and void of detail. At 2½ cents per word, subjects gave careful consideration to what they would emphasize. The vast majority devoted at least half their space to their lives before Yolo County—childhood experiences, removals, and often three or four sentences describing a military feat or other adventure. They seemed determined to let readers know that they had established their identities elsewhere, the Midwest

The Chiles Ranch, as depicted in *The Illustrated Atlas and History of Yolo County* (San Francisco: De Pue & Co., 1879). Larkey Collection #1-1. Courtesy of the Yolo County Archives, Woodland.

in most cases. Their descriptions of life in Yolo County, in contrast, were much more mundane—when they settled, current acreage of their farms, when and whom they had married, number of and names of children—almost as though they were following a template. There was also a stoic quality to the entries—very little heroism, nostalgia, or glorification of the past. This stood in sharp contrast to the new genre of county history that was already becoming popular throughout much of the Midwest. The so-called mug books abandoned the detailed township maps and lithographs of the illustrated atlas in favor of hugely expanded narrative and biographical sections devoted much more to promoting subscribers' egos.

The key dynamic shaping both the substance and the tone of the biographies in *The Illustrated Atlas and History of Yolo County*, by virtue of its conspicuous absence, was the gold rush. The unsuspecting reader, once again, would never have guessed that the vast majority of these individuals were lured westward by dreams of striking it rich. Instead, as stated in William Marden's sketch, they merely "came to California in 1850 and settled in Yolo County in 1851." As in Pierce's diaries, the defining moment in most of their lives seemed never to have happened. With a hole that gaping separating the present from the past, nostalgia did not come easily for these miners-turned-farmers. That may also be the reason why farmers in Yolo County and elsewhere in rural California rarely, if ever, formed the kinds of "Old Settler" societies and reunions that were so popular among contemporary midwesterners. Their present-day needs were better served by forgetting, rather than reliving, the glory days of El Dorado.[20]

Gilbert's history complemented the lithographs and biographies very nicely. Remarkably, it was largely devoid of the romanticism and hyperbole that dominated much of nineteenth-century historical writing. Local newspaper editors praised it for its careful research in land, court, school, church, and other county records; for correcting the "errors and inaccuracies" of a few earlier histories of the Sacramento Valley; and in general for being "reliable, full, accurate . . . and extremely interesting and instructive." Of course, Gilbert could not escape the narrow perceptions and ethnocentrism of his time when deciding what constituted history or who to include. He simply did not concern himself with Indian and Hispanic cultures or the experiences of women, laborers, and townspeople—only the "better men of Yolo County." Still, later historians found Gilbert's chapters on elections, schools, fraternal societies, churches, agriculture, stock raising, swamplands, and other matters very useful—and still do today.[21]

Among the "formidable array of authorities" whom Gilbert interviewed for his history, none proved more valuable than Charles Greene. Nor, by the same token, did any of the fifty "old settlers" who contributed, including eight from Putah Township, seek to influence Gilbert's history more than Charles Greene. Not wanting to risk any misunderstanding or ambiguity, Greene wrote down his recollections of early agriculture in the county in a long letter to Gilbert, the only one of the fifty to do so, and also gave Gilbert access to his daily journals from the 1850s and 1860s. Extended excerpts from both the letter and the journals, neither needing "any comment at our hand," Gilbert insisted, fill the pages of the three core chapters of his history.[22]

Greene was bound and determined to give the Big Ranch its just due. In a year-by-year account, he described the many accomplishments of Hutchinson, Greene, and Co. They put in operation the first gang plows in the county, the first reapers, the first threshing machines, and the first on-site blacksmith shop to build and repair their own machines. They raised the first crop of barley in 1852 and the first crop of wheat two years later. In considerable detail, Greene also recalled the yield of each harvest, the number of workers employed and their wages, and the prices paid by various Sacramento millers and brokers for each crop. Though he did not blame the volatile weather for the Big Ranch's financial problems, Greene's journal entries informed the discerning reader of the floods and droughts that farmers endured, as did Gilbert's detailed description of these disasters. Indeed, Greene did not explicitly mention any of the Big Ranch's numerous problems, except for the fire that destroyed the crop in 1852. He wanted the Big Ranch to be remembered only for marking "the commencement of agriculture in the county," and Gilbert obliged him.[23]

Greene did not avoid hardships and controversies altogether, however. He also contributed substantially to the Grange Movement, by far the most openly critical chapter in Gilbert's history. Having just won his lawsuit against Morgan's Sons but having lost much of his settlement to his attorneys, Greene seemed bent on deriving some measure of satisfaction by exposing every last detail of the sordid affair. Gilbert, once again, let Greene's account speak for itself. He praised farmers' efforts to combine their crops, charter their own vessels, and in general "get rid of the middlemen" in the wheat trade. The "wisdom" of this "co-operative united body," Gilbert maintained, revealed itself in no uncertain terms when sack prices fell dramatically in the early 1870s. Farmers then put their trust in Morgan's Sons to ship their crops but, through no fault of their own, "fell victim" to the company's unscrupulous business practices. With Greene's blessing, Gilbert printed a list of the "losers" from Yolo County and, down to the last penny, how much Morgan's Sons had "robbed" from them. The intent was not to embarrass (though one wonders if some on the list felt that way) or even just to publicize the outcome of the trial; it was to show the great resiliency of these "aggrieved" farmers. Their confidence in "this great and good cause" and in themselves, however "misplaced" it may have seemed, reflected "the spirit of the time" much more than their temporary lapse in judgment, Gilbert concluded. "I am not discouraged," he quoted one farmer as saying at the end of the chapter. The 3,500 sacks of wheat that this farmer lost to Morgan's Sons, however, suggests that he may only have been telling Gilbert what he wanted to hear.[24]

While Greene and Gilbert tried to put a good face on the Big Ranch and the Granger disaster, none of the contributors cared to look back from any angle at the land problems that had so befuddled them in the 1850s and 1860s. Rancho Laguna de Santos Callé and other Mexican land grants in the area received mention only in passing and without reference to the California Land Act of 1851, the long and trying hearings before the Land Commission, or the mass of confusion over titles that often resulted. Squatters were also nowhere to be found in the *Illustrated Atlas*. Migrants to the area "settled" as though the region had been wide open to homesteaders and preemptors. Even those patrons who were well known to have been squatters (and there were more than a few) refused to identify themselves as such. H. P. Merritt, for example, whose initial claim to fame was his involvement in the Willow Slough murder in 1860, paid for a half-page lithograph of his 2,000-acre stock farm but in his biography did not tell readers that he had squatted on that very site for more than ten years while waiting for title to Rancho Laguna de Santos Callé to be resolved. Nor did the county's largest landholders merit much, if any, attention. R. S. Carey and George W. Chapman, who owned more than 22,000 acres (most of it swampland) between them by 1880, played no role in Gilbert's history.[25]

Why, the question remains, were such matters of paramount importance to the county's history left out? Part of the answer can be found, perhaps, in the *Illustrated Atlas* itself—in the lithographs, in particular. The image of neatness, order, and progress that farmers wanted to project to themselves and outsiders might well have been muddied by long depictions of their messy land problems. But there had to be more to this omission than meets the eye. It could not have been simply to shield subscribers' egos from unpleasant memories or humbling experiences. After all, Greene, Drummond, Chiles, or just about any of the patrons could have turned their early land struggles into epic tales of persistence triumphing over turmoil on the frontier. Gilbert, in fact, did just that in his detailed descriptions of farmers coping with the great flood and drought of the early 1860s, yet he all but avoided their land problems.[26]

One reason he might have done so was that squatters and Anglo grant claimants were not faring well in the larger histories that were just then appearing from California's first generation of historians. In the eyes of John Hittell and, shortly thereafter, Hubert Howe Bancroft and Josiah Royce, the disputes over land titles that marked the first two decades of statehood left a permanent stain of social irresponsibility on California. They sympathized with the plight of the Mexican grantees and portrayed the "American intruders" as greedy men bent on defying authority and obstructing justice. Above all, they associated Anglo settlers with the violence and "immorality" that characterized the Sacramento squatter riot of 1850, as depicted in the sensational newspaper accounts upon which they relied. "Squatterism," concluded Bancroft, was "only a phase of mob law"— hardly a view that someone like H. P. Merritt would have wanted to embrace. Indeed, evidence of the more enterprising and less confrontational squatters of Putah Creek remained buried in the assessment rolls and county court case files that nineteenth-century historians (and most of their successors in the twentieth century) did not examine.[27]

As for large landholders, contemporary sentiments did not bode well for them either. While most everything big was good in the 1850s—the Big Ranch, at least on the surface, being a prime example—large landholders had become the bane of existence in the 1870s. Social critics, strongly influenced by the writings of San

Francisco journalist Henry George, decried the "problem of monopoly" in rural California. Inspired at the beginning of the decade by George's first major work, *Our Land and Land Policy, National and State* (1871), and at the end by his classic *Progress and Poverty* (1879), reformers debated ways to break up giant holdings—from graduated land taxes, to restrictions on the amount of land that could be inherited, to direct limitations on the size of farms. Putah Creek ranchers scoffed at such proposals, as did most state lawmakers in the end. Cultivation of 160-acre homesteads (some critics allowed for 320) may have suited conditions in the Midwest, they argued, but such homesteads were unworkable for purposes of grazing or wheat farming in the Sacramento Valley. Large tracts—which the *Sacramento Daily Union* defined as "500 acres and upwards" in 1873—were essential for these agricultural pursuits. The vast majority of wheat farmers were not "land grabbers," insisted the *Yolo County Democrat* in defense of its readers against George's "rants," but "productive contributors to the General Welfare of the State." As for Carey, Chapman, and other truly large (however defined) landholders in their midst, local farmers tended to turn a blind eye. Land monopoly, in their minds, was a problem that existed elsewhere, in the concentrated holdings of Hugh Glenn, Henry Miller and Charles Lux, and William Chapman, not in Yolo County. As one newspaper editor put it, "Everybody is opposed to all species of monopoly except their own."[28]

There was one other reason, by far the most tangible, why farmers chose not to address their earlier land problems: they did not want to call attention to what they feared might develop into a public scandal. As production for the *Illustrated Atlas* proceeded, more than a hundred landowners north of Putah Creek, all of whom *thought* they could trace their titles back to Rancho Laguna de Santos Callé, found themselves in the middle of a series of lawsuits that called into question their very property rights. Having long ago thought to have put their troubles with Mexican land grants behind them, Putah Creek farmers had to look back at that turbulent time once more, whether they wanted to or not.

That turbulent time took its toll on just about everyone, but none more than E. L. Brown. The once proud purchaser of a large claim on the north bank of Putah Creek, with the Big Ranch on one side and the Davis stock farm on the other, Brown never recovered from the financial problems that prompted creditors to seize all but 200 acres of his estate in the late 1850s. He and his son, William, tried to hold on, but could not withstand the devastation of the great flood of 1862. After selling their farm, William fled to the Comstock silver mines in Nevada, while his father remained in the area as a laborer. The founding of Davisville in

1868 gave the elder Brown a chance to reestablish himself. He purchased a lot, opened a saloon, became an Odd Fellow, and joined the Presbyterian church. When his neighbors elected him to the office of Justice of the Peace in October 1869, Brown seemed to regain his self-respect. For four years, he was "Judge Brown," with farmers and townspeople alike praising his "commitment and good sense." But when he lost his bid for reelection by just a few votes in the spring of 1874, Brown found himself devastated once again. He began telling friends that he "was tired of life" and wanted to "put himself out of the way." On November 12, he committed suicide by taking poison.[29]

Still in Nevada, William rushed back to Davisville upon receiving the news to settle his father's estate. Brown's assets totaled $700, which turned out to be $27 short of covering his debts and expenses. Before paying the balance, William rode to Woodland to examine his father's land records at the county courthouse. There, in Deed Book A, were his father's two purchases from the summer of 1851—one from Charles De Pendray for half his interest in Rancho Laguna de Santos Callé, the other from Juan Manuel Vaca and Juan Felipe Peña for 980 acres in Rancho Los Putos on the north bank of Putah Creek. Joseph B. Chiles, Brown noticed, had also purchased his league from Vaca and Peña. Wait a minute, he thought; that did not make any sense. Everyone knew that Vaca and Peña's Rancho Los Putos had been located south of Putah Creek while Marcos Vaca and Victor Prudon's Rancho Laguna de Santos Callé lay to the north. The county recorder seemed to verify that when he told Brown that he would have to go to the Solano County courthouse in Fairfield to find copies of the Los Putos survey papers.[30]

Brown made the trip the next day, but to his surprise somebody already had the papers when he asked to see them. David Bouldin was also looking into the affairs of his recently deceased father, who had also purchased several hundred acres of a Mexican land grant in Solano County in the early 1850s without ever acquiring title. Bouldin recommended that Brown talk to his lawyer, John B. Mhoon, whose firm (Mhoon and Flournoy) specialized in such matters. Mhoon was skeptical at first because Bouldin had not been able to produce his father's original deeds, but he agreed to ride with Brown back to Woodland to look at county documents and, a few weeks later, to San Francisco to examine the records of the Land Commission. To his astonishment, he found everything he needed to mount a lawsuit of mammoth proportions. The only problem, he told Brown, was that it promised to be very costly. Frustrated by his own case, Bouldin decided that perhaps the best way to honor his father would be to help Brown. He fronted him $5,000 in exchange for half of Brown's settlement, should he win his lawsuit.[31]

Mhoon took Brown through their case step by step. Everything rested on the

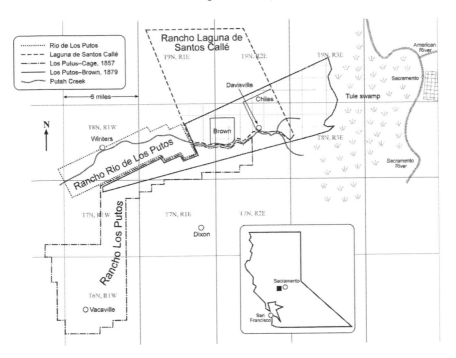

Putah Creek land grants, including William W. Brown's version of Rancho Los Putos. Based on the map in U.S. Land Department, Office of the U.S. Surveyor-General of the State of California, "In the Matter of the Rancho Los Putos . . . Applicants' Brief" (San Francisco: Spaulding, Barto & Co., 1879), Los Putos docket.

fact that Rancho Los Putos had been surveyed incorrectly in 1857. The key document was the settlement that Vaca and Peña had reached with William Wolfskill back in 1845 to resolve their dispute over the boundary between Rancho Los Putos and Rancho Rio de los Putos. While the two grants had previously overlapped each other (the *diseños* were even difficult to tell apart), Los Putos now would be defined directly in relation to Rio de los Putos—"on the margins of the river adjourning at the east the Rancho of Guillermo Wolfskill." That meant, Mhoon emphasized, "that the Vaca Grant should be to the east of the Wolfskill Grant, and should be on the margins of Putah Creek, the two sides. It says 'margins'—the plural—of Putah Creek." When Rio de los Putos was surveyed by Henry Hancock, first in 1852 and again in 1857, when the patent was issued, the northern boundary of Los Putos should have been determined by the so-called Wolfskill line—his northern boundary extended eastward.

Complicating matters all the more, Mhoon continued, the original grant papers in 1842 specified that Rio de los Putos contained equal portions of land north and south of Putah Creek. This had posed quite a problem for Hancock. Because the creek meandered to the north as it flowed through Wolfskill's grant, he had to tilt his survey to the north, about twenty-six degrees above the true east-west axis. The Wolfskill line, therefore, extended not due east, but northeastward, right through the heart of what had been considered Laguna de Santos Callé, north of the land that Brown and Chiles had purchased from Vaca and Peña. That land, Mhoon insisted, had been part of Los Putos all along and thus should have been included in Dewitt C. Cage's official survey of 1857. By Mhoon's reasoning, upwards of two-thirds of Los Putos—roughly 31,000 acres—lay *north* of Putah Creek.[32]

At the very least, Mhoon thought initially, Brown ought to be given the opportunity to purchase, at the government minimum of $1.25 per acre, the 980-acre tract that Vaca and Peña had deeded his father. The Conness Act of 1866, after all, gave that option to those who had purchased grant land but were "left out" of the final survey. Upon further study, however, Mhoon decided to try for more—much more. Had Los Putos been surveyed correctly, he asked himself, who rightfully should have held title to this 31,000-acre mass of land? The answer, he found, lay in an agreement dated December 8, 1851. The signers—E. L. Brown, C. I. Hutchinson, Joshua Bailey, Joseph B. Chiles, Jerome C. Davis, Gabriel Brown, Simon Lettner, and Nathaniel Sharp—were well aware that ranchos Los Putos and Laguna de Santos Callé covered much of the same ground north of Putah Creek. On that day, they agreed "to make certain concessions each to the other, for the purpose of avoiding difficulty and dispute." They recognized all previous purchases from both Los Putos and Laguna de Santos Callé north of Putah Creek and agreed to hold the unclaimed land as tenants in common, primarily for grazing purposes. Had the land been surveyed correctly six years later, Mhoon concluded, title would have reverted back to those eight men who had either claimed under Los Putos or been tenants in common under this agreement. Each would have been entitled to the possession of an undivided one-eighth interest. The current landowners—all 105 of them—were, in effect, "unlawfully withholding the possession from these individuals." Mhoon urged Brown to file suit against every last one of them. Demand the land, he counseled, but settle for its value.[33]

Determined to make sense of his father's suicide and convinced by the logic and sheer boldness of Mhoon's plan, Brown gave his lawyer permission to proceed. Mhoon's first course of action was to hire Vitus Wackenreuder, a surveyor experienced with Mexican grants, to draw up a detailed, professional map of the *real* Los Putos as determined by the Wolfskill line. Mhoon then had to decide on the proper venue and figured it would be best to avoid Yolo County altogether and file at a neutral site—the Twelfth District Court for the City and County of San Francisco. He also contacted the other seven tenants in common to see if they were interested in joining the suit. Not one wanted anything to do with it. Six of the seven, however, gladly took the $100 that Mhoon offered in exchange for their deed to Brown for "all their remaining interest to Vaca and Peña lands north of Putah Creek." The seventh, Jerome C. Davis, found the scheme "ludicrous" and told Mhoon that he would not relive that particular time in his life for any amount of money. Charles Greene, upon hearing of the deeds, called them "utterly worthless" and Brown a "menace" to the community. Fine, both Brown and Mhoon thought. Their suit, filed in San Francisco on March 3, 1875, demanded all seven-eighths of the land in question, listed Greene as first defendant, and named Bouldin co-plaintiff. *Brown v. Greene* had begun.[34]

Neither Greene nor the other 104 defendants took the case very seriously at first. Any judge with an ounce of sense, they thought, would see the absurdity of Mhoon's argument. That it took Mhoon two years to prepare his case left the defendants all the more complacent. In the spring of 1877, Mhoon carefully and methodically presented the judge with all the pertinent documents from the previous thirty-three years, including the original grant petitions and *diseños*, the 1845 agreement between Wolfskill and Vaca and Peña, the trail of deeds from the early 1850s, the "fraudulent" Cage survey, and finally, with the drama mounting, Wackenreuder's "corrected" map. The defendants merely demurred, still confident that the plaintiffs had no case. The judge seemed to agree when he hesitated to rule on whether Brown and Bouldin should be awarded seven-eighths of the 31,000 acres in question. But Mhoon's more general argument that Cage had surveyed Rancho Los Putos incorrectly in 1857 persuaded, indeed bewildered, the judge. On December 14, 1877, after several weeks of deliberation, he declared the "perplexing case" a federal matter and transferred it to the U.S. Circuit Court (Ninth Circuit) in San Francisco.[35]

While the plaintiffs declared victory, the defendants scrambled to respond. Spurred into action by the district judge's ruling and fearful now that the plaintiffs could "shake their very titles," the defendants held a meeting in Davisville to decide what to do. On the insistence of Greene and R. S. Carey, they hired J. H. McKune, one of the more prominent attorneys in the Sacramento Valley, to represent them—agreeing to defray expenses pro rata on the basis of their property taxes from the previous year. McKune not only prepared their defense but also filed a countersuit to recover damages from lost property values caused by the plaintiffs' "inflammatory insinuations." But if McKune thought he could scare

Brown, Bouldin, and Mhoon with his aggressive action, he was mistaken. Both attorneys laid out their cases in federal court in February 1878. As in the San Francisco district court two months earlier, the federal judge knew that the easy way out was to dismiss Mhoon's claims, but he could not in good conscience find fault with his reasoning. Rather than make a ruling, however, he ordered the plaintiffs to go upstairs (literally) to the U.S. surveyor general's office and petition for a new survey of Rancho Los Putos.[36]

Then, before the surveyor general, Mhoon once again presented the case, document by document, and once again, McKune refuted it, point by point. At first, the plaintiffs appeared to have found an even more sympathetic audience. "There is no question in my mind," wrote Surveyor General Theodore Wagner on July 10, 1878, "that the land surveyed and patented as the Rancho Los Putos is not the land described in the decree of confirmation of that rancho, and I am at a loss to account for the manner in which this survey of said rancho has been made." But Wagner was also at a loss as to what to do about it. Literally hundreds of transactions, after all, had been made in good faith over the years based not on the plaintiffs' version of Los Putos but on Cage's survey, however inaccurate. "It would be a great hardship," he stated, "to disturb those rights." But he, too, then insisted that the case was outside his jurisdiction and kicked it upstairs (metaphorically this time) to the secretary of the interior in Washington, D.C., who threw up his hands as well. The issues at hand, he declared on May 31, 1880, "can only be contested in the Courts having jurisdiction thereof."[37]

This was not what Brown, Bouldin, and Mhoon wanted to hear. The secretary's ruling left them with only one option—the hostile environment of the newly established Yolo County Superior Court.[38] Greene, Carey, and the other defendants, on the other hand, were so energized by the turn of events that McKune filed their countersuit at the courthouse in Woodland several weeks before Mhoon. Both sides agreed to try the two cases concurrently and without a jury. The trial took over two years, with both lawyers pulling out all the stops. In addition to once again laying out all the petitions, deeds, and other documents, both sides also called a number of witnesses—including Brown, Wackenreuder, Greene, and Jerome C. Davis—a strategy that, not surprisingly, favored the defense. With 105 landowners in danger of losing their property should Mhoon's version of Los Putos prevail, the trial quickly became a local cause célèbre, with seemingly everyone in the county focused on the proceedings and recalling their own version of events.[39]

Looking back proved particularly painful for Brown, who spent several hours on the witness stand, mostly under cross-examination. With a large crowd spilling out of the courtroom onto the streets of Woodland, McKune picked apart Brown's testimony bit by bit. In excruciating detail, Brown reluctantly recounted his father's legal and financial struggles. If all but 200 acres of his land "had passed to another party," McKune asked Brown incredulously, "how can you now, twenty-five years later, make any claim to the property?" Brown offered no response. "Did you or your father," continued McKune, "try to convince federal authorities *at the time* that the Cage survey ought to be located so as to include the land north of the Putah?" "No," answered Brown. "Mr. Brown," McKune asked, "why did not you and E. L. Brown proceed to get your title under the Conness Act, or the special Act passed for the Laguna Santos Callé, while the others were getting them?" "I was absent from the State," Brown could only reply. And so the questioning proceeded. Brown stepped off the stand thoroughly humiliated and, so it seemed, thoroughly defeated.[40]

Brown, however, was not the only witness who had a rough time on the stand. So too did Jerome Davis. Subpoenaed by the defense to testify against Brown, Davis traveled from Sacramento to the Woodland courthouse in December 1880. By all accounts, he had not set foot in Yolo County in almost twelve years. McKune's intent was to first establish Davis as "the most public figure" along Putah Creek at the time and then to have him describe his relationship with Brown's father. For a while, Davis seemed to enjoy the moment. "It was not certain as to who owned the land," he recalled, but that did not stop him from developing his prize-winning stock farm. He admitted to having been tenants in common with Brown but only "up to a time." "He had an interest in the whole thing until the Sheriff sold him out," Davis stated, referring to his former neighbor's mortgage foreclosures. After McKune built up Davis's reputation, Mhoon then tried to tear it down to undermine his testimony. Under cross-examination, Davis reluctantly recounted his struggles to confirm Rancho Laguna de Santos Callé, his swampland troubles, his financial collapse, and the sale of his property to "the Railroad people." He, too, left the courtroom humiliated and distraught. Though it may have only been a coincidence, Davis died in Sacramento just a few weeks later.[41]

Though the trial had been a disaster for his client, Mhoon did not give up. The judge decreed in no uncertain terms that "the plaintiffs take nothing by their said action," but he unintentionally left them an opening. In his zeal to "put an end and a finality to these proceedings," the judge denounced every last argument that Mhoon had made, including two in particular that were undeniably true. Brown, Bailey, Hutchinson, and the others, the judge insisted, "never at any time" agreed to become tenants in common. And Rancho Los Putos, he claimed, "never at any time" contained land north of Putah Creek. Armed with plenty of evidence to the contrary, Mhoon filed an appeal with the California Supreme Court for a new trial. There, the ordeal seemed finally to come to an end, perhaps fittingly, on a technicality. Immersed in the details of preparing his case, Mhoon failed to officially notify his adversary of the appeal within one year of the judgment and, as a result, gave the court no alternative but to dismiss the case, which it did on May 8, 1884.[42]

Still, Mhoon refused to give up, especially with his own reputation now on the line. On May 27, 1885, he appealed to the U.S. Supreme Court, claiming that the writ of error issued the previous year was his fault, not that of his clients, who still deserved a fair hearing. When the highest court in the land turned him down Mhoon, in one last desperate attempt, went back to the secretary of the interior who, in turn, threw the case back in the lap of the U.S. surveyor general of California. Clearly annoyed—"I have already rendered a ruling on this," he complained—the surveyor general sat on the case for two full years. At last, on March 19, 1887, he declared "the whole matter to be *res judicata*" (a thing adjudicated), thus finally, if anticlimactically, bringing down the curtain on the long drama of *Brown v. Greene*, twelve years after it had begun.[43]

Charles Greene did not live to witness the final resolution of the case that bore his name—nor did about a third of the other 104 defendants. Another third did not survive far into the next decade. Indeed, in the fifteen years since Montgomery's death in 1877, roughly two-thirds of the first generation of Putah Creek farmers died. "Another pioneer gone," the local newspapers bemoaned seemingly week after week—L. C. Drummond on April 23, 1882; Joseph B. Chiles, June 25, 1885; Greene, July 10, 1886; Bartlett Guthrie, April 27, 1887; James T. Lillard, January 7, 1889; Pierce, February 24, 1890; and so on down the list. On more than a few occasions, a pallbearer at one funeral became the deceased at the next. The Davisville cemetery, a small, unkempt lot before 1885, had to hire a full-time superintendent to attend to "the business of death," care for the grounds, and polish the "newly-erected costly monuments" that had become "increasingly conspicuous."

Thus, even before the surveyor general put *Brown v. Greene* to rest, fewer and fewer farmers were paying much attention any more. The case seemed cut-and-dried and Mhoon's appeals, in the words of one observer, were "downright silly." Moreover, the new generation that emerged in the 1880s was not all that interested in looking back. The trial was over, the *Illustrated Atlas of Yolo County* was gathering dust on subscribers' bookshelves, and pondering the past seemed to serve little purpose. The gold rush, perhaps most importantly, no longer shaped this new generation's outlook on life—or so it appeared. New dreams took hold in the last two decades of the nineteenth century and, along with them, a host of new problems as well. Even with all the changes, however, fathers and sons had much more in common than they cared to admit.[44]

PART FOUR

THE NEW GENERATION EMERGES

CHAPTER ELEVEN

Gold—Wheat—Fruit

While plowing the family's new, enlarged vineyard on "the overflowed land" along the creek in May 1885, George Pierce Jr. suddenly heard a loud clank. He stopped and walked over to remove the large rocks that he presumed had impeded his progress. He found not only rocks but several other large objects that looked like bone fragments. It was not unusual for farmers near Putah Creek to plow up portions of old Patwin burial grounds, but these bones looked much too large to be human. Believing his discovery might be "of scientific value," Pierce contacted Professor George Davidson, the renowned geographer, whom he had met in Berkeley at a recent university gathering. Anxious to see what Pierce had found, Davidson took the next train to Davisville. As soon as he saw the fragments, he knew they were extraordinary. Though he could not be certain just yet, Davidson believed the remains were "of some extinct animal"—perhaps even a mastodon. When Pierce plowed up a lower jaw bone "in an almost perfect state" several months later, Davidson confirmed his hypothesis. The "creature" caused quite a sensation, as visitors rode out to the Pierce ranch in droves to catch a glimpse. Soon thereafter, Pierce donated his findings to the California Academy of Sciences in San Francisco, where the "Putah Creek mastodon" remained on display for several years.[1]

Locally, the excitement took farmers' minds off their problems, but only for a short time. The wheat market continued to confound them. In 1884, they grew more wheat than ever before—almost 10 percent more than in 1880, the previous record-breaking year, and 35 percent more than in the boom of 1873. Every farmer took great pride in knowing that California had been the nation's leading wheat-producing state five times between 1872 and 1884. Nor was shipping a problem. In response to the increased production, nine firms established a new state-of-the-art warehousing and loading complex at Port Costa, across Carquinez Strait from Vallejo and Benicia. "Demand will never cease so long as there are mouths to feed in other lands," both farmers and shippers continued to declare.

Yet, prices continued to fall, year after year, down to $1.25 per cental in 1884 and $1.20 in 1885. More and more farmers began to ask the question none of them wanted to hear: "Does it pay to raise wheat, our bread and butter for so long?"[2]

Their answers split them along generational lines. "Old-timers" argued that the market had bottomed out and that wheat would surely "reign king in our district" again. For their sons, however, the question was more complicated. They feared that the bottom had in fact dropped out of the market. Wheat's price decline, moreover, came just as they were beginning to emerge from their fathers' shadows. They were determined, as one put it, to look forward with "fresh energy and clear vision." For years, their fathers had tended small orchards and vineyards to supplement their grain incomes. Although the new generation did not abandon wheat in the 1880s and 1890s, they turned increasingly to fruits and nuts both as cash crops and as the means to cultivate their own identities.[3]

The younger Pierce was enlarging his vineyard for those very reasons when his plow unearthed the Putah Creek mastodon. It was "a stroke of good fortune," he later recalled, that the same soils that preserved the great prehistoric beast produced such bountiful and diverse crops. Pierce's choice of words was telling. Though a generation removed from the "days of '49," he and his neighbors still spoke the language of the gold rush. They had inherited their fathers' dreams of striking it rich in California, and they pursued those dreams with equal, perhaps even greater, passion. With boldness and a little luck (not necessarily in that order), they still believed that they could succeed materially and, just as importantly, bring stability and prosperity to their community. Thus, as they dramatically transformed agriculture along Putah Creek, they also preserved the strong cultural ties that linked them to the previous generation—more so than they realized. A gold-wheat-fruit continuum, in other words, transcended generational conflicts and marked the gradual but determined shift from staple- to specialty-crop production.[4]

"Bread the world must have." So spoke one Davisville farmer in 1891, capturing the mindset of most wheat farmers in the region. They were well aware of "the depressed state of the wheat market" that began in the late 1870s, but found it difficult to come to terms with the realization that the fruits of their success often proved bitter. In their day-to-day lives, wheat farming remained tantalizingly seductive. In the midst of this steady decline in prices, political developments, technological innovation, and new shipping facilities actually encouraged farmers to produce to their hearts' content. Their success blinded them to the harsh realities of global supply and demand—not only the simple economics of overproduction but also the fact that farmers elsewhere in the United States and thousands of miles away in Europe, Asia, South America, and Australia were beating them at their own game.[5]

In politics, particularly at the state level, Davisville farmers benefitted quite handsomely, even though they were in large part nonparticipants. Still fuming over the Morgan's Sons debacle, they avoided the Grange like the plague, even as the Patrons of Husbandry exerted considerable influence, including elsewhere in Yolo and Solano counties. Granger participation in state politics proved much more potent than their more direct efforts to break Isaac Friedlander's shipping and sack monopolies. A Grange-inspired third party movement—the People's Independent Party, or "Dolly Vardens," as dubbed by their critics—made significant inroads during the 1870s, especially in a special election held in 1879 to ratify a new state constitution. This extraordinarily long and extremely detailed document (one of world's longest and most complex constitutions) had something for everyone. It embodied many of the reforms demanded by the Grange over the course of the decade, chief among them a new railroad commission and changes in the state's tax structure.[6]

Wheat farmers stood to gain from both measures. The new constitution declared railroads "subject to legislative control" by establishing a three-member commission elected by the voters and endowed with the power to set maximum transportation rates. Overall railroad rates did fall in the 1880s, though probably because of increased competition and more efficient operations rather than the commission's power to regulate. That distinction was not important to Davisville farmers, who, as one put it, "cherished the opportunity to put money back into our farms [rather] than give it to the Central Pacific." The new constitution also transferred mortgage tax obligations from borrowers to lenders, significantly lowering most farmers' annual payments. Pierce, for example, paid just $41 in taxes after deducting his mortgage in 1880, as compared to $478 two years earlier. In time, lenders would simply raise their interest to a rate large enough to cover their new tax obligation, but for at least the first half of the decade, farmers' tax burden became considerably lighter. Pierce and his neighbors in Putah Township, who viewed the new constitution as the handiwork of the Grange and, worse yet, of Denis Kearney and other "radical San Francisco insurgents" in the Workingmen's Party of California, voted almost two-to-one against it. That did not stop them, however, from reaping the benefits it provided and growing more wheat.[7]

In addition to taxes and railroad rates, harvest costs also dropped considerably for wheat farmers—by as much as half over the course of the decade. Though estimates (and boasts) varied widely, figures from the Pierce ranch seemed typical for Davisville farmers. In 1884, Pierce Sr.'s accounts revealed that harvest costs, including reaping, threshing, labor, and sacks, came to about $3.30 per acre. Five years later, Pierce Jr. harvested the crop for just $1.75. The difference was that Pierce Jr. purchased a Best combined harvester in May 1888—"a Jack-of-all-trades implement," as a contemporary described it, "that cuts, threshes, separates, re-cleans, and sacks the wheat at one operation."[8]

The combined harvester, or simply "combine," had been around since at least the 1850s—the Pierces themselves saw one on display at the state fair in Sacramento in 1868. But the many drawbacks of the machine, not the least of which were its massive size (about twenty tons), hefty price tag ($2,500), and frequent breakdowns, scared farmers away. The low prices they received for the bountiful harvest of 1884, however, convinced many that the best, if not only, way to increase their profit margins was to cut production costs. Competition among several manufacturers in the state brought down the price (by about $800), but the machine's bulk still made it very difficult to navigate. Before Pierce could put his combine to work, for example, he had to widen all the gates in his fences to get from one field to the next. While cumbersome, the combine's great advantage was that it allowed farmers to substitute horsepower for manpower. It required the services of twenty to thirty horses both to pull it and to rotate the wheels that operated the machinery, but only three or four men to manage it. The result, in one farmer's words, was "less waste in handling, no fire risk from steam threshers, and a great economy of labor." Few doubted the machine's efficiency. "It has been asserted, and probably truthfully," remarked one writer, "that wheat has been harvested, flour made of it, and bread made of that and eaten at breakfast the same morning, all within a few hours."[9]

Because of its high purchase price, however, the combine still took some selling. Daniel Best, whose San Leandro–based company (along with Benjamin Holt's Stockton firm) dominated sales in northern California, knew just what to do. In the mid-1880s, he toured wheat communities in the Sacramento Valley, not with the intent of making sales himself but to find others to sell his combines for him. The best person, he believed, would have deep roots in the community, ambition, and his neighbors' utmost respect. In Davisville, Best found his man in George Pierce Jr. He first contacted Pierce in February 1886 and asked him to try out one of his combines to see how he liked it. Amazed by what the machine could do, Pierce not only bought one (for $1,650) but also agreed to become Best's "local agent." He sold four in 1887, fourteen in 1888, and by 1890, a reported two-thirds of all farmers in the region had purchased a Best combined harvester. Pierce helped buyers unpack their machines, set them up, start them, and fix

Best combined harvester on the Pierce ranch, 1891. Pierce Family Papers, Department of Special Collections, University of California Library, Davis.

them. To generate still more interest, he entered one of them at the state fair in 1890 and won a first premium and a gold medal. Once one's neighbor had one of these "mighty harvesters," as Pierce called them, they were difficult to resist. Just about everyone went deeper in debt to buy one, including several smaller farmers and tenants who pooled their resources together to share ownership— all of them determined to grow more wheat. In 1889, under optimal conditions, they grew almost as much as they had in 1884.[10]

Davisville farmers also took advantage of the "lively competition" among local grain merchants over the course of the decade. After William Dresbach left in 1879, no one firm dominated the local market. Three grain dealers operated shipping houses and general stores in Davisville along the tracks just north of the depot: Henry Stelling, a Tremont farmer who took over the abandoned Granger warehouse and moved into Dresbach's old mansion; William Bullard, a former employee of Dresbach's; and Malford Drummond, son of one of the region's prominent pioneers, who later formed a partnership with B. F. Ligget. Farmers could also sell their wheat to merchants in Dixon, Winters, Woodland, and Merritt's Station. Most, such as Pierce Jr., spent several days every year shopping around for the best deal, not only for selling their wheat but for purchasing sacks, twine, insurance, and other merchandise as well.[11]

Even greater changes took place among the ranks of the middlemen further down the tracks. By 1884, Davisville wheat, along with most of the state's grain, no longer passed through San Francisco, where Isaac Friedlander had reigned the previous two decades. Nine firms now exported wheat to the United Kingdom directly from the waterfront at Port Costa, a booming shipping center on the south shore of Carquinez Strait. George Washington McNear, the grain broker who many said came closest to inheriting Friedlander's mantle, led the way. Seeking to avoid high hauling, transfer, and port charges at San Francisco, one of the most expensive ports in the world, McNear opened the Port Costa Warehouse and Dock Company in 1881. The enterprise provided storage for 55,000 tons of grain and room for at least nine ships to load. The other warehousing concerns, some of them with even larger capacities, came in quick succession. Seemingly overnight, grain dealers in Liverpool spoke of their ships leaving Port Costa, not San Francisco, and for good reason—it had become the leading wheat port on the west coast.[12]

The southern shore of Carquinez Strait seemed a most unlikely location for the new facilities. There had been no previous development in the area, where hills rose steeply from the water's edge to heights of 700 feet, leaving no room, it appeared, for warehouses or wharves. Adapting to the awkward shoreline location, McNear and his associates constructed, out over the water, long, narrow warehouses, each measuring only 100 feet wide but up to 3,000 feet from end to end. They looked more like tunnels than granaries. One contemporary, from his vantage point on the other side of the strait, wrote that "the long rows of buildings" seemed to "cling to the hillsides, in constant danger of falling."[13]

Yet, when McNear first stood at this inhospitable setting early in 1880, he thought that building the new port was well worth the gamble. The state's main arteries of transportation, he knew, were about to converge at this deep, narrow channel. As the only navigable waterway connecting California's two great interior valleys with the sea, Carquinez Strait provided the only outlet for water traffic on the Sacramento and San Joaquin rivers. Moreover, there had been just enough level ground along the south side of the channel for the Central Pacific to lay its tracks two years earlier as part of a new route from Stockton, in the San Joaquin Valley, to Oakland. Shortly thereafter, the existing line to the north between Sacramento and Vallejo (the old California Pacific) was rerouted to a new terminus at Benicia, across Carquinez Strait from where McNear stood. The last piece of the puzzle was a long rail ferry across the channel (one of the longest in the world at the time), linking the two lines and in the process creating a more fully integrated system of transportation for northern California. Four-fifths of all the state's wheat could now be funneled to this new deep-water port, where ocean-bound ships could be loaded simultaneously from river barges, on one side, and railroad cars, on the other. Once success touched McNear's new enterprise, warehouse after warehouse followed at Port Costa. In the 1880s, it was not unusual for dozens of ships to be docked for loading and anchored in the strait waiting for wharf space, with long lines of railroads delivering carload after carload of wheat—literally millions of sacks, year after year.[14]

The success of this unique and unlikely port revitalized wheat farming not only in Davisville but around the state as well. The combination of lower freight charges and competition between shippers, the *Yolo Weekly Mail* predicted, would bring farmers higher prices for their wheat. Of even greater significance, Port Costa generated "an excitement in wheat" that had been largely missing since the boom years of the early 1870s. "Having fallen into a very bad way, wheat is on its way back," proclaimed the *Pacific Rural Press*. "We now have a port," declared Pierce, "worthy of our superior grain." "We cannot help believing," wrote another farmer, "that our wheat culture is yet in its infancy, and that the next twenty or forty years will witness great development in industry and large increase in our wheat crops."[15]

All the optimism in the world, however, could not stem the tide of low prices. Wheat farmers yearned for the days of $2.00 per cental, which they had received as late as 1878. From that year on, however, there was an almost steady downward movement. As prices at the end of the 1880s hovered at just over $1.00 per cental, which most equated with the cost of production, the "excitement in wheat" stemming from lower freight rates and taxes, the combine, and Port Costa began to wane. When local prices plummeted to 73 cents in 1894, even the most hopeful farmers had to concede that, as one writer put it succinctly, "wheat does not pay." That same writer felt it necessary to rush to record the history of wheat in California that year, "before it has faded from our memories."[16]

Part of the reason for wheat's precipitous decline can be traced directly to Port Costa. McNear and the other shippers did save large sums of money by leaving San Francisco; they did not, however, pass those savings on to farmers, as many had hoped. Instead, they wielded their power recklessly and, in the process, exerted a tremendously disruptive influence on California's wheat market. Most damaging were the six separate attempts between 1882 and 1895 to corner the market on wheat. The idea was to capitalize on their prime location on Carquinez Strait by attempting to buy up northern California's entire wheat supply and then hold it for higher prices from merchants overseas.

The most notorious of these attempts, in 1887, involved John Rosenfeld of the

Nevada Warehouse and Dock Company at Port Costa and none other than William Dresbach, now President of the San Francisco Produce Exchange. To secure the wheat, they drove tidewater prices back up to the magical $2.00 per cental mark in mid summer—$2.17 at their peak—a staggering 80 cents more than Liverpool buyers were offering. Few farmers celebrated, however. By the time most of them harvested their crop, the bubble had burst. Panicky bankers, realizing how much Rosenfeld and Dresbach had inflated prices, cut off their credit. Once word got out that the corner was off, prices plummeted back to just over $1.00, well below the Liverpool price. No one could determine exactly how much Dresbach, Rosenfeld, and other speculators in the "wheat ring" had lost in this dubious venture, though the *San Francisco Chronicle* estimated "millions and millions of dollars."[17]

"When a big tree falls," the *Chronicle* added, "it carries with it the small trees in its path." Such was the case in Davisville. As the price of wheat began to climb in the spring of 1887, optimism filled the air once again. A "lively competition" developed among the town's three grain merchants, all of whom greatly reduced storage costs, gave large advances, and offered farmers "attractive prices" for their wheat. When the flurry in the market came to an abrupt end, however, Bullard, Stelling, and Drummond and Ligget were left holding the bag. All three firms fell deeply into the red, and one of them, Bullard's, did not recover. With liabilities totaling $132,000 and with little hope of climbing out of debt with wheat prices so low, Bullard filed for insolvency. The others held on, though Drummond and Ligget went under in 1894 after McNear tried to run a corner himself with similar results. The "Dresbach Failure" also wreaked havoc on Davisville farmers, most of whom received far less for their wheat than they had anticipated. Many, expecting a big payoff, took out mortgages and loans that kept them in financial straits for years to come. There was also an emotional cost. Having had their hopes and dreams revived when prices climbed over $2.00 that July, farmers could only watch in agony when the market crashed a few days later. "We are tired of wheat," one groaned.[18]

Far more damaging to farmers' collective psyche and their pocketbooks, though far less tangible to them, was the competition they faced from within the United States and from at least a dozen other wheat-producing countries. The opening up of millions of acres of fresh grain lands around the world in the 1880s was unquestionably the primary reason for the fall of prices. The wheat belt on the western edge of the Midwest, from North Dakota down to Kansas and into northern Texas, began to take shape and by the turn of the century would produce nearly three-fifths of the nation's total crop and a sizeable surplus. Pacific Northwest wheat, which had to be shipped from San Francisco at great expense before the northern transcontinental railroads were built and before the dredging of the Columbia River eased transportation difficulties, became an important factor in the Liverpool trade. India, Argentina, Russia, Australia, Canada, and several other countries, taking advantage of improved internal transportation, low oceanic freight rates, cheap labor, and high yields, not to mention techniques and machines imported from California, sent huge surpluses to Britain over the course of the decade. As one astute observer noted in 1894, "the wheat harvest is going on every day somewhere on the globe." California farmers often complained that there was "no war nor any famine" in Europe at the time to drive up prices, not realizing the full extent of the problem.[19]

Indeed, having long watched their wheat leave the Davisville depot for Port Costa, whence it sailed out the Golden Gate to the United Kingdom, local farmers still clung to their fundamental assumption that supply somehow created its own demand. Ironically, the worldwide depression of the mid-1890s reinforced that fallacy in their minds. The economy, they felt, was bound to recover, and when it did, so too would the wheat market. The vast majority of Davisville farmers, though tired of "ruinous prices," as Pierce put it, continued to grow wheat. In the meantime, however, they had already begun to look for more profitable opportunities in their vineyards and orchards. The laws of supply and demand, they would find, could be just as unforgiving for fruit as they were for wheat.[20]

The shift from wheat to fruit in Davisville and around the state was slow, uneven, and contingent. It took place over a twenty- to twenty-five-year period, with farmers often assuming dual identities—"agriculturists as well as horticulturists," as a local newspaper put it. Though gradual and often tentative, the transformation was as dramatic and complete as any in American agricultural history. Overall, California was the nation's second leading wheat-producing state in 1889, with almost three million acres harvested and exports totaling 840,000 tons. By 1909, wheat acreage had fallen to less than 400,000 acres, with the state becoming a net importer. Over the same period, California emerged as one of the world's principal producers of deciduous and citrus fruits, grapes, vegetables, and nuts. In Putah and Tremont townships, the shift, if not quite as pronounced, significantly altered the region's economy and landscape. When Pierce and other longtime wheat farmers began calling themselves "orchardists" and "vineyardists" as early as the mid-1880s, they seemed to know that they were part of something special—just as their fathers had during the gold rush.[21]

Yet, the impetus to experiment with alternative cash crops came not from local farmers themselves but from outside the community, beginning as far back as 1869, when "silk mania" briefly took hold in Davisville. That winter, a group of San Francisco capitalists purchased 343 acres of prime land just east of town along Putah Creek from Isaac S. Chiles and formed the California Silk Culture Association. Under the watchful eye of manager Charles Reed, a farmer from nearby Washington Township, the company's "plantation" flourished. In 1871, it contained 600,000 mulberry trees, two large cocooneries, and at least two million silkworms, netting an astounding $760 per acre, according to one report. Enthusiasts from as far away as Europe insisted that Davisville produced "some of the finest raw silk ever shown in any country." But, in June 1871, when the thermometer reportedly stood at 110 degrees in the shade for ten consecutive days, every last silkworm perished, despite heroic efforts to save them. The association abandoned the silk business, but the excitement and the profits generated by this exotic enterprise were not soon forgotten. In a manner reminiscent of the Big Ranch and the Davis Stock Farm in the 1850s, the "Silk Ranch," as locals called it, made Davisville famous.[22]

The same group of San Francisco businessmen on the same 343-acre tract undertook their next "great experiment" the following year. Borrowing $25,000, the owners dug up their mulberries and planted 27,000 fruit and nut trees—10,000 pear, 9,000 almond, 4,500 peach, 1,000 plum, 800 apricot, 500 cherry, 500 fig, 500 nectarine, 500 walnut, and 400 apple—making it one of the largest orchard operations in the state. Shortly thereafter, they converted much of the rest of their grounds into vineyards. When the trees and vines started bearing in 1876, the Silk Ranch officially changed its name to the Oak Shade Fruit Company, incorporated with a capital stock of $200,000, and began shipping carloads of dried and fresh fruit down the Central Pacific tracks to vendors in Oakland and San Francisco. The proprietors also sold trees and vines locally, though the nursery was a much smaller part of the business. Surrounded for miles around by wheat fields, the Oak Shade Fruit Company stood apart from the community, though farmers continued to enjoy the attention that, as one said, this "curiously intriguing" enterprise brought to their region.[23]

Just a few months after the Silk Ranch began operations in 1869, George G. Briggs of Marysville, who had already established a reputation as a "noted horticulturist," purchased 200 acres on the Solano side of Putah Creek opposite Davisville and took up residence there. Intending to take advantage of both the fertile soil and the close proximity to the railroad, he too began planting numerous varieties of fruit trees and grapevines. Briggs made substantial profits when his orchards and vineyards began producing in 1874, but his fruit did not command the prices he had hoped to receive. No single wheat grower posed much of a threat to him but, when combined, their small orchards provided more competition than he had anticipated. And all he had to do was gaze across the creek at the rapidly maturing trees and vines of the Oak Shade Fruit Company to realize that the competition would only increase. Seeking his own niche in the market, Briggs began, as he later recalled, "making a few raisins of my grapes" in 1875. These "rare Mediterranean delights" proved so remunerative that by 1879 Briggs had converted his entire grape crop into raisins and replaced half his orchards with vineyards. The following year, he installed a $20,000 "sub-irrigation system," the first of its kind in the Sacramento Valley. It consisted of three large reservoirs, 200 miles of twelve-inch cement pipes laid two feet underground, and a 30-horsepower steam engine capable of pumping 2,600 gallons of water per minute out of Putah Creek. When Briggs died in 1885, he left an estate worth $150,000 and, in the words of one local farmer, a reputation around the state for "innovation and success" that "serves as an inspiration to us all."[24]

The success of the Briggs vineyard and the Oak Shade Fruit Company notwithstanding, Davisville farmers did not become converts all at once or all together. It took one of their own, Jacob E. La Rue, to begin to convince the others that fruit was the future. Jacob was the son of Hugh M. La Rue, a gold-rush migrant from Kentucky who purchased the old E. L. Brown tract in 1866, expanded it to 2,000 acres over the years, and, like his neighbors, grew wheat as his staple crop. One of the state's more prominent Democrats, Hugh had held a number of public positions, including sheriff of Sacramento County, state assemblyman, president of the state agricultural society, delegate to the second constitutional convention in 1879, and regent of the University of California. Though he spent a considerable amount of time on the farm, his main residence was in Sacramento, opposite the governor's mansion on Sixteenth Street. Jacob took over the management of the farm in 1880, the year he graduated from the University of California. Discouraged by falling wheat prices and two disastrous fires in his fields, envious of the success that Briggs had achieved a few miles downstream, and determined to make his own mark, Jacob decided in the fall of 1881 to gamble on grapes. By 1885, his ninety-acre vineyard, the largest in the county, proved so profitable ($50 per acre, net) that he gave up wheat altogether to concentrate on grapes and, to a lesser degree, stock and feed crops. "There are men," he quipped, after harvesting 100 tons of grapes that year, "who still believe that fruit-growing will not pay."[25]

La Rue might well have been chiding his neighbor and rival, Pierce Jr. Both were sons of prominent pioneer farmers, graduates of the state university, and emerging community leaders. Not surprisingly, a sometimes friendly, sometimes fierce competition developed between them over the years, with Pierce, being the older of the two by several years, usually holding the upper hand. Pierce held a number of leadership positions in the university alumni association, whereas La Rue played no visible role and often did not even attend meetings; Pierce frequently read the Declaration of Independence at Fourth of July celebrations, but La Rue was just another face in the crowd; Pierce became a high-ranking officer in the Davisville Odd Fellows, while La Rue remained in the rank and file. Even the Putah Creek mastodon, by virtue of where it was found, seemed to favor Pierce. But La Rue seized the advantage upon becoming a self-proclaimed vineyardist. Local newspapers carefully followed the progress of "the Arlington Farm," as La Rue now called his expanding operations, which in 1888 produced no fewer than 850 tons of grapes. That year, La Rue married Sacramento socialite Adeline Rankin, built a magnificent Victorian farmhouse overlooking his now 200-acre vineyard, and began planting the "Alameda" (later, "Avenue of Trees")— a mile-long stretch of soon-to-be towering black walnuts lining the public road (Davisville Road West) that bisected his ranch.[26]

Green with envy, Pierce yearned to become a vineyardist himself. Unlike La Rue's, however, Pierce's father still made the important decisions on the Pierce Ranch. Grapes had their place, Pierce Sr. acknowledged. The September harvest brought in several hundred dollars a year, and it filled a gap in the yearly cycle between the wheat harvest at the end of the June and the start of fall plowing. But the Pierces were wheat men, he insisted, not grape men. The resulting family feud reached a climax in 1884. That winter, both father and son visited the Oak Shade Fruit Company "to see them earigate [sic]," as Pierce Sr. wrote that evening. Both were impressed but came away with vastly different objectives in mind. While the son wished to expand the family's vineyard and orchard operations, the father wanted to raise alfalfa to feed the growing number of stock and workhorses on the ranch. "Sowed alfalfa in the orchard lot," wrote Pierce Sr. in March, making clear whose opinion still mattered most. Thereafter, however, Pierce Jr. asserted himself more forcefully. As his father's health declined, he gradually, over the next four years, enlarged the vineyard from 25 to 112 acres—nowhere near the size of La Rue's, but big enough for the *Dixon Tribune* to call him a "horticulturist" in 1888. That September, moreover, a month after his marriage to schoolteacher Susie Gilmore, when his parents moved to a house in Davisville, Pierce Jr. assumed full control of the ranch. Having finally become his own man at age thirty-eight, Pierce Jr. let the rivalries with both father and neighbor subside. When the newlyweds gave their first dinner party in the home they now called their own, the La Rues joined the elder Pierces as their guests.[27]

With La Rue and Pierce leading the way, many of their peers along Putah Creek also caught "fruit fever" by the end of the decade. With one notable exception, they were all second-generation farmers. In 1886, William O. Russell and James Campbell, Pierce's and La Rue's immediate neighbors, became the next to plant orchards and vineyards of at least fifty acres. They were followed by Napoleon Miner, James Chiles (son of Isaac and stepson of Phineas), Charles Greene Jr., Grant Cecil, and Lee Jackson Montgomery—each one, observed a Davisville merchant, "inducing others in their vicinity to follow their example." The only "argonaut" among them, the same merchant noted, was longtime swamplander William H. Marden, whose sixty-acre raisin vineyard in Putah Sink became "a mine of wealth." So many farmers—upwards of forty with land along the creek—"made the transition" by 1890 that the county assessor that year began counting the "number of fruit trees" and "acres of grape vines" when making his annual rounds. "Our farmers," a local newspaper correspondent declared, "are gradually becoming converted to the belief that fruit-raising pays better than wheat-farming."[28]

These developments in Davisville reflected a process that occurred throughout much of California in the 1880s. News of a "fruit boom" in Fresno, Riverside, Santa Clara, Newcastle, Vacaville, and other emerging communities reinforced the sense among Davisville orchardists and vineyardists that they were part of a "growing movement of progressive farmers." Many were jealous of all the attention the eastern press was giving citrus in southern California while barely acknowledging "that there is such a place as the Sacramento Valley." "Here in Yolo, 400 or 500 miles north of Los Angeles," one farmer boasted, "we will show you a land of milk and honey—pears, peaches, apricots, figs, almonds, walnuts, and grapes, native and foreign, raisin and wine, in endless variety." Two events held in Sacramento late in 1886 shone the limelight on the north, however briefly—the State Fruit Growers' Convention in November and the Northern California Citrus Fair a month later (the name for the latter being rather misleading, given the strong emphasis on deciduous fruit and grapes). Taking advantage of reduced fares offered by the Southern Pacific Railroad, Pierce, La Rue, and many other Davisville farmers went to both. They listened intently to papers delivered by "fruit experts," placed "fine examples" of their own crops on exhibit, and socialized with "like-minded people" from around the state. Caught up in the hoopla of all the activities, the *Yolo Weekly Mail* published a lengthy "citrus fair supplement," detailing the many accomplishments of local "pioneers," including Briggs and La Rue. Declaring fruit to be "a leading industry in the county," the *Mail* devoted all of one paragraph to wheat. "Our great wealth is not to be, in the future, in our wheat crop, but rather in fruits, vines, olives, and nuts," it editorialized. Four years later, the paper put out an even longer "horticultural edition," echoing the same sentiments.[29]

The *Mail*'s enthusiasm notwithstanding, most Davisville farmers, while reveling in the attention, had not yet given up on wheat—far from it. While they took great pride in their orchards and vineyards, they were also buying Best combined harvesters, producing huge wheat crops, and hoping that the market would somehow turn around. They were just beginning to realize, moreover, that life as a horticulturist was not all "milk and honey," either. Though county boosters rarely mentioned them, fruit growing produced problems of its own—water, labor, and falling prices in particular—that made farmers more than a little wary of "making the transition" outright.

The subject of irrigation prompted much discussion, speculation, innovation, and conflict along Putah Creek, but little resolution. Farmers, who had long enjoyed the cost-free form of irrigation that the creek's annual overflows provided their wheat fields, were well aware that their new orchards and vineyards required a more dependable, controllable source of water. With that in mind, La Rue and Briggs proposed the region's first "irrigation scheme," in December 1882. They envisioned building a dam in Putah canyon, twenty miles west of Davisville, where the creek begins its sharp descent into the Sacramento Valley, and running a ditch along the north bank of the creek twenty-five miles, all the way to the Tule. The "Putah Creek Water Company" incorporated and, at La Rue's expense, hired an engineer to survey the site, but it never evolved beyond the initial stage of planning. Only five other farmers—Pierce, Russell, and Chiles, among them—took stock in the company, leaving it far short of the engineer's very conservative estimate of $250,000 needed for the project. No one seemed to question the engineering feasibility of building the huge dam (which would eventually be constructed, but not until the 1950s); they had a complete, if not quite blind, faith in technology. But farmers on the Solano side of the creek threatened a massive lawsuit against the company should it attempt to "steal" their water, and even on the Yolo side several landholders refused to grant a right-of-way through their farms for the ditch.[30]

The failure of the Putah Creek Water Company left orchardists and vineyardists to their own devices, but because of an exceptionally wet cycle in the

Sacramento Valley for most of the 1880s, not even the former company stock-holders seemed particularly concerned. One by one, farmers proceeded to water their crops on an individual basis. The Oak Shade Fruit Company, following Briggs's lead, purchased an 85-horsepower engine to pump water out of Putah Creek and constructed an equally sophisticated system of "sub-irrigation." Steam engines and cement pipes, however, were beyond the reach of most of the others, who instead relied on windmills and ditches to secure the means of irrigation. Campbell's windmill, for example, powered a rotary pump that directed water to his vineyard at about one-tenth the speed of Briggs' system, but it was more than sufficient for his smaller operation. Campbell's method became so popular that the Sinclair Company began manufacturing windmills in Davisville in 1887, thus becoming the town's "first industrial enterprise." As long as the wind kept blow-ing and the water flowing, everyone seemed content.[31]

Indeed, when the state legislature passed the Wright Irrigation Act in 1887, Putah Creek farmers all but ignored it. Derived directly from swampland legisla-tion two decades earlier, the Wright Act authorized the formation of local irriga-tion districts with the approval of a majority of landowners in the area, and em-powered the districts to acquire water rights and to levy taxes and sell bonds to build dams, canals, and reservoirs. Davisville farmers considered forming a Putah Irrigation District, but nothing much came of their discussions. "In their present frame of mind," a correspondent for the *Dixon Tribune* explained in No-vember 1887, "the near approach of the winter rains put a damper on the sub-ject." In addition to the abundance of water that they currently enjoyed, Davisville orchardists and vineyardists also did not embrace the Wright Act's ultimate ob-jective—the subdivision of large estates. Wheat farmers and cattle ranchers, leg-islators presumed, would sell their land to small farmers both to reap the profits that their irrigated tracts would bring as well as to avoid the taxes imposed by the new districts. But most Davisville horticulturists were wheat farmers themselves, who, once they understood the key elements of the law, were of no mind to pay for something that they did not think they needed.[32]

The end of the cycle of good weather the following year exposed the folly of ir-rigation on a farm-by-farm basis, but only briefly. Less than ten inches of rain fell during the winter of 1887–88. The drought created a pumping frenzy, as irri-gators tried to drain as much water as they could from the creek. By July, only a few small pools remained in the channel. The "meager waters of Putah Creek" prompted a small-scale replay of *Lux v. Haggin*, the already famous lawsuit from earlier in the decade in which two giant land interests had fought for control of the Kern River in the San Joaquin Valley. In that case, the state supreme court in

1886 determined that the riparian rights of downstream landowners (the Miller-Lux Land and Cattle Company) superseded the appropriation rights of upstream water users (James Haggin and Lloyd Trevis). Citing *Lux v. Haggin* as precedent, R. S. Carey and William W. Montgomery sued Webster Treat, the manager of the Oak Shade Fruit Company, for $10,000, for "stopping the natural flow of the creek and depriving them of their downstream water rights." The resulting lack of water in Putah Sink, they complained, compelled them to drive their stock into the mountains at great expense.

Treat's lawyer countered that *Lux v. Haggin* was not relevant to the case. He admitted that his client had pumped water out of the creek for irrigation, "but no more than was reasonable and necessary for said purpose," and as a riparian owner himself, not an appropriator. As such, Treat had as much right to the water as Carey or Montgomery. Nonetheless, the superior court judge granted an injunction to stop "the defendant and anyone else" from pumping and set a trial date for April 28, 1889. By then, however, the rains had returned in full force, causing Putah Creek to spill its banks on several occasions. With more water than they knew what to do with, the litigants settled their differences out of court. The drought of 1888 also revived an interest in the irrigation district, but that too was washed away by the raging waters of 1889. Not until after the turn of the century would the subject be broached again.[33]

Labor posed another set of problems that these novice horticulturists preferred would just go away. An inkling of what lay ahead came in 1879, when Briggs began preparations for his massive subirrigation system. On December 13, he signed a contract with an engineer from Napa named R. W. Biggerstaff, who agreed to dig Briggs's 200 miles of ditches and lay his cement pipes for $40 a mile. But when Biggerstaff returned to Napa for his crew and implements, Briggs received a better offer from Ah Hai, a Chinese contractor who guaranteed to do the job for half the cost. Biggerstaff arrived a week later to find two dozen Chinese laborers hard at work in Briggs's vineyard. Angry and humiliated, he filed suit in Yolo Superior Court for $7,340 to recover the lost wages. When asked on the witness stand why he had made the change, Briggs answered that he had found not only a cheaper alternative but a better one. The Chinese, he elaborated, "put in a little rounding on the bottom . . . before putting in the pipes, just the way I wanted it." Though awarding him only one-tenth the damages he had demanded, the jury found in favor of Biggerstaff, as did the state supreme court on Briggs's appeal. In the end, however, Briggs did indeed get just what he wanted—inexpensive, readily available, attentive, fast, and skilled labor. When his vines were ready to harvest that fall, he went right back to Ah Hai, as he would do for many seasons to come.[34]

Most of Briggs's neighbors, having long concentrated on wheat, did not adapt as quickly. They were simply unprepared for the intensiveness of their orchard and vineyard crops. Over the years, maintaining an adequate labor force had become almost routine, with most farmers employing a small number of full-time hands and then hiring temporary workers as needed for the wheat harvest. Despite the dangerous and unpleasant conditions, many harvesters returned year after year to the same farms, and regular hands remained loyal to their employers for years at a time—twelve years in the case of one of La Rue's prized workers. When the combined harvester "enabled farmers to do with less help," as one put it, labor became even less of a concern. The same could not be said for fruit, however. While the average wheat harvest in the area required "about half a dozen workers," the same farmer estimated that "our orchards and vineyards necessitate two-to-three times that many, sometimes more." The Oak Shade Fruit Company already employed 208 laborers at the height of the season in 1885, when most trees and vines in the area were just beginning to bear. "I find it very difficult to obtain laborers to gather my grape crop," lamented La Rue that same year. "What am I to do?"[35]

Eventually, La Rue and his counterparts reached the same conclusion as Briggs—hire Chinese workers. By the fall of 1887, "large hordes of Chinamen," observed a reporter from the *Yolo Weekly Mail,* were "engaged in picking and packing fruit of all kinds along Putah Creek." Unlike white workers, explained Jean Gould, manager of the Briggs vineyard, the Chinese were "easily hired" through contractors, "abundant," and perhaps most importantly, "painstaking and neat in their work." Yet, the presence of "so many Celestials employed in and around Davisville" concerned farmers and townspeople alike, all of whom admitted to "a deep-rooted prejudice against the Chinaman." Few doubted the orchardists and vineyardists who insisted that the fruit would drop and rot unless Chinese were there to pick it, but no one wanted them in their community. They were just as adamant about avoiding the mob violence that had recently accompanied a number of anti-Chinese uprisings in other Sacramento Valley towns. By 1890, they reached something of a compromise. Farmers continued to hire Chinese orchard and vineyard workers, who came and went with the fall harvest and were expected to be invisible even then. But in their packinghouses, many of which were in town, they hired local women and children, not Chinese. For the moment, the image of "Davisville girls—laughing, singing, talking, and working" hid the harsh realities of labor and race relations along Putah Creek. But as the number of bearing trees and vines continued to multiply in the coming years, the demand for proficient workers would empower Asian contractors and simply bewilder their employers.[36]

In the meantime, farmers faced an even more pressing concern: rapidly declining prices for their fruit. During the boom of the 1880s, marketing posed few problems. Orchardists and vineyardists simply delivered their crops to the Oak Shade Fruit Company, where San Francisco merchants and, beginning in 1885, J. K. Armsby, Porter Brothers, and other national brokerage firms paid "very satisfactory" prices (4 to 7 cents per pound for raisins, often twice that for other fruits). In 1890, shipments from Oak Shade totaled fifty carloads (625 tons), with fully 80 percent going to eastern and midwestern urban markets via the Southern Pacific Railroad. When Gould reported a profit margin of $100 an acre that year, several farmers bragged that they had netted even more. James Chiles became so giddy that in January 1891 he bet his stepfather "a tidy sum" that his seventy-five-acre orchard would clear more than Phineas's several hundred acres of wheat. Though the contest was "watched with much interest," neither James nor Phineas reported the result. Neither felt as if he had won, as both wheat and fruit prices declined sharply that season. They tumbled again the following year and again in 1893. The nationwide depression that began that year only exacerbated the situation. For the next four years, neither James nor Phineas nor any of their counterparts broke even, with fruit prices declining even more than wheat prices.[37]

Lawsuits, bankruptcies, and foreclosures became "all the rage in Davisville," as farmers invariably tried to borrow their way out of trouble. Andrew McClory, one of the few forty-niners still alive in the area, was among the first to have his land seized by the county sheriff, in 1893. He resorted to hunting and fishing for sustenance, just as he had in the 1850s, when he first arrived in Putah Creek. The celebrated Sinclair Windmill Company went out of business in 1894, as did many stores, hotels, and saloons in Davisville. No one fell harder or further, however, than Emma Briggs, who had become the proprietor of her husband's vineyard upon his death in 1885. She spent much of 1895 in court, defending herself against five different creditors. Since 1891, she had borrowed a total of $84,000 to keep the business alive, but she had yet to pay back a dime of interest. Even Ah Hai, the family's longtime labor contractor, sued her for $780 in back wages. By the summer, the judge saw no choice but to attach all her property—the land itself, more than 35,000 drying trays, 2,800 sweatboxes, all 200 miles of subirrigation pipe, and every last tool, implement, work animal, scale, and wagon. That

December, a newspaper reporter spent a day rambling through the once-prized vineyard, "disheartened at the spectacle" before him. "The vines run wild and untrained on the uncultivated ground, . . . the warehouses stand with open doors, . . . and cows graze idly as they did fifty years past." "This is not a sign of returning prosperity," he lamented.[38]

Despite the hard economic times, Davisville farmers, even the twenty or so who had filed for insolvency, eschewed the most sweeping farmer movement of the late nineteenth century—Populism. Traveling lecturers from the Farmers' Alliance tried to precipitate a mass protest in the Sacramento Valley, as they did throughout much of the American South and Midwest, but the four or five meetings held in Davisville "excited but little interest," in the words of one local. The Granger debacle with Morgan's Sons, now fifteen years past, no longer accounted for the indifference, though farmers continued to bring it up on occasion. That they identified so strongly with the "natural advantages of soil and climate" of their particular region may have deterred mass organization; and their more favorable relationship with the Southern Pacific left them without a unifying target of protest. But farmers elsewhere joined the Farmers' Alliance and the People's Party for reasons deeper than economics alone. For many, social isolation, a beaten self-image, and little means of self-expression made Alliance communities appealing. Indeed, Populism engendered within millions of American farmers a "sense of somebodiness." Two generations of Davisville farmers, however, did not find that sense lacking.[39]

The years had brought plenty of disappointment and dampened expectations, but little overt despondency or despair. Deep discontent of the kind that led to insurgent movements elsewhere was rare indeed among Davisville farmers of either generation. Those of the first had their dreams broken time and time again, but they passed on to their sons the thirst for excitement, the sheer energy, and the unyielding drive to succeed that had so animated them in both the goldfields and the wheat fields. That temperament compelled those of the second generation to cling to their own dreams, seemingly in defiance of the harsh realities before them. It seemed not to matter that fruit was still by and large a luxury crop, one of the first items consumers scratched off their grocery lists in hard times. While everyone ate bread, American buying habits had only just begun to change toward better nutrition and fewer calories. "Our orchards are our hope," insisted one Tremont farmer anyway, "if starve we must."[40]

Davisville farmers ended up placing their hopes and dreams in, of all things, almonds, perhaps the least likely orchard crop at the time to become a staple of the American diet. Several small almond orchards dotted the region as early as 1885, with the average harvest securing, in the words of Webster Treat, "a decent competence"—no more and no less than walnuts or any one fruit. With their spectacular pink bloom early in the spring, almond trees were known more for their esthetic than their remunerative value. But in 1887, Treat discovered—by accident, he later admitted—that eastern confectioners, by far the nut's largest consumers, favored two varieties in particular—the Nonpareil paper shell and the Ne Plus Ultra soft shell—which he just happened to have planted for the Oak Shade Fruit Company three years earlier. When his first crop the following year paid 13 cents a pound, Treat began a one-man almond-booster campaign. He went from farm to farm along Putah Creek touting the nut and gave papers at fruit-grower conventions, citrus fairs, and other prominent venues around the state detailing its advantages. He budded another 150,000 young almond trees in 1888 and by 1893 had converted the Oak Shade Fruit Company into one huge almond orchard. As many as twenty other Davisville farmers followed his lead, including Pierce, who dug up his 132-acre vineyard in the summer of 1892 and replanted the land with almond trees—half Nonpareil, half Ne Plus Ultra.[41]

Treat's pitch emphasized not only high prices but also the ease of raising almonds compared to other orchard crops. The trees themselves, he said, took less time to mature; they required minimal pruning; their product was neither perishable nor fragile; they did not need as much water; and they could be harvested with a significantly smaller labor force. "It is the most easily cared for of any kind of nut or fruit-bearing tree," he maintained. The depression, however, exposed almonds as no less vulnerable to the forces of supply and demand than any other product, as prices dropped to $7\frac{1}{2}$ cents a pound in 1896. In time, farmers would also learn that the peculiarities of the almond that Treat omitted—its erratic blooming behavior, irregular bearing habits, and strict soil and climate requirements—limited production to "about two good crops out of five," according to another expert. And Treat's assessments of water and labor requirements would prove to be the biggest myths of all. Nonetheless, those farmers who had committed themselves to almonds were bound and determined to, as Pierce later put it, "make them pay."[42]

But as the economy began to recover at the end of 1896, almond prices remained low. Believing as their fathers had that supply makes its own demand, Davisville growers blamed their predicament on the same brokerage firms who had paid them so well the previous decade but were now, in their minds, "gouging" them. "We were easily imposed upon," Pierce recalled. Resolving to seize control of the marketing process themselves, fifteen growers holding about 600 acres between them met in the Davisville Odd Fellows' Hall on January 23, 1897, to discuss "the benefits to be derived by organization." A week later, proclaiming that almonds had become "one of the leading industries of this section," they formed California's first almond cooperative, the Davisville Almond Growers' Association. For leadership, members turned to a trio of experienced men whom they trusted implicitly, electing La Rue president, Pierce vice president, and Chiles secretary-treasurer. In fact, no fewer than eleven of the fifteen charter members were sons of pioneer wheat farmers from the 1850s and 1860s—La Rue, Pierce, Chiles, W. O. Russell, Charles E. Greene Jr., L. J. Montgomery, G. K. Swingle, W. H. Marden, W. Montgomery, J. Campbell, and J. G. Cecil. A new generation of prominent citizens, most of them direct descendants of the gold rush, had arrived.[43]

Determined to play a more aggressive role in setting the price of their almonds, members quickly discovered that they could increase their bargaining power by storing the crop in a centralized warehouse, entertaining bids for the total crop, rejecting bids deemed "not up to market," and copyrighting their own brand. Over the next six years, they took credit for doubling the price of their almonds, to 13 cents, not realizing that higher prices were more the product of the vigorous economic recovery at the turn of the century than of the cooperative's efforts to control the market. La Rue and Pierce did realize, however, that their association could "never make us complete master of the market, struggling by itself," so they proceeded to organize several other almond locals in the Sacramento Valley, intending ultimately to form a statewide cooperative. Over the same period, Davisville growers, now twenty-six in number, increased their yields almost 50 percent (to more than 300 tons, 20 percent of the state's crop), to make their district the leader in production as well as marketing.[44]

Cooperation brought more than just economic gain. "We had nothing but almonds and a determination to succeed," Pierce recalled. In an era in which middle-class Americans held the "associative impulse" in high esteem, that determination—the desire to be "progressive"—brought Davisville growers and their community statewide and even national recognition. Indeed, when the prestigious *Overland Monthly* proclaimed in 1902 that "this pioneer association" was setting "the standard for the state," it referred not only to improved almond prices but also to what this band of horticulturists had collectively accomplished. Almonds made Davisville famous, once again.[45]

"There is no reason that the same cannot be done for wheat!" exclaimed Pierce in an interview published in newspapers throughout northern California in January of 1902. Inspired by the success of the Davisville Almond Growers' Association, Pierce led one last concerted effort to revive the wheat market. There had been a brief recovery when the economy rebounded in 1897. Prices rose to $1.35 per cental but dropped back below the cost of production just two years later. "Everybody in California is getting richer but the wheat farmer," declared Pierce. "Something must be done." Hoping to secure cheaper rates of transportation and eventually to market their own wheat, about 150 farmers from the Sacramento and San Joaquin valleys convened at the state capitol on September 25, 1901, to organize the California Grain Growers' Association. With Pierce as president, membership tripled over the next few months, with the association garnering considerable publicity. At the end of the summer, however, low prices killed whatever momentum the association might have generated. As a result, hundreds more farmers in the Sacramento and San Joaquin valleys withdrew land from wheat production than paid the $5 subscription fee. "Organization seems to us like the straw to the drowning man," one said.[46]

The following season, Pierce saw no choice but to cut back on wheat himself. The writing was on the wall. In 1902, his wheat harvest of 138 tons earned only $2,600, while his 14 tons of almonds netted over $3,000—the first time his nut income surpassed his grain income. That fall and every year thereafter until the end of the decade, he replanted portions of his wheat acreage with barley, as did all his neighbors. By 1910, the cultivation of wheat on the Pierce ranch, mirroring the statewide trend, had dwindled to insignificance. For the first time in half a century, the land along Putah Creek was largely devoid of wheat.[47]

By then, however, Pierce and his fellow growers had turned heart and soul to almonds. They began referring to Davisville as "the home of the almond," and with abundant evidence to back their claim: Their almonds won a gold medal at the St. Louis World's Fair in 1905; they routinely took home blue ribbons from the California State Fair; they were the state's top-producing region almost every year, more than doubling production over the course of the decade; and their marketing cooperative was "the parent body which blazed the way" for others. On May 6, 1910, representatives elected from each of the nine local associations that Pierce and La Rue had helped organize met in Sacramento, determined "to steady the market through cooperation." The next day, they incorporated the California Almond Growers' Exchange (CAGE) and elected officers, including Pierce as vice president. The Exchange proved enormously successful. Between 1910 and 1914, CAGE expanded its membership from 230 to 900, inspired an "almond boom" that increased the number of acres in the state from 11,000 to 35,000, gained control of 80 percent of the crop, and helped advance prices from 12 to 18 cents a pound. Pierce, whose fellow growers elected him CAGE president in 1913, sang the praises of the Exchange up and down the state, brushing aside the claims of contemporary economists that rising agricultural prices throughout the United States accounted for the prosperity much more than the efforts of CAGE or any one marketing association. "Co-operation," insisted Pierce, "is a glorious achievement. The situation is full of hope."[48]

Pierce's pronouncement harkened back to Judge Stephen J. Field's memory of his first day in San Francisco in December 1849. Here again, it seemed that anything was possible. The intensity of expectation, in many ways, burned just as bright for Pierce during the almond boom as it had for Field during the gold rush. Perhaps it was only a coincidence that just a few years later, during the 1920s, with the agricultural economy in deep recession, economists and farmers alike would look back at the period 1910–14 as the "golden age" of American agriculture—a time when farm prices achieved "parity" with the prices of other goods and services. And just a few years after that the concept of parity prices and income would become the hallmark of American agricultural policy. For the time being, however, almond growers basked in a spirit of optimism so "glorious" they could hardly contain themselves. Pierce took to literally idolizing the fruits of his profession when addressing his fellow growers in convention. The almond, he maintained, was an instrument of civility: "As far back as authentic history takes us we read of the Almond. It is frequently referred to in Scripture and has played no small part in ministering to the needs and pleasures of mankind. Its food value is important and its bloom, following closely on the heels of Winter, has probably appealed to the esthetic side of mankind more strongly than has the bloom of any other orchard tree." No one in the audience blushed. To the contrary, they all believed they were on the verge of striking it rich.[49]

CHAPTER TWELVE

Legacies

"Five years," wrote nineteenth-century humorist Prentice Mulford of the gold rush, "was the longest period any one expected to stay." The first generation of California farmers, it must be remembered, had not intended to farm at all, but having failed in the mines, they became desperate to succeed on the land. In their haste to adapt to their new surroundings, they committed themselves not only to the market but to community life as well—and with a resolve and a sense of permanence that can only be described as remarkable.

The fact that a community of any sort emerged along Putah Creek defies conventional wisdom about rural California, which has emphasized "wheat kings," "land barons," and "farm factories." This was a community, moreover, of considerable stability, as evidenced by the eleven enterprising charter members of the Davisville Almond Growers' Association, whose fathers were among the first miners-turned-farmers to settle the region. Such persistence was driven by capitalist as well as cultural values. Capitalism, to put it another way, was an integral part of Putah Creek culture. Separating the two or, worse yet, opposing capitalism and culture discounts the power and saliency of human agency in making history—in this case, how a diverse group of displaced forty-niners, their families, and their descendants perceived one another and experienced the events, personalities, and broad range of economic and environmental forces that shaped their lives.[1]

That said, perhaps the most powerful agent of change and certainly the most persistent was Putah Creek itself. Periodic flooding through the end of the century—most notably in 1885, 1889, and again in 1895—continued to baffle residents. Every time the creek spilled its banks, farmers seemed caught by surprise, with someone invariably saying something to the effect of "the overflow is the most destructive ever known in this section" or "the flood was so sudden and so unexpected that no time was given for preparation." Particularly conspicuous was the railroad engineer who, in the midst of a fierce downpour, left Davisville on the afternoon of January 5, 1895, driving the northbound Southern Pacific line. Barely a mile from the depot, he encountered, much to his chagrin, the "big lake," the result of overflow from both Putah Creek and Willow Slough, which once filled the swampy region of the old Jerome C. Davis ranch. With the tracks ahead of him deep under water, the engineer stopped the train and started to return to Davisville, backing up. At a small trestle in the embankment, through which the water was rushing, the roadbed gave way under the weight of the coaches, causing the entire locomotive to topple over the bank on its side. No one was injured too severely, though several people had to be pulled out of the rapidly rising water. The passengers waited on high ground near the tracks until boats sent from Sacramento took them back to Davisville.[2]

Nor did the Putah canal, constructed by landowners back in the 1870s, provide much in the way of flood control; it simply created another channel whose banks could not contain the fierce torrents of water. This provided a source of endless frustration for the Southern Pacific, which rebuilt its bridge over the canal several times, only to see it wiped out by the next big flood. Tremont residents often could not ford the canal for weeks on end after a bad storm, which meant that to get to Davisville, they had to ride several miles southeast to Dixon across the soggy prairie and then take the train. Their repeated cries for a public bridge fell on deaf ears, as the Solano County Board of Supervisors continued its tradition of refusing to spend even a dime on these outlying residents while gladly taking their tax dollars. As late as 1897, Tremont farmers were still trying to "secede" from their county to escape the clutches of "the Vallejo-Fairfield ring that oppresses us."[3]

No one battled Putah Creek longer, harder, and with greater futility than R. S. Carey. At least five times over the course of his life, flooding forced Carey to reconstruct the ten miles of levees designed to protect his 1,500-acre Putah Sink ranch. About one-third of the them bordered the tule margin on the east, while the other two-thirds held back the waters of "the old Putah Creek" to the north and the canal to the south. In recent years, Carey was never sure just how to utilize this productive land—whether for cultivating wheat or raising sheep. He was, moreover, "a poor guesser," as one observer put it. "If he sowed, the flood came; if he failed to sow the flood failed to come and a favorable season was lost." His luck was never worse than in 1895. Hoping to ride out the depression with a huge crop of wheat, Carey instead met his nemesis once again. On January 5, the raging waters of Putah Creek, with virtually no warning, roared through "the break" at La Rue's bend and poured into the canal on a collision course toward Carey's ranch. Their destructive impact, mighty enough already, was made even greater because landowners upstream from Carey had not been maintaining the canal very well, allowing its width to shrink from 200 to 100 feet. The "ocean of water" that came down from the mountains burst through the narrow channel and shot forward onto Carey's land, exploding over the top of his levees, which then "merely served to keep in the water." Another "huge lake" drowned Carey's crop and 300 of his sheep. "You could not see the fences, which were at least four feet high," recalled one of his hands.[4]

This time, Carey would not recover. In this season as never before, he was in dire need of a big crop and a big payoff. Back in 1886, embarking on his latest effort to reclaim Putah Sink, Carey had borrowed $50,000 from Henry Cowell, a San Francisco financier. The terms were steep—8 percent interest, compounded yearly, with one-third of the principal due in three years, another third after five, and the last third in seven. To secure the loan, Carey mortgaged much of his land—not only the 1,500 acres he intended to levee off but another 4,500 of surrounding swamp and overflowed land as well. The subsequent flood of 1889, falling prices, and the onset of economic depression prevented him from making even a single payment. In July 1893, with Carey owing him over $66,000, Cowell decided he could wait no longer and filed suit in the Yolo Superior Court. Though his lawyers managed to delay attachment for a couple of years, the flood of 1895 spelled certain doom for Carey. On the afternoon of June 18, while sitting in his favorite chair on the rear porch of his home, overlooking his swamp-ridden ranch, he drew a pistol from his pocket and, placing the muzzle just beneath his right ear, sent a bullet crashing through his head.[5]

Obituaries, while trying to explain Carey's suicide in the context of his "rich, full life," maintained that pulling the trigger on himself was an act of nobility. "He had no choice but to die," insisted one. In detailing his accomplishments, writers omitted Carey's struggles in the mines of El Dorado County in the early 1850s, as was customary, but the gold rush resonated throughout their accounts of the rest of his life. "Mr. Carey was a proud man," one emphasized. "He had always controlled great interests; he had filled high places; his honor was dearer to him than life. The downfall of all his cherished plans, the prospect of seeing his name dragged in the dust by remorseless creditors, was too much for him. He possessed the courage to face death, but not the courage to face dishonor." "In his state of desperation," stated another more bluntly, "it was a wise choice." With the stakes so high, admitting failure was simply not an option—either for Carey or for his peers.[6]

Not all legacies of the gold rush were so harsh. The same mania to succeed that drove Carey to suicide compelled George W. Pierce Jr. to heights beyond anything his father had attained. Pierce, too, suffered through a number of personal crises. When his father died on February 24, 1890, the blow was softened somewhat by a sense of relief that Pierce Sr.'s suffering had ended. Just twelve days later, however, the death of his infant son, Gilmore, devastated Pierce and sent his wife, Susie, into a severe depression that left her bedridden for several months. The couple then relived their horror when their infant daughter, Eunice, met the same fate five years later. Only the birth of two healthy sons in the interim helped ease the pain. Pierce's mother lived for eighteen years beyond her husband's death but was confined to her home in Davisville with rheumatism for much of the time. Shortly after her mother-in-law's death, Susie became "weak and frail" herself, with an undiagnosed illness that made the remaining eight years of her life miserable. Pierce did not ignore these tragedies—quite the contrary—but they did seem to motivate him all the more toward the "extreme achievement," as one observer described it, that characterized his life.[7]

Politics beckoned first. After abandoning hope of a professional career off the farm because of family responsibilities, Pierce longed to utilize the critical thinking and speaking skills that he had developed in college in public office. As a steadfast member of the Republican Party, however, he found campaigning in a district that remained about 60 percent Democratic all his life not very fruitful. During the 1890s he ran, unsuccessfully, for several different local and state positions, confident throughout that, as he once put it, "this is a Republican year." That prediction finally came true in 1898, when he was elected to the state assembly. But after one uneventful term, the Democrats prevailed once again. Pierce's most memorable moment of his brief political career surely came when, one month before the 1896 presidential election, he infiltrated a meeting of Davisville Democrats and shouted, "Three cheers for McKinley!"[8]

Disappointed but far from discouraged, Pierce resolved to find other ways to distinguish himself. He applied the same ingenuity exhibited in his wheat and almond affairs to numerous public ventures. He participated in regional and state booster organizations such as the Sacramento Valley Development Association, the California Promotion Committee, and the California Development Board, "always hammering industriously on some proposition for the benefit and advancement of his section," the local paper boasted. On at least one such occasion, he derived a measure of personal satisfaction as well. Traveling with a group of enthusiasts to the World's Fair in Chicago in 1893 to promote northern California fruit, Pierce took three days by himself and "saw the old homestead" in

Kenosha—the trip his father had dreamed about but never taken. When the opportunity arose in 1902 for Davisville farmers to access water through the Yolo County Consolidated Water Company (from Cache Creek to the north, not Putah Creek), Pierce seized it. Declaring, "I am an irrigationist," he recounted the demise of the Putah Creek Water Company twenty years earlier "with such passion and grace" at a local "mass meeting" that many of his most skeptical neighbors subscribed, to their ultimate benefit. It was Pierce who made certain in 1911 that the section of the transcontinental Lincoln Highway between Sacramento and San Francisco passed through his hometown, in part to enhance his status as Davisville's first automobile owner. He also found the time to serve as trustee of the San Jose State Normal School for five years, to arrange Yolo County's exhibit at San Francisco's Panama Pacific International Exposition in 1915, and to travel to Alaska, Canada, Europe (twice), Asia, and Central America promoting the advantages of life in the Sacramento Valley.[9]

But of all Pierce's accomplishments, none proved more lasting or far-reaching than persuading University of California officials to choose Davisville as the site for a new agricultural college in 1906. At first, Jacob La Rue assisted him, but when his onetime rival and now best friend died suddenly at the age of forty-seven, Pierce was left to marshal the Davisville efforts on his own. Taking advantage of his status as an influential alumnus, Pierce drafted the original proposal to locate the University Farm in Davisville, arranged for the sale of a fertile tract of land along Putah Creek (part of the old Davis stock farm), personally chauffeured university president Benjamin Ide Wheeler on a full-day tour of Yolo County, and conducted a virtual one-man-chamber-of-commerce campaign to persuade Governor George C. Pardee, other influential officeholders, and the public at large of Davisville's advantages. He helped close the deal by paying the property taxes on the tract out of his own pocket and was intimately involved in all the key transactions regarding title, water rights, deeds, and abstracts. Not even the great San Francisco earthquake, which came in the middle of negotiations, slowed him down.[10]

Two years later, Pierce explained to a gathering of influential farmers and state officials the utmost importance of the University Farm: "The College of Agriculture is more necessary to the state than the school of medicine, law or theology. If we lived a more natural life in the fresh air, we could get along without medicine. If we had no lawyers, we might get along with justice. If we had no theology, we could get along with religion. But we could not live at all without an adequate supply of food, and for that we are dependant upon an intelligent system of agriculture." Here was a classic expression of agricultural fundamentalism, in the words of a supremely confident individual. The University Farm gave a coherency to Pierce's life that theretofore had been lacking. He knew well the value of education, but until then had felt largely detached from the university he so loved. As an agriculturist and horticulturist of considerable renown locally, he nonetheless longed for greater recognition within wider social and political circles. Most importantly, the establishment of the University Farm in Davisville satisfied, to some degree, Pierce's insatiable appetite for achievement—rooted in his Yankee heritage, intensified and consolidated by his father's relentless quest for gold, both literally on Weber Creek and metaphorically on Putah Creek, and boosted by his own life experiences. Having long searched for the good life, Pierce appeared to have found it.[11]

The same month that Pierce landed the University Farm for Davisville, he and his neighbors mourned the passing of "one of the pioneer mothers of Yolo County" and Davisville's oldest resident at the time, Susan Montgomery. No one left a larger legacy, in terms of sheer numbers, than Mrs. Montgomery. Since migrating to California from Missouri in 1853 to join her husband, Alexander, father-in-law, William, and brothers-in-law William W. and Hugh, Susan bore fifteen children, eleven of whom survived into adulthood and married children of other pioneer families. Inheriting the title "matron of Putah Creek" from her mother-in-law, Rebecca, upon the latter's death in 1886, Susan also left thirty grandchildren and twenty great-grandchildren. So many of these boys and girls came of age in the 1870s and 1880s that the Yolo County Board of Supervisors felt it necessary to form the Montgomery School District in Putah Sink to accommodate them. Weddings, housewarmings, and parties of a hundred guests and more on the Montgomery Ranch were commonplace. Four generations of Putah Creek residents, family and friends alike, attended this matron's funeral. In the Montgomery tradition, the procession that followed "was without doubt the longest ever known here," a local newspaper reported.[12]

The changes in the landscape that Susan witnessed on the ranch over the years were nothing short of phenomenal. For half a century, the Montgomerys "fought the brush," as one longtime resident of Davisville put it. When the senior William Montgomery arrived with his three sons in 1851, "their land was an impenetrable tangle of weeds, briars, and forest trees, a home for the deer, the elk, the jack rabbit, and the grizzly bear." Over the years, the "jungle" had been replaced by, in succession, cattle pasture, wheat fields, vineyards, and now almond orchards—

each change, in the minds of the Montgomerys and their neighbors, "marking a healthful progress." Farmers routinely congratulated themselves on having conquered their environment. In their minds, they had made the land better both productively and esthetically. "The beauties of our surrounding country so struck me," the same observer wrote of the orchards and vineyards near Davisville, "that mere words cannot describe them adequately." It was easy to wax poetic in this manner in June, when Putah Creek was "a beautiful stream from three to ten feet in depth"—and easy to forget that heavy rains spelled disaster for the Montgomerys nearly every bit as much as the Careys.[13]

The Montgomerys left their deepest imprint on the tradition of fine horsemanship they had brought with them from Missouri. Rattler the trotting stallion was a tough act to follow after all his success in the late 1850s and early 1860s. Rattler, in fact, left a lasting legacy of his own. Many of his offspring, identified as sired by their famous father, went on to celebrated careers, and horse racing itself became something of an obsession in the region. "Turfmen" of all backgrounds, Yankees, southerners, and immigrants alike, raised thoroughbred horses with as much or more passion than they felt for their wheat or fruit, and even Presbyterians as devout as the Pierces experienced the "unparalleled excitement" that awaited them at the Davisville racecourse. While the Pierces refrained from gambling, most others went to the track eager to place a wager or two. So enamored was one of the Montgomery clan with gambling that, in 1884, he borrowed $100 to make a bet and then refused to pay it back when his horse lost the race. When his lender took him to court, Montgomery insisted that anyone with a sense of honor would have given him another chance to pick a winner, and a jury of his peers agreed with him. Raising horses and gambling at the track had a cultural meaning to its participants beyond the chance to make money. These activities allowed them to entertain the same impulse that had failed them during the gold rush.[14]

That impulse persisted well into the twentieth century. Local ranchers won so many royal-purple grand-champion ribbons at state, national, and international competitions in the 1910s and 1920s that the entire area within a twelve-mile radius of the city of Davis (the local newspaper announced "the dropping of the ville" on April 14, 1906) became known as the "Purple Circle." Among its members was John Elmo Montgomery, one of William W.'s sons. John Elmo trained a number of award-winning trotters and pacers, but "Jim Logan" was his prize horse. Between 1909 and 1917, Jim Logan won dozens of races, not only in Davis, Woodland, and Sacramento, but on the East Coast circuit as well. The most memorable, by most accounts, came on Thursday afternoon, September 10, 1914, on the Woodland track. Pitted against local upstarts Eleta J and Don Pronto, Jim Logan fell well behind out of the gate, but on the home stretch "made a fine burst of speed" to beat both competitors by a nose, breaking the Pacific Coast record once held by Rattler himself.[15]

When Jim Logan died at the old age of twenty-six in 1932, local newspapers published his obituary as a feature news story, just as they had Rattler's sixty-nine years earlier. In minute detail, they described his greatest races, "nationally-known" reputation, and numerous offspring—some of them champions in their own right and all of them treated as family pets by the Montgomerys. "Elmo Montgomery," stated one writer, "breeds them, feeds them, breaks them, races them, and sells them" for as much as $10,000 a colt. The obituaries also focused intently on Jim Logan's impact on his community. "This fine, fiery, fast, magnificent piece of thoroughbred horseflesh," one maintained, "made remarkable history for himself and this section." Another called him "the Man of War of Pacific Coast pacers" and simply "the horse that made Yolo Famous." In earning for himself a legendary place in the annals of California horse racing, Jim Logan brought home the gold to Davisville.[16]

And thus the allegory continued. For more than half a century, life along Putah Creek seemed to imitate drama, and vice-versa. Each character, object, and event—from Carey, Pierce, and Montgomery, to gold, wheat, and almonds, to the floods, droughts, and bankruptcies—seemed designed to mock the classic American values of optimism and hard work. But the analogy between allegory and history ends there. An allegory, after all, is supposed to illustrate an overarching idea or principle, usually moral or religious in substance and tone. The history of Putah Creek, however, offers no such definitive message or legacy. One might be tempted to conclude that the region's farmers were greedy capitalists who, upon failing as greedy miners, took up the most easily and profitably produced frontier crop. That same unquenchable thirst then led them to oppress their workers, rape the land, and in general help launch California agriculture in the wrong direction. Such a conclusion is too simplistic, although Putah Creek farmers were hardly symbols of Jeffersonian virtue.

What we have, then, is neither allegory nor any other grand literary device, but simply a cautionary tale. It may sound trite to say that while some dreams can indeed be golden, most are invariably tarnished. To a man, the miners-turned-farmers along Putah Creek believed that if just one of the golden dreams came true, then all the broken dreams would be worth it. Their capacity to appreciate what they had rarely matched their capacity to dream for more. Whether that was a strength or a flaw in their character often depended on the circumstances at hand, be they economic, environmental, political, or just pure luck. That fate captured the essence of rural life in California after the gold rush.

Remnants

Driving from Davis to Winters today would seem to pose few complications. The land is flat, and Russell Boulevard, the road between these two bedroom communities in the lower Sacramento Valley, heads due west along the section lines, about a mile north of Putah Creek. On the left, as the trip begins, lies the sprawling campus of UC Davis. Two miles down the road on the right, along the 120-year-old "Avenue of Trees," sits the magnificently preserved Victorian farmhouse built by the La Rues in 1888, though surrounded by apartment houses, not vineyards. Two miles farther along, on the left, two tall pillars still mark the entrance to the former Pierce ranch, both of them made of stones collected by George Jr. and Susie on their extensive world travels. All along, thus far, Russell Boulevard looks to be a straight shot to Winters, just as it did when it served wheat farmers in the 1870s as Davisville Road West and motorists in the early twentieth century as the transcontinental Lincoln Highway. Then and now, however, almost halfway to Winters, three-quarters of a mile past Pierce Ranch Road, the boulevard suddenly zigzags at slanted ninety-degree angles—not once but three times—before resuming a more direct course. The detour is caused by Rancho Rio de los Putos, the Mexican land grant awarded to William Wolfskill in 1842, confirmed by the California Land Commission in 1854, subdivided into twenty-one lots by the end of the 1870s, and to this day never surveyed by the federal government in the customary 640-acre sections.[1]

Heading in the opposite direction, Russell Boulevard changes course again when it crosses A Street in downtown Davis. Here, it parallels the original streets of Davisville, which, in 1868, were aligned not with the section lines but with the east and west boundaries of another Mexican rancho, Laguna de Santos Callé. Of course, whether Davisville itself and surrounding areas had actually been part of Laguna de Santos Callé and not part of still another grant, Los Putos, was not determined conclusively until *Brown v. Greene* reached a final resolution in 1887.[2]

Remnants of the past also await those who prefer the train. On the Amtrak line from Davis to Oakland, in the six-mile stretch between Martinez and Crockett, the tracks still cling to the inhospitable hillside along Carquinez Strait, where, even amidst the explosive housing market of recent years in the San Francisco Bay Area, there has been little development. At low tide, however, train passengers can still see the outlines of the old wharves of the Port Costa Warehouse and Dock Company and the other former shipping firms, marked by hundreds of charred pilings protruding from the water. The wheat-shipping capital of the Pacific Coast in its heyday, Port Costa operated against the grain from the outset as declining prices ensured its eventual demise. Wheat farmers themselves produced in prodigious amounts, not realizing, as we can in retrospect, that their enterprise—and the days of $2 per cental, in particular—was destined to fail even before Port Costa came to life in the early 1880s. Today's farmers might be the only ones who, without hesitation, would empathize with their predecessors' struggle to resolve the great paradox of agriculture in the modern economic world: farmers' very identity—their inner drive to produce, produce, produce—invariably gluts the market, brings low prices, and spreads misery and frustration.[3]

Their predecessors would have marveled at the soaring dams, many hundreds of miles of high levees, numerous bypass channels, and maze of canals that now protect the Sacramento Valley from the terrifying floods that so often disrupted their lives. The Sacramento Flood Control Project, constructed over the course of the first half of the twentieth century, stands today as one of the most complex and massive systems of its kind ever built. While this engineering wonder prevents the valley from routinely becoming an inland sea, it is by no means foolproof—witness the immense devastation caused by the floods of 1986 and 1997. Should any of us succumb to the temptation to chide our nineteenth-century counterparts for their arrogant and ultimately futile quest to control nature, we need only look at the huge new housing developments that now spread across the expansive American River floodplain north of Sacramento, where, for almost 150 years, no one dared build at all. Another "flood of the century" awaits only a break or two in the levee.[4]

The same dangers, on a smaller scale, exist along Putah Creek. Even after the U.S. Army Corps of Engineers sealed off the entrance of the "old" creek at La Rue's bend in 1948, making Carey's canal the only through channel, both "forks" continued to flood during heavy rains. In 1973, for example, Davis residents for several blocks in the vicinity of Seventh and B streets gained access to their homes by boat only—not unlike George and Eunice Pierce upon their arrival in the winter of 1854. Evidence of the many small sloughs that used to carry off the floodwaters of Putah Creek can still be found in backyards, the cemetery, and other un-developed locations in town. The dam that La Rue, Briggs, and Pierce envisioned at the top of Putah canyon in 1882 was in fact built in the mid-1950s to control flooding and to divert water south to the growing cities of Fairfield and Vacaville via the Putah South Canal. Yet, should Monticello Dam break, as dams are prone to do after a century or so in use, tens of thousands of acres of land north and south of Putah Creek, both cultivated and urbanized, would be buried under a veritable avalanche of water more explosive and more destructive than anything witnessed by Pierce, Carey, and their contemporaries.[5]

If the laws of nature, the laws of supply and demand, and the lay of the land itself still often elude our comprehension today, we can only imagine the fear and confusion they generated 100 to 150 years ago among Putah Creek farmers. With the stigma of having failed in the gold rush added to the already daunting obsta-cles of natural disaster, uncertain land titles, contradictory land policy, and eco-nomic chaos, the odds of striking it rich in the Sacramento Valley seemed remote indeed. There was an unmistakable harshness to rural life, but it was balanced by a profound, if often exaggerated, even misguided, sense of hope. The Pierces, William Montgomery and his three sons, Charles Greene, R. S. Carey—they all felt that they *had* to succeed. With little to show for themselves after their treach-erous overland journeys and hard work in the goldfields, none of them cared to look failure in the eye again. Thus motivated, they made Putah Creek and later Davisville into one of the most prominent rural communities in the state and helped transform the Sacramento Valley into one of the most productive agricul-tural regions in the world. Theirs is not a heroic story—even the participants did not like to talk much about their checkered pasts and fortunes—but it illustrates the extent to which dreams, for better or for worse, drive the entrepreneur in the modern age of American agriculture.

Prologue. "Glorious"

1. Quoted in Rodman W. Paul, ed., *The California Gold Discovery: Sources, Documents, Accounts, and Memoirs Relating to the Discovery of Gold at Sutter's Mill* (Georgetown, CA: Talisman Press, 1966), 199.

2. This short narrative of events draws from the following: Hubert Howe Bancroft, *History of California*, 7 vols. (San Francisco: History Co., 1884–90), 6:26–428; H. W. Brands, *The Age of Gold: The California Gold Rush and the New American Dream* (New York: Doubleday, 2002); John Walton Caughey, *The California Gold Rush* (1948; reprint, Berkeley: Univ. of California Press, 1975); J. S. Holliday, *The World Rushed In: The California Gold Rush Experience* (New York: Simon & Schuster, 1981); Rodman W. Paul, *California Gold: The Beginning of Mining in the Far West* (Cambridge: Harvard Univ. Press, 1947); Paul, *The California Gold Discovery*; James J. Rawls and Walton Bean, *California: An Interpretive History*, 6th ed. (New York: McGraw-Hill, 1993), 82–95; Richard B. Rice, William A. Bullough, and Richard J. Orsi, *The Elusive Eden: A New History of California*, 2nd ed. (New York: McGraw-Hill, 1996), 185–204; Malcolm J. Rohrbough, *Days of Gold: The California Gold Rush and the American Nation* (Berkeley: Univ. of California Press, 1997); Kevin Starr, *Americans and the California Dream, 1850–1915* (New York: Oxford Univ. Press, 1973), 49–68; Richard T. Stillson, "Golden Words: Communications and Information Dispersal in the California Gold Rush" (Ph.D. diss., Johns Hopkins University, 2003).

3. Quoted in Paul, *The California Gold Discovery*, 129.

4. Quoted in Bancroft, *History of California*, 6:56.

5. Ibid., 6:60.

6. Quoted in Paul, *The California Gold Discovery*, 101.

7. Quoted in Caughey, *The California Gold Rush*, 40.

8. Ibid.

9. Quoted in Paul, *The California Gold Discovery*, 97.

10. Quoted in Rohrbough, *Days of Gold*, 27.

11. Ibid., 26.

12. Stephen J. Field, *Personal Reminiscences of Early Days in California* (1893; reprint, New York: Da Capo Press, 1968), 6–7.

13. E.g, *Missouri Whig* (Palmyra), Feb. 14, 1850.

14. Quoted in Rawls and Bean, *California*, 146.

15. Quoted in Caughey, *The California Gold Rush*, 293.

16. Quoted in Starr, *Americans and the California Dream*, 55.

17. Ibid., 57.

18. In addition to Brands, *The Age of Gold*, and Rohrbough, *Days of Gold*, see, among many others, Susan L. Johnson, *Roaring Camp: The Social World of the California Gold Rush* (New York: Norton, 2000); Brian Roberts, *American Alchemy: The California Gold Rush and Middle-Class Culture* (Chapel Hill: Univ. of North Carolina Press, 2000); Kenneth N. Owens, ed., *Riches for All: The California Gold Rush and the World* (Lincoln: Univ. of Nebraska Press, 2002); and the four-volume California History Sesquicentennial Series, published by the University of California Press: Ramón A. Gutiérrez and Richard J. Orsi, eds., *Contested Eden: California before the Gold Rush* (1997); James J. Rawls and Richard J. Orsi, eds., *A Golden State: Mining and Economic Development in Gold Rush California* (1999); Kevin Starr and Richard J. Orsi, eds., *Rooted in Barbarous Soil: People, Culture, and Community in Gold Rush California* (2000); and John F. Burns and Richard J. Orsi, eds., *Taming the Elephant: Politics, Government, and Law in Pioneer California* (2003).

19. Quoted in Bancroft, *History of California*, 6:118.

20. Holliday, *The World Rushed In*.

21. Rohrbough, *Days of Gold*, 6.

22. Joyce Oldham Appleby, "The Vexed Story of American Capitalism Told by American Historians," *Journal of the Early Republic* 21 (Spring 2001): 1–18; Starr, *Americans and the California Dream*, 49–68; Brands, *The Age of Gold*, esp. 441–43; Jackson Lears, *Something for Nothing: Luck in America* (New York: Viking Penguin, 2003), esp. 1–24; David Vaught, "State of the Art—Rural History, or Why Is There No Rural History of California?" *Agricultural History* 74 (Fall 2000): 759–74.

Chapter One. Removals

1. George W. Pierce, Daily Journals, 1867–90, entries for Feb. 16 and 17, 1882; Feb. 16 and 17 (quote), 1884; Apr. 19, 1887, Pierce Family Papers, Department of Special Collections, University of California Library, Davis (hereafter Pierce journal); *Sacramento Daily Union*, Feb. 17, 1854; Joann Leach Larkey, *Davisville '68: The History and Heritage of the City of Davis, Yolo County, California* (Davis: Davis Historical and Landmarks Commission, 1969), 200–202.

2. Pierce journal, Apr. 20, 1882; Apr. 20 and July 8, 1884; Apr. 20 and July 8, 1886; Apr. 20, 1887; July 4 and 8, 1888; July 8, 1889; *Yolo Weekly Mail*, Mar. 1, 1890; *Mail of Woodland*, Oct. 27, 1908; C. W. Butterfield, *History of Racine and Kenosha Counties, Wisconsin* (Chicago: Western Historical Co., 1879), 331–40; Carrie Cropley, *Kenosha: From Pioneer Village to Modern City, 1835–1935* (Kenosha, WI: Kenosha County Historical Society, 1958), 2–7; Frank H. Lyman, *The City of Kenosha and Kenosha County Wisconsin: A Record of Settlement, Organization, Progress, and Achievement* (Chicago: S. J. Clarke Publishing Co., 1916), 12; Robert Hugh Downes, "Economic and Social Development of Kenosha County," *Transactions of the Wisconsin Academy of Sciences, Arts, and Letters, 1901* (Madison: State Printer, 1902), 550–

52; Mary D. Bradford, *Memoirs of Mary D. Bradford* (Evansville, WI: Antes Press, 1993), 1; Wallace Mygatt, "First Settlement of Kenosha," in *Collections of the State Historical Society of Wisconsin*, vol. 3, ed. Lyman Copeland Draper (Madison: State Historical Society of Wisconsin, 1904), 395.

3. George Rogers Taylor, *The Transportation Revolution, 1815–1860* (New York: Rinehart, 1951); Charles Sellars, *The Market Revolution: Jacksonian America, 1815–1846* (New York: Oxford Univ. Press, 1991); John G. Clark, *The Grain Trade in the Old Northwest* (Urbana: Univ. of Illinois Press, 1966); R. Douglas Hurt, *The Ohio Frontier: Crucible of the Old Northwest, 1720–1830* (Bloomington: Indiana Univ. Press, 1996), esp. 388–96; Martin Bruegel, *Farm, Shop, Landing: The Rise of a Market Society in the Hudson Valley, 1780–1860* (Durham, NC: Duke Univ. Press, 2002); Charles E. Brooks, *Frontier Settlement and Market Revolution: The Holland Land Purchase* (Ithaca: Cornell Univ. Press, 1996).

4. Pierce journal, July 4, 1884.

5. Alan Taylor, *William Cooper's Town: Power and Persuasion on the Frontier of the Early American Republic* (New York: Vintage Books, 1995), 88–95; Susan E. Gray, *The Yankee West: Community Life on the Michigan Frontier* (Chapel Hill: Univ. of North Carolina Press, 1996), 1–16; Jon Gjerde, *The Minds of the West: Ethnocultural Evolution in the Rural Middle West, 1830–1917* (Chapel Hill: Univ. of North Carolina Press, 1997), chap. 1.

6. Pierce journal, July 8, 1884; July 8, 1886; Lyman, *City of Kenosha and Kenosha County Wisconsin*, 13–14, 27; Cropley, *Kenosha*, 12–21; Mygatt, "First Settlement of Kenosha," 398; Larkey, *Davisville '68*, 200; Patent Records, Kenosha County, WI, from the U.S. Bureau of Land Management web site: http://www.glorecords.blm.gov; G. Washington Pierce, Account Book, Southport, 1845–50, box 2, Pierce Family Papers (hereafter Pierce Southport Account Book).

7. Lyman, *City of Kenosha and Kenosha County Wisconsin*, 15–17, 52–89; Cropley, *Kenosha*, 1–11, 17; Taylor, *William Cooper's Town*, 88–95; Gray, *The Yankee West*, 1–16.

8. Taylor, *William Cooper's Town*, 90–91; John Giffin Thompson, *The Rise and Decline of the Wheat Growing Industry in Wisconsin*, Bulletin of the University of Wisconsin, no. 292, May 1907, 28–30, 123–28.

9. Clark, *The Grain Trade in the Old Northwest*, 82, 96; Cropley, *Kenosha*, 1, 7; Lyman, *City of Kenosha and Kenosha County Wisconsin*, 65; Downes, "Economic and Social Development of Kenosha County," 552; Thompson, *The Rise and Decline of the Wheat Growing Industry in Wisconsin*, 25–26 (quote at 25).

10. Pierce Southport Account Book, 6, 9, 17, 22, 25, 35, 39, 41; George Washington Pierce, Tax receipt, Racine County, WI, Jan. 3, 1844, box 2, Pierce Family Papers; Thompson, *The Rise and Decline of the Wheat Growing Industry in Wisconsin*, 22, 32; R. Douglas Hurt, *American Agriculture: A Brief History* (Ames: Iowa State Univ. Press, 1994), 133–47.

11. Pierce journal, Sept. 29, 1880; Pierce Southport Account Book, 18, 42, 49, 53; Larkey, *Davisville '68*, 200.

12. Thompson, *The Rise and Decline of the Wheat Growing Industry in Wisconsin*, 20–26, 35 (quote at 21–22); Pierce Southport Account Book, passim; Cropley, *Kenosha*, 12, 22, 26.

13. Pierce journal, Apr. 15, 1886; Larkey, *Davisville '68*, 200; Cropley, *Kenosha*, 22.

14. Pierce journal, Apr. 19, 1886. On the decisions that faced Washington, Eunice, and

their contemporaries, see Malcolm J. Rohrbough, *Days of Gold: The California Gold Rush and the American Nation* (Berkeley: Univ. of California Press, 1997), 33–39, 172–74; Jo Ann Levy, *They Saw the Elephant: Women in the California Gold Rush* (Norman: Univ. of Oklahoma Press, 1992), pref. and intro.; and Brian Roberts, *American Alchemy: The California Gold Rush and Middle-Class Culture* (Chapel Hill: Univ. of North Carolina Press, 2000), 69–92.

15. Pierce's overland diary is in box 2, Pierce Family Papers. The literature on the overland route is extensive; for a lively synthesis, see H. W. Brands, *The Age of Gold: The California Gold Rush and the New American Dream* (New York: Doubleday, 2002), 122–90.

16. Pierce journal, Apr.19, 1888; Apr. 19, 1889 (quotes); *Yolo Weekly Mail*, Mar. 1, 1890; *Mail of Woodland*, Oct. 27, 1908. A long list of provisions can be found at the beginning of Pierce's overland diary. On what life in the gold country might have been like for the Pierces, see Rohrbough, *Days of Gold*, 172–96; Levy, *They Saw the Elephant*, 53–70; Susan L. Johnson, "The Last Fandango: Women, Work, and the End of the California Gold Rush," in *Riches for All: The California Gold Rush and the World*, ed. Kenneth N. Owens (Lincoln: Univ. of Nebraska Press, 2002), 230–63; Brands, *The Age of Gold*, 193–242; Roberts, *American Alchemy*, 197–219; Rodman W. Paul, *California Gold: The Beginning of Mining in the Far West* (Cambridge: Harvard Univ. Press, 1947), 69–90.

17. *Mail of Woodland*, Oct. 27, 1908. On Sacramento, see Mark A. Eifler, *Gold Rush Capitalists: Greed and Growth in Sacramento* (Albuquerque: Univ. of New Mexico Press, 2002); and Kenneth N. Owens, "Begun by Gold: Sacramento and the Gold Rush Legacy after 150 Years," in Owens, *Riches for All*, 328–54. On failure in the goldfields and its consequences, see Rohrbough, *Days of Gold*, 185–96; and Roberts, *American Alchemy*, 156–60.

18. On Greene, see *A Memorial and Biographical History of Northern California* (Chicago: Lewis Publishing Co., 1891), 439; and on Hutchinson, see note 19. The other Kenoshans (and identifying sources) were as follows: Benjamin Cahoon, in *H. O. Beatty v. R. C. Clark* (1861), California Supreme Court, no. 3223, "Transcript on Appeal," 141–43, California State Archives, Sacramento, and Lyman, *City of Kenosha and Kenosha County Wisconsin*, 86; Russell Crary, in *George W. Pierce v. Henry E. Robinson* (1859), California Supreme Court, no. 2329, "Transcript on Appeal," 116–20, California State Archives, and Patent Records, Kenosha County, Wis.; Hudson Fox, in *Davisville Advertiser*, Dec. 18, 1869, and Pierce journal, Jan. 1, 1867; Frederick W. Hatch, in Winfield J. Davis, *An Illustrated History of Sacramento County, California* (Chicago: Lewis Publishing Co., 1890), 736–37; Catharine Hutchinson, in *Sacramento Daily Record–Union*, Sept. 24, 1884; Richard and Thomas Hext, in *Beatty v. Clark*, "Transcript on Appeal," 155–57, and *Mail of Woodland*, Nov. 5, 1903; and Gilbert L. Luddington, in J. M. Guinn, *History of the State of California and Biographical Record of the Sacramento Valley, California* (Chicago: Chapman Publishing Co., 1906), 835, and Patent Records, Kenosha County, Wis. For wages on the Big Ranch, see Frank T. Gilbert, *The Illustrated Atlas and History of Yolo County* (San Francisco: De Pue & Co., 1879), 46.

19. *Sacramento Daily Record–Union*, Sept. 24, 1884; *San Francisco News Letter*, Aug. 26, 1876; Alonzo Phelps, *Contemporary Biography of California's Representative Men* (San Francisco: A. L. Bancroft, 1881–82), 364; Lyman, *The City of Kenosha and Kenosha County Wisconsin*, 87; Cropley, *Kenosha*, 21–24; Bradford, *Memoirs of Mary D. Bradford*, 10–13 (quote at 11).

20. Owens, "Begun by Gold"; Eifler, *Gold Rush Capitalists.*

21. *Sacramento Daily Union,* Apr. 23, 1851; May 6, 1851; Mar. 24, 1852; Apr. 1, 1852; Apr. 3, 1852; Apr. 5, 1852; Mar. 31, 1853; *Sacramento Daily Record–Union,* Sept. 24, 1884; *San Francisco News Letter,* Aug. 26, 1876; *Sacramento Bee,* Aug. 5, 1950; Phelps, *Contemporary Biography of California's Representative Men,* 365–67.

22. Yolo County, "Deeds," Book A, 288, Yolo County Archives, Woodland, CA (hereafter YCA); C. I. Hutchinson to James Warren, Sept. 29, 1852, box 3, James L. Warren Papers, Bancroft Library, University of California, Berkeley; *Sacramento Daily Union,* Oct. 8, 1852; May 7, 1853; Gilbert, *Illustrated Atlas and History of Yolo County,* 43; Horace S. Foote, *Pen Pictures from the Garden of the World, or Santa Clara County, California* (Chicago: Lewis Publishing, 1888), 617; Rodman W. Paul, "The Beginnings of Agriculture in California: Innovation vs. Continuity," *California Historical Quarterly* 52 (Spring 1973): 23.

23. *Sacramento Daily Union,* Apr. 3 and 5, 1852.

24. *Missouri Whig* (Palmyra), Feb. 20, 1850.

25. G. F. Wright, *History of Sacramento County, California* (Oakland: Thompson & West, 1880), 282; Larkey, *Davisville '68,* 161–62; *Davis Enterprise,* Mar. 19, 1970.

26. Larkey, *Davisville '68,* 161–62; *Sacramento Daily Union,* Oct. 6, 1881; *Davis Enterprise,* Aug. 19, 1971. On the Bear Flag Revolt, see Neal Harlow, *California Conquered: War and Peace on the Pacific, 1846–1850* (Berkeley: Univ. of California Press, 1982), 61–114; and Richard B. Rice, William A. Bullough, and Richard J. Orsi, *The Elusive Eden: A New History of California* (New York: McGraw-Hill, 1996), 113–27.

27. Wright, *History of Sacramento County,* 282; *Davis Enterprise,* Aug. 19, 1971.

28. *Sacramento Daily Record–Union,* Oct. 6, 1881; *W. W. Brown v. C. E. Greene* (1884), California State Supreme Court, no. 9443, "Transcript on Appeal," 199–204, California State Archives; Yolo County, "Board of Supervisors Minutes," Court of Sessions Book, July 8, 1850, YCA; Helen S. Giffen, *Trail-Blazing Pioneer: Colonel Joseph Ballinger Chiles* (San Francisco: John Howell Books, 1969), 77–78; Wright, *History of Sacramento County,* 282; William O. Russell, ed., *History of Yolo County, California: Its Resources and Its People* (Woodland: n.p., 1940), 133; Larkey, *Davisville '68,* 37, 153, 161–62.

29. *Brown v. Greene,* "Transcript on Appeal," 200–201, 204; *Sacramento Daily Union,* May 7, 1853; *Davisville Enterprise,* Jan. 5, 1900; *Davis Enterprise,* Feb. 26, 1970 (quote); Larkey, *Davisville '68,* 161–62 (quote).

30. Larkey, *Davisville '68,* 159–62; Hurt, *The Ohio Frontier,* 211–24; Yolo County, "Marks and Brands," YCA (for the Davis earmark); Yolo County, "Deeds," Book B, 208, YCA.

31. Guinn, *History of the State of California,* 1521, 1698; Larkey, *Davisville '68,* 192; U.S. Census, Population Schedules for Russellville, Logan County, Kentucky, 1820, microfilm (Washington, DC: National Archives, 1967); Thomas D. Clark, *Agrarian Kentucky* (Lexington: Univ. of Kentucky Press, 1977), 1–63; Paul W. Gates, "Tenants of the Log Cabin," *Mississippi Valley Historical Review* 49 (June 1962): 1–18 (quote at 4); R. Douglas Hurt, *Agriculture and Slavery in Missouri's Little Dixie* (Columbia: Univ. of Missouri Press, 1992), 24–50 (quote at 50).

32. Guinn, *History of the State of California,* 1521, 1698; R. I. Holcombe, *History of Marion County, Missouri* (1884; reprint, Hannibal: Marion County Historical Society, 1979),

146–295, 716–18 (quote at 716); Hurt, *Agriculture and Slavery in Missouri's Little Dixie*, 24–50, 62; Paul W. Gates, *History of Public Land Law Development* (Washington, DC: Zenger Publishing Co., 1968), 104–8.

33. Patent Records, Marion County, Missouri, from the U.S. Bureau of Land Management web site: http://www.glorecords.blm.gov; U.S. Census, Population and Slave Schedules for Union Township, Marion County, Missouri, 1840 and 1850, microfilm (Washington, DC: National Archives, 1967); Hurt, *Agriculture and Slavery in Missouri's Little Dixie*, 215–44.

34. Patent Records, Marion and Shelby counties, Missouri; Holcombe, *History of Marion County, Missouri*, 248–95; William H. Bingham, *General History of Shelby County, Missouri* (Chicago: Henry Taylor & Co., 1911), 39, 47; Guinn, *History of the State of California*, 1521, 1698; Hurt, *Agriculture and Slavery in Missouri's Little Dixie*, 138–44.

35. Holcombe, *History of Marion County, Missouri*, 249; Hurt, *Agriculture and Slavery in Missouri's Little Dixie*, 213; T. H. Breen, "Horses and Gentlemen: The Cultural Significance of Gambling among the Gentry of Virginia," *William and Mary Quarterly* 34 (Apr. 1977): 239–57; Bertram Wyatt-Brown, *Southern Honor: Ethics and Behavior in the Old South* (Oxford: Oxford Univ. Press, 1982), 339–50; Kenneth S. Greenberg, *Honor and Slavery* (Princeton: Princeton Univ. Press, 1996), 135–40; Melvin L. Adelman, *A Sporting Time: New York City and the Rise of Modern Athletics, 1820–70* (Urbana: Univ. of Illinois Press, 1986), 27–89; Jackson Lears, *Something for Nothing: Luck in America* (New York: Viking, 2003), esp. 1–24.

36. Holcombe, *History of Marion County, Missouri*, 295–96 (quote); Guinn, *History of the State of California*, 1521, 1698; Bingham, *General History of Shelby County, Missouri*, 49–50. The referenced letters were all printed in the *Missouri Whig* (Palmyra) in 1849 and 1850 and are available on-line at http://www.rootsweb.com/~momarion. Many of the transcriptions are dated by month and year but not by specific day. Monte is a card game in which two cards are chosen from four laid out; a player then bets that one of the two will be matched by the dealer before the other one.

37. Guinn, *History of the State of California*, 1521, 1698; E. Dyer, Deputy Surveyor, "Field Notes of the Subdivision Lines in Township 8 North, Range 2 East of the Mt. Diablo Base and Meridian in the State of California," 1862, Surveyor Records, Bureau of Land Management, California State Office, Sacramento (quote); Yolo County, "Assessment Rolls," 1853, YCA.

38. The breakdown by the end of the decade was approximately 42 percent Yankees, 30 percent upland southerners, 7 percent midlanders, 13 percent German immigrants, and 7 percent British immigrants; see U.S. Census, Population Schedules for Putah Township, Yolo County and Tremont Township, Solano County, California, 1860, microfilm (Washington, DC: National Archives, 1967).

39. Unlike the federal census schedules for 1850 or 1860, the special census taken by the state of California in 1852 (a transcribed copy is available in the California Room, California State Library, Sacramento) listed both place of birth *and* previous place of residence. For those who arrived after 1852, however, previous place of residence is not readily available. The assessment rolls that have survived (1850, 1853, 1856–60), reveal approximately

300 individuals who paid taxes in Putah Township over the course of the decade—almost all of them male (Yolo County, "Assessment Rolls," YCA). I have been able to identify removal patterns for 105 of them (including 18 women not on the assessment rolls) from a variety of biographical sources, among them newspaper obituaries (many from the extensive file at the Yolo County Archives), county, district, and state court cases, and the following local and county histories: *A Memorial and Biographical History of Northern California; History of Solano County* (San Francisco: Wood, Alley & Co., 1879); Davis, *An Illustrated History of Sacramento County;* Gilbert, *Illustrated Atlas and History of Yolo County;* Tom Gregory, *History of Solano and Napa Counties, California* (Los Angeles: Historic Record Co., 1912); Tom Gregory, *History of Yolo County* (Los Angeles: Historic Record Co., 1913); Guinn, *History of the State of California;* Larkey, *Davisville '68;* G. Walter Reed, *History of Sacramento County, California, with Biographical Sketches* (Los Angeles: Historic Record Co., 1923); Russell, *History of Yolo County;* and Wright, *History of Sacramento County*. Of the 105 individuals, 86 migrated to California from the Midwest (esp. WI, OH, and MO, but also IL, IN, IA, and MI).

Chapter Two. Seduced

1. C. I. Hutchinson to James Warren, Sept. 29, 1852, box 3, James L. Warren Papers, Bancroft Library, University of California, Berkeley; *Sacramento Daily Union*, Oct. 8, 1852 (quote); May 7, 1853; Frank T. Gilbert, *Illustrated Atlas and History of Yolo County* (San Francisco: De Pue & Co., 1879), 43; Rodman W. Paul, "The Beginnings of Agriculture in California: Innovation vs. Continuity," *California Historical Quarterly* 52 (Spring 1973): 18, 23; Yolo County, "Mortgages," Book A, 9, 395, Yolo County Archives, Woodland, CA (hereafter YCA); *Charles E. Greene v. His Creditors* (1861), Yolo County, County Court Case Files, Civil Case no. 107, YCA. On fencing in the Midwest, see John Mack Faragher, *Sugar Creek: Life on the Illinois Prairie* (New Haven: Yale Univ. Press), 70–71, 132; and William Cronon, *Nature's Metropolis: Chicago and the Great West* (New York: Norton, 1991), 101.

2. *Sacramento Daily Union*, June 4, 1852; *California Farmer*, May 24, 1855; *California Culturist*, June 1858; *Daily Alta California*, July 30, 1853; Will S. Green, "The Upper Sacramento," *Hutchings' Illustrated California Magazine* (Apr. 1857): 493–96; C. P. Sprague and H. W. Atwell, *The Western Shore Gazetteer and Commercial Directory, for the State of California . . . Yolo County* (San Francisco: Press of Bancroft, 1870), 1–5, 43; Elna Bakker, *An Island Called California: An Ecological Introduction to Its Natural Communities* (Berkeley: Univ. of California Press, 1971), 146–57; Paul, "The Beginnings of Agriculture in California," 16–17.

3. Bakker, *An Island Called California*, 123–57; Stephen Johnson, Gerald Haslam, and Robert Dawson, *The Great Central Valley: California's Heartland* (Berkeley: Univ. of California Press, 1993), 5–11, 27, 34, 87; John Muir, *The Mountains of California* (New York: Anchor Books, 1961), 260–62; Robert Kelley, *Battling the Inland Sea: American Political Culture, Public Policy, and the Sacramento Valley, 1850–1986* (Berkeley: Univ. of California Press, 1989), 3–6; Joseph A. McGowan, *History of the Sacramento Valley* (New York: Lewis Historical Publishing, 1961), 1:3–16; Kenneth Thompson, "Riparian Forests of the Sacramento

Valley, California," *Annals of the Association of American Geographers* 51 (Sept. 1961): 294–314; Thompson, "Historic Flooding of the Sacramento Valley," *Pacific Historical Review* 29 (Sept. 1960): 349–60.

4. In addition to the sources cited in note 3, see Sprague and Atwell, *Western Shore Gazetteer*, 54–55, 86–91, 98; *Pacific Rural Press*, Aug. 21, 1880; Sue Coggins, *Puta-To to North Fork of Putah Creek* (n.p., 1970), 1–2, Department of Special Collections, University of California Library, Davis; Ann Brice, *Exploring Putah Creek: From Monticello Dam to the Yolo Wildlife Area* (Davis: Putah Creek Council, 2001), 4–5, 21–23; Joann Leach Larkey, *Davisville '68: The History and Heritage of the City of Davis, Yolo County, California* (Davis: Davis Historical and Landmarks Commission, 1969), 6–9; Mike Madison, *A Sense of Order: The Rural Landscape of Lower Putah Creek* (Winters, CA: Yolo Press, 2002), 15–16; Michael P. Marchetti and Peter B. Moyle, "Conflicting Values Complicate Stream Protection: The Case of Putah Creek," *California Agriculture* 49 (Nov.–Dec. 1995): 73–78.

5. McGowan, *History of the Sacramento Valley*, 1:12, 159; Faragher, *Sugar Creek*, 61–67; Cronon, *Nature's Metropolis*, 101–3; Joann Leach Larkey, *Winters: A Heritage of Horticulture, a Harmony of Purpose* (Woodland: Yolo County Historical Society, 1991), 10; William Cronon, *Changes in the Land: Indians, Colonists, and the Ecology of New England* (New York: Hill & Wang, 1983); 159–70; Richard B. Rice, William A. Bullough, and Richard J. Orsi, *The Elusive Eden: A New History of California* (New York: McGraw-Hill, 1996), 98–99; Muir, *The Mountains of California* (quote at 260).

6. Tom Gregory, *History of Yolo County* (Los Angeles: Historic Record Co., 1913), 60 (quote). See also U.S. Land Case no. 411, Northern District, Laguna de Santos Callé Grant, 10–11, 15–37, Bancroft Library, on the emptiness of the area.

7. *Dixon Tribune*, Feb. 23, 1878; *W. W. Brown v. C. E. Greene* (1884), California State Supreme Court, no. 9443, "Transcript on Appeal," 62 (quote), California State Archives, Sacramento; Alfred C. Grover, *Indians of the Yolo County Area* (Woodland: Yolo County Historical Society, 1965); A. L. Kroeber, *The Patwin and Their Neighbors* (Berkeley: Univ. of California Press, 1932); Sherburne F. Cook, "The Epidemic of 1830–1833 in California and Oregon," *University of California Publications in American Archaeology and Ethnology* 3 (1955): 318; Joann L. Larkey and Shipley Walters, *Yolo County: Land of Changing Patterns* (Northridge, CA: Windsor Publications, 1987), 9–13; Rice, Bullough, and Orsi, *The Elusive Eden*, 30–45; James Sandos, "Between Crucifix and Lance: Indian-White Relations in California, 1769–1848," in *Contested Eden: California before the Gold Rush*, ed. Ramón A. Gutiérrez and Richard J. Orsi (Berkeley: Univ. of California Press, 1997), 216; William Preston, "Serpent in the Garden: Environmental Change in Colonial California," ibid., 264–66; Erwin Gudde, *California Place Names: The Origin and Etymology of Current Geographical Names* (Berkeley: Univ. of California Press, 1969), 259.

8. McGowan, *History of the Sacramento Valley*, 13, 17–23; Kenneth Thompson, "The Agricultural Promise of the Sacramento Valley: Some Early Views," *Journal of the West* 18 (Oct. 1979): 33–41; Thompson, "Riparian Forests of the Sacramento Valley, California," 301–4 (quotes); Thompson, "Historic Flooding of the Sacramento Valley," 354–59 (quote at 355); Col. J. J. Warner, "Reminiscences of Early California From 1831 to 1846," *Publications of the Historical Society of Southern California* 7 (1909): 176–93; Francis P. Farquhar,

"The Topological Reports of Lieutenant George H. Derby," *California Historical Society Quarterly* 11 (June 1932): 118–19 (quote).

9. Sherburne F. Cook, "Smallpox in Spanish and Mexican California, 1770–1845," *Bulletin of the History of Medicine* 12 (Feb. 1939): 182–87; Larkey and Walters, *Yolo County*, 13–15; Alan Rosenus, *General Vallejo and the Advent of the Americans* (Berkeley: Heyday Books, 1999), 14–16, 33; Sandos, "Between Crucifix and Lance," 213–15.

10. Edward Wolfskill, "A Few Things I Remember as Told Me by my Father, the Late J. R. Wolfskill," 1925, 1–10, unpublished MS, box 6, Ned Wolfskill Collection, Department of Special Collections, University of California, Davis; Iris Higbie Wilson, *William Wolfskill, 1798–1866: Frontier Trapper to California Ranchero* (Glendale, CA: Arthur H. Clark Co., 1965), 19–118; Larkey, *Winters*, 9–10; H. D. Barrows, "A Pioneer of Sacramento Valley," *Publications of the Historical Society of Southern California* 4 (1899): 11–17; Warner, "Reminiscences of Early California," 185, 187 (quote); Anne Foster Baird, "The Wolfskills of Winters," *Pacific Historian* 21 (Winter 1977): 351–53; Ellen Lamont Wood, "Samuel Green McMahan: Member of the Bidwell Party and Owner of Bartlett Springs," *California Historical Society Quarterly* 23 (Dec. 1944): 295.

11. U.S. Land Case no. 232, Northern District, Rio de los Putos Grant, 6–18, Bancroft Library; Wolfskill, "A Few Things I Remember," 10, 14, 17; *Dixon Tribune*, June 4, 1897; Tom Gregory, *History of Solano and Napa Counties, California* (Los Angeles: Historic Record Co., 1912), 57; Larkey, *Winters*, 10; Wilson, *William Wolfskill*, 128–29; Wood, "Samuel Green McMahan," 295.

12. David Hornbeck, "Land Tenure and Rancho Expansion in Alta California, 1784–1846," *Journal of Historical Geography* 4 (1978): 377–83; David Weber, *The Mexican Frontier, 1841–1846: The American Southwest under Mexico* (Albuquerque: Univ. of New Mexico Press, 1982), 162, 180–81; Michael J. Gillis and Michael F. Magliari, *John Bidwell and California: The Life and Writings of a Pioneer, 1841–1900* (Spokane, WA: Arthur H. Clark Co., 2003), 73–75; Larkey and Walters, *Yolo County*, 17–20.

13. U.S. Land Case no. 74, Northern District, Los Putos Grant, 1–62 (quote at 25), 94–100, 130–36, 201, Bancroft Library; John Currey, "History of the Spanish Grants of Solano County," unpublished MS, 1907, 5–9, Law Library, University of California, Berkeley; G. W. Hendry and J. N. Bowman, "The Spanish and Mexican Adobe and other Buildings in the nine San Francisco Bay Counties, 1776 to about 1850," unpublished MS, 1945, part 4, 424i–k, Bancroft Library; Wilson, *William Wolfskill*, 130–32; Larkey, *Davisville '68*, 14, 16, 219–21; Larkey, *Winters*, 11; Wood Young, *Vaca-Peña Los Putos Rancho and the Peña Adobe* (Vallejo: Wheeler Printing and Publishing, 1971), 1–3, 11–13. The *diseños* are held in the Bancroft Library. On the differences between Mexican and American law, see Donald J. Pisani, "Squatter Law in California, 1850–1858," in Pisani, *Water, Land, and Law in the West: The Limits of Public Policy, 1850–1920* (Lawrence: Univ. Press of Kansas, 1996), 65; and David J. Langum, *Law and Community on the Mexican California Frontier: Anglo-American Expatriates and the Clash of Legal Traditions, 1821–1846* (Norman: Univ. of Oklahoma Press, 1987), esp. 268–77.

14. U.S. Land Case no. 74, 96–99; U.S. Land Case no. 232, 22–25; U.S. Land Case no. 411, Northern District, Laguna de Santos Callé Grant, 251–54, Bancroft Library; Wolfskill, "A Few Things I Remember," 19–20; Young, *Vaca-Peña Los Putos Rancho*, 6–15; Douglas

Monroy, *Thrown among Strangers: The Making of Mexican Culture in Frontier California* (Berkeley: Univ. of California Press, 1990), 134–54; Rice, Bullough, and Orsi, *The Elusive Eden*, 137–45; Gillis and Magliari, *John Bidwell and California*, 155–56.

15. U.S. Land Case no. 411, 10–11 (quotes), 112–16, 308–16, 325–79; Larkey, *Davisville '68*, 17; Hendry and Bowman, "The Spanish and Mexican Adobe," part 4, 424m.

16. Yolo County, "Deeds," Book A, 288, YCA; Merrill G. Burlingame, "The Contribution of Iowa to the Formation of the State Government of California in 1849," *Iowa Journal of History and Politics* 30 (Apr. 1932): 182–218; Kenneth N. Owens, "Begun by Gold: Sacramento and the Gold Rush Legacy after 150 Years," in *Riches for All: The California Gold Rush and the World*, ed. Kenneth N. Owens (Lincoln: Univ. of Nebraska Press, 2002), 334–35.

17. Sprague and Atwell, *Western Shore Gazetteer*, 89 (quote); Young, *Vaca-Peña Los Putos Rancho*, 20 (quote).

18. *Sacramento Daily Union*, Oct. 8, 1852; Jan. 15, 1853; May 7, 1853; *Yolo Democrat*, Oct. 12, 1872; *Dixon Tribune*, Jan. 10, 1896; *Davisville Enterprise*, Jan. 5, 1900; Gilbert, *Illustrated Atlas and History of Yolo County*, 43, 44 (quote); Winfield J. Davis, *An Illustrated History of Sacramento County, California* (Chicago: Lewis Publishing Co., 1890), 139; *Brown v. Greene*, "Transcript on Appeal," 198–99; Yolo County, "Deeds," Book A, 204, 232, 261; Book C, 73, YCA; Yolo County, "School Lands Record Book," Book 1, 8–9, YCA; *California Statutes* (1850), 131; Hazel Adele Pulling, "California's Fence Laws and the Range-Cattle Industry," *Historian* 8 (Spring 1946): 140–41.

19. *Brown v. Greene*, "Transcript on Appeal," 134–37; *Transactions of the California State Agricultural Society during the Year 1858* (Sacramento: State Printer, 1859), 237; Yolo County, "Marks and Brands," Book A, passim, YCA; Yolo County, "Estrays," Book A, passim, YCA; *California Statutes* (1850), 131; Gilbert, *Illustrated Atlas and History of Yolo County*, 40; Ray August, "Cowboys v. Ranchers: The Origins of Western American Law," *Southwestern Historical Quarterly* 96 (Apr. 1993): 457–88; Hazel Adele Pulling, "A History of California's Range-Cattle Industry, 1770–1912" (Ph.D. diss., University of Southern California, 1944), 78–100; Paul W. Gates, *The Farmer's Age: Agriculture, 1815–1860* (New York: Harper & Row, 1960), 202, 393; Faragher, *Sugar Creek*, 132; Terry G. Jordan, *North American Cattle-Ranching Frontiers: Origins, Diffusion, and Differentiation* (Albuquerque: Univ. of New Mexico Press, 1993), 279–81.

20. *Sacramento Daily Union*, July 21, 1852; Jan. 12, 1853 (quote); *California Statutes* (1854), 56–58; Phelps, *Contemporary Biography of California's Representative Men*, 368; *Official Report of the California State Agricultural Society's Third Annual Agricultural Fair, Cattle Show and Industrial Exhibition* (San Francisco: California Farmer Office, 1856), 4–5, 69–73; *Official Report of the California State Agricultural Society's Fourth Annual Fair, Cattle Show and Industrial Exhibition in 1857* (San Francisco: O'Meara & Painter, 1858), 16–17; *Transactions of the California State Agricultural Society during the Year 1858*, 235–39; *Transactions of the California State Agricultural Society during the Year 1860* (Sacramento: State Printer, 1861), 55; C. I. Hutchinson to James Warren, Jan. 14 and Feb. 12, 1855, box 3, Warren Papers; F. Hal Higgins, "Col. Warren, Father of California Agriculture," *Pacific Rural Press*, Aug. 28, 1937, 209; Higgins, "Prize Farms of the Fifties," ibid., 226; Walton E. Bean, "James Warren and the Beginnings of Agricultural Institutions in California," *Pacific Historical Review* 13 (Dec. 1944): 361–75.

21. On boosterism, see Cronon, *Nature's Metropolis,* 31–54; and Richard J. Orsi, "Selling the Golden State: A Study of Boosterism in Nineteenth-Century California" (Ph.D. diss., University of Wisconsin, 1973), 1–113, 152–63.

22. Morton Rothstein, "The Big Farm: Abundance and Scale in American Agriculture," *Agricultural History* 49 (Oct. 1975): 583–97; Rothstein, "The American West and Foreign Markets, 1850–1900," in *The Frontier in American Development: Essays in Honor of Paul Wallace Gates,* ed. David M. Ellis (Ithaca: Cornell Univ. Press, 1969), 381–406; John Giffin Thompson, *The Rise and Decline of the Wheat Growing Industry in Wisconsin,* Bulletin of the University of Wisconsin, no. 292, May 1907, 16–36; Gates, *The Farmer's Age,* 279–93; Clarence H. Danhof, *Change in Agriculture: The Northern United States, 1820–1870* (Cambridge: Harvard Univ. Press, 1969), 181–250; Peter D. McClelland, *Sowing Modernity: America's First Agricultural Revolution* (Ithaca: Cornell Univ. Press, 1997), 129–84; Reynold M. Wik, "Some Interpretations of the Mechanization of Agriculture in the Far West," *Agricultural History* 49 (Jan. 1975): 73–83.

23. *Greene v. His Creditors; H. O. Beatty v. R. C. Clark* (1861), California Supreme Court, no. 3223, "Transcript on Appeal," 104–5, California State Archives; *E. D. Kennedy and W. T. Kennedy v. C. I . Hutchinson, W. W. Cozzens, and C. E. Greene* (1853), Sacramento County, District Court Case Files, no. 2065, Sacramento Archives and Museum Collection Center, Sacramento, California (hereafter SAMCC); Yolo County, "Mortgages," Book A, 9–12, 16–17, 29–30, 90–92, YCA; *Sacramento Daily Union,* Nov. 6, 1852; Gilbert, *Illustrated Atlas and History of Yolo County,* 43 (quote), 46. On the other ranches along Putah Creek, see *Joseph B. Chiles and Jerome C. Davis v. James M. Calvert* (1852), Yolo County, County Case Files, Civil Case no. 12, YCA; *John W. Myrick v. W. W. Brown* (1853), Yolo County, District Court Case Files, 1st ser., no. 58, YCA.

24. *Greene v. His Creditors; Kennedy and Kennedy v. Hutchinson, Cozzens, and Greene; John Wilkins v. C. I. Hutchinson, C. E. Greene, and Jacob McKinney* (1854), Yolo County, District Court Case Files, 1st ser., no. 91, YCA; *A. T. Hamilton v. C. I. Hutchinson, C. E. Greene, and W. W. Cozzens* (1853), Sacramento County, District Court Case Files, no. 2112, SAMCC; *Sacramento Daily Union,* May 7, 1853 (quote); *Daily Alta California,* July 30, 1853; Gilbert, *Illustrated Atlas and History of Yolo County,* 43.

25. Gilbert, *Illustrated Atlas and History of Yolo County,* 48; *Sacramento Daily Union,* Jan. 10, 1853; May 7, 1853 (quote); Sprague and Atwell, *Western Shore Gazetteer,* 102–3 (quote); Faragher, *Sugar Creek,* 70–71; Jeffrey F. Mount, *California Rivers and Streams: The Conflict between Fluvial Process and Land Use* (Berkeley: Univ. of California Press, 1995), 55–57, 246–56.

26. Yolo County, "Deeds," Book B, 78, 84, 86, 94, YCA; G. Walter Reed, *History of Sacramento County, California, with Biographical Sketches* (Los Angeles: Historic Record Co., 1923), 610.

27. *Greene v. His Creditors; Beatty v. Clark,* "Transcript on Appeal," 7; *Charles K. Smith v. Hutchinson, Greene, and Co.* (1855), California Supreme Court, no. 602, "Transcript on Appeal," 2–10, 15–24, California State Archives; Gilbert, *Illustrated Atlas and History of Yolo County,* 43–44; *Daily Alta California,* Aug. 6, 1854 (quoting the *Stockton Argus,* at length); *Sacramento Daily Union,* Feb. 11, 1854; June 27, 1854 (quote); *Transactions of the California State Agricultural Society during the Year 1858,* 237.

28. *Greene v. His Creditors;* Ira B. Cross, *Financing an Empire: History of Banking in California* (Chicago: S. J. Clarke Publishing Co., 1927), 1:151–53; Gerald D. Nash, *State Government and Economic Development: A History of Administrative Policies in California, 1849–1933* (Berkeley: Institute of Government Studies, 1964), 83–87; Wolfskill, "A Few Things I Remember," 15–16 (quote).

29. *Greene v. His Creditors;* Frank H. Lyman, *The City of Kenosha and Kenosha County Wisconsin: A Record of Settlement, Organization, Progress and Achievement* (Chicago: S. J. Clarke Publishing Co., 1916), 86; Cross, *Financing an Empire,* 1:78–82; *Beatty v. Clark,* "Transcript on Appeal," 141–43; Mills (D. O.) & Company, "Ledgers," vol. 1, 250, vol. 2, 174, 185, 273, 291, California Room, California State Library, Sacramento; Yolo County, "Mortgages," Book A, 100, 158, 193, 233, 283, 351, 357; Book B, 30, 93, YCA; *Benjamin Cahoon v. E. L. Brown and W. W. Brown and Haines L. Roby* (1856), Yolo County, District Court Case Files, 2nd ser., no. 33, YCA; *B. Cahoon v. J. C. Davis* (1862), Yolo County, District Court Case Files, 2nd ser., no. 348, YCA; *B. Cahoon v. W. W. Brown, Adelia Brown, and I. M. Hubbard* (1863), Yolo County, District Court Case Files, 2nd ser., no. 400, YCA; *W. W. Brown v. B. Cahoon* (1856), Sacramento County, District Court Case Files, no. 4215, SAMCC; *Benjamin Cahoon v. J. B. Chiles and G. F. Brown* (1858), Sacramento County, District Court Case Files, no. 6472, SAMCC; *B. Cahoon v. Jerome C. Davis and Isaac Davis* (1867), Sacramento County, District Court Case Files, no. 11590, SAMCC; *Benjamin Cahoon v. Henry E. Robinson* (1856), California Supreme Court, no. 1090, "Transcript on Appeal," California State Archives; Allan G. Bogue, *From Prairie to Corn Belt: Farming on the Illinois and Iowa Prairies in the Nineteenth Century* (1963; reprint, Ames: Iowa State Univ. Press, 1994), 170–81; Alan Taylor, *William Cooper's Town: Power and Persuasion on the Frontier of the Early American Republic* (New York: Vintage Books, 1995), 107–14.

30. Yolo County, "Deeds," Book B, 245, 257, YCA; *Wilkens v. Hutchinson, Greene, and McKinney; Beatty v. Clark,* Exhibits H, I, J, K, and L; *Cahoon v. Robinson,* "Transcript on Appeal"; *George W. Pierce v. Henry E. Robinson* (1859), California Supreme Court, no. 2329, "Transcript on Appeal," 1–50, California State Archives; *Greene v. His Creditors; Sacramento Daily Union,* Feb. 21, 1855; Oct. 1, 1858; Apr. 28, 1859; *California Farmer,* Mar. 1, 1855.

31. *Pierce v. Robinson,* "Transcript on Appeal," 35; Yolo County, "Deeds," Book B, 432–36, YCA; Yolo County, "Mortgages," Book A, 231, YCA; *Beatty v. Clark,* "Transcript on Appeal," 3–8, "Opinion" (quotes), Exhibit A.

32. *Beatty v. Clark,* "Transcript on Appeal," 26–36 (quote at 28), 94–103, 130–40, 174–80, "Opinion," "Deposition of A. W. Hall," Exhibits O and P; *Greene v. His Creditors; Official Report of the California State Agricultural Society's Fourth Annual Fair, Cattle Show and Industrial Exhibition in 1857,* 17 (quote); *Daily Alta California,* Oct. 4, 1857; *Sacramento Daily Union,* Apr. 2, 1857; May 13, 1858; May 24, 1858.

33. *Beatty v. Clark,* "Transcript on Appeal," 94–103; "Opinion"; *Transactions of the California State Agricultural Society during the Year 1858,* 237–39; *Greene v. His Creditors; C. I. Hutchinson v. His Creditors* (1861), Sacramento County, District Court, "Minutes," Book J, 283, SAMCC; *Sacramento Daily Union,* July 16, 1861.

34. Yolo County, "Deeds," Book A, 311; Book C, 154, YCA; Yolo County, "Mortgages," Book A, 48–50, 357–58, YCA; Sacramento County, "Mortgages," Book D, 219, 389, SAMCC; Edmund L. Brown to Myra R. Clark, Bond, Mar. 7, 1853, Yolo County, "Probate

Case Files," o.s., misc. folder, YCA; *Myrick v. Brown; Jerome C. Davis v. W. H. Donaldson and Ira B. Severe* (1854), Yolo County, District Court Case Files, 1st ser., no. 62, YCA; *Alexander Kent v. E. L. Brown and Charles Sackett* (1857), Yolo County, District Court Case Files, 1st ser., no. 68, YCA; *Cahoon v. Brown, Brown, and Roby; E. L. Brown and W. W. Brown v. C. E. Greene and R. L. Crary* (1857), Yolo County, District Court Case Files, 2nd ser., no. 76, YCA; *Jerome C. Davis v. E. L. Brown, W. W. Brown, H. L. Roby, J. C. Steele* (1857), Yolo County, District Court Case Files, 2nd ser., no. 105, YCA; *Robert C. Clark v. E. L. Brown, W. W. Brown and J. C. Steele* (1857), Yolo County, District Court Case Files, 2nd ser., no. 106, YCA; *Benjamin Cahoon v. E. L. Brown and W. W. Brown* (1857), Yolo County, District Court Case Files, 2nd ser., no. 107, YCA; *John C. Morrison and William P. Morrison v. E. L. Brown* (1854), Sacramento County, District Court Case Files, no. 2668, SAMCC; *John W. Myrick v. Edmund L. Brown and Henry Winkle* (1854), Sacramento County, District Court Case Files, no. 2670, SAMCC; *E. L. Brown v. Robert Robinson and Charles Crocker* (1857), Sacramento County, District Court Case Files, no. 5223, SAMCC.

35. *Beatty v. Clark,* "Transcript on Appeal," 183, 193; Yolo County, "Mortgages," Book B, 230, YCA; Yolo County, "Deeds," Book D, 391, YCA; Yolo County, "Assessment Rolls," 1858, YCA; *Dixon Tribune,* Jan. 10, 1896; Larkey, *Davisville '68,* 29; Reed, *History of Sacramento County,* 610.

36. Jordan, *North American Cattle-Ranching Frontiers,* 241–49, 279–82 (on the "mid-westernization" of cattle ranching in northern California); Pulling, "A History of California's Range-Cattle Industry," 78–121; Paul W. Gates, *California Ranchos and Farms, 1846–1862* (Madison: State Historical Society of Wisconsin, 1967), 17–27; Gilbert, *Illustrated Atlas and History of Yolo County,* 40–41, 54; *Sacramento Daily Union,* June 15, 1853; Feb. 28, 1855; Nov. 2, 1855; May 28, 1859; *Joseph B. Chiles and Jerome C. Davis v. P. H. Clark and W. D. Clark* (1853), Yolo County, District Court Case Files, 1st ser., no. 48, YCA; *Transactions of the California State Agricultural Society during the Year 1858,* 235–36 (quote); Allan R. Ottley, "Some Notes on Early Yolo County and Davisville," speech given at the annual meeting of the Friends of the Davis Public Library, Feb. 5, 1860, 8–9, Department of Special Collections, University of California Library, Davis; Jerome C. Davis, "Ledger; general farm, October 1, 1856–December 31, 1859, Putah Creek, Calif.," 12; Davis, "Ledger; general farm, January 1, 1860–June 14, 1867, Putah Creek, Calif.," 91, California Room, California State Library.

37. Jim Gerber, "The Origin of California's Export Surplus in Cereals," *Agricultural History* 67 (Fall 1992): 40–57.

38. Greed is emphasized in Gates, *California Ranchos and Farms,* esp. 12–13; Carey McWilliams, *Factories in the Field: The Story of Migratory Farm Labor in California* (Boston: Little, Brown, 1939), 49–59; and Cletus Daniel, *Bitter Harvest: A History of California Farmworkers: 1870–1941* (Ithaca: Cornell Univ. Press, 1981), 15–39.

Chapter Three. Farms without Titles

1. Paul W. Gates, "Adjudication of Spanish-Mexican Land Claims in California," in Gates, *Land and Law in California: Essays on Land Policy* (Ames: Iowa State Univ. Press, 1991), 3–23; Christian G. Fritz, *Federal Justice in California: The Court of Ogden Hoffman,*

1851–1891 (Lincoln: Univ. of Nebraska Press, 1991), 134–39; Lewis Grossman, "John C. Frémont, Mariposa, and the Collision of Mexican and American Law," *Western Legal History* 6 (Winter/Spring 1993): 17–25; Donald J. Pisani, "Squatter Law in California, 1850–1858," in *Water, Land, and Law in the West: The Limits of Public Policy, 1850–1920* (Lawrence: Univ. Press of Kansas, 1996), 64–67; Michael J. Gillis and Michael F. Magliari, *John Bidwell and California: The Life and Writings of a Pioneer, 1841–1900* (Spokane, WA: Arthur H. Clark Co., 2003), 131.

2. U.S. Land Case no. 232, Northern District, Rio de los Putos Grant, 6–18, Bancroft Library, University of California, Berkeley; Ogden Hoffman, *Reports of Land Cases Determined in the United States District Court for the Northern District of California* (San Francisco: Numa Hubert, 1862), app., 32; Gillis and Magliari, *John Bidwell and California*, 132; Beverly E. Bastian, "'I Heartily Regret that I Ever Touched a Title in California': Henry Wager Halleck, the *Californios*, and the Clash of Legal Cultures," *California History* 72 (Winter 1993/ 94): 318; David Hornbeck, "The Patenting of California's Private Land Claims, 1851–1885," *Geographical Review* 69 (Oct. 1979): 444.

3. U.S. Land Case no. 74, Northern District, Los Putos Grant, 63–73 (quote at 72), Bancroft Library; John Currey, "History of the Spanish Grants of Solano County," unpublished MS, 1907, 9–10, Law Library, University of California, Berkeley; Wood Young, *Vaca-Peña Los Putos Rancho and the Peña Adobe* (Vallejo: Wheeler Printing and Publishing, 1971), 13; Fritz, *Federal Justice in California*, 150–51; Paul W. Gates, "The Fremont-Jones Scramble for California Land Claims," in Gates, *Land and Law in California*, 77.

4. Interview with Jack Phillips (great-grandson of John Currey), July 18, 1998, Oral Histories, Dixon Public Library, Dixon, California; U.S. Land Case no. 74, 74–128 (quote at 126), 175–78; Currey, "History of the Spanish Grants of Solano County," 9–11; Young, *Vaca-Peña Los Putos Rancho*, 19–21; Fritz, *Federal Justice in California*, 148–49.

5. Solano County, "Deeds," Book I, 438; Book M, 542, Solano County Archives, Fairfield, California; Interview with Jack Phillips; Currey, "History of the Spanish Grants of Solano County," 11; U.S. Land Case no. 74, 112–23 (quote at 116); Hoffman, *Reports of Land Cases Determined in the United States District Court*, app., 8–9; Dewitt C. Cage, "Field Notes of the Final Survey of Rancho Los Putos," May 19, 1857, Surveyor Records, Bureau of Land Management, California State Office, Sacramento; John Wilson to Thomas A. Hendricks, Feb. 19, 1858, docket no. 53, Los Putos Rancho, United States District Court (California), "Documents pertaining to the adjudication of private land claims in California, ca. 1852– 1892," Bancroft Library (hereafter Los Putos docket); "Los Putos Rancho, Files and Charges," Mar. 22, 1858, Los Putos docket; Affidavit of H. Patton, Mar. 18, 1858 (quotes), Los Putos docket; *James H. Long v. A. H. Dollarhide* (1864), California State Supreme Court (no number in original), California State Archives, Sacramento; Young, *Vaca-Peña Los Putos Rancho*, 17, 20.

6. The *diseños* are held in the Bancroft Library. U.S. Land Case no. 74, 25 (quote at 25); U.S. Land Case no. 411, Northern District, Laguna de Santos Callé Grant, 6–7, 10–11, 14– 17, 70–81, 92–98, 112–16, 180–85, Bancroft Library.

7. U.S. Land Case no. 411, 126–37, 229–34, 419–36; Neal Harlow, *California Conquered: War and Peace on the Pacific, 1846–1850* (Berkeley: Univ. of California Press, 1892), 61–114; Gates, "Adjudication of Spanish and Mexican Land Claims in California," 14–15;

Gates, "The California Land Act of 1851," in *Land and Law in California,* 25; Gates, "California's Embattled Settlers," in ibid., 156.

8. Fritz, *Federal Justice in California,* 144–55; U.S. Land Case no. 411, 251–55 (quote at 252).

9. U.S. Land Case no. 411, 6–14, 18–27, 39–41, 82–87, 92–98, 180–85, 197–99, 230 (quote), 325–79 (quote at 372), 419–36; Louis Blanding to Jeremiah S. Black, Aug. 19, 1859, box 2, Correspondence on Land Claims, Records Relating to California Land Claims, Records of the Attorney General's Office, General Records of the Department of Justice (RG 60), National Archives at College Park, College Park, Maryland (hereafter CLC). On Howard and other prosecutors who jumped ship to defend claimants in these land grant cases, see Paul W. Gates, "Carpetbaggers Join the Rush for California Land," in Gates, *Land and Law in California,* 128–29. See also Samuel Lanner Kreider, "Volney Erskine Howard: California Pioneer," *Historical Society of Southern California Quarterly* 31 (Mar.–June 1949): 119–34.

10. Yolo County, "Deeds," Book A, 204–5, 228–29, 232–33, 261, 306–7, YCA; *W. W. Brown v. C. E. Greene* (1884), California State Supreme Court, no. 9443, "Transcript on Appeal," 63–146, 198–216, California State Archives; John Wilson to Edward Bates, Apr. 9, 1861, box 3, CLC.

11. Gilbert C. Fite, *The Farmers' Frontier, 1865–1900* (New York: Holt, Rinehart & Winston, 1966), 160–62; Paul W. Gates, *The Farmer's Age: Agriculture, 1815–1860* (New York: Harper & Row, 1960), 395–96.

12. Pisani, "Squatter Law in California," 57–85; Paul W. Gates, *History of Public Land Law Development* (Washington, DC: Zenger Publishing Co., 1968), 219–47; Gates, "Adjudication of Spanish-Mexican Land Claims in California," 3–23; Gates, *The Farmer's Age,* 387 (quote).

13. U.S. Land Case no. 411, 14–37, 246–55; *Pacific Rural Press,* Aug. 21, 1880; *Duvis v. Donaldson and Severe; James W. Chiles v. William Flanders* (1852), Yolo County, County Court Case Files, Civil Case no. 21, YCA; *Sacramento Daily Union,* Jan. 25, 1854; Paul W. Gates, *California Ranchos and Farms, 1846–1862* (Madison: State Historical Society of Wisconsin, 1967), 11; Gates, "Pre–Henry George Land Warfare in California," in *Land and Law in California,* 188–91; Pisani, "Squatter Law in California," 68; Fritz, *Federal Justice in California,* 144–55; Yolo County, "Assessment Rolls," 1853, YCA. Squatters are identified from the assessment rolls as taxpayers with no real estate but with improvements and personal property valued at $100 or more.

14. *Official Report of the California State Agricultural Society's Fourth Annual Fair, Cattle Show and Industrial Exhibition in 1857* (San Francisco: O'Meara & Painter, 1858), 17; *Transactions of the California State Agricultural Society during the Year 1858* (Sacramento: State Printer, 1859), 236–37; *Transactions of the California State Agricultural Society during the Year 1859* (Sacramento: State Printer, 1860), 61; *Sacramento Daily Union,* Feb. 11, 1854; Aug. 8, 1857 (quote); Mar. 19, 1867; *Davisville Enterprise,* Aug. 15, 1901; *Davis Enterprise,* Aug. 27, 1970; Sept. 17, 1970; Sept. 24, 1970; Oct. 1, 1970; Stephen Johnson, Gerald Haslam, and Robert Dawson, *The Great Central Valley: California's Heartland* (Berkeley: Univ. of California Press, 1993), 131; Gates, "California's Embattled Settlers," 158.

15. U.S. Land Case no. 411, esp. the Land Commission's decision, 92–98; *Sacramento*

Daily Union, June 27, 1860; Gates, "California's Embattled Settlers," 178–79; Fritz, *Federal Justice in California*, 163–73.

16. Yolo County, "Assessment Rolls," 1856 and 1860, YCA; *C. I. Hutchinson and Jerome C. Davis v. Henry Conner* (1859), Sacramento County, District Court Case Files, no. 6372, Sacramento Archives and Museum Collection Center, Sacramento, California; *Sacramento Daily Union*, Feb. 11, 1854, Aug. 8, 1857; *San Francisco Bulletin*, Jan. 22, 1858; Gates, "California's Embattled Settlers," 158, 164–65.

17. *George H. Peck v. Lewis Horton* (1856), Yolo County, District Court Case Files, 2nd ser., no. 24, YCA; *George H. Peck v. William H. Horton* (1857), Yolo County, District Court Case Files, 2nd ser., no. 79, YCA; *Richard Hext v. James Lillard and William Horton* (1857), Yolo County, District Court Case Files, 2nd ser., no. 116, YCA. Other ejection suits included *Simon H. Lettner v. John Wolff* (1859), Yolo County, District Court Case Files, 2nd ser., no. 182, YCA; *Henry Conner v. Charles Edsell and Alph Gandy* (1859), Yolo County, County Court Case Files, Civil Case no. 80, YCA.

18. By focusing so strongly on violence, historians of California land have all but ignored motives for cooperation. See, in particular, Gates, *Land and Law in California*, esp. "Pre–Henry George Land Warfare in California," 185–208, and "The Suscol Principle, Preemption, and California Latifundia," 209–28; and Pisani, "Squatter Law in California."

19. U.S. Land Case no. 411, 325–72, 388–94 419–35 (quotes at 393); *Henry Conner v. C. I. Hutchinson* (1859), California Supreme Court, no. 2100, "Transcript on Appeal," 6–12, California State Archives; *Brown v. Greene* (1884), "Transcript on Appeal," 198–216; *H. O. Beatty v. R. C. Clark* (1861), California Supreme Court, no. 3223, "Transcript on Appeal," 151–53, 158–59; California State Archives; Yolo County, "Deeds," Book B, 432–36, 441–42, 446–49; Book C, 2, 10–41, 44–45, 59, 70–73, 141–42, 175–76, 197–98, 250–53, 261–62, 315–16, 537; Book D, 47, 154–55, YCA; Yolo County, "Mortgages," Book A, 287–89, 322–23; Book B, 112–13, 224–28, 357–58, 564–65, YCA; Yolo County, "Articles of Agreement," 58–60, 107–8, YCA; William Minis, County Surveyor, "Plat of a legal subdivision of the Laguna de Santos Callé grant," Apr. 1856, YCA; Gates, *California Ranchos and Farms*, 15.

20. *Transactions of the California State Agricultural Society during the Year 1858*, 238. Several lists of workers, though not comprehensive, can be found in the following: Yolo County, "Assessment Rolls," 1858—esp. the unnumbered back pages in which the assessor listed workers whose poll taxes were paid by Hutchinson and Greene; *Beatty v. Clark*, "Transcript on Appeal," 181; U.S. Census, Population Schedules for Putah Township, Yolo County, California, 1860, microfilm (Washington, DC, 1967)—noting that workers were generally listed after their employers; Jerome C. Davis, "Ledger; general farm, October 1, 1856–December 31, 1859, Putah Creek, Calif.," 12, California Room, California State Library, Sacramento; *Fred Lloyd v. Henry Conner* (1858), Yolo County, County Court Case Files, Civil Case no. 72, YCA. The names on these lists were then cross-checked with the assessment rolls to determine which workers were also squatters. On Lillard, see Yolo County, "Assessment Rolls," 1857, 1858, YCA; *Catharine Mehan v. James T. Lillard* (1858), Yolo County, District Court Case Files, 2nd ser., no. 151, YCA; Larkey, *Davisville '68*, 187; *A Memorial and Biographical History of Northern California*, 724.

21. A. W. Von Schmidt, Deputy Surveyor, "Field Notes of the Subdivision Lines in Township 8 North, Range 1 East of the Mt. Diablo Base and Meridian in the State of California,"

1858; Von Schmidt, "Field Notes of the Subdivision Lines in Township 9 North, Range 2 East of the Mt. Diablo Base and Meridian of the State of California," 1858; Von Schmidt, "Field Notes of the Subdivision Lines in Township 9 North, Range 3 East of the Mt. Diablo Base and Meridian Line of the State of California," 1858—Surveyor Records, Bureau of Land Management, California State Office, Sacramento.

22. Albert H. Hurtado, *Indian Survival on the California Frontier* (New Haven: Yale Univ. Press, 1988), 1, 149–68; Hurtado, "John A. Sutter and the Indian Business," in *John Sutter and a Wider West*, ed. Kenneth N. Owens (Lincoln: Univ. of Nebraska Press, 2002), 51–75; Gillis and Magliari, *John Bidwell and California*, 146, 256–57; Gates, *California Ranchos and Farms*, 45–48; David E. Schob, *Hired Hands and Plowboys: Farm Labor in the Midwest, 1815–60* (Urbana: Univ. of Illinois Press, 1975). For a different perspective, see Richard Steven Street, *Beasts in the Field: A Narrative History of California Farmworkers, 1769–1913* (Stanford: Stanford Univ. Press), esp. 133. The current literature suggests that variable local conditions—the size of the labor market, in particular—make it difficult to assert unqualified generalizations about the use of Indian labor for all of California in the 1850s. See esp. Michael Magliari, "Free Soil, Unfree Labor: Cave Johnson Couts and the Binding of Indian Workers in California, 1850–1870," *Pacific Historical Review* 73 (Aug. 2004): 349–89.

23. Yolo County, "Assessment Rolls," 1858; C. P. Sprague and H. W. Atwell, *The Western Shore Gazetteer and Commercial Directory, for the State of California . . . Yolo County* (San Francisco: Press of Bancroft, 1870), 60–65, 73; *Annual Report of the Surveyor-General of California for the Year 1861* (Sacramento: State Printer, 1862), 49 (quote); *Sacramento Daily Union*, Oct. 19, 1859; Nov. 14, 1859. The 1860 agricultural census confirms what the assessor found in 1858. The value of farming implements and machinery among settlers—excluding the large landholders—ranged from $50 to $500, averaging about $150; see U.S. Census, Agricultural Schedules for Putah Township, Yolo County, California, 1860, on microfilm in the California Room, California State Library. On the wide variety of crops grown by contemporary midwestern farmers, see Bogue, *From Prairie to Corn Belt*, 123–47; and on shared purchases of expensive machinery, see Alan Olmstead, "The Mechanization of Reaping and Mowing in American Agriculture, 1833–1870," *Journal of Economic History* 35 (June 1975): 327–52.

24. E. Dyer, Deputy Surveyor, "Field Notes of the Subdivision Lines in Township 8 North, Range 3 East of the Mt. Diablo Base and Meridian in the State of California," 1862, Surveyor Records, Bureau of Land Management, California State Office; Gates, *The Farmer's Age*, 181–82, 395.

25. J. M. Guinn, *History of the State of California and Biographical Record of the Sacramento Valley, California* (Chicago: Chapman Publishing Co., 1906), 581–82; *Davis Enterprise*, Oct. 15 and 22, 1970; Larkey, *Davisville '68*, 188–89.

26. *California Statutes* (1855), 189; Yolo County, "Swampland Surveys," Book A, 28 (quote), County Surveyor's Office, Woodland, CA; Yolo County, "Swamp and Overflowed Lands Record Book," YCA; *Sacramento Daily Union*, May 19, 1853; Sprague and Atwell, *Western Shore Gazetteer*, 48–51.

27. Yolo County, "Swampland Surveys," Book A, 14, 20, 40, 41; Yolo County, "Swamp and Overflowed Lands Record Book," YCA; *Sacramento Daily Union*, Apr. 18, 1855; Sept. 21, 1855; Oct. 12, 1858; Sept. 9, 1862; Dec. 29, 1862; *Knights Landing News*, Apr. 28, 1860; Rus-

sell, *History of Yolo County,* 61; Larkey, *Davisville '68,* 166–68; Sprague and Atwell, *Western Shore Gazetteer,* 48–51.

28. *U.S. Statutes at Large,* 10:519; John Wilson to Samuel D. King, Jan. 13, 1853, Letters from the Commissioner of the General Land Office to the Surveyor General of California, 1851–98, microfilm, Survey Records, Bureau of Land Management, California State Office, Sacramento; Richard H. Peterson, "The Failure to Reclaim: California State Swamp Land Policy and the Sacramento Valley, 1850–1866," *Southern California Quarterly* 56 (Spring 1874): 46–48; McGowan, *History of the Sacramento Valley,* 1:283–84; *Knights Landing News,* Jan. 23, 1864; Yolo County, "Swamp Land Surveys," Book A; Yolo County, "Swamp and Overflowed Lands Record Book," YCA.

29. *Daily Alta California,* May 11, 1860.

Chapter Four. *"A Very Public Place"*

1. *Sacramento Daily Union,* Oct. 5, 1857; Apr. 26, 1860; Sept. 29, 1862; Mar. 13, 1863; Apr. 13, 1863 (quote); *Knights Landing News,* Mar. 24, 1860; "Rattler Mare Account, 1861," MS box 305, Jerome C. Davis Collection, California Room, California State Library, Sacramento; *Transactions of the California State Agricultural Society during the Year 1858* (Sacramento, 1859), 84–85, 115, 160, 236–37; *Transactions of the California State Agricultural Society during the Year 1859* (Sacramento: State Printer, 1860), 61; *Transactions of the California State Agricultural Society during the Year 1861* (Sacramento: State Printer, 1862), 82–83, 122; Yolo County, "Assessment Rolls," 1862, Yolo County Archives, Woodland, CA (hereafter YCA); *Oliver and Belinda Scudder v. J. C. Davis and J. B. Chiles* (1866), Sacramento County, District Court Case Files, no. 11469, Sacramento Archives and Museum Collection Center, Sacramento, California (hereafter SAMCC); "Fine Horses" folder, box 12, James L. Warren Papers, Bancroft Library, University of California, Berkeley.

2. On the phenomenon of the "instant city" in California, see Roger W. Lotchin, *San Francisco, 1846–1856: From Hamlet to City* (Oxford: Oxford Univ. Press, 1974).

3. John Mack Faragher, *Sugar Creek: Life on the Illinois Prairie* (New Haven: Yale Univ. Press, 1986).

4. See John Mack Faragher, "Open-Country Community: Sugar Creek, Illinois, 1820–1850," in *The Countryside in the Age of Capitalist Transformation: Essays in the Social History of Rural America,* ed. Steven Hahn and Jonathan Prude (Chapel Hill: Univ. of North Carolina Press, 1985), 233–58, for an extended discussion of the sociology of open-country settlements.

5. Jim Gerber, "The Origin of California's Export Surplus in Cereals," *Agricultural History* 67 (Fall 1992): 40.

6. *W. W. Brown v. C. E. Greene* (1884), California State Supreme Court, no. 9443, "Transcript on Appeal," 134–37, California State Archives, Sacramento; Hazel Adele Pulling, "A History of California's Range-Cattle Industry, 1770–1912" (Ph.D. diss., University of Southern California, 1944), 82–85; Robert C. McMath Jr., "Sandy Land and Hogs in the Timber: (Agri)cultural Origins of the Farmers' Alliance in Texas," in *The Countryside in the Age of Capitalist Transformation,* 208–10, 214; Ray August, "Cowboys v. Ranchers: The Origins of Western American Law," *Southwestern Historical Quarterly* 96 (Apr. 1993): 457–88.

7. *California Statutes* (1850), 214; *California Statutes* (1851), 299–301, 411–13; Yolo

County, "Estrays," Book A, 56–57, YCA; Yolo County, "Marks and Brands," Book A, passim; *Sacramento Daily Union,* Apr. 4, 1851; Oct. 24, 1855; Nov. 16, 1860; Feb. 6, 1863; Feb. 9, 1863; *Joseph B. Chiles and Jerome C. Davis v. P. H. Clark and W. D. Clark* (1853), Yolo County, District Court Case Files, 1st ser., no. 48, YCA; Frank T. Gilbert, *The Illustrated Atlas and History of Yolo County* (San Francisco: De Pue & Co., 1879), 40–42.

8. *Transactions of the California State Agricultural Society during the Year 1858,* 238; *Transactions of the California State Agricultural Society during the Year 1860* (Sacramento: State Printer, 1861), 55; *Daily Alta California,* May 11, 1860 (quote); *California Culturist* (Aug. 1860), 69–70; *Sacramento Daily Union,* May 17, 1855; May 25, 1858; May 13, 1868; *California Farmer,* May 24, 1855; *Benjamin Cahoon v. E. L. Brown, W. W. Brown, and Haines L. Roby* (1856), Yolo County, District Court Case Files, 2nd ser., no. 33, YCA (price of threshing machine); Gilbert, *Illustrated Atlas and History of Yolo County,* 42–44; Horace Davis, "Wheat in California," *Overland Monthly* 1 (Nov. 1868): 447–49; F. Hal Higgins, "Plows and Plowmen at the Fair," *Pacific Rural Press,* Aug. 28, 1937, 208; Joseph A. McGowan, *History of the Sacramento Valley* (New York: Lewis Historical Publishing, 1961), 1:247–49; Reynold M. Wik, "Some Interpretations of the Mechanization of Agriculture in the Far West," *Agricultural History* 49 (Jan. 1975): 79.

9. Yolo County, "Mortgages," 259–60, YCA; Yolo County, "Assessment Rolls," 1856, 1858, 1859, YCA; *Official Report of the California State Agricultural Society's Third Annual Agricultural Fair, Cattle Show and Industrial Exhibition* (San Francisco: California Farmer Office, 1856), 16–17; *Transactions of the California State Agricultural Society during the Year 1858,* 235–36; *Sacramento Daily Union,* June 1, 1854; Jerome C. Davis, "Ledger; general farm, October 1, 1856–Dec. 31, 1859, Putah Creek, Calif.," esp. 17, 24, 86, 91–92, 103, 106, 117–20, 122; and Davis, "Journal; general farm, January 1, 1860–June 30, 1863, Putah Creek, Calif.," 1–164, both in the California Room, California State Library, Sacramento; U.S. Census, Population Schedules for Putah Township, Yolo County, and Tremont Township, Solano County, California, 1860, microfilm (Washington, DC: National Archives, 1967); *H. O. Beatty v. R. C. Clark* (1861), California Supreme Court, no. 3223, "Transcript on Appeal," 193, California State Archives.

10. U.S. Census, Population Schedules for Putah Township, Yolo County, and Tremont Township, Solano County, California, 1860; Yolo County, "Board of Supervisors Minutes," Book A, May 11, 1855; May 6, 1856, Mar. 3, 1857, YCA; Yolo County, "Roads and Highways," Book A, 27–28 (quote), 137–38; Book C, 72–78; C. P. Sprague and H. W. Atwell, *The Western Shore Gazetteer and Commercial Directory, for the State of California . . . Yolo County* (San Francisco: Press of Bancroft, 1870), 86, 93; Joann Leach Larkey, *Davisville '68: The History and Heritage of the City of Davis, Yolo County, California* (Davis: Davis Historical and Landmarks Commission, 1969), 147, 191, 192, 196–97, 207, 213; Joann L. Larkey and Shipley Walters, *Yolo County: Land of Changing Patterns* (Northridge, CA: Windsor Publications, 1987), 33–34; Faragher, "Open-Country Community," 237–42. On Tremont, see *Vacaville Reporter,* Sept. 10, 1995, and the other clippings and materials in the Tremont file, Dixon Public Library, Dixon, California.

11. *Brown v. Greene,* "Transcript on Appeal," 204 (quote); Davis, "Ledger; general farm, October 1, 1856–December 31, 1859," passim; Davis, "Journal; general farm, January 1, 1860–June 30, 1863," passim; *Davisville Enterprise,* Jan. 5, 1900.

12. U.S. Census, Population Schedules for Yolo County and Solano County, California, 1850, microfilm (Washington, DC: National Archives, 1967); California Census of 1852, Counties of Yolo and Solano, transcribed copy in the California Room, California State Library; U.S. Census, Population Schedules for Putah Township, Yolo County, and Tremont Township, Solano County, California, 1860; *Sacramento Daily Union*, Apr. 7, 1858.

13. *Sacramento Daily Union*, July 9, 1856; *Davisville Enterprise*, Jan. 5, 1900; Jan. 19, 1900; Gilbert, *Illustrated Atlas and History of Yolo County*, 58–59; Larkey, *Davisville '68*, 76, 105, 106, 120, 122.

14. *Davis Enterprise*, Jan. 23, 1915 (quote); Larkey, *Davisville '68*, 162.

15. George W. Pierce, "Ranch Accounts, 1856–1861," box 2, Pierce Family Papers, Department of Special Collections, University of California Library, Davis; *California Culturist* (Aug. 1860), 69–70 (quotes); *Daily Alta California*, May 11, 1860; *Solano Press*, Oct. 4, 1862; *Transactions of the California State Agricultural Society during the Year 1858*, 238; *Transactions of the California State Agricultural Society during the Year 1860*, 55; *Beatty v. Clark*, "Transcript on Appeal," 113–20; Larkey, *Davisville '68*, 166–68, 187.

16. Yolo County, "Marriage Documents," box 1, YCA; Sprague and Atwell, *Western Shore Gazetteer*, 179–86; Faragher, *Sugar Creek*, 80.

17. Faragher, "Open-Country Community," 250; Susan Sessions Rugh, *Our Common Country: Family Farming, Culture, and Community in the Nineteenth-Century Midwest* (Bloomington: Indiana Univ. Press, 2001), 28–30; Jon Gjerde, *The Minds of the West: Ethnocultural Evolution in the Rural Middle West, 1830–1917* (Chapel Hill: Univ. of North Carolina Press, 1997), 108; *Solano Herald*, Nov. 30, 1861; *Solano Press*, Oct. 4, 1862; *Vacaville Reporter*, June 11, 2000, and other clippings and materials in the Silveyville file, Dixon Public Library; Gilbert, *Illustrated Atlas and History of Yolo County*, 58–59; *Davisville Enterprise*, Jan. 19, 1900; George W. Pierce, Daily Journals, 1867–90, entry for June 16, 1867, Pierce Family Papers; Larkey, *Davisville '68*, 105–7.

18. *Sacramento Daily Union*, Sept. 26, 1855; Sept. 30, 1855; Oct. 13, 1856; Oct. 5, 1857; July 10, 1858; Aug. 27, 1858; Sept. 9, 1858; Sept. 16, 1859; Sept. 20, 1859; *Transactions of the California State Agricultural Society during the Year 1858*, passim; *Transactions of the California State Agricultural Society during the Year 1859*, passim; I. N. Hoag, "History of the State Agricultural Society of California," in *Transactions of the State Agricultural Society during the Year 1879* (Sacramento: State Printer, 1880), 176–211; *California Culturist* (Aug. 1860), 69–70; Gerald L. Prescott, "The California State Fair in the Gilded Age," *Southern California Quarterly* 60 (Spring 1978): 17–27; Walton E. Bean, "James Warren and the Beginnings of Agricultural Institutions in California," *Pacific Historical Review* 13 (Dec. 1944): 363–64. Earlier, the state fair had been held in San Francisco, San Jose, Stockton, and Marysville.

19. *California Statutes* (1850), esp. 56, 80, 85, 93, 112, 115, 117, 151, 170, 179, 199, 203, 210, 217, 261, 263, 264, 275; Merrill G. Burlingame, "The Contribution of Iowa to the Formation of the State Government of California in 1849," *Iowa Journal of History and Politics* 30 (Apr. 1932): 182–218; Yolo County, "Board of Supervisors Minutes," Court of Sessions Book, June 30, 1851; Book A, Aug. 10, 1855, YCA; W. N. Davis, Jr., "Research Uses of County Court Records, 1850–1879, and Incidental Glimpses of California Life and Society," *California Historical Quarterly* 52 (Fall/Winter 1973): 241, 261; David Alan Johnson, *Founding*

the Far West: California, Oregon, and Nevada, 1840–1890 (Berkeley: Univ. of California Press, 1992), 102, 108.

20. Yolo County, "Assessment Rolls," 1850–60, YCA (rolls for 1851, 1852, 1854, and 1855 are missing). Payment status was usually marked right next to the name, with "paid," "refused to pay," or the like.

21. Yolo County, "Board of Supervisors Minutes," Book A, esp. Dec. 6 and 7, 1854; Apr. 11, 1855; Nov. 20, 1855; Aug. 14, 1856; Nov. 17, 1856; Feb. 22, 1858; Book B, Feb. 9, 1860; Sept. 6, 1860, YCA; Yolo County, "Assessment Rolls," 1850–63, YCA; Allan R. Ottley, "Some Notes on Early Yolo County and Davisville," speech given at the annual meeting of the Friends of the Davis Public Library, Feb. 5, 1960, 8–9, Department of Special Collections, University of California Library, Davis.

22. Yolo County, "Board of Supervisors Minutes," Book A, Oct. 3, 1854; Mar. 11, 1855; Apr. 11, 1855; June 22, 1855; Aug. 10, 1855; Sept. 13, 1855; Nov. 5, 1855; Feb. 5, 1856; May 6, 1856; Aug. 17, 1856; Nov. 17, 1856; Mar. 3, 1856; Aug. 10, 1857; Sept. 15, 1857; Feb. 24, 1858; Aug. 20, 1858; Sept. 10, 1859; Book B, Nov. 8, 1859; Feb. 9, 1860; Aug. 6, 1860, YCA; Yolo County, "Estrays," Book A, 40, 41, 56, 66, 89, 131, YCA; *California Statutes* (1850), 200; *California Statutes* (1855), 192; Yolo County, "Roads and Highways," Book A, 9, 27, 31, 33, 34, 35, 38, 40, 43, 61, YCA; Yolo County, "Leases," Book A, 109, YCA; *Sacramento Daily Union*, June 24, 1853; Apr. 16, 1857; Mar. 25, 1863; *Knights Landing News*, May 11, 1861; Sept. 21, 1861; Nov. 29, 1862; Rugh, *Our Common Country*, 25–28; Paul Bourke and Donald DeBats, *Washington County: Politics and Community in Antebellum America* (Baltimore: Johns Hopkins Univ. Press, 1995), 95–115; Hal S. Barron, *Mixed Harvest: The Second Great Transformation in the Rural North, 1870–1930* (Chapel Hill: Univ. of North Carolina Press, 1997), 21–22.

23. Yolo County, "Board of Supervisors Minutes," Book A, Sept. 13, 1855; Nov. 17, 1856; Sept. 15, 1857; Sept. 9, 1858; Sept. 10, 1859; Book B, Nov. 16, 1860, YCA; *California Statutes* (1850), 179; Gilbert, *Illustrated Atlas and History of Yolo County*, 36–39; Larkey, *Davisville '68*, 200.

24. *George W. Pierce v. Henry E. Robinson* (1859), California Supreme Court, no. 2329, "Transcript on Appeal," 1–50, California State Archives; Larkey, *Davisville '68, 200; Knights Landing News*, Sept. 13, 1862; George W. Pierce, Account Book, 1858–69 (containing justice of the peace case records), box 2, Pierce Family Papers; Pierce, "Ranch Accounts, 1856–1861" (containing justice of the peace office records); *Richard Hext v. Henry H. Hartley* (1858), Yolo County, District Court Case Files, 2nd ser., no. 137, YCA; *Fred Lloyd v. Henry Conner* (1858), Yolo County, County Court Case Files, Civil Case no. 72, YCA; *Davis Enterprise*, Mar. 14, 1930; Tom Gregory, *History of Yolo County* (Los Angeles: Historic Record Co., 1913), 229–30.

25. Calculated from U.S. Census, Population Schedules for Putah Township, Yolo County, California, 1860, and the local and county histories cited in chap. 1, n. 39.

26. On Yankee culture in the Midwest, see Susan E. Gray, *The Yankee West: Community Life on the Michigan Frontier* (Chapel Hill: Univ. of North Carolina Press, 1996); Gjerde, *The Minds of the West*; R. Douglas Hurt, *The Ohio Frontier: Crucible of the Old Northwest, 1720–1830* (Bloomington: Indiana Univ. Press, 1996), 249–50. On the relative slowness of mi-

grants from the upland South to develop local institutions, with the notable exception of churches, in new settlements, see Faragher, *Sugar Creek*, chaps. 9–12.

27. Bertram Wyatt-Brown, *Southern Honor: Ethics and Behavior in the Old South* (Oxford: Oxford Univ. Press, 1982), 339–50; Kenneth S. Greenberg, *Honor and Slavery* (Princeton: Princeton Univ. Press, 1996), 135–40; Paul W. Gates, *Farmer's Age: Agriculture, 1815–1860* (New York: Harper & Row, 1960), 228–30; Allan G. Bogue, *From Prairie to Corn Belt: Farming on the Illinois and Iowa Prairies in the Nineteenth Century* (1963; reprint, Ames: Iowa State Univ. Press, 1994), 121–22.

28. "Rattler Mare Account, 1861," Davis Collection; *Sacramento Daily Union*, Apr. 26, 1860; Apr. 13, 1863.

29. Based on a thorough survey of the near-complete case files housed in the Yolo County Archives. Only the justice of the peace files are missing, though many of them can be found in cases that were appealed or assigned to higher courts, and a few can be found in Pierce, Account Book, 1858–69. For the period 1850 to 1879, there were five local courts—the justice court, county court, court of sessions, probate court, and district court. The justice of the peace had both civil and criminal jurisdiction, with the former limited to actions in which the amount claimed did not exceed $200—though, as already stated, the limit was rarely enforced. The county court initially had only civil jurisdiction (primarily in cases appealed from the justice court) while the court of sessions handled criminal cases. In 1863, the court of sessions was abolished and its criminal jurisdiction assigned to the county court. The district court was the highest trial court in the county and operated as a circuit court generally covering two or more counties. It held jurisdiction in law and equity in all civil cases in which the amount in dispute exceeded $200 and in all criminal cases not otherwise provided for. In 1879, the new state constitution consolidated all these jurisdictions and responsibilities into a single superior court in each county. For a thorough discussion, see Davis, "Research Uses of County Court Records, 1850–1879," 241–66, 338–65.

30. *The People v. Solomon Thorn* (1855), Yolo County, Court of Sessions Case Files, YCA; Davis, "Research Uses of County Court Records, 1850–1879," 346; Altina L. Waller, *Feud: Hatfields, McCoys, and Social Change in Appalachia, 1860–1900* (Chapel Hill: Univ. of North Carolina Press, 1988), 85–93; Faragher, *Sugar Creek*, 112–13.

31. *C. I. Hutchinson and Jerome C. Davis v. Henry Conner* (1859), Sacramento County, District Court Case Files, no. 6372, SAMCC (second quote from the deposition of W. W. Stow); *Henry Conner v. C. I. Hutchinson* (1859), California State Supreme Court, no. 2100, "Transcript on Appeal," 6–12 (first quote at 10), California State Archives; *Brown v. Greene*, "Transcript on Appeal," 198–216; U.S. Land Case no. 411, Northern District, Laguna de Santos Callé Grant, 101–2, 256–63, Bancroft Library.

32. *Daily Alta California*, May 11, 1860.

33. Two cases, among many, document Pierce's mediating skills: *Henry Conner v. Charles Edsell and Alph Gandy* (1859), Yolo County, County Court Case Files, Civil Case no. 80, YCA; and *James Mills v. William Wright* (1864), Yolo County, County Court Case Files, Civil Case no. 148, YCA. In both cases, the angry litigants resolved their differences after long discussions with Pierce, who persuaded them to drop their appeals to the County Court.

34. *Pierce v. Robinson,* "Transcript on Appeal," passim; *Beatty v. Clark,* "Transcript on Appeal," 116–20, 142–47, 151–57, 181–86, and "G. W. Pierce account with R. C. Clark"; Pierce, "Ranch Accounts, 1856–1861"; *Daily Alta California,* May 11, 1860.

35. Yolo County, "Deeds," Book D, 47, YCA; "Lease," David M. Oakes to George W. Pierce, May 27, 1859, box 2, Pierce Family Papers; *Davis Enterprise,* Mar. 14, 1930; *Daily Alta California,* Sept. 13, 1863; Larkey, *Davisville '68,* 200–201; Gregory, *History of Yolo County,* 230.

Chapter Five. *"To Begin Again"*

1. The *Sacramento Daily Union* covered the flood extensively. For a concise overview, see its one-year "anniversary" stories, Dec. 9, 1862 (quote), and Jan. 10, 1863. See also *Knights Landing News,* Jan. 18, 1862 (quote); *California Farmer,* Dec. 20, 1861; Jan. 3, 17, 24, 1862; Frank T. Gilbert, *The Illustrated Atlas and History of Yolo County* (San Francisco: De Pue & Co., 1879), 54; G. F. Wright, *History of Sacramento County, California* (Oakland: Thompson & West, 1880), 69–72; "Drought in California," in Commonwealth Club of California, *Transactions* 21 (Dec. 1926): 477–78; Joseph A. McGowan, *History of the Sacramento Valley* (New York: Lewis Historical Publishing, 1961), 1:84; Robert Kelley, *Battling the Inland Sea: American Political Culture, Public Policy, and the Sacramento Valley, 1850–1986* (Berkeley: Univ. of California Press, 1989), 72; Thor Severson, *Sacramento, An Illustrated History: 1839–1875—From Sutter's Fort to Capital City* (San Francisco: California Historical Society, 1973), 108–9; Francis P. Farquhar, ed., *Up and Down California in 1860–1864: The Journal of William H. Brewer* (Berkeley: Univ. of California Press, 1974), 241–44.

2. *Knights Landing News,* Jan. 25, 1862 (quote); Feb. 15, 1862; Mar. 15, 1862; *Sacramento Daily Union,* Dec. 14, 1861 (quote); Jan. 17, 1862; Gilbert, *Illustrated Atlas and History of Yolo County,* 40, 54.

3. *Transactions of the California State Agricultural Society during the Year 1860* (Sacramento: State Printer, 1861), 55; *Daily Alta California,* May 11, 1860; *California Culturist* (Aug. 1860), 69–70 (quote).

4. *Sacramento Daily Union,* Sept. 18, 1857–Jan. 15, 1858.

5. About fifty landowners from Yolo County, including Hutchinson, purchased conditional stock in the company. Lists of stockholders and other materials are in box 1, MS 114, California Pacific Railroad and Other Subsidiary Companies Collection, Southern Pacific Railroad Company Records, California State Railroad Museum, Sacramento. See also Yolo County, "Mortgages," Book A, 465, Yolo County Archives, Woodland, CA (hereafter YCA); *Transactions of the California State Agricultural Society during the Year 1860,* 55; *Solano County Herald,* Mar. 13, 1858; *Knights Landing News,* Nov. 5, 1859; Dec. 3, 1859; Mar. 17, 1860; Dec. 26, 1863; *Sacramento Daily Union,* Nov. 27, 1860; McGowan, *History of the Sacramento Valley,* 1:207–8; Joann Leach Larkey, *Davisville '68: The History and Heritage of the City of Davis, Yolo County, California* (Davis: Davis Historical and Landmarks Commission, 1969), 41.

6. See *Charles E. Greene v. His Creditors* (1861), Yolo County, County Court Case Files, Civil Case no. 107, YCA; and *H. O. Beatty v. R. C. Clark* (1861), California Supreme Court, no. 3223, California State Archives, Sacramento, for discussions of these cases. Most of the case files themselves are available at the Yolo County Archives, the Sacramento Archives

and Museum Collection Center (hereafter SAMCC), and the Placer County Archives, Auburn, California.

7. *W. A. McWilliams and John Redmond v. C. I. Hutchinson et al.* (1861), Sacramento County, District Court Case Files, no. 8106, SAMCC.

8. Yolo County, "Minutes—District Court," Book A, 222–27, YCA.

9. Paul Kens, *Justice Stephen Field: Shaping Liberty from the Gold Rush to the Gilded Age* (Lawrence: Univ. Press of Kansas, 1997); Carl Brent Swisher, *Stephen J. Field: Craftsman of the Law* (Washington, DC: Brookings Institution, 1930).

10. *Beatty v. Clark,* "Opinion," 6–13.

11. Ibid., 26–28; *Solano Herald,* Nov. 30, 1861; John Mack Faragher, *Sugar Creek: Life on the Illinois Prairie* (New Haven: Yale Univ. Press, 1986), 204.

12. *I. M. Hubbard v. S. E. Herrick and L. F. Reed* (1868), Sacramento County, District Court Case Files, no. 11878, SAMCC; *Lester L. Robinson v. S. E. Herrick and I. M. Hubbard* (1869), Yolo County, District Court Case Files, 2nd ser., no. 532, YCA; *Sacramento Daily Union,* Feb. 12, 1872; Winfield J. Davis, *An Illustrated History of Sacramento County, California* (Chicago: Lewis Publishing Co., 1890), 805; Robert D. Livingston, "Mixed Personalities: Wells, Fargo & Co.'s Agents in Early Sacramento," *Golden Notes* 42 (Winter 1996): 1–8; Yolo County, "Deeds," Book B, 206, 225, YCA.

13. Yolo County, "Deeds," Book D, 560; Book L, 5, YCA; *Knights Landing News,* Nov. 29, 1862; Yolo County, "Assessment Rolls," 1861, YCA.

14. *Sacramento Daily Record–Union,* Jan. 29, 1883; Davis, *An Illustrated History of Sacramento County,* 799.

15. *Sacramento Daily Union,* Aug. 14, 1860; July 16, 1861; Mar. 7, 1867; *California Statutes* (1851), 296; *California Statutes* (1852), 69; Gordon Morris Bakken, *The Development of Law in Frontier California: Civil Law and Society, 1850–1890* (Westport, CT: Greenwood Press, 1985), 97–101.

16. *Greene v. His Creditors; Knights Landing News,* July 20, 1861; Yolo County, "Minutes—County Court," Book C, 163, 172, YCA; Yolo County, "Homesteads," Book A, 3; *California Statutes* (1860), 311; *C. I. Hutchinson v. His Creditors* (1861), Sacramento County, "Minutes—District Court," Book J, 283, SAMCC; *San Francisco News Letter,* Aug. 26, 1876; Paul Goodman, "The Emergence of Homestead Exemption in the United States: Accommodation and Resistance to the Market Revolution, 1840–1880," *Journal of American History* 80 (Sept. 1993): 470–98.

17. *Beatty v. Clark,* "Transcript on Appeal," 113–16, 151–53, 181–86; "Lease," David M. Oakes to George W. Pierce, May 27, 1859, box 2, Pierce Family Papers, Department of Special Collections, University of California, Davis; Hogs receipt, Oct. 15, 1859; Hutchinson promissory note, June 3, 1860; and Beef account, 1860, box 1, Pierce Family Papers; George W. Pierce, "Ranch Accounts, 1856–1861," box 2, Pierce Family Papers.

18. George W. Pierce, Daily Journals, 1867–90, entry for May 7, 1867, Pierce Family Papers, Department of Special Collections, University of California, Davis (hereafter Pierce journal); U.S. Census, Industrial Schedules for Putah Township, Yolo County, California, 1860, on microfilm in the California Room, California State Library, Sacramento; *Woodland News,* July 14, 1866; Shipley Walters, *Knights Landing: The River, the Land, and the People* (Woodland: Yolo County Archives, 1992), 20–21.

19. "Old Maine Prairie, Once a Busy Shipping Point" (unidentified clipping), "History of Maine Prairie" (unidentified manuscript), *Vacaville Reporter,* June 18, 1995, and several other clippings and documents in the Maine Prairie file, Dixon Public Library, Dixon, California; Mrs. Amelia Ransome Neville Scrapbooks, San Francisco Society, 1878–80, 56–58 (for many unidentified clippings on Friedlander's life), California Historical Society, San Francisco (hereafter Friedlander clippings); *Historical Atlas Map of Solano County, California* (San Francisco: Thompson & West, 1878), 13; J. P. Munro Fraser, *History of Solano County* (San Francisco: Wood, Alley & Co., 1879), 308–9; *Oakland Tribune,* June 1, 1930; *J. C. Merrithew v. Isaac McCoy* (1860), Solano County, District Court Case Files, no. 753, Solano County Archives, Fairfield, California; Morton Rothstein, *The California Wheat Kings* (Davis: University of California, Davis, 1987), 4–5; Rothstein, "A British Firm on the American West Coast, 1869–1914," *Business History Review* 37 (Winter 1963): 395–86; Albert Shumate, "Isaac Friedlander, Wheat Merchant," in *Breadbasket of the World: California's Great Wheat-Growing Era, 1860–1890* (San Francisco: Book Club of California, 1984).

20. Merrithew receipts, 1861, box 1, Pierce Family Papers; George W. Pierce, Account Book, 1858–69, box 2, Pierce Family Papers; *Historical Atlas Map of Solano County, California,* 13; Fraser, *History of Solano County,* 308–9; Rodman W. Paul, "The Wheat Trade between California and the United Kingdom," *Mississippi Valley Historical Review* 45 (Dec. 1958): 391–95; Horace Davis, "Wheat in California," *Overland Monthly* 1 (Nov. 1868): 442 (quote).

21. *Knights Landing News,* Jan. 25, 1862; *Sacramento Daily Union,* Dec. 11, 1861; Dec. 14, 1861; Jan. 17, 1862; Dec. 9, 1862; Pierce journal, Feb. 21, 1867; Edward Wolfskill, "A Few Things I Remember as Told Me by my Father, the Late J. R. Wolfskill," 1925, 22–23, unpublished MS, box 6, Ned Wolfskill Collection, Department of Special Collections, University of California, Davis; Gilbert, *Illustrated Atlas and History of Yolo County,* 54.

22. In addition to the sources in note 19, see *Solano Herald,* Jan. 11, 1862; *Sacramento Daily Union,* Jan. 15, 1862.

23. Friedlander clippings; Paul, "The Wheat Trade between California and the United Kingdom," 393, 395, 400–402; Rothstein, *California Wheat Kings,* 4–5; *Sacramento Daily Union,* Apr. 5, 1862.

24. *Historical Atlas Map of Solano County, California,* 13; *Weekly Solano Herald,* July 24, 1869.

25. J. C. Merrithew account, 1862; Cook, Dunning, and Co. account, 1862; Drury Melone accounts, 1862 and 1863—all in Pierce, Account Book, 1858–69; Pierce-Melone contract, Apr. 17, 1862, box 1, Pierce Family Papers; *California Farmer,* June 27, 1862.

26. Merrithew account, 1862, Pierce Account Book, 1858–69; *Sacramento Daily Union,* May 5, 1860; June 16, 1862; *California Farmer,* Aug. 15, 1862; *Pacific Rural Press,* Mar. 29, 1890; Paul, "The Wheat Trade between California and the United Kingdom," 392.

27. Cook, Dunning, and Co. account, 1862, Pierce Account Book, 1858–69; C. P. Sprague and H. W. Atwell, *The Western Shore Gazetteer and Commercial Directory, for the State of California . . . Yolo County* (San Francisco: Press of Bancroft, 1870), 262.

28. *Knights Landing News,* Aug. 16, 1862 (quote); *California Farmer,* June 27 and July 18, 1862; Merrithew account, 1862; Grape and peach accounts, 1865; "Two Chinamen" account, 1862—all in Pierce Account Book, 1858–69; Furniture receipt, J. G. Clark and Co., Aug. 29, 1862, box 1, Pierce Family Papers.

29. W. H. Fraser, "Rainfall and Wheat in California," *Overland Monthly* 33 (Jan. 1899): 521–23; J. M. Guinn, "Exceptional Years: A History of California Floods and Drought," *Publications of the Historical Society of Southern California* 1 (1890): 36–37; "Drought in California," 494; *Knights Landing News*, May 30, 1863; Hazel Adele Pulling, "California's Fence Laws and the Range-Cattle Industry," *Historian* 8 (Spring 1846): 144; Terry G. Jordan, *North American Cattle-Ranching Frontiers: Origins, Diffusion, and Differentiation* (Albuquerque: Univ. of New Mexico Press, 1993), 248; Gilbert, *Illustrated Atlas and History of Yolo County*, 40–41; *Historical Atlas Map of Solano County, California*, 13; *Sacramento Bee*, Sept. 27, 1941 (quote); Davis, "Wheat in California," 446, 449 (quote).

30. *Daily Alta California*, Sept. 13, 1863; Pierce Account Book, 1858–69, passim; *Sacramento Daily Union*, Dec. 2, 1867; Yolo County, "Board of Supervisors Minutes," Book C, July 1, 1867, YCA; Pierce journal, May 10, 1867 (quote); Oct. 27 and 30, 1867; Nov. 16, 1867; Yolo County, "Deeds," Book E, 342, YCA; Larkey, *Davisville '68*, 200; Shipley Walters, *Woodland, City of Trees: A History* (Woodland: Yolo County Historical Society, 1995), 17–27.

31. Yolo County, "Assessment Rolls," 1861–64, YCA; Yolo County, "Assessment List Books," 1864, YCA; Paul, "The Wheat Trade between California and the United Kingdom," 396; Pulling, "California's Fence Laws," 144; *Solano Press*, July 25, 1866; Wheat accounts, 1865, 1866 in Pierce Account Book, 1858–69.

32. Pierce journal, June 10, 17, 24 (quote), 1867; June 10, 1870 (quote); *Woodland News*, July 7 and 21, 1866; *Sacramento Daily Union*, Mar. 19, 1866; *California Farmer*, Jan. 30, 1868; Davis, "Wheat in California," 449; McGowan, *History of the Sacramento Valley*, 1:207–8; Leo Rogin, *The Introduction of Farm Machinery in Its Relation to the Productivity of Labor in the Agriculture of the United States during the Nineteenth Century* (Berkeley: Univ. of California Press, 1941), 110–15; Michael Frederick Magliari, "California Populism, a Case Study: The Farmers' Alliance and People's Party in San Luis Obispo County, 1885–1903" (Ph.D. diss., University of California, Davis, 1992), 112–13; Kenneth A. Smith, "California: The Wheat Decades" (Ph.D. diss., University of Southern California, 1969), 171–74; C. Daniel Elliott, "The Harvest," in *Breadbasket of the World: California's Great Wheat-Growing Era: 1860–1890* (San Francisco: Book Club of California, 1984).

33. *Davisville Advertiser*, Dec. 18, 1869; Pierce journal, Jan. 1, 1867 (quote); Apr. 26 and 30, 1867; Jan. 14, 1870; June 8, 1870; George W. Pierce Jr., "Schoolboy diary, 1866," box 4, Pierce Family Papers.

34. *Solano Press*, Jan. 2 and 9, 1867; *Sacramento Union*, Dec. 25, 1866; Jan. 5, 1867; Mar. 22, 1867; *Woodland News*, Mar. 9, 1867; June 29, 1867; Pierce journal, Apr. 8, 1867; Gilbert, *Illustrated Atlas and History of Yolo County*, 51, 54; Kelley, *Battling the Inland Sea*, 82–83.

35. Pierce journal, Jan. 1, 2, 3, 4, 19, Feb. 2, 4, 21, 28, May 4, 27, June 3, 14, 15, 27, July 8, 30, Aug. 14, Nov. 21, 24, 1867; *Solano Press*, Oct. 16, 1867 (quote).

36. Pierce journal, Dec. 22, 1867 (quote); *Yolo County Democrat*, Dec. 21, 28, 1867; *Solano Press*, Jan. 1, 15, 22, 29, 1868; *Sacramento Daily Union*, Jan. 3, 4, and 8, 1868; Gilbert, *Illustrated Atlas and History of Yolo County*, 51, 55; Kelley, *Battling the Inland Sea*, 83; *Davis Enterprise*, Feb. 12, 1970.

37. *The People of the State of California v. S. E. Herrick* (1864), Yolo County, District Court Case Files, 2nd ser., no. 414½, YCA; *Lester L. Robinson v. I. M. Hubbard* (1864), Yolo County, District Court Case Files, 2nd ser., no. 531, YCA; *Lester L. Robinson v. S. E. Herrick and I. M.*

Hubbard (1867), Yolo County, District Court Case Files, 2nd ser., no. 532, YCA; *James P. Robinson v. S. E. Herrick and I. M. Hubbard* (1868), U.S. Circuit Court, District of California, no. 559, National Archives, Pacific Sierra Region, San Bruno, California; *I. M. Hubbard v. S. E. Herrick and L. F. Reed* (1868), Sacramento County, District Court Case Files, no. 11878, SAMCC; Yolo County, "Deeds," Book E, 227, YCA.

38. Yolo County, "Miscellaneous Records," Book A, 26, YCA; Yolo County, "Deeds," Book H, 484, YCA; *Solano Press*, Aug. 26, 1868. See also the township map for Township 8 North, Range 1 East, Mt. Diablo Base and Meridian, May 12, 1865, National Archives, Pacific Sierra Region—which provides "eye sketches" of improvements, including grain fields.

39. Yolo County, "Miscellaneous Records," Book A, 26, YCA; Yolo County, "Assessment List Books," 1868, YCA; Big Ranch accounts, 1868–69, box 2, Pierce Family Papers; Big Ranch accounts, 1868–69, in G. Washington Pierce, Account Book, Southport, 1845–50, box 2, Pierce Family Papers (back pages); George W. Pierce, Monthly Time Book, 1868–82, box 3, Pierce Family Papers.

40. Big Ranch accounts, 1868–69, in Pierce, Account Book, Southport, 1845–50 (back pages); Pierce Monthly Time Book; Campbell lease, Dec. 18, 1868, box 1, Pierce Family Papers; Vineyard account, 1869, in Pierce Account Book, 1858–69; Pierce journal, Jan. 24, 1867; *Solano Press*, Aug. 26, 1868 (quote).

41. Yolo County, "Deeds," Book J, 558, 560, YCA; Agreement with Capital Savings Bank, May 31, 1870, box 1, Pierce Family Papers; Yolo County, "Assessment Rolls," 1869, 1870, YCA; *Davisville Advertiser*, Jan. 9, 1870; *Sacramento Daily Union*, Feb. 8, 1869; Feb. 26, 1870; *Daily Alta California*, Oct. 29, 1872; Roger C. Lister, *Bank Behavior, Regulation, and Economic Development: California, 1860–1910* (New York: Garland Publishing, 1993), 23–25.

42. Pierce journal, May 31, 1870; W. H. Fraser, "Rainfall and Wheat in California," 523.

43. *Solano Press*, May 13, 1868; *Weekly Solano Herald*, Mar. 6, 1869; July 24, 1869 (quote); *Oakland Tribune*, June 1, 1930.

44. *Solano Press*, Aug. 26, 1868 (quote); Sept. 2, 1868 (quote).

45. Ibid., Aug. 26, 1868; Sept. 2, 1868.

Chapter 6. Favorite Son

1. U.S. Census, Agricultural Schedules for Putah Township, Yolo County, California, 1860, on microfilm in the California Room, California State Library, Sacramento; U.S. Census, Industrial and Manufacturing Schedules for Putah Township, Yolo County, California, 1860, ibid.; Allan R. Ottley, "Some Notes on Early Yolo County and Davisville," speech given at the annual meeting of the Friends of the Davis Public Library, Feb. 5, 1960, 8–9, Department of Special Collections, University of California Library, Davis; *Sacramento Daily Union*, Sept. 22, 1860. For a more detailed list of Davis's holdings, see his inventory of Jan. 1, 1860, in Jerome C. Davis, "Journal; general farm, January 1, 1860–June 30, 1863, Putah Creek, Calif.," 1–5, California Room, California State Library.

2. U.S. Land Case no. 411, Northern District, Laguna de Santos Callé Grant, 427 (quote), Bancroft Library, University of California, Berkeley; *U.S. Statutes at Large*, 9:631–34 (quote

at 633); Paul W. Gates, "California's Embattled Settlers," in *Land and Law in California: Essays on Land Policy* (Ames: Iowa State Univ. Press, 1991), 172–73.

3. *W. W. Brown v. C. E. Greene* (1884), California State Supreme Court, no. 9443, "Transcript on Appeal," 198–209, California State Archives, Sacramento.

4. *Brown v. Greene*, "Transcript on Appeal," 209; U.S. Land Case no. 411, 300–301; Paul W. Gates, "The Suscol Principle, Preemption, and California Latifundia," in *Land and Law in California*, 210; Alston G. Field, "Attorney-General Black and the California Land Claims," *Pacific Historical Review* 4 (1935): 235–45; Christian G. Fritz, *Federal Justice in California: The Court of Ogden Hoffman, 1851–1891* (Lincoln: Univ. of Nebraska Press, 1991), 173–79.

5. *Sacramento Daily Union*, Sept. 21, 1860; Yolo County, "Assessment Rolls," 1861, Yolo County Archives, Woodland, CA (hereafter YCA). Ditch and brush fences are identified on the detailed township map for Township 9 North, Range 2 East, Mt. Diablo Base and Meridian (T9NR2E), Mar. 31, 1868, Township Survey Plats, Marysville Land Office, California, General Land Office Records, Records of the Bureau of Land Management (RG 49), National Archives, Pacific Sierra Region, San Bruno, California (hereafter Township Survey Plats, Marysville, NA-PSR).

6. *The People of the State of California v. H. P. Merritt, J. M. McClerg, John Haines, F. Bullard, C. Olds, and A. Merritt* (1860), Yolo County, Court of Sessions Case Files, YCA; *Knights Landing News*, Oct. 20, 1860; *Sacramento Daily Union*, Oct. 16, 17 (quote), 18, 19 (quote), 20, 22, and 23, 1860; *Woodland Daily Democrat*, Mar. 20, 1893; Frank T. Gilbert, *Illustrated Atlas and History of Yolo County* (San Francisco: De Pue & Co., 1879), 91.

7. *John C. Morrison and William P. Morrison v. E. L. Brown* (1854), Sacramento County, District Court Case Files, no. 2668, Sacramento Archives and Museum Collection Center, Sacramento (hereafter SAMCC); *Drury Melone v. James Lillard* (1862), Placer County, District Court Case Files, no. 9064, Placer County Archives, Auburn, California; *Brown v. Greene*, "Transcript on Appeal," 210–11; Yolo County, "Assessment Rolls," 1861, YCA; *Sacramento Daily Union*, Sept. 25, 1861; *San Francisco Chronicle*, May 26, 1903.

8. Drafts of the petition are in box 4, Pierce Family Papers, Department of Special Collections, University of California Library, Davis. See also Solano County, "Board of Supervisors Minutes," Book 2, 12, 40, County Administrator's Office, Fairfield, California. Davis's ledgers reveal that most of the twenty-five farmers who signed the petition, including Pierce, Hext, and Greene, held substantial accounts prior to 1861 but maintained only minimal balances thereafter. See esp. Davis, "Ledger; general farm, October 1, 1856–December 31, 1859, Putah Creek, Calif.," and "Ledger; general farm, January 1, 1860–June 14, 1867, Putah Creek, Calif.," California Room, California State Library.

9. Yolo County, "Assessment Rolls," 1861, 1862, YCA; *Sacramento Daily Union*, May 28, 1859; *Knights Landing News*, Feb. 15, 1862; Mar. 15, 1862; Gilbert, *Illustrated Atlas and History of Yolo County*, 40–41; *B. F. Hastings v. I. S. Chiles* (1864), Yolo County, District Court Case Files, 2nd ser., no. 419, YCA; *John Ehrhardt v. Jerome C. Davis et al* (1865), Sacramento County, District Court Case Files, no. 10010, SAMCC; Davis, "Ledger; general farm, January 1, 1860–June 14, 1867," esp. 213, 226, 235; Terry G. Jordan, *North American Cattle-Ranching Frontiers: Origins, Diffusion, and Differentiation* (Albuquerque: Univ. of New Mex-

ico Press, 1993), 248–49; Hazel Adele Pulling, "A History of California's Range-Cattle Industry, 1770–1912" (Ph.D. diss., University of Southern California, 1944), 110–19.

10. "Docket of Trials in the matter of the Rancho Laguna de Santos Callé," box 816, U.S. Land Office, Sacramento, Records, California Room, California State Library; *Sacramento Daily Union*, Dec. 25, 1865; *Knights Landing News*, Mar. 15, 1862; Davis, "Ledger; general farm, October 1, 1856–December 31, 1859," 43, 60, 63, 94, 157.

11. *Congressional Globe*, 37th Cong., 2nd sess., 1862, 2639–46 (quote at 2640); *Solano Herald*, Apr. 5 and 12, 1862; *Knights Landing News*, July 19, 1862; Gates, "The Suscol Principle," 210–14.

12. *Congressional Globe*, 37th Cong., 2nd sess., 1863, 1485; *U.S. Statutes at Large*, 12:808; *Solano Herald*, May 23, 1863; *Knights Landing News*, Apr. 16, 1864; *Brown v. Greene*, "Transcript on Appeal," 208–9; Gates, "The Suscol Principle," 216–17.

13. *Sacramento Daily Union*, Feb. 9, 1859; May 22, 1861; Sept. 20, 1862; Jan. 9, 1909; *Daily Alta California*, May 18, 1867; Oct. 12, 1884; John Conness Bio-Information file, California Room, California State Library.

14. E. F. Beale to A. J. Snyder, Apr. 10, 1863 (quote); Jerome C. Davis to Beale, Apr. 10, 1863; Davis to Beale, Aug. 18, 1863 (quote); Beale to Snyder, Aug. 25, 1863; Beale to Snyder, Sept. 30, 1863—all in box 816, U.S. Land Office, Sacramento, Records; Beale to J. M. Edmunds, Aug. 5, 1863; Edmunds to Edward Bates, Sept. 1, 1863, box 4, Correspondence on Land Claims, Records Relating to California Land Claims, Records of the Attorney General's Office, General Records of the Department of Justice (RG 60), National Archives at College Park, College Park, Maryland. On the president's proclamation and subsequent suspension, see the handwritten notes on township maps T8NR1E, T8NR2E, T8NR3E, T9NR1E, T9NR2E, and T9NR3E, Mt. Diablo Base and Meridian, Township Survey Plats, Marysville, NA-PSR; *Sacramento Daily Bee*, Oct. 27, 1858; *Sacramento Daily Union*, Oct. 28, 1857; and Paul W. Gates, "Public Land Disposal in California," in *Land and Law in California*, 262. On the maladministration of land policy in California, see Gerald D. Nash, "The California State Land Office, 1858–1898," *Huntington Library Quarterly* 27 (Aug. 1964): 347–56.

15. *Brown v. Greene*, "Transcript on Appeal," 208–9; *Sacramento Daily Union*, Apr. 25, 1864; Fritz, *Federal Justice in California*, 194–201.

16. *Knights Landing News*, Jan. 23, Mar. 19, and Apr. 30, 1864; *Sacramento Daily Union*, Apr. 25, 1864; *Brown v. Greene*, "Transcript on Appeal," 209.

17. *Congressional Globe*, 38th Cong., 2nd sess., 1864, 3360, 3370, 3375, 3388 (quote), 3420; *U.S. Statutes at Large*, 13:372; John Conness to J. P. Usher, box 2, Miscellaneous Letters Received, Lands and Railroads Division, Records of the Department of the Interior (RG 48), National Archives at College Park, College Park, Maryland; *Sacramento Daily Union*, Apr. 16, 1864; July 26 and 27, 1864; Gates, "The Suscol Principle," 220–21.

18. *U.S. Statutes at Large*, 12:409; 13: 372; Joseph S. Wilson to Register and Receiver, Marysville, CA, Aug. 17, 1864, box 816, U.S. Land Office, Sacramento, Records (quotes).

19. C. I. Hutchinson to Jerome C. Davis, June 8, 1865, box 305, Jerome C. Davis Collection, California Room, California State Library; Yolo County, "Deeds," Book E, 16, 78, 106, 501, 571, 589; Book F, 140, 353; Book I, 186, 223, 636, YCA; "Docket of Trials in the

matter of the Rancho Laguna de Santos Callé." See also the untitled sheet of paper detailing the transactions between Pierce, Hext, and Herrick in box 1, Pierce Family Papers. Three of the maps drawn by U.S. Deputy Surveyor Amos Matthews in 1865 are available in the California Room, California State Library: "Map of the Jerome C. Davis Ranch," "Field Notes of the S. E. Herrick Tract" (includes tracts of Pierce, Hext, and Melone), and "Map showing the Exterior lines of the Rejected Claims, Laguna de Santos Callé." See also the patent maps for T8NR1E, T8NR2E, and T9NR2E Mount Diablo Meridian, California, Surveyor Records, Bureau of Land Management, California State Office, Sacramento.

20. "Decisions of Register and Receiver in Application to enter Land in Rancho Laguna de Santos Callé under Act of 2 July 1864" (no pagination) box 816, U.S. Land Office, Sacramento, Records, California Room, California State Library; Hutchinson to Davis, June 8, 1865; *Marysville Daily Appeal,* Dec. 22, 1865; *Sacramento Daily Union,* Dec. 25, 1865.

21. Joseph S. Wilson to Register and Receiver, Marysville, CA, Aug. 17, 1864; *Sacramento Daily Union,* May 24, 1867; Case file of George W. Pierce, no. 1732, Dec. 6, 1866, Marysville land office, California, Land Entry Files, General Land Office Records, Records of the Bureau of Land Management (RG 49), National Archives Building, Washington, DC (hereafter Marysville Land Entry Files). Copies of the patents themselves, available on-line from the National Archives, were also kept by the county; see Yolo County, "Patents," Book A, 85 (Herrick), 87 (Hext), 112 (Greene), 153 (Pierce), 221 (Melone), 223 (J. Davis), 351 (Chiles), 369 (I. Davis); Book B, 42 (Lettner), 119 (Keithley), YCA.

22. *Solano Press,* Mar. 13, 1867; May 8, 1867; *Woodland News,* Mar. 30, 1867; May 18, 1867; Case file of Jerome C. Davis, no. 1985, Jan. 7, 1869, Marysville Land Entry Files (hereafter Davis land entry file); Township Tract Books for Townships 8 and 9 North, Range 2 East, Mt. Diablo Base and Meridian, Marysville Land Office, California, General Land Office Records, Records of the Bureau of Land Management (RG 49), National Archives, Pacific Sierra Region.

23. *Brown v. Greene,* "Transcript on Appeal," 256–60; Yolo County, "Swampland District No. 18 Boundary Petition Description," YCA (for a survey of Davis's swamp and overflowed land); Samuel A. Smith to J. W. Mandeville, Dec. 13, 1859 (quote), Correspondence, Board of Swampland Commissioners, Predecessor Agencies, Reclamation Board Records, California State Archives; Horace A. Higley to Board of Swampland Commission, Dec. 27, 1861, ibid.; "Report of Hon. William H. Parks, as Land Commissioner, to Visit the City of Washington," in California, *Journals of the Senate and Assembly* (Sacramento: State Printer, 1863), appendix 14, 27–37; *Knights Landing News,* Nov. 16, 1861; *Sacramento Daily Union,* May 22, 1862; Richard H. Peterson, "The Failure to Reclaim: California State Swamp Land Policy and the Sacramento Valley, 1850–1866," *Southern California Quarterly* 56 (Spring 1974): 48–56; Joseph A. McGowan, *History of the Sacramento Valley* (New York: Lewis Historical Publishing, 1961), 1:283–84; Joseph Ellison, *California and the Nation, 1850–1869* (Berkeley: Univ. of California Press, 1927), 38–45.

24. Yolo County, "Assessment Rolls," 1861, 1862, YCA; "Decisions of Register and Receiver in Application to enter Land in Rancho Laguna de Santos Callé" (quote); Davis land entry file (quote); Case file of Isaac S. Chiles, no. 2032, Aug. 5, 1869, Marysville Land Entry Files.

25. *U.S. Statutes at Large,* 14:218; *Congressional Globe,* 39th Cong., 1st sess., 1866, 3026,

3077–80, 3564–67, 3590–95, 3650–55, 3760; Joseph S. Wilson to O. H. Browning, July 15, 1868, box 17, Letters Received from the Commissioner of the General Land Office, Lands and Railroads Division, Records of the Department of the Interior (RG 48), National Archives at College Park, College Park, Maryland; *Sacramento Daily Union*, May 19, May 25, July 23, and Dec. 16, 1866; *Woodland News*, June 23, 1866; Gates, "The Suscol Principle," 221–23; Michael J. Gillis and Michael F. Magliari, *John Bidwell and California: The Life and Writings of a Pioneer, 1841–1900* (Spokane, WA: Arthur H. Clark Co., 2003), 191–92, 212–13.

26. Yolo County, "Deeds," Book F, 435, YCA; *Sacramento Daily Union*, Dec. 2, 1867; Yolo County, "Board of Supervisors Minutes," Book C, July 1, 1867, YCA; *Anna Tryon v. J. C. Davis, et al* (1866), Yolo County, District Court Case Files, 2nd ser., no. 492, YCA.

27. Yolo County, "Deeds," Book G, 500, YCA; Yolo County, "Mortgages," Book D, 461, YCA; *In the Matter of the Estate of Isaac Davis*, Sacramento County, "Probate Case Files," no. 1243 (1869), SAMCC; *Brown v. Greene*, "Transcript on Appeal," 209–12; Gilbert, *Illustrated Atlas and History of Yolo County*, 76; *Solano Press*, Mar. 27 and Apr. 13, 1867; May 20 and Aug. 26, 1868; *Yolo County Democrat*, Feb. 15, 1868; Joann Leach Larkey, *Davisville '68: The History and Heritage of the City of Davis, Yolo County, California* (Davis: Davis Historical and Landmarks Commission, 1969), 49–51.

28. Wilson to Browning, July 15, 1868 (quote); Davis land entry file; *Brown v. Greene*, "Transcript on Appeal," 212. See also the handwritten notes on the township map for T8NR2E, Mt. Diablo Base and Meridian, Township Survey Plats, Marysville, NA-PSR.

29. *Davisville Advertiser*, Dec. 4, 1869 (quotes); Dec. 18, 1869; Yolo County, "Mortgages," Book E, 13, YCA; Yolo County, "Deeds," Book H, 242, YCA; *Solano Press*, Aug. 19, 1868; Aug. 26, 1868; Sept. 2, 1868 (quote); Oct. 14, 1868; *Yolo County Democrat*, July 4, 1868; Sacramento *Daily Union*, July 7, 1868; *Davis Enterprise*, Dec. 10, 1970; Sept. 30, 1871; Sept. 28, 1872; Gilbert, *Illustrated Atlas and History of Yolo County*, 76; Ottley, "Some Notes on Early Yolo County and Davisville," 10–12; Larkey, *Davisville '68*, 49–52.

30. *Yolo County Democrat*, Oct. 30, 1869 (quote). The Central Pacific Railroad, owned by the famed "Big Four," purchased the California Pacific in the fall of 1871, though locals called the line the Cal-P for years to come; Ward McAfee, *California's Railroad Era, 1850–1911* (San Marino, CA: Golden West Books, 1973), 99.

31. *In the Matter of the Estate of Isaac Davis; In the Matter of the Estate of Jerome C. Davis*, Sacramento County, "Probate Case Files," no. 196 (1881), SAMCC; *Elnora S. Mitchell v. Milton Dale et al.* (1874), Yolo County, District Court Case Files, Civil Case no. 1125, YCA; *Elnora S. Mitchell v. Joseph F. Mitchell et al* (1890), Yolo County, Superior Court Case Files, Civil Case no. 1004, YCA; *Yolo County Democrat*, Oct. 30, 1869; *Davis Enterprise*, Jan. 23, 1915. The county and regional histories are cited at chap. 1, n. 39.

Chapter Seven. Prominent Citizens

1. The year 1858 was chosen because of the wealth of information provided by the county assessor that year (see chap. 3, nn. 20, 23). Persistence was then calculated by comparing Yolo County, "Assessment Rolls," 1858, Yolo County Archives, Woodland, CA (hereafter YCA); to the Township Tract Books for T8NR1E, T8NR2E, T8NR3E, T9NR1E,

T9NR2E, and T9NR3E, Mt. Diablo Base and Meridian, Township Tract Books, Marysville Land Office, California, General Land Office Records, Records of the Bureau of Land Management (RG 49), National Archives, Pacific Sierra Region, San Bruno, California; to Yolo County, "Patents," Books A and B, YCA; and to U.S. Census, Population Schedules for Putah Township, Yolo County, and Tremont Township, Solano County, California, 1870 and 1900, microfilm (Washington, DC: National Archives, 1967). See also "Tremont Township" (no author given), Tremont file, Dixon Public Library, Dixon, California, which claims that almost one-third of the families listed in the township in the 1860 census were represented by descendants still living in the area late in the twentieth century.

2. Hal S. Barron, *Those Who Stayed Behind: Rural Society in Nineteenth-Century New England* (Cambridge: Cambridge Univ. Press, 1984); John Mack Faragher, *Sugar Creek: Life on the Illinois Prairie* (New Haven: Yale Univ. Press, 1986), 249, n. 14; Susan Sessions Rugh, *Our Common Country: Family Farming, Culture, and Community in the Nineteenth-Century Midwest* (Bloomington: Indiana Univ. Press, 2001), 71–78.

3. R. Douglas Hurt, *The Ohio Frontier: Crucible of the Old Northwest, 1720–1830* (Bloomington: Indiana Univ. Press, 1996), 176.

4. E.g., *A Memorial and Biographical History of Northern California* (Chicago: Lewis Publishing Co., 1891).

5. Yolo County, "Assessment Rolls," 1853, 1861, 1864, YCA; *In the Matter of the Estate of John McClory*, Yolo County, "Probate Case Files," o.s., no. 124 (1867), YCA; Yolo County, "Title Abstracts," R-35, YCA; *Sacramento Daily Union*, June 25, 1855.

6. *Annual Report of the Surveyor General of California for 1858* (Sacramento: State Printer, 1859), 22–23; *California Statutes* (1858), 248; *U.S. Statutes at Large*, 5:455; Yolo County, "Mortgages," Book C, 7, YCA; Gerald D. Nash, *State Government and Economic Development: A History of Administrative Policies in California, 1849–1933* (Berkeley: Institute of Government Studies, 1964), 128.

7. *Annual Report of the Surveyor General of California for 1857* (Sacramento: State Printer, 1858), 14 (quote); George W. Gift, *The Settler's Guide* (Stockton, CA: Rasey Biven, 1857), California Room, California State Library, Sacramento; *Sacramento Daily Union*, Jan, 23 and May 14, 1858; Gerald D. Nash, "Problems and Projects in the History of Nineteenth-Century California Land Policy," *Arizona and the West* 2 (1960): 337.

8. *In the Matter of the Estate of John McClory; Andrew McClory v. Thomas McClory* (1869), Yolo County, District Court Case Files, 2nd ser., no. 548, YCA; *Thomas McClory v. Andrew McClory* (1870), Yolo County, District Court Case Files, 2nd ser., no. 622, YCA; *Amos Mathews v. Andrew McClory* (1870), Yolo County, District Court Case Files, 2nd ser., no. 680, YCA; Yolo County, "Mortgages," Book E, 21, 23, 58; Book F, 496, YCA; Yolo County, "Patents," Book B, 140, YCA; Yolo County, "Title Abstracts," R-35, YCA.

9. Case file of Jacob W. Oeste, no. 4161, Feb. 1, 1872, Marysville land office, California, Land Entry Files, General Land Office Records, Records of the Bureau of Land Management (RG 49), National Archives Building, Washington, DC (hereafter Marysville Land Entry Files); *George W. Derman v. J. H. Oeste and Gottfried Schmeiser* (1874), Sacramento County, District Court Case Files, no. 13984, Sacramento Archives and Museum Collection Center, Sacramento (hereafter SAMCC); U.S. Census, Population Schedules for Putah Township, Yolo County, California, 1860, microfilm (Washington, DC: National Archives,

1967); *The People of the State of California v. John W. Markely* (1864), Yolo County, Court of Sessions Case Files, YCA; *Knights Landing News,* July 18, 1863.

10. Oeste land entry file; Case file of Gottfried Schmeiser, no. 4834, June 1, 1872, Marysville Land Entry Files; *Jacob W. Oeste v. Frank Slocum* (1870), Yolo County, District Court Case Files, 2nd ser., no. 607, YCA; *Gottfried Schmeiser v. Richard Thomas* (1871), Yolo County, District Court Case Files, 2nd ser., no. 608, YCA; *Gottfried Schmeiser v. Charles Thomas and Frank Slocum* (1870), Yolo County, District Court Case Files, 2nd ser., no. 631; *Jacob W. Oeste v. W. F. Slocum* (1870), Yolo County, District Court Case Files, 2nd ser., no. 633; *Derman v. Oeste and Schmeiser;* Township Tract Book for T8NR1E; Yolo County, "Patents," Book B, 298, 359, YCA; Joann Leach Larkey, *Davisville '68: The History and Heritage of the City of Davis, Yolo County, California* (Davis: Davis Historical and Landmarks Commission, 1969), 196–97, 213–14.

11. Case file of Charles E. Greene, no. 1848, Nov. 1, 1867, Marysville Land Entry Files; "Decisions of Register and Receiver in Application to enter Land in Rancho Laguna de Santos Callé under Act of 2 July 1864" (no pagination) box 816, U.S. Land Office, Sacramento, Records, California Room, California State Library; *U.S. Statutes at Large,* 10:244 (quote at 246); *Sacramento Daily Union,* May 6, 1861; Yolo County, "Seminary Lands" Record Book, YCA; Yolo County, "Patents," Book A, 88, 112, 113, YCA; *Report of the Surveyor General of California from November 1st, 1865, to November 1st, 1867* (Sacramento: State Printer, 1867), 1–11; Joseph Ellison, *California and the Nation, 1850–1869* (Berkeley: Univ. of California Press, 1927), 36–38.

12. C. P. Sprague and H. W. Atwell, *The Western Shore Gazetteer and Commercial Directory, for the State of California . . . Yolo County* (San Francisco: Press of Bancroft, 1870), 64–67 (quotes), 469; *Sacramento Daily Union,* Oct. 19, 1859; *Woodland News,* Oct. 27, 1866; Yolo County, "Assessment Lists," 1864, 1865, 1871, YCA; U.S. Census, Population Schedules for Putah Township, Yolo County, 1860.

13. William O. Russell II, "Notes on FXR," Russell Ranch Papers, in possession of Marilyn C. Russell, Ft. Lauderdale, Florida; *A Memorial and Biographical History of Northern California,* 663–64; J. M. Guinn, *History of the State of California and Biographical Record of the Sacramento Valley, California* (Chicago: Chapman Publishing Co., 1906), 1387–88; *Winters Express,* Sept. 28, 1906; *Mail of Woodland,* Feb. 13, 1907; *Yolo Democrat,* Feb. 14, 1907; Yolo County, "Deeds," Book F, 362, YCA; Yolo County, "Assessment Rolls," 1860, YCA; U.S. Census, Agricultural Schedules for Putah Township, Yolo County, California, 1860, on microfilm in the California Room, California State Library; Yolo County, "Patents," Book C, 150, YCA; Joann Leach Larkey, *Winters: A Heritage of Horticulture, a Harmony of Purpose* (Woodland: Yolo County Historical Society, 1991), 20; Larkey, *Davisville '68,* 210–11.

14. Yolo County, "Board of Supervisors Minutes," Book B, Nov. 16, 1860; June 17, 1861; Aug. 13, 1861; Sept. 9, 1861; Sept. 8, 1862; Oct. 31, 1863; Sept. 11, 1865; Feb. 5, 1866; July 1, 1867; Sept. 2, 1867; Sept. 23, 1867; Oct. 8, 1867; May 5, 1868; Sept. 6, 1869; *Knights Landing News,* June 9, 1860, YCA; *Sacramento Daily Union,* Nov. 19, 1861 (quote); *Woodland News,* Sept. 21, 1867; *Yolo County Democrat,* Sept. 11, 1869.

15. U.S. Census, Population Schedules for Putah Township, Yolo County, and Tremont Township, Solano County, California, 1860, microfilm (Washington, DC: National Archives, 1967); Yolo County, "Board of Supervisors Minutes," Book B, June 17, 1861; May 7, 1866,

YCA; Yolo County, "Marriage Documents," box 1, YCA; Frank T. Gilbert, *Illustrated Atlas and History of Yolo County* (San Francisco: De Pue & Co., 1879), 68–71; Sprague and Atwell, *Western Shore Gazetteer*, 135, 179–96; Larkey, *Davisville '68*, 85.

16. *Caroline Heinz v. Lorenz Heinz* (1868), Yolo County, District Court Case Files, 2nd ser., no. 589, YCA; Yolo County, "Judgment Books, Civil Court," Book A, 412, YCA; Yolo County, "Minutes, District Court," Book B, 210.

17. *A Memorial and Biographical History of Northern California*, 327–28; Jon Gjerde, *The Minds of the West: Ethnocultural Evolution in the Rural Middle West, 1830–1917* (Chapel Hill: Univ. of North Carolina Press, 1997), esp. chap. 6; Rugh, *Our Common Country*, 147–53; Faragher, *Sugar Creek*, 79–86; Robert L. Griswold, *Family and Divorce in California, 1850–1890* (Albany: State Univ. of New York Press, 1982), 1–31 (quote at 19).

18. *Heinz v. Heinz; A Memorial and Biographical History of Northern California*, 328; "In the Matter of the Claim of Jerome C. Davis to West ½ of Section 31 T9NR2E, Lorenz Heinz and the State of California, Contestants," box 816, U.S. Land Office, Sacramento, Records; Rugh, *Our Common Country*, 152; Griswold, *Family and Divorce in California*, 1–2, 21.

19. Sprague and Atwell, *Western Shore Gazetteer*, 59–64; *Ephraim H. Cone v. John Hynes* (1868), Yolo County, District Court Case Files, 2nd ser., no. 526, YCA; *Ephraim H. Cone v. John Hynes* (1873), Yolo County, District Court Case Files, 2nd ser., no. 568, YCA; *Samuel Ogburn v. Edward Connor* (1872), California Supreme Court, no. 3453, "Transcript on Appeal," 1–11, California State Archives, Sacramento.

20. *Cone v. Hynes* (1873); Yolo County, "Assessment Rolls," 1858, 1862, 1867, 1869, YCA; Yolo County, "Board of Supervisors Minutes," Book B, Sept. 11, 1865; Book C, Sept. 2, 1867, YCA; *Yolo Weekly Mail*, May 25, 1871.

21. *Cone v. Hynes* (1873). See also the various township maps for T9NR2E, Township Survey Plats, Marysville Land Office, California, General Land Office Records, Records of the Bureau of Land Management (RG 49), National Archives, Pacific Sierra Region; those dated before 1873 designate all the southeast quarter of section 24 as swampland, while the segregation line splits the quarter section in half on all maps thereafter.

22. *Cone v. Hynes* (1873); *California Statutes* (1861), 355–61 (quotes at 359); *Sacramento Daily Union*, Jan. 1, 1862; May 22, 1862; S. Smith to J. W. Mandeville, Dec. 15, 1859, "Instructions to Surveyor General," Correspondence, Board of Swamp Land Commissioners, Predecessor Agencies, Reclamation Board Records, California State Archives (quote); Thomas A. Hendricks to J. W. Mandeville, July 15, 1859, reprinted in Francois D. Uzes, *Chaining the Land: A History of Surveying in California* (Sacramento: Landmark Enterprises, 1977), 135–36 (quote).

23. *Ogburn v. Connor* (1872), "Transcript on Appeal," 3–5, 11, "Opinion"; Yolo County, "Patents," Book B, 194, 248, YCA; Yolo County, "Assessment Rolls," 1870, YCA.

24. *Ogburn v. Connor* (1872), "Transcript on Appeal," 9–11 (quote), "Opinion" (quote).

25. Ibid., 12–13, "Opinion"; Yolo County, "Assessment Rolls," 1890, YCA; Guinn, *History of the State of California*, 484.

26. Copies of the deeds are in William H. J. Brooks, "Abstract of Deeds and Existing Encumbrances on the Undivided Interests in the Rancho Los Putos under Conveyances from Manuel Vaca and Juan Felipe Pena; together with all deeds made by said Vaca and Pena on said Rancho," 1872, Bancroft Library, University of California, Berkeley (hereafter

Los Putos deeds); and "Abstract of Title to 565 Acres, Los Putos Rancho, Solano County, belonging to R. B. Armstrong in T8NR2E, MDM," 1891, YCA (hereafter Armstrong title abstract). The deed books themselves are in the Solano County Archives, Fairfield, California (hereafter SCA). For the quote, see, e.g., Book E, 9, 138. See also, Wood Young, *Vaca-Peña Los Putos Rancho and the Peña Adobe* (Vallejo: Wheeler Printing and Publishing, 1971), 24.

27. U.S. Land Case no. 74, Northern District, Los Putos Grant, 137–206, Bancroft Library; *Dixon Tribune,* Mar. 5, 1897; *Vacaville Reporter,* Sept. 10, 1995; Larkey, *Davisville '68,* 220. See also the map accompanying the Armstrong title abstract.

28. Los Putos deeds; Armstrong title abstract; Young, *Vaca-Peña Los Putos Rancho,* 24–29; Larkey, *Davisville '68,* 217; *Davis Enterprise;* Dec. 11, 1969; Tom Gregory, *History of Solano and Napa Counties, California* (Los Angeles: Historic Record Co., 1912), 653–55.

29. Township Tract Book for T8NR2E; Solano County, "Patents," Books A and B, SCA.

30. Compare Yolo County, "Deeds," Books C, D, E, F, G, H, I, J, YCA to Los Putos deeds, Armstrong property abstract, and Solano County, "Deeds," Books N, O, P, Q, R, S, T, U, V, W, X, Y, Z, A-1, B-1, C-1, D-1, E-1, F-1, SCA.

31. U.S. Census, Population Schedules for Tremont Township, Solano County, 1860, 1870. See also *Historical Atlas Map of Solano County, California* (San Francisco: Thompson & West, 1878), 27.

32. U.S. Census, Agricultural Schedules for Tremont Township, Solano County, California, 1860, 1870, on microfilm in the California Room, California State Library; "Tremont Township"; Gilbert C. Fite, *The Farmers' Frontier, 1865–1900* (New York: Holt, Rinehart & Winston, 1966), 161.

33. "Tremont Township"; *Solano Press,* Sept. 2, 1868; *Sacramento Daily Union,* Nov. 6, 1869; *Vacaville Reporter,* Sept. 10 and Oct. 29, 1995; Larkey, *Davisville '68,* 175, 217; Los Putos deeds.

34. *Solano Press,* Apr. 10, 1867; Sept. 2, 1868 (quote); *Yolo County Democrat,* July 4, 1868 (quote); *Davisville Advertiser,* Dec. 4, 1869; *Davis Enterprise,* Dec. 11, 1969; Dec. 10, 1970.

35. *Sacramento Bee,* Apr. 8, 10 (quote), 13, 17, 1865; *Sacramento Daily Union,* Apr. 10 and 17, 1865; Joseph A. McGowan, *History of the Sacramento Valley* (New York: Lewis Historical Publishing, 1961), 1:170, 194–204.

36. *Sacramento Daily Union,* Aug. 1, 1860; Dec. 4, 1860; Sept. 4, 1862; Aug. 1, 1865; *Solano Press,* Aug. 26, 1868; McGowan, *History of the Sacramento Valley,* 1:194–95; James J. Rawls and Walton Bean, *California: An Interpretive History,* 6th ed. (New York: McGraw-Hill, 1993), 106–7.

37. U.S. Census, Population Schedules for Putah Township, Yolo County, 1860, 1870; Township Tract Books for T8NR2E and T8NR3E; Yolo County, "Swamp and Overflowed Lands Record Book," YCA.

38. *Knights Landing News,* June 15, 1861; *Yolo County Democrat,* Aug. 15, 1868; Apr. 10, 1869; *Sacramento Daily Union,* Aug. 2, 1858; Sept. 24, 1866; Yolo County, "Board of Supervisors Minutes," Book B, Aug. 6, 1860; Aug. 22, 1865, YCA; Larkey, *Davisville '68,* 193.

39. *Sacramento Daily Union,* Mar. 15, 1859 (quote); *Knights Landing News,* Apr. 28, 1860; Aug. 9, 1862.

40. *California Statutes* (1861), 355–61; Robert Kelley, *Battling the Inland Sea: American Political Culture, Public Policy, and the Sacramento Valley, 1850–1986* (Berkeley: Univ. of Cal-

ifornia Press, 1989), 47–48; McGowan, *History of the Sacramento Valley*, 1:284; Richard H. Peterson, "The Failure to Reclaim: California State Swamp Land Policy and the Sacramento Valley, 1850–1866," *Southern California Quarterly* 56 (Spring 1974): 50.

41. *California Statutes* (1861), 355–61 (quotes); *Sacramento Daily Union*, May 16, 1861; Jan. 1, 1862; Kelley, *Battling the Inland Sea*, 48–50; Peterson, "The Failure to Reclaim," 50–51.

42. A small portion of the southern end of the district (less than 10,000 acres) lay in Solano County.

43. Yolo County, "Swampland District No. 18 Boundary Petition Description," YCA; *Sacramento Daily Union*, Mar. 15, 1859 (quote); "Annual Report to the Governor by the Board of Swamp Land Commissioners," draft MS, Dec. 1, 1864, Land Grant Litigation, A–Z, Land Office Papers, Governor's Office, California State Archives; *First Annual Report of Swamp Land Commissioners for 1861* (Sacramento: State Printer, 1862), 23–24; *Annual Report of the Swamp Land Commissioners for the Year 1862* (Sacramento: State Printer, 1863), 3–6; *Report of the Board of Swamp Land Commissioners for the Years 1864 and 1865* (Sacramento: State Printer, 1866), 10–11; *Sacramento Daily Union*, Jan. 1, 1862; Jan. 1, 1864; Nov. 24, 1864; Jan. 2, 1865; Jan. 1, 1866; Dec. 25, 1866; Gilbert, *Illustrated Atlas and History of Yolo County*, 57; Peterson, "The Failure to Reclaim," 53.

44. Yolo County, "Board of Supervisors, Swampland District No. 18, Supervisors' Record, 1866–1873," 81–159 (quote at 157), YCA; Gilbert, *Illustrated Atlas and History of Yolo County*, 54–55; *Woodland News*, Mar. 9, 1867; *Sacramento Daily Union*, Jan. 20, 1868; Apr. 10, 1869.

45. Kelley, *Battling the Inland Sea*, 52–53; Yolo County, "Board of Supervisors, Swampland District No. 18, Supervisors' Record, 1866–1873," 159–61, YCA; *California Statutes* (1865–66), 799–801; *California Statutes* (1867–68), 514–21.

46. *Sacramento Daily Record–Union*, June 19, 1895; U.S. Census, Agricultural Schedules for Putah Township, Yolo County, 1860; *Mail of Woodland*, Oct. 6, 1911; Yolo County, "Board of Supervisors, Swampland District No. 18, Supervisors' Record, 1866–1873," 3–80; Yolo County, "Assessment Rolls," 1866, YCA; *California Statutes* (1865–66), 799–800; Kelley, *Battling the Inland Sea*, 57.

47. Yolo County, "Board of Supervisors, Swampland District No. 18, Supervisors' Record, 1866–1873," 79–80, 119–26; Kelley, *Battling the Inland Sea*, 57–59.

48. *California Statutes* (1867–68), 514–21; Kelley, *Battling the Inland Sea*, 560–61.

49. *Yolo County Democrat*, May 30, 1868; Yolo County, "Swamp and Overflowed Lands Record Book," YCA; U.S. Census, Agricultural Schedules for Putah Township, Yolo County, 1870.

50. *Knight's Landing News*, Nov. 14, 1863 (quote); *California Statutes* (1863–64), 170–71 (quote); *California Statutes* (1865–66), 440–43; Wilson Flint, "The Fence Question," *Transactions of the California State Agricultural Society during the Year 1863* (Sacramento: State Printer, 1864), 146–55; *Solano Herald*, Jan. 18, 1862; Hazel Adele Pulling, "California's Fence Laws and the Range-Cattle Industry," *Historian* 8 (Spring 1946): 144–45; Bentham Fabian, *The Agricultural Lands of California: A Guide to the Immigrant as to the Productions, Climate, and Soil of Every County of the State* (San Francisco: H. H. Bancroft & Co., 1869), 20; *Solano Press*, Jan. 8, 1868; *Yolo County Democrat*, Dec. 14, 1867 (quote). The Township Tract Books for T8NR1E, T8NR2E, T8NR3E, T9NR1E, T9NR2E, and T9NR3E and Yolo

County, "Swamp and Overflowed Lands Record Book," YCA, confirm the *Democrat*'s assessment.

51. Horace Davis, "California Breadstuffs," *Journal of Political Economy* 2 (Sept. 1894): 526–29; Rodman W. Paul, "The Beginnings of Agriculture in California: Innovation vs. Continuity," *California Historical Quarterly* 52 (Spring 1973): 22; Paul, "The Wheat Trade between California and the United Kingdom," *Mississippi Valley Historical Review* 45 (Dec. 1958): 396–97; Morton Rothstein, *The California Wheat Kings* (Davis: University of California, Davis, 1987), 3–5; Yolo County, "Assessment Rolls," 1866, 1869, YCA.

Chapter Eight. *"As Good As Wheat"*

1. "Unidentified Store at Davisville," 2 vols., Aug. 1868–Sept. 1868 and May 1869–Sept. 1869, Yolo County Archives (YCA), Woodland, CA (hereafter Dresbach ledgers); *Solano Press,* Oct. 2, 1867; June 23 and 30, 1869; *Yolo Weekly Mail,* Nov. 24, 1870. By this time, wheat merchants in California had adopted the English cental as the standard unit of measure rather than the more familiar bushel.

2. *Sacramento Daily Union,* Aug. 20, 1868 (quote); Dec. 24, 1868; *Yolo Weekly Mail,* Nov. 5, 1868 (quote); *Yolo County Democrat,* Feb. 15, 1868; May 15, 1869; *Weekly Solano Herald,* Aug. 14, 1869; *Davisville Advertiser,* Dec. 11, 1869; *Solano Press,* June 23, 1869; Morton Rothstein, "Frank Norris and Popular Perceptions of the Market," *Agricultural History* 56 (Jan. 1982): 53.

3. Dresbach ledgers, passim; C. P. Sprague and H. W. Atwell, *The Western Shore Gazetteer and Commercial Directory, for the State of California . . . Yolo County* (San Francisco: Press of Bancroft, 1870), 126 (quotes); *Davisville Advertiser,* Mar. 12, 1870; Apr. 16, 1870; *Yolo County Democrat,* July 31, 1869; *Weekly Solano Herald,* Nov. 25, 1869.

4. *Yolo County Democrat,* Aug. 21, 1869 (quotes).

5. Horace Davis, "Wheat in California: A Retrospect and Prospect," *Overland Monthly* 32 (July 1898): 61 (quote); Davis, "California Breadstuffs," *Journal of Political Economy* 2 (Sept. 1894): 529; Kenneth Aubrey Smith, "California: The Wheat Decades" (Ph.D. diss., University of Southern California, 1969), 202–3, 284–85.

6. *Pacific Rural Press,* Sept. 9, 1876; *Yolo Weekly Mail,* July 25, 1872 (quote, my emphasis); Aug. 31, 1876.

7. George W. Pierce, Daily Journals, 1867–90, entries for June 8, 1870 (quote); Oct. 1, 6, 12, 19, 1870; Mar. 11, 1871; Apr. 6, 10, 11, 12, 1871; and Aug. 30, 1871; Pierce Family Papers, Department of Special Collections, University of California, Davis (hereafter Pierce journal); *Yolo Weekly Mail,* Oct. 13, 1870; Nov. 24, 1870; May 30, 1872; *Sacramento Daily Union,* Aug. 6 and Nov. 25, 1870; *California Farmer,* Jan. 7, 1870; June 1, 1871; Joseph Hutchinson, "California Cereals," *Overland Monthly* 2 (July–Aug. 1883): 148–49 (quote); Horace Davis, "Wheat in California," *Overland Monthly* 1 (Nov. 1868): 448; Smith, "California: The Wheat Decades," 54–56, 210; Hugh Myron Hoyt Jr., "The Wheat Industry in California, 1850–1910" (M.A. thesis, Sacramento State College, 1953), 2, 13–15, 33–40; Michael Frederick Magliari, "California Populism, a Case Study: The Farmers' Alliance and People's Party in San Luis Obispo County, 1885–1903" (Ph.D. diss., University of California, Davis, 1992), 126.

8. *Henry Linton v. William D. Wristen* (1872), Yolo County, County Court Case Files, Civil Case no. 689, YCA; *William D. Wristen v. Henry Dawson and Robert Dawson* (1869), Yolo County, District Court Case Files, 2nd ser., no. 601, YCA; *John P. Jackson v. Henry K. Mitchell* (1875), Yolo County, District Court Case Files, 2nd ser., no. 1046, YCA; *William Dresbach v. William Minis and William D. Wristen* (1872), California Supreme Court, no. 3475, California State Archives, Sacramento; *Yolo County Democrat*, May 18, 1872; *Weekly Solano Republican*, Sept. 7, 1871; *Pacific Rural Press*, June 1, 1872; Yolo County, "Assessment Lists," 1885, YCA (quote); Hutchinson, "California Cereals," 150; Smith, "California: The Wheat Decades," 212–14. On the convoluted title history of the Davis ranch, see Yolo County, "Title Abstracts," R-40, YCA; and Abstract D-32, box 1, Davis Land Records and Abstract D-344, ledger no. 2, City of Davis Collection, Department of Special Collections, University of California Library, Davis, California.

9. Pierce journal, Sept. 10, 1870 and Sept. 4, 1871; Davis, "Wheat in California" (1868), 448; *Pacific Rural Press*, Dec. 6, 1879; Smith, "California: The Wheat Decades," 58, 81; Magliari, "California Populism," 95.

10. Pierce journal, Mar. 10, 1877; Jan. 2, 1879; Jan. 21, 1882; Feb. 15, 1884; *Davisville Advertiser*, Feb. 26, 1870; *Yolo County Democrat*, Dec. 12, 1873; *Pacific Rural Press*, Dec. 20, 1873; Feb. 12, 1887; Mar. 3, 1888; *Dixon Tribune*, Oct. 13, 1877.

11. Pierce journal, Nov. 21 and Dec. 2, 1870; Jan. 5, 6, 7, 28, 1871; Mar. 15, 21, 30, 1871; Apr. 3, 1871; *Yolo Weekly Mail*, Dec. 22, 1870 (quote); Apr. 13 and 27, 1871; May 25, 1871 (quote); *Sacramento Daily Union*, Apr. 25, 1871; *Pacific Rural Press*, May 27, 1871.

12. Pierce journal, Mar.–Nov., 1871 (quote, Oct. 6); *Yolo Weekly Mail*, July 27, 1871. On farmers' efforts to diversify, see esp. Yolo County, "Assessment Lists," 1871, YCA.

13. *Yolo Democrat*, June 8, 1872; *Yolo Weekly Mail*, Apr. 18, 1872 (quote); June 18, 1872; *Dixon Tribune*, June 21, 1879; Aug. 14, 1880; *Report of the Surveyor-General of California, from November 1, 1867, to November 1, 1869* (Sacramento: State Printer, 1870), 16–17; *Biennial Report of the Surveyor-General of the State of California, from August 1, 1875 to August 1, 1877* (Sacramento: State Printer, 1877), 20–21; Yolo County, "Assessment Lists," 1868, 1875, YCA; U.S. Census, Agricultural Schedules for Putah Township, Yolo County, and Tremont Township, Solano County, California, 1870, on microfilm in the California Room, California State Library, Sacramento; George W. Pierce, "Monthly Time Book for Employers and Workmen," 1868–82, no pagination, box 3, Pierce Family Papers, Department of Special Collections, University of California, Davis (hereafter Pierce Monthly Time Book); Pierce journal, Feb. 1, 1871; Oct. 4 and Dec. 28, 1872; July 7 and 9, 1873; Mar. 17 and May 25, 1874; Joseph A. McGowan, *History of the Sacramento Valley* (New York: Lewis Historical Publishing, 1961), 1:250.

14. *Yolo County Democrat*, June 27, 1868; June 26, 1869 (quote); May 15, 1874; Yolo County, "Assessment Lists," 1875, YCA; McGowan, *History of the Sacramento Valley*, 1:249; Smith, "California: The Wheat Decades," 177–81; Reynold M. Wik, *Steam Power on the American Farm* (Philadelphia: Univ. of Pennsylvania Press, 1953), 52–59.

15. *Dixon Tribune*, June 9, 1877; July 10, 1879; July 21, 1883; May 21, 1887; Pierce journal, July 24, 1872; Joann Leach Larkey, *Davisville '68: The History and Heritage of the City of Davis, Yolo County, California* (Davis: Davis Historical and Landmarks Commission, 1969), 35; McGowan, *History of the Sacramento Valley*, 1:249.

16. Pierce Monthly Time Book, passim; *William Francis v. R. S. Carey* (1870), Yolo County, County Court Case Files, Civil Case no. 631, YCA; *Yolo Weekly Mail*, July 1, 1875; *Yolo County Democrat*, July 3, 1869; *Davisville Advertiser*, Apr. 23, 1870; *California Farmer*, July 11, 1872; *Dixon Tribune*, Jan. 25, 1878; Aug. 16, 1879; *Sacramento Daily Union*, Apr. 22, 1870; Pierce journal, July 26, 1870; McGowan, *History of the Sacramento Valley*, 1:249–50; Richard Steven Street, "Tattered Shirts and Ragged Pants: Accommodation, Protest, and the Coarse Culture of California Wheat Harvesters and Threshers, 1866–1900," *Pacific Historical Review* 67 (Nov. 1998): 581–83.

17. Pierce journal, Oct. 3 and Nov. 7, 1871; Feb. 28, Mar. 8, Sept. 29, and Nov. 10, 1873; June 15 and Oct. 8, 1874; Pierce Monthly Time Book, esp. entries for Sept. 1870; *Yolo County Democrat*, Aug. 6, 1870; *Yolo Weekly Mail*, Oct. 27, 1870; *Sacramento Daily Union*, Jan. 1, 1862 (quote); *Dixon Tribune*, May 13, 1876 (quote); *California Farmer*, May 21, 1874; Michael J. Gillis and Michael F. Magliari, *John Bidwell and California: The Life and Writings of a Pioneer, 1841–1900* (Spokane, WA: Arthur H. Clark Co., 2003), 311–42. In other, more isolated regions in the Sacramento Valley with less access to large numbers of urban white workers, farmers were more likely to hire Chinese laborers—but even then usually as binders or cooks, not machine operators. See Davis, "Wheat in California" (1868), 449–50; Smith, "California: The Wheat Decades," 181–83; Richard Steven Street, *Beasts in the Field: A Narrative History of California Farmworkers, 1769–1913* (Stanford: Stanford Univ. Press, 2004), 235–36.

18. *Yolo County Democrat*, Sept. 26, 1868; *Yolo Weekly Mail*, July 25, 1872 (quote); Aug. 22, 1872 (quote); July 13, 1873; Aug. 31, 1876; *Pacific Rural Press*, Jan. 14, 1871; Oct. 2, 1875; Sept. 9, 1876; Smith, "California: The Wheat Decades," 196–200; Gilbert C. Fite, *The Farmers' Frontier, 1865–1900* (New York: Holt, Rinehart & Winston, 1966), 171.

19. *Yolo Weekly Mail*, June 23 and 30, 1870; July 21, 1870; Sept. 1, 1870 (quote); Dec. 1, 1870; Nov. 7, 1872; *Yolo County Democrat*, July 23, 1870; Oct. 1, 1870; *Sacramento Daily Union*, Dec. 24, 1868; Nov. 18, 1870; *Pacific Rural Press*, Sept. 23, 1874; Smith, "California: The Wheat Decades," 196–200; Magliari, "California Populism," 122.

20. Pierce journal, Apr. 5, 6, 22, and 27, 1873; May 22–27, 1873; June 14, 1873 (quote); Aug. 12–28, 1873 (quotes).

21. Pierce journal, Aug. 29, 1873; Sept. 1, 12, 14, 16, 22, and 29, 1873; Yolo County, "Deeds," Book Q, 45, YCA; Yolo County, "Mortgages," Book K, 244, YCA; George W. Pierce, Agreement with Capital Savings Bank, May 31, 1870 (scribbled payment notations), box 1, Pierce Family Papers; Yolo County, "Assessment Lists," 1871, 1875, YCA; *Yolo County Democrat*, Feb. 6, 1869; *Yolo Weekly Mail*, July 17, 1873.

22. *Yolo Weekly Mail*, Feb. 16, 1871 (quote); *Yolo County Democrat*, Oct. 9, 1874 (quote).

23. *Solano Press*, June 23, 1869. Pierce, for example, often solicited bids from dealers in these locations; see Pierce journal, Apr. 11, 1870; Aug. 16, 1873.

24. *Yolo County Democrat*, Mar. 27, 1868; June 13, 1868; Oct. 17, 1868; Dec. 4, 1869; *Weekly Solano Republican*, Dec. 2, 1869; *Dixon Tribune*, Nov. 9, 1878; Clare L. Childers, transcriber, "Presbyterian Church of Davisville, California: Minutes of the Session and Register of Communicants, 13 November 1873–14 April 1918," 1997, 3, 6, 7, YCA; Yolo County, "Articles of Incorporation," Davisville Town Hall Association, Sept 28, 1876, YCA; Yolo County, "Board of Supervisors Minutes—Roads and Highways," Book A, 116, 137–38; Book C, 48–51, 72–78, 269–83, 286–88, 357–58, 400–406, YCA.

25. *Dixon Tribune*, Dec. 5, 1874; June 23, 1877; Nov. 9, 1878; *Yolo County Democrat*, July 17, 1869 (quotes); July 31, 1869; *Solano Press*, Aug. 26, 1868; *Davisville Advertiser*, Feb. 19, 1870; Dresbach ledgers, passim; Sprague and Atwell, *Western Shore Gazetteer*, 126.

26. *Dixon Tribune*, Dec. 5, 1874; *Solano Press*, Oct. 14, 1868; *Yolo Weekly Mail*, July 31, 1869; Oct. 16, 1869; Jan. 5, 1871; *Yolo County Democrat*, July 31, 1869; *Davisville Advertiser*, Dec. 4 and 25, 1869; Sprague and Atwell, *Western Shore Gazetteer*, 238, 388, 462; Yolo County, "Assessment Rolls," 1858, YCA; Pierce journal, Jan. 8, 1870 (quote); *Davis Enterprise*, Dec. 19, 1969; Larkey, *Davisville '68*, 57.

27. My thanks to Professor John Lofland, for sharing his unpublished research of Davisville with me in the summer of 2002. His work, now in print, is entitled *Davis: Radical Changes, Deep Constants* (Charleston, SC: Arcadia Publishing, 2004); see esp. 13–44.

28. Clare L. Childers, transcriber, "First Presbyterian Church of Davisville, California: Board of Trustees, Minutes of the Meetings, 22 June 1873–3 March 1897," 1997, 1–10, YCA; Childers, "First Presbyterian Church of Davisville: Minutes of the Session," 1–7; Yolo County, "Deeds," Book J, 458, YCA; Yolo County, "Miscellaneous Records," Book A, 75, YCA; *Dixon Tribune*, Dec. 5, 1874; Jan. 9, 1875; Apr. 24, 1875; May 31, 1877; *Davisville Advertiser*, Jan. 22, 1870; Larkey, *Davisville '68*, 105–7; John Lofland and Phyllis Haig, *Davis, California, 1910s–1940s* (Charleston, SC: Arcadia Publishing, 2000), 65.

29. Frank T. Gilbert, *The Illustrated Atlas and History of Yolo County* (San Francisco: De Pue & Co., 1879), 70; Yolo County, "Board of Supervisors Minutes," Book C, Sept. 7, 1868, YCA; Yolo County, "Deeds," Book K, 67, YCA; *Yolo Weekly Mail*, Apr. 14, 1870; Jan. 5, 1871; *Yolo County Democrat*, Nov. 21, 1868; Larkey, *Davisville '68*, 83.

30. Gilbert, *Illustrated Atlas and History of Yolo County*, 62–64; *Davisville Advertiser*, Apr. 16, 1870; *Sacramento Daily Union*, Apr. 14, 1870; *Yolo Weekly Mail*, Sept. 9, 1876; Feb. 7, 1878; *Davis Enterprise*, Apr. 9, 1970; Larkey, *Davisville '68*, 118–19; Pierce journal, Apr. 9, 12, 29, and 30, 1870; June 15 and 29, 1871; July 6, 1871; Feb. 8, 1872 (draft of his speech). See also Alan Taylor, *William Cooper's Town: Power and Persuasion on the Frontier of the Early American Republic* (New York: Vintage Books, 1995), 210–12.

31. *Dixon Tribune*, Dec. 12, 1874; Feb. 6, 1875 (quote); June 23, 1877; Oct. 27, 1877; Nov. 24, 1877; *Yolo Daily Democrat*, Mar. 5, 1875; *Yolo Weekly Mail*, Apr. 18, 1878.

32. *Weekly Solano Herald*, Oct. 2 and 16, 1869; *Sacramento Daily Union*, Sept. 28, 1869; *Yolo Weekly Mail*, May 11, 1871; May 8, 1879; *Weekly Solano Republican*, May 1, 1878; *Dixon Tribune*, Feb. 6, 1875; Apr. 17, 1875; Aug. 28, 1879; May 16 and 23, 1885; June 6, 1885; Larkey, *Davisville '68*, 121–22; Kevin Nelson, *The Golden Game: The Story of California Baseball* (San Francisco: California Historical Society Press, 2004), 2–11.

33. Pierce journal, May 7, 1870; Jan. 9, 1871; May 7, 1871; May 13, 1872 (quote); June 7, 1872; July 13, 1874; Aug. 21, 1874; Oct. 20, 1882; Aug. 21, 1886; *Davisville Advertiser*, May 7, 1870; *Yolo Weekly Mail*, Nov. 6, 1879; *Dixon Tribune*, Sept. 24, 1887.

34. *Yolo Weekly Mail*, Oct. 3, 1872; *R. B. Armstrong v. California Pacific Railroad Company* (1872), California Supreme Court, no. 3340, California State Archives; *S. M. Enos v. California Pacific Railroad Company* (1870), Yolo County, District Court Case Files, 2nd ser., no. 810, YCA; *Jonathan A. Sikes v. California Pacific Rail Road Company* (1871), Yolo County, County Court Case Files, Civil Case no. 672, YCA; *William H. Marden v. California Pacific Railroad Company* (1870), Yolo County, County Court Case Files, Civil Case no. 624, YCA;

Yolo County, "Articles of Incorporation," California Pacific Railroad Company, 1869, YCA; Yolo County, "Board of Supervisors Minutes," Book C, Aug. 23, 1870, YCA.

35. *Yolo County Democrat*, June 19, 1869 (quote); *Davisville Advertiser*, Feb. 19, 1870 (quote); Yolo County, County Court Case Files, Criminal Cases, 1867–75, YCA; *Dixon Tribune*, July 6, 1878; Larkey, *Davisville '68*, 76.

36. Pierce journal, Feb. 28, 1871; Yolo County, "Board of Supervisors Minutes," Book D, June 8, 1874, YCA; *Yolo County Democrat*, June 12, 1874; *Yolo Weekly Mail*, Feb. 8, 1877; May 8, 1879; Oct. 16, 1879; *Dixon Tribune*, Apr. 13, 1877; May 4, 1878; Sept. 28, 1878; Oct. 26, 1878; Apr. 12, 1879; Mar. 27, 1880; Apr. 10, 1880; Childers, "First Presbyterian Church of Davisville: Minutes of the Session," 14, 19; Gilbert, *Illustrated Atlas and History of Yolo County*, 65–67 (quote 66); Larkey, *Davisville '68*, 119.

37. Pierce journal, Feb. 28, 1871; July 20, 1874; Childers, "First Presbyterian Church of Davisville: Minutes of the Session," 19; Childers, "First Presbyterian Church of Davisville: Board of Trustees, Minutes of the Meetings," 8, 10–11; Dresbach ledgers, passim; Pierce journal, 1870 (worker accounts at end of volume); *Yolo County Democrat*, June 12, 1874; *Dixon Tribune*, July 28, 1878; Nov. 9, 1878.

38. Yolo County, "District Court Case Files," 1869–79, YCA; Yolo County, "Marriage Documents," box 1, YCA; *Dixon Tribune*, May 20, 1876; Robert L. Griswold, "Apart But Not Adrift: Wives, Divorce, and Independence in California, 1850–1890," *Pacific Historical Review* 49 (May 1980): 265–83; Susan Gonda, "Not a Matter of Choice: San Diego Women and Divorce, 1850–1880," *Journal of San Diego History* 37 (1991): 195–213.

39. *Magdaline Glockler v. Charles Glockler* (1873), Yolo County, District Court Case Files, 2nd ser., no. 987, YCA; *Odd Fellows Bank of Saving v. Charles Glockler, Magdaline Glockler, and Carl Strobel* (1873), Yolo County, District Court Case Files, 2nd ser., no. 878, YCA; Yolo County, "Deeds," Book K, 222, YCA; *California Statutes* (1869–70), 291; *Sacramento Daily Union*, Mar. 19, 1870.

40. *Caroline Greiner v. Jacob Greiner* (1880), Yolo County, District Court Case Files, 2nd ser., no. 1575, YCA; Yolo County, "Assessment Lists," 1885, YCA; Yolo County, "Deeds," Book 31, 504, YCA; *Mail of Woodland*, July 28, 1916.

41. Yolo County, "Board of Supervisors, Swampland District No. 18, Supervisors' Record, 1866–1873," 161–232, YCA; Yolo County, "Board of Supervisors, Swampland District No. 18, Accounts," 228, 230, YCA; *Henry Cowell v. R. S. Carey* (1895), Yolo County, Superior Court Case Files, no. 1531, YCA; *S. H. Cowell v. Lydia T. Armstrong* (1930), California State Supreme Court, no. 4341 (SAC), "Transcript on Appeal," 73–75, 312, California State Archives; *Biennial Report of the Treasurer of California for the Twenty-first and Twenty-second Fiscal Years* (Sacramento: State Printer, 1871), 23; *Sacramento Daily Union*, Jan. 20, 1868; June 2, 1868; *Weekly Solano Republican*, Feb. 16, 1871; *Davisville Advertiser*, Feb. 26, 1870; *Pacific Rural Press*, July 5, 1875.

42. *Yolo County Democrat*, Dec. 23, 1871 (quotes); *Dixon Tribune*, Nov. 5, 1887; *Cowell v. Armstrong*, "Transcript on Appeal," 73.

43. Gilbert, *Illustrated Atlas and History of Yolo County*, 50; Yolo County, "Board of Supervisors Minutes," Book C, Feb. 4, 1868; Mar. 9, 1868, YCA; Yolo County, "Board of Supervisors, Swampland District No. 18, Supervisors' Record," 39, 50, 60, 81, 166, YCA; *Cowell v. Armstrong*, "Transcript on Appeal," 66–75, 85; Pierce journal, Dec. 19, 1871; "Why

Putah Creek Changed Its Course," undated clipping (1968) from the *Dixon Tribune* on file at the Dixon Public Library, Dixon, California; *Woodland News*, Mar. 9, 1867; *Yolo Weekly Democrat*, Dec. 23, 1871; *Yolo Weekly Mail*, Jan. 4, 1872; *Dixon Tribune*, Sept. 18, 1886; Nov. 5, 1887.

44. *Cowell v. Armstrong*, "Transcript on Appeal," 68, 80; Pierce journal, Dec. 19, 1871; "Why Putah Creek Changed Its Course"; *Yolo Weekly Democrat*, Dec. 23, 1871; *Dixon Tribune*, Sept. 18, 1886; Nov. 5, 1887.

45. Yolo County, "Board of Supervisors, Swampland District No. 18, Accounts," 230, YCA; Yolo County, "Board of Supervisors Minutes," Book D, Feb. 7, 1872, YCA; Yolo County, "Reclamation District Formation," Book A, 23, YCA.

46. *California Statutes* (1872), 941; *Sacramento Daily Union*, Mar. 28, 1872; *Weekly Solano Republican*, May 2, 1872; *Yolo County Democrat*, Aug. 21, 1869; May 11, 1872; California, *Journal of the Assembly* (Sacramento: State Printer, 1872), 833, 846, 875.

47. *California Statutes* (1872), 941–45 (quotes); *Yolo County Democrat*, May 11, 1872.

48. Yolo County, "Board of Supervisors Minutes," Book D, Apr. 22, 1872; May 7, 1872, YCA; *Yolo County Democrat*, May 11, 1872 (quotes).

49. Solano County, "Board of Supervisors Minutes," Book 4, Apr. 25 and 30, 1872, County Administrator's Office, Fairfield, California; *Yolo County Democrat*, May 11, 1872 (quote); *Dixon Tribune*, Sept. 18, 1886; Nov. 5, 1887; *California Statutes* (1874), 84.

50. "Why Putah Creek Changed Its Course"; *Cowell v. Armstrong*, "Transcript on Appeal," 312–13; *Dixon Tribune*, Nov. 29, 1884; Sept. 18, 1886; Nov. 5, 1887.

51. "Why Putah Creek Changed Its Course"; *Cowell v. Armstrong*, "Transcript on Appeal," 69–75; *Dixon Tribune*, Jan. 19, 1878; *Yolo Weekly Mail*, May 16, 1878; *Historical Atlas Map of Solano County, California* (San Francisco: Thompson & West, 1878), 27.

52. *Sacramento Bee*, Dec. 31, 1873; *Marysville Daily Appeal*, Jan. 3, 1874; Pierce journal, Nov. 25, 1874; *Cowell v. Armstrong*, "Transcript on Appeal," 69–87 (quote at 85), 312–13; *Yolo Weekly Mail*, Jan. 21, 1875; Feb. 21, 1878; May 16, 1878; *Dixon Tribune*, Nov. 11, 1876; Jan. 19, 1878 (quotes); Feb. 2 and 23, 1878; Mar. 8, 1879; Mar. 15, 1879; Jan. 17, 1880; Apr. 24, 1880; Gilbert, *Illustrated Atlas and History of Yolo County*, 55–56.

53. *Dixon Tribune*, Mar. 15, 1879; "Why Putah Creek Changed Its Course"; *Cowell v. Armstrong*, "Transcript on Appeal," 69–76; *Historical Atlas Map of Solano County, California*, 27; Edward Nelson Eager, *Official Map of the County of Solano* (San Francisco: Britton & Rey, 1890); California Commissioner of Public Works, *Yolo Basin* (San Francisco: Britton & Rey, 1895); P. N. Ashley, *Official Map of the County of Yolo* (San Francisco: Britton & Rey, 1900); C. F. Weber, *Weber's Map of Solano County, California* (San Francisco: C. F. Weber & Co., 1914); Edward Denny, *Denny's Pocket Map of Solano County, California* (San Francisco: Edward Denny & Co., 1915); Jeffrey F. Mount, *California Rivers and Streams: The Conflict between Fluvial Process and Land Use* (Berkeley: Univ. of California Press, 1995), 52–82.

54. *Dixon Tribune*, Feb. 23, 1878 (quote).

55. *Sacramento Daily Union*, Jan. 3, 1876, quoted in McGowan, *History of the Sacramento Valley*, 1:244.

Chapter Nine. *"A Devil's Opportunity"*

1. *Wheat: An Illustrated Description of California's Leading Industry* (San Francisco: Commercial Publication Co., 1887), Bancroft Library, University of California, Berkeley (author unknown); Rodman W. Paul, *The Far West and the Great Plains in Transition, 1850–1900* (New York: Harper & Row, 1988), 225–31; Morton Rothstein, "West Coast Farmers and the Tyranny of Distance: Agriculture on the Fringes of the World Market," *Agricultural History* 49 (Jan. 1975): 275–76; Michael Frederick Magliari, "California Populism, a Case Study: The Farmers' Alliance and People's Party in San Luis Obispo County, 1885–1903" (Ph.D. diss., University of California, Davis, 1992), 84; and esp. Forest G. Hill, "Place of the Grain Trade in California Economic Development, 1870–1900," Social Science Research Council, Western Committee on Regional Economic Analysis, Proceedings, 1954, 13–33, Bancroft Library.

2. Ezra S. Carr, *The Patrons of Husbandry on the Pacific Coast* (San Francisco: A. L. Bancroft & Co., 1875), 66–67; Morton Rothstein, *The California Wheat Kings* (Davis: University of California, Davis, 1987), 2–5 (quote 5); Rothstein, "A British Firm on the American West Coast, 1869–1914," *Business History Review* 37 (Winter 1963): 395–96; Horace Davis, "Wheat in California: A Retrospect and Prospect," *Overland Monthly* 32 (July 1898): 60 (quote); Joseph Hutchinson, "California Cereals," *Overland Monthly* 2 (July–Aug. 1883): 10–11; Albert Shumate, "Isaac Friedlander, Wheat Merchant," in *Breadbasket of the World: California's Great Wheat-Growing Era, 1860–1890* (San Francisco: Book Club of California, 1984), no pagination; Rodman W. Paul, "The Wheat Trade between California and the United Kingdom," *Mississippi Valley Historical Review* 45 (Dec. 1958): 400–401; Paul, "The Great California Grain War: The Grangers Challenge the Wheat King," *Pacific Historical Review* 27 (Nov. 1958): 336–39; *Wheat: An Illustrated Description,* 34 (quote); Magliari, "California Populism," 131.

3. "Unidentified Store at Davisville," 2 vols., Aug. 1868–Sept. 1868 and May 1869–Sept. 1869, Yolo County Archives, Woodland, CA (YCA) (hereafter Dresbach ledgers); *William Dresbach v. William Minis and William D. Wristen* (1872), California Supreme Court, no. 3475, California State Archives, Sacramento; *William D. Wristen v. Isaac Friedlander and William Dresbach* (1873), Yolo County, District Court Case Files, 2nd ser., no. 690, YCA; Yolo County, "Chattel Mortgages," Book A, 122, 135, 139, 157, 213, YCA; *William Dresbach v. His Competitors* (1879), Yolo County, County Court Case Files, Civil Case no. 788, YCA; *Yolo Weekly Mail*, Sept. 25, 1873; Jan. 2, 1879 (quote); *Yolo County Democrat*, Oct. 9, 1873 (quote); *Dixon Tribune*, Nov. 21, 1874; Dec. 5, 1874 (quote); Oct. 8, 1887; Nov. 2, 1894.

4. "The Terrible Seventies" is the title of chapter 19 of Gertrude Atherton, *California: An Intimate History* (New York: Blue Ribbon Books, 1927). Frank T. Gilbert, *Illustrated Atlas and History of Yolo County* (San Francisco: De Pue & Co., 1879), 46 (quote); *Yolo County Democrat*, Nov. 23, 1876 (quote).

5. *Solano Press*, Apr. 29, 1868 (quote); *Sacramento Daily Union*, Apr. 23, 1868; Aug. 24, 1868; *Yolo County Democrat*, May 2, 1868; Jan. 1, 1870; *Wristen v. Friedlander and Dresbach*; Margery Holburne Saunders, "California Wheat, 1867–1910: Influences of Transportation on the Export Trade and the Location of Producing Areas" (M.A. thesis, University of Cal-

ifornia, Berkeley, 1960), 56–60; Morton Rothstein, "American Wheat and the British Market, 1860–1905" (Ph.D. diss., Cornell University, 1960), 72–75.

6. *Sacramento Daily Union*, Apr. 23, 1868 (quotes); Rothstein, "American Wheat and the British Market," 72–99; John Giffin Thompson, *The Rise and Decline of the Wheat Growing Industry in Wisconsin*, Bulletin of the University of Wisconsin, no. 292, May 1907, 112–20; William Cronon, *Nature's Metropolis: Chicago and the Great West* (New York: Norton, 1991), 104–19.

7. *Solano Press*, Apr. 29, 1868 (quote); July 29, 1868; Apr. 7, 1869; *Weekly Solano Herald*, Jan. 2, 1869; Jan. 30, 1869; Feb. 6, 1869; *Weekly Solano Republican*, Aug. 11, 1870; *Sacramento Daily Union*, Apr. 23, 1868; May 23, 1868; Aug. 24, 1868; Jan. 15, 1869; Feb. 20, 1869; *Yolo County Democrat*, May 2, 1868; Mar. 20, 1869; *Yolo Weekly Mail*, May 23, 1872; Rothstein, "American Wheat and the British Market," 91–95; Cronon, *Nature's Metropolis*, 120–27.

8. *Solano Press*, Apr. 29, 1868; *Sacramento Daily Union*, Apr. 23, 1868; J. P. Munro Fraser, *The History of Solano County* (Oakland: Wood, Alley & Co., 1879), 231–35 (quotes); Saunders, "California Wheat," 59.

9. *Solano Press*, Apr. 29, 1868 (quotes); *Sacramento Daily Union*, May 23, 1868 (quotes); *San Francisco Commercial Herald*, May 18, 1868; *Yolo Daily Democrat*, Jan. 1, 1870; Feb. 13, 1874; *Yolo Weekly Mail*, May 23, 1872; *Wristen v. Friedlander and Dresbach*; Rothstein, "American Wheat and the British Market," 83–85.

10. *Sacramento Daily Union*, May 23, 1868 (quotes); *Yolo County Democrat*, Jan. 1, 1870 (quote); *Yolo Weekly Mail*, May 30, 1872; *Wristen v. Friedlander and Dresbach*.

11. *Yolo County Democrat*, Jan. 1, 1870.

12. *Wristen v. Friedlander and Dresbach*; *William D. Wristen v. Isaac Friedlander and William Dresbach* (1873), Yolo County, District Court Case Files, 2nd ser., no. 690½, YCA; *F. S. Freeman v. William Dresbach* (1871), Yolo County, District Court Case Files, 2nd ser., no. 796, YCA.

13. *Yolo County Democrat*, Jan. 1, 1870; Horace Davis, "California Breadstuffs," *Journal of Political Economy* 2 (Sept. 1894): 527; Saunders, "California Wheat," 59; Paul, "The Wheat Trade between California and the United Kingdom," 391, 393, 403–5.

14. *Vallejo Chronicle*, reprinted in *Yolo County Democrat*, Sept. 21, 1872; Fraser, *The History of Solano County*, 234–35.

15. *Yolo Weekly Mail*, May 30, 1872 (quote); June 20, 1872; Mar. 20, 1873; *Yolo County Democrat*, June 29, 1872; Mar. 20, 1874; *Marysville Daily Appeal*, July 16, 1876; *Pacific Rural Press*, Sept. 28, 1872; Nov. 2, 1872; Mar. 29, 1890; Jan. 13, 1894; Magliari, "California Populism," 130–31; Paul, "The Great California Grain War," 332–33; Joseph A. McGowan, *History of the Sacramento Valley* (New York: Lewis Historical Publishing, 1961), 1:268–69.

16. *Dixon Tribune*, Dec. 5, 1874; *Yolo Weekly Mail*, Sept. 25, 1873; *Yolo County Democrat*, Nov. 23, 1872 (quote); Oct. 9, 1873; George W. Pierce, Daily Journals, 1867–90, entry for Mar. 6, 1872, Pierce Family Papers, Department of Special Collections, University of California, Davis (hereafter Pierce journal); Gilbert, *Illustrated Atlas and History of Yolo County*, 46; Magliari, "California Populism," 128.

17. *William Dresbach v. Andrew McClory* (1874), Yolo County, District Court Case Files, 2nd ser., no. 1092, YCA.

18. *Dresbach v. McClory;* Yolo County, "Mortgages," Book C, 500; Book K, 244, YCA; Gilbert, *Illustrated Atlas and History of Yolo County,* 46; Morton Rothstein, "Technological Change and American Farm Movements," in *Technology, the Economy, and Society: The American Experience,* ed. Joel Colton and Stuart Bruchey (New York: Columbia Univ. Press, 1987), 195–96.

19. *Yolo County Democrat,* Jan. 6, 1872 (quote); Oct. 5, 1872; Nov. 23, 1872 (quote); Dec. 14, 1872; Dec. 28, 1872; Jan. 11, 1873 (quote); Jan. 18, 1873; Jan. 25, 1873; Feb. 22, 1873; Mar. 22, 1873; *Yolo Weekly Mail,* Sept. 26, 1872; Dec. 12, 1872; Jan. 2, 1873; Mar. 6, 1873; Apr. 24, 1873 (quote); *Pacific Rural Press,* Jan. 18, 1873; *California Farmer,* Feb. 13, 1873; Gilbert, *Illustrated Atlas and History of Yolo County,* 46; Solon Justus Buck, *The Granger Movement: A Study of Agricultural Organization and its Political, Economic, and Social Manifestations, 1870–1880* (Cambridge: Harvard Univ. Press, 1913), 59–60, 73–79; McGowan, *History of the Sacramento Valley,* 1:269; Carr, *Patrons of Husbandry on the Pacific Coast,* 75–103; Paul, "The Great California Grain War," 335, 341.

20. *Yolo Weekly Mail,* Apr. 24, 1873; *Pacific Rural Press,* Apr. 19, 1873; July 12, 1873; July 19, 1973; July 26, 1873; Oct. 18, 1873; Carr, *Patrons of Husbandry on the Pacific Coast,* 103; Paul, "The Great California Grain War," 343; Gerald L. Prescott, "Farm Gentry vs. the Grangers: Conflict in Rural America," *California Historical Quarterly* 56 (Winter 1977/78): 330.

21. *Yolo County Democrat,* May 23, 1873; Oct. 10, 1873 (quote); *Pacific Rural Press,* Oct. 11, 1873; Jan. 17, 1874 (quote); Jan. 31, 1874; Carr, *Patrons of Husbandry on the Pacific Coast,* 237; Pierce journal, Sept. 23, 1873; Gilbert, *Illustrated Atlas and History of Yolo County,* 46.

22. Fred A. Shannon, *The Farmer's Last Frontier: Agriculture, 1860–1897* (New York: Rinehart & Co., 1945), 329–32; Paul, "The Great California Grain War," 345; Pierce journal, Sept. 29, 1873.

23. Gilbert, *Illustrated Atlas and History of Yolo County,* 46 (quote); *Pacific Rural Press,* Mar. 28, 1874; Apr. 25, 1874 (quote; emphasis in original); *Yolo Weekly Mail,* Mar. 19, 1874; Yolo County, "Deeds," Book R, 277, YCA; Yolo County, "Articles of Incorporation," Davisville Grangers Warehousing Association, May 16, 1874, YCA; Paul, "The Great California Grain War," 345.

24. Gilbert, *Illustrated Atlas and History of Yolo County,* 46 (quote); *Pacific Rural Press,* Aug. 8, 1874 (quote); Oct. 21, 1874; Carr, *Patrons of Husbandry on the Pacific Coast,* 159–61; Paul, "The Great California Grain War," 345–46.

25. *Charles E. Greene v. John H. Campbell* (1880), California State Supreme Court, no. 6806, "Transcript on Appeal," 10–12, 14 (quote), California State Archives; Mrs. Amelia Ransome Neville Scrapbooks, San Francisco Society, 1878–80, 56–58 (for many unidentified clippings on Friedlander's life), California Historical Society, San Francisco (hereafter Friedlander clippings); *Pacific Rural Press,* July 18, 1874; Aug. 1, 1874; Aug. 8, 1874; *Sacramento Daily Union,* Oct. 21, 1874; Gilbert, *Illustrated Atlas and History of Yolo County,* 47; Paul, "The Great California Grain War," 346–48.

26. *Sacramento Daily Union,* Oct. 21, 1874; Oct. 22, 1874 (quote); *San Francisco Market Review,* Aug. 27, 1874 (quote); *San Francisco Bulletin,* Oct. 20, 1874; *Pacific Rural Press,* Oct. 17, 1874 (quote); Oct. 24, 1874; *Yolo County Democrat,* July 24, 1874; Aug. 21, 1874; Oct. 16, 1874; Gilbert, *Illustrated Atlas and History of Yolo County,* 47 (quote); Carr, *Patrons of Hus-*

bandry on the Pacific Coast, 202–5 (quote 204); McGowan, History of the Sacramento Valley, 1:270; Paul, "The Great California Grain War," 348–49.

27. Pacific Rural Press, Aug. 29, 1874; Sept. 12, 1874; Sept. 19, 1874; Oct. 31, 1874 (quote); California Farmer, July 22, 1875; Sacramento Daily Union, Oct. 21, 1874; Gilbert, Illustrated Atlas and History of Yolo County, 47; Charles E. Greene v. Daniel Meyer and Jonas Meyer (1877), Yolo County, District Court Case Files, 2nd ser., no. 1352, YCA; Yolo County Democrat, Aug. 7, 1874; Oct. 16, 1874.

28. Greene v. Meyer (district); Charles E. Greene v. Daniel Meyer and J. F. Baker (1877), California State Supreme Court, no. 4879, "Transcript on Appeal," 3–4, 27–46, California State Archives; California Farmer, July 22, 1875; Carr, Patrons of Husbandry on the Pacific Coast, 204; Gilbert, Illustrated Atlas and History of Yolo County, 47.

29. Greene v. Meyer (state), "Transcript on Appeal," 1–3; George W. Pierce, Agreement with Capital Savings Bank, May 31, 1870 (see attached extension and scribbled payment notations), box 1, Pierce Family Papers; Pierce, Promissory note to Woodland Bank, box 1, Pierce Family Papers; Harriet E. Mowe v. George W. Pierce (1875), Yolo County, District Court Case Files, 2nd ser., no. 1251, YCA; Pierce journal, Oct. 27, 1874; Dec. 14, 1874; Dec. 29; 1874; Dec. 30, 1874; Gilbert, Illustrated Atlas and History of Yolo County, 47 (quote).

30. Greene v. Meyer (state), "Transcript on Appeal," 4–16 (quote 14); "Brief of Respondent," 1–14 (quote at 10); "Petition for Rehearing," 1–34; California Farmer, July 22, 1875; Gilbert, Illustrated Atlas and History of Yolo County, 47; McGowan, History of the Sacramento Valley, 1:270; Pacific Rural Press, Jan. 10, 1880. Greene himself, in a separate case involving 310 sacks of wheat that had not been loaded on the Pride of Port, found himself mired in additional litigation through September 1880; see Greene v. Campbell. See also, e.g., William Hayes v. John H. Campbell (1880), California State Supreme Court, no 6807, California State Archives; and J. H. Dodge v. Daniel Meyer (1882), California State Supreme Court, no. 7241, California State Archives.

31. Friedlander clippings; Gilbert, Illustrated Atlas and History of Yolo County, 47 (quotes), 76; Sacramento Daily Union, Oct. 22, 1874 (quote); "Friedlander's Annual Grain Circular," June 30, 1878, in Transactions of the California State Agricultural Society during the year 1878 (Sacramento: State Printer, 1879), 143; Daily Alta California, July 3, 1877; Sacramento Daily Record–Union, July 9, 1878; Yolo Weekly Mail, July 20, 1876; Mar. 15, 1877; Yolo County Democrat, Nov. 23, 1876 (quote); Pacific Rural Press, Sept. 23, 1876; Davisville Enterprise, Jan. 19, 1900.

32. Pierce journal, Jan. 16, 1877; Oct. 19, 1877; May 1, 1877; Sept. 2, 1880; Dixon Tribune, Mar. 10, 1877; Aug. 18, 1877; May 4, 1878; Yolo County Democrat, Jan. 11, 1877; Yolo Weekly Mail, Mar. 15, 1877.

33. Friedlander clippings; Dixon Tribune, Jan. 1, 1876; Rothstein, California Wheat Kings, 5 (quote); Paul W. Gates, "Public Land Disposal in California," in Land and Law in California: Essays on Land Policy (Ames: Iowa State Univ. Press, 1991), 262–66; Gerald D. Nash, "Henry George Reexamined: William S. Chapman's Views on Land Speculation in Nineteenth-Century California," Agricultural History 33 (July 1959): 133–37; Charles W. Clough and William B. Secrest Jr., Fresno County—The Pioneer Years: From the Beginning to 1900 (Fresno: Panorama West Books, 1984), 118.

34. Friedlander clippings; Shumate, "Isaac Friedlander, Wheat Merchant"; Rothstein, *California Wheat Kings*, 5–6.

35. Friedlander clippings; "Friedlander's Annual Grain Circular," 143–44, 147; Pierce journal, 1877 (notes on drought in back); *Yolo Weekly Mail*, Jan. 4, 1877; Mar. 8, 1877; *Yolo County Democrat*, Apr. 12, 1877; *Dixon Tribune*, Apr. 7, 1877; July 9, 1878; July 28, 1877; Aug. 17, 1878; Aug. 24, 1878; *California Farmer*, June 21, 1877; *Sacramento Daily Record–Union*, Apr. 5, 1877; Rothstein, *California Wheat Kings*, 6; Rothstein, "A British Firm on the American West Coast, 398–99; Kenneth Aubrey Smith, "California: The Wheat Decades" (Ph.D. diss., University of Southern California, 1969), 137; Magliari, "California Populism," 131–32.

36. Friedlander clippings; Rothstein, *California Wheat Kings*, 6; Shumate, "Isaac Friedlander, Wheat Merchant"; *Dixon Tribune*, Aug. 24, 1878 (quote).

37. *San Francisco Post*, quoted at length in the *Dixon Tribune*, Aug. 24, 1878.

38. *Dresbach v. His Competitors* (county); *William Dresbach v. His Creditors* (1881), California State Supreme Court, no. 8048, "Transcript on Appeal," 4–25, California State Archives; Yolo County, "Deeds," Book J, 157; Book N, 354; Book Q, 284; Book V, 295, YCA; Yolo County, "Leases," Book B, 52, YCA (Dresbach and his "croppers" did not record most of their leases with the county); *William Dresbach v. F. W. Houx and S. N. Mering* (1874), Yolo County, District Court Case Files, 2nd ser., no. 903, YCA; *William Dresbach v. D. A. Hudson* (1876), Yolo County, District Court Case Files, 2nd ser., no. 1318, YCA; *R. P. Davidson v. William Dresbach* (1878), Yolo County, District Court Case Files, 2nd ser., no. 1365, YCA; *Pacific Rural Press*, June 28, 1873; June 17, 1876; *Weekly Solano Republican*, July 18, 1872; *Dixon Tribune*, Nov. 21, 1874; Jan. 23, 1875; Mar. 6, 1875; *Yolo Weekly Mail*, Jan. 6, 1876; Joann Leach Larkey, *Davisville '68: The History and Heritage of the City of Davis, Yolo County, California* (Davis: Davis Historical and Landmarks Commission, 1969), 61; Larkey, *Winters: A Heritage of Horticulture, a Harmony of Purpose* (Woodland: Yolo County Historical Society, 1991), 23–28.

39. *Pacific Rural Press*, June 28, 1873; Jan. 30, 1875; May 6, 1876; Oct. 25, 1946; *Dixon Tribune*, Mar. 27, 1875 (quote); *Yolo Weekly Mail*, July 3, 1874; *San Francisco Call*, Oct. 14, 1883; Charles Davis McComish and Rebecca T. Lambert, *History of Colusa and Glenn Counties, California* (Los Angeles: Historic Record Co., 1918), 441–45; Rothstein, *California Wheat Kings*, 7–8 (quote); McGowan, *History of the Sacramento Valley*, 1:258–60; Richard Steven Street, "Dr. Glenn, 'Wheat King,'" in *Breadbasket of the World*; Street, "The Murder of Hugh Glenn," *Sacramento Magazine* 11 (July 1985): 49–54; Jimmy V. Allen, "Hugh Glenn" (M.A. thesis, Sacramento State College, 1969), 1–15; Smith, "California: The Wheat Decades," 145–48.

40. *Dresbach v. His Creditors* (state), "Transcript on Appeal," 1–27, 54–95 (like the leases in Yolo County, the crop mortgages were generally not recorded with the counties); I. Friedlander to S. Franklin, Apr. 27, 1877, box 2, John T. Doyle Papers, California Historical Society; *Dixon Tribune*, Mar. 27, 1875; Feb. 8, 1879; *Colusa Sun*, Nov. 18, 1876, quoted at length in the *Yolo Weekly Mail*, Nov. 23, 1876 (quote).

41. *Dresbach v. His Creditors* (state), "Transcript on Appeal," 3–15; *Dixon Tribune*, Oct. 13, 1877; Feb. 23, 1878; Feb. 8, 1879; Jan. 10, 1880; *Yolo Weekly Mail*, Apr. 19, 1877; Feb. 7,

1878; *Yolo County Democrat*, Feb. 28, 1878; *Pacific Rural Press*, Mar. 9, 1878; Gilbert, *Illustrated Atlas and History of Yolo County*, 55–56 (quote).

42. *Dresbach v. His Creditors* (state), "Transcript on Appeal," 28–52 (quote at 31), 60–69, 79–95; Yolo County, "Deeds," Book Y, 519 (quote); Book Z, 111, YCA; *Dixon Tribune*, Nov. 9, 1878; Nov. 29, 1879; Dec. 27, 1879; Jan. 10, 1880.

43. *Yolo Weekly Mail*, Jan. 2, 1879; Sept. 9, 1880; Aug. 6, 1887; *Dixon Tribune*, May 22, 1880; Sept. 11, 1880; *San Francisco Chronicle*, June 29, 1901; *Davis Enterprise*, Dec. 3, 1970; *Wheat: An Illustrated Description*, 25–26; Rothstein, *California Wheat Kings*, 12–13.

44. U.S. Census, Population Schedules for Putah Township, Yolo County, and Tremont Township, Solano County, California, 1870 and 1880, microfilm (Washington, DC: National Archives, 1967). In calculating persistence, I did not include the townspeople of Davisville, who came and went much more frequently.

45. *Yolo County Democrat*, Feb. 28, 1878; *Pacific Rural Press*, Mar. 9, 1878; *Dixon Tribune*, Feb. 23, 1878 (quote); Jan. 6, 1899; Gilbert, *Illustrated Atlas and History of Yolo County*, 55–56 (quote).

46. Pierce journal, June 19, 1879; June 23, 1879; July 15, 1879; July 30, 1879; Aug. 8, 1879; (quote from the summary of the season on separate page tucked into the volume); *Yolo Weekly Mail*, June 15, 1878; *Pacific Rural Press*, May 17, 1879; June 21, 1879; June 28, 1879; Aug. 9, 1879 (quote); *Dixon Tribune*, June 15, 1878; July 6, 1878; Oct. 4, 1879; *Sacramento Daily Record–Union*, Aug. 2, 1879; Davis, "California Breadstuffs," 529–30; Smith, "California: The Wheat Decades," 58–60, 235–36.

47. George W. Pierce, Record of Account with Dresbach & Co., Feb. 22, 1877, and Sept. 16, 1878; Record of Account with Eppinger & Co., Dec. 31, 1879; Receipt from Bullard and Pearce, Jan. 1, 1880, and Aug. 17, 1881; Sacramento Savings Bank to Pierce, Aug. 5, 1879; Agreement between George Fiske and Pierce, Apr. 19, 1880—all in box 1, Pierce Family Papers; Pierce journal, May 23, May 31, July 15, Aug. 11, Aug. 12, Aug. 23, Aug. 28, Sept. 10, Sept. 20, Oct. 13, Nov. 5, Nov. 10, Nov. 12, Nov. 20, Dec. 9, Dec. 22, and accounts at end of volume—all in 1879; Sept. 16, 1880. The Sacramento Savings Bank assumed the Pierce loan from the Capital Savings Bank in August 1878; Yolo County, "Mortgages," Book Q, 312, YCA.

48. *Yolo Weekly Mail*, Mar. 15, 1879 (quote); Apr. 8, 1880; May 6, 1880; *Yolo County Democrat*, Jan. 11, 1877 (quote); *Davisville Enterprise*, Jan. 19, 1900; U.S. Census, Population Schedules for Putah Township, Yolo County, and Tremont Township, Solano County, 1870 and 1880; Yolo County, "Deeds," Book L, 3, YCA; Yolo County, "Assessment Rolls," 1870, 1880; Gilbert, *Illustrated Atlas and History of Yolo County*, 76; Larkey, *Davisville '68*, 61.

49. Pierce journal, Apr. 5, 1880 (quote); Sept. 2, 1880; Davis, "California Breadstuffs," 530–31; Davis, "Wheat in California," 61 (quote).

50. Pierce journal, Apr. 19 and 20, 1880.

Chapter Ten. Looking Back

1. *Yolo County Democrat*, July 17, 1874; George W. Pierce, Daily Journals, 1867–90, entry for May 9, 1877, Pierce Family Papers, Department of Special Collections, University of California, Davis (hereafter Pierce journal); J. M. Guinn, *History of the State of California*

and Biographical Record of the Sacramento Valley, California (Chicago: Chapman Publishing Co., 1906), 1698.

2. Yolo County, "Probate Case Files," o.s., no. 323 (1877), Yolo County Archives, Woodland, CA (YCA; quote from the will itself); Yolo County, "Assessment Rolls," 1876, YCA; Yolo County, "Mortgages," Book X, 84, YCA; *R. S. Carey v. W. H. Marden* (1888), Yolo County, Superior Court Case Files no. 769, YCA; *Yolo County Democrat*, July 26, 1877.

3. Surviving death records, though incomplete, indicate that fewer than fifteen residents of Putah Township over the age of fifty died prior to 1877; see Yolo County, "Death Records" and "Probate Case Files," o.s., YCA. See also, *Yolo Weekly Mail*, Aug. 21, 1866, for the editor's extended comment on the subject.

4. Pierce journal, May 9, 1877.

5. Ibid., Feb. 5 and 6, 1877 (quotes); Aug. 17, 1879 (quote); Oct. 31, 1879 (quote); Nov. 1, 1879; Dec. 10, 1879; July 8, 1880; Feb. 21, 1884; June 28, 1884; *Mail of Woodland*, Oct. 27, 1908 (quote).

6. George W. Pierce Jr., "Schoolboy diary, 1866," box 4, Pierce Family Papers; Guinn, *History of the State of California*, 555; Tom Gregory, *History of Yolo County* (Los Angeles: Historic Record Co., 1913), 230; *Davis Enterprise*, Mar. 14, 1930; Joann Leach Larkey, *Davisville '68: The History and Heritage of the City of Davis, Yolo County, California* (Davis: Davis Historical and Landmarks Commission, 1969), 201; Jon Gjerde, *The Minds of the West: Ethnocultural Evolution in the Rural Middle West, 1830–1917* (Chapel Hill: Univ. of North Carolina Press, 1997), chap. 7 (quote at 198).

7. Pierce journal, Oct. 23, 1877; Nov. 17, 1877; Dec. 23, 1877; May 30, 1881; June 9, 1882 (quote; the 1875 diary is missing from the collection); June 9, 1884; Gregory, *History of Yolo County*, 230; *Davis Enterprise*, Mar. 14, 1930.

8. Pierce journal, Oct. 28 and 29, 1879 (quotes); Nov. 28, 1879; Dec. 23, 1879.

9. Ibid., Sept. 29, 1874; Sept. 29, 1881; Gjerde, *The Minds of the West*, 198–99.

10. Pierce journal, Apr. 19 and 20, 1880; Feb. 16, 1882; Apr. 19, 1883; Apr. 20, 1884; July 8, 1886.

11. Ibid., July 21, 1885; Apr. 15, 1886; Apr. 19, 1889.

12. Ibid., July 8, 1884; Jan. 20, 1885; July 8, 1885.

13. *Yolo Weekly Mail*, Jan. 23, 1879; Feb. 20, 1879; Mar. 20, 1879; Frank T. Gilbert, *The Illustrated Atlas and History of Yolo County* (San Francisco: De Pue & Co., 1879); Michael P. Conzen, "Maps for the Masses: Alfred T. Andreas and the Midwestern County Atlas Trade," in *Chicago Mapmakers: Essays on the Rise of the City's Map Trade*, ed. Michael P. Conzen (Chicago: Chicago Historical Society, 1984), 50. Although the *Illustrated Atlas and History of Yolo County* has a publishing date of 1879, it did not appear in print until August 1880; *Yolo Weekly Mail*, Aug. 29, 1880.

14. *Yolo Weekly Mail*, Jan. 23, 1879; Mar. 20, 1879 (quote); July 10, 1879 (quotes); Aug. 5, 1880; *Moore and De Pue's Illustrated History of San Mateo County, California, 1878* (San Francisco: G. T. Brown & Co., 1878); Yolo County, "Board of Supervisors Minutes," Book E, Oct. 14, 1879, YCA; Conzen, "Maps for the Masses," 50.

15. *Yolo Weekly Mail*, Mar. 20, 1879; Apr. 3, 1879; May 29, 1879; Gilbert, *Illustrated Atlas and History of Yolo County*, 82–105; Michael P. Conzen, "The County Landownership Map in America: Its Commercial Development and Social Transformation, 1814–1939,"

Imago Mundi 36 (1984): 17–23; Conzen, "Landownership Maps and County Atlases," *Agricultural History* 58 (Spring 1984): 118–22; Conzen, "The All-American County Atlas: Styles of Commercial Landownership Mapping and American Culture," in *Images of the World: The Atlas through History*, ed. John A. Wolter and Ronald E. Grim (Washington, DC: Library of Congress, 1997), 331, 348–50; Steven Hoelscher, "Mapping the Past: Historical Atlases and the Mingling of History and Geography," *Public Historian* 23 (Winter 2001): 77; Richard V. Francavilia, "Rediscovering Your County's Historical Atlases," Ohio Association of Historical Societies and Museums *Local History Notebook*, May–June 1991.

16. *Yolo Weekly Mail*, Apr. 3, 1879; May 29, 1879; July 24, 1879; Oct. 9, 1879; Apr. 1, 1880; Apr. 29, 1880; May 6, 1880; Yolo County, "Board of Supervisors Minutes," Book E, Jan. 12, 1880, YCA; Gilbert, *Illustrated Atlas and History of Yolo County*, 26 (quote); Conzen, "Maps for the Masses," 50.

17. *Yolo Weekly Mail*, Mar. 20, 1879; Gilbert, *Illustrated Atlas and History of Yolo County*, 26. On the production of "collective memory" in late-nineteenth-century California, see John Walton, *Storied Land: Community and Memory in Monterey* (Berkeley: Univ. of California Press, 2001).

18. Gilbert, *Illustrated Atlas and History of Yolo County*, plate nos. 25, 26, 33, 39, 48, 50. The total value of Drummond's taxable property fell from $10,135 in 1876 to $6,760 in 1878; Yolo County, "Assessment Rolls," 1876, 1878, YCA. On the accuracy of this genre of lithographs, see Conzen, "Landownership Maps and County Atlases," 120–21; Francavilia, "Rediscovering Your County's Historical Atlases." See also Allison Preston and William Preston, "Pictured Landscapes of the South San Joaquin Valley, California: Lithographs of the 1880s and 1890s," *California History* 83 (2005): 41–58.

19. Gilbert, *Illustrated Atlas and History of Yolo County*, 85, plate no. 39, portrait facing page 85; U.S. Census, Agricultural Schedules for Putah Township, Yolo County, California, 1860, on microfilm in the California Room, California State Library, Sacramento; *Pacific Rural Press*, Sept. 22, 1888; *Dixon Tribune*, June 15, 1889.

20. Gilbert, *Illustrated Atlas and History of Yolo County*, 82–105 (quote 102); *Yolo Weekly Mail*, Aug. 21, 1866; Conzen, "The County Landownership Map in America," 17–23; James C. Malin, "Notes on the Writing of General Histories of Kansas—Part Five: The 'Vanity' Histories," *Kansas Historical Quarterly* 21 (Winter 1955): 616–17; Nadine Ishitani Hata, *The Historic Preservation Movement in California, 1940–1976* (Sacramento: California Department of Parks and Recreation, Office of Historic Preservation, 1992), 1–5; John Mack Faragher, *Sugar Creek: Life on the Illinois Prairie* (New Haven: Yale Univ. Press, 1986), 216–33; Susan Sessions Rugh, *Our Common Country: Family Farming, Culture, and Community in the Nineteenth-Century Midwest* (Bloomington: Indiana Univ. Press, 2001), 178.

21. *Yolo Weekly Mail*, Apr. 1, 1880 (quotes); Aug. 5, 1880; Gilbert, *Illustrated Atlas and History of Yolo County*, 26–27; Gregory, *History of Yolo County*; William O. Russell, ed., *History of Yolo County, California: Its Resources and Its People* (Woodland: n.p., 1940); Joseph A. McGowan, *History of the Sacramento Valley* (New York: Lewis Historical Publishing, 1961); Larkey, *Davisville '68*; not to mention my research as well.

22. *Yolo Weekly Mail*, Apr. 29, 1880 (quote); Gilbert, *Illustrated Atlas and History of Yolo County*, 26, 42–52.

23. Gilbert, *Illustrated Atlas and History of Yolo County*, 40–57.

24. Ibid., 46–47; *Yolo Weekly Mail*, Aug. 5, 1880.

25. Gilbert, *Illustrated Atlas and History of Yolo County*, 91, 98, plate no. 33; *Sacramento Daily Record–Union*, Oct. 19, 1891; Yolo County, "Assessment Rolls," 1880, YCA.

26. Gilbert, *Illustrated Atlas and History of Yolo County*, 40–41, 52.

27. *Dixon Tribune*, Apr. 18, 1885; John S. Hittell, "Mexican Land-Claims in California," *Hutchings' California Magazine* 2 (July 1857–June 1858): 442–48; Hittell, *The Resources of California* (San Francisco: A. Roman & Co., 1863), 453–61; Hubert Howe Bancroft, *California Inter Pocula: A Review of Some Classical Abnormalities* (San Francisco: History Co., 1888), 396–412 (quotes); Bancroft, *History of California, 1848–1859* (San Francisco: History Co., 1888), 529–81; Josiah Royce, *California: From the Conquest in 1846 to the Second Vigilance Committee in San Francisco, A Study in American Character* (Boston: Houghton, Mifflin & Co., 1886), 467, 469, 489–90, 499; *Pacific Rural Press*, Mar. 26, 1881; Gerald D. Nash, "California and Its Historians: An Appraisal of the Histories of the State," *Pacific Historical Review* 50 (Aug. 1981): 387–92; Donald J. Pisani, "Squatter Law in California, 1850–1858," in *Water, Land, and Law in the West: The Limits of Public Policy, 1850–1920* (Lawrence: Univ. Press of Kansas, 1996), 61–63; Leonard Pitt, *The Decline of the Californios: A Social History of the Spanish-Speaking Californians, 1846–1890* (Berkeley: Univ. of California Press, 1966), 88–89; Lawrence J. Jelinek, *Harvest Empire: A History of California Agriculture*, 2nd ed. (San Francisco: Boyd & Fraser, 1982), 25–27.

28. Henry George, *Our Land and Land Policy, National and State* (San Francisco: White & Bauer, 1871); George, *Progress and Poverty* (San Francisco: W. M. Hinton & Co., 1879); *Sacramento Daily Union*, Feb. 15, 1873 (quote); *Yolo Weekly Democrat*, Feb. 25, 1871 (quote); Aug. 12, 1871; *Yolo Weekly Mail*, Feb. 23, 1871; Nov. 16, 1871; Oct. 2, 1879; *Dixon Tribune*, Aug. 6, 1887; *Sacramento Daily Record–Union*, Oct. 19, 1891 (quote); Gerald D. Nash, "Henry George Reexamined: William S. Chapman's View on Land Speculation in Nineteenth-Century California," *Agricultural History* 33 (July 1959): 133–37; Donald J. Pisani, "Land Monopoly in Nineteenth-Century California," in *Water, Land, and Law in the West*, 86–87; McGowan, *History of the Sacramento Valley*, 1:256–67.

29. *Yolo County Democrat*, Oct. 12, 1872; Nov. 13, 1874 (quotes); Yolo County, "Deeds," Book D, 796, YCA; Yolo County, "Board of Supervisors Minutes," Book C, Oct. 25, 1869; Book D, July 6, 1871; Oct. 23, 1871; Apr. 14, 1871, YCA; C. P. Sprague and H. W. Atwell, *The Western Shore Gazetteer and Commercial Directory, for the State of California . . . Yolo County* (San Francisco: Press of Bancroft, 1870), 236; *W. W. Brown v. C. E. Greene* (1884), California State Supreme Court, no. 9443, "Transcript on Appeal," 118, 133, California State Archives, Sacramento.

30. Yolo County, "Probate Case Files," o.s., no. 295 (1874), YCA; Yolo County, "Deeds," Book A, 232, 261, YCA; *Brown v. Greene*, "Transcript on Appeal," 82–85, 87–89, 115–20.

31. *Brown v. Greene*, "Transcript on Appeal," 105–6, 115–20; Yolo County, "Deeds," Book U, 528; *Dixon Tribune*, July 28, 1877; Matthew Fountain, "The Mare Island Case," *Solano Historian* (Dec. 1997): 7–10; *Vacaville Reporter*, Feb. 2, 2003.

32. *Brown v. Greene*, "Transcript on Appeal," 2–14, 45–79 (quote at 74), 248 (quote); U.S. Land Department, Office of the U.S. Surveyor-General of the State of California, "In the Matter of the Rancho Los Putos . . . 'Applicant's Brief'" (San Francisco: Spaulding, Barto & Co, 1879), 1–87, in Docket no. 53, Los Putos Rancho, United States District Court

(California), "Documents pertaining to the adjudication of private land claims in California, ca. 1852–1892," Bancroft Library, University of California, Berkeley (hereafter Los Putos docket); Mike Madison, *A Sense of Order: The Rural Landscape of Lower Putah Creek* (Winters, CA: Yolo Press, 2002), 21.

33. *Brown v. Greene*, "Transcript on Appeal," 2–6 (quotes), 79, 115–46, 154–55; Yolo County, "Deeds," Book A, 228 (quote), 329, YCA.

34. *Brown v. Greene*, "Transcript on Appeal," 100–105, 146–58; *William W. Brown v. Charles E. Greene* (1878), U.S. Circuit Court, Ninth Circuit, District of California, no. 1856, National Archives, Pacific Sierra Region, San Bruno, California (contains the papers from the Twelfth District Court); Yolo County, "Deeds," Book W, 339 (quote), 434, 453, YCA.

35. *Brown v. Greene* (federal); *Dixon Tribune*, July 28, 1877; Sept. 15, 1877.

36. *Brown v. Greene* (federal); *R. S. Carey v. William W. Brown* (1878), U.S. Circuit Court, Ninth Circuit, District of California, no. 1857, National Archives, Pacific Sierra Region; *R. S. Carey v. William W. Brown* (1880), California State Supreme Court, no. 7080, "Transcript on Appeal," 6–7 (quote), California State Archives; *Dixon Tribune*, Aug. 25, 1877 (quote); Sept. 5, 1877; Oct. 26, 1878.

37. U.S. Land Department, Office of the U.S. Surveyor-General of the State of California, "In the Matter of the Rancho Los Putos . . . ,"Applicant's Brief," 87–89 (quotes); U.S. Department of the Interior, "Petition for Rehearing Rancho Los Putos," May 31, 1880 (quote), Los Putos docket; *Brown v. Greene* (state), "Transcript on Appeal," 111–13; *Yolo Weekly Mail*, July 25, 1878; *Dixon Tribune*, Oct. 26, 1878.

38. California's new constitution of 1879 had abolished the state's county and district courts and replaced them with the new superior courts.

39. *Brown v. Greene* (state), "Transcript on Appeal," passim.

40. Ibid., 115–46 (quotes at 130, 132, 133, 140).

41. Ibid., 198–216, 256–60 (quotes at 204, 209, 211); *Sacramento Daily Record–Union*, Oct. 6, 1881.

42. *Brown v. Greene* (state), "Transcript on Appeal," 32–62 (quotes at 33 and 58), 112, and "Opinion," May 8, 1884; Pierce journal, June 7, 1884.

43. U.S. Department of the Interior, "In the Matter of Mexican Land Grant Rancho Los Putos," 1885–1887, Los Putos docket; R. P. Hammond Jr. to Commissioner, General Land Office, Mar. 19, 1887, Los Putos docket (quotes). Mhoon's appeal to the U.S. Supreme Court is filed in *Carey v. Brown* (state).

44. Yolo County, "Death Records," YCA; *Dixon Tribune*, May 26, 1884 (quote); Oct. 10, 1885 (quote); Feb. 27, 1886 (quotes); July 17, 1886; Apr. 30, 1887; May 21, 1887; Jan. 12, 1889; Jan. 19, 1889; Apr. 27, 1889; Mar. 1, 1890.

Chapter Eleven. Gold—Wheat—Fruit

1. George W. Pierce, Daily Journals, 1867–90, entries for May 9 and 25, 1885, Jan. 14, 1886, and Apr. 15, 1887, Pierce Family Papers, Department of Special Collections, University of California Library, Davis (hereafter Pierce journal); *Dixon Tribune*, May 30, 1885 (quote); June 27, 1885; July 4, 1885; Jan. 30, 1886; Feb. 20, 1886 (quote); Apr. 23, 1887 (quote); Mar. 17, 1888.

2. *Dixon Tribune,* Aug. 9, 1884; Jan. 3, 1885 (quote); Nov. 14, 1891 (quote); *Yolo Weekly Mail,* Nov. 12, 1887; *Pacific Rural Press,* Jan. 21, 1885; *Wheat: An Illustrated Description of California's Leading Industry* (San Francisco: Commercial Publication Co., 1887), 35, Bancroft Library, University of California, Berkeley (author unknown); Horace Davis, "Wheat in California: A Retrospect and Prospect," *Overland Monthly* 32 (July 1898): 60–63; Davis, "California Breadstuffs," *Journal of Political Economy* 2 (Sept. 1894): 530–32; Alfred Bannister, "California and Her Wheat Culture," *Overland Monthly* 12 (July–Aug. 1888): 67; Margery Saunders Hellmann, "Port Costa, California Wheat Center," *California Geographer* 4 (1963): 63–65.

3. *Dixon Tribune,* Nov. 14, 1891 (quote); *Yolo Weekly Mail,* Jan. 1, 1892 (quote).

4. *Yolo Weekly Mail,* Jan. 1, 1892 (quote).

5. *Dixon Tribune,* Jan. 3, 1885 (quote); Morton Rothstein, "The American West and Foreign Markets, 1850–1900," in *The Frontier in American Development: Essays in Honor of Paul Wallace Gates,* ed. David M. Ellis (Ithaca: Cornell Univ. Press, 1969), 381–406.

6. *Yolo Weekly Mail,* May 8, 1879; Michael J. Gillis and Michael F. Magliari, *John Bidwell and California: The Life and Writings of a Pioneer, 1841–1900* (Spokane, WA: Arthur H. Clark Co., 2003), 199–202. Dolly Varden was a female character in Charles Dickens' novel *Barnaby Rudge* whose name was later applied to a popular style of women's clothing. Democrats and Republicans used the name as a reference to members of the Independent party.

7. *Yolo Weekly Mail,* May 8, 1879; June 19, 1879 (quotes); *Dixon Tribune,* Mar. 20, 1880; Jan. 3, 1885; Yolo County, "Assessment Rolls, 1878, 1880, 1885, Yolo County Archives, Woodland, CA (hereafter YCA); Yolo County, "Board of Supervisors Minutes," Book E, Apr.14, 1879; May 12, 1879, YCA; Pierce journal, May 7, 1879; Carl Plehn, "The Taxation of Mortgages in California, 1849–1899," *Yale Review* 8 (May 1899): 31–67; Bannister, "California and Her Wheat Culture," 65; Richard B. Rice, William A. Bullough, and Richard J. Orsi, *The Elusive Eden: A New History of California* (New York: McGraw-Hill, 1996), 298–99 (quote at 298). The new tax was not, properly speaking, a mortgage tax. Farmers now paid property tax on the difference between the total assessed value of their real estate minus the value of the mortgage; lenders paid property tax on the amount of assessed value covered by the mortgage. Lawmakers intended to restructure the property tax to provide some relief to indebted farmers.

8. Pierce journal, 1884 (estimated from accounts at end of volume); May 5 and 7, 1888; George W. Pierce Jr., Daily Journals, 1888–1930, 1889 (estimated from accounts at end of volume), Pierce Family Papers, Department of Special Collections, University of California Library, Davis (hereafter Pierce Jr. journal); *Dixon Tribune,* Jan. 3, 1885; May 12, 1888; *Yolo Weekly* Mail, Nov. 12, 1887; *Wheat: An Illustrated Description,* 22 (quote); Bannister, "California and Her Wheat Culture," 66; Joseph Hutchinson, "California Cereals," *Overland Monthly* 2 (July–Aug. 1883): 145; Kenneth A. Smith, "California: The Wheat Decades" (Ph.D. diss., University of Southern California, 1969), 112–24, 174–79.

9. Pierce journal, May 25, 1888; July 25, 1888; Davis, "Wheat in California," 63 (quote); Bannister, "California and Her Wheat Culture," 66 (quote); *Pacific Rural Press,* Aug. 16, 1884; July 21, 1888; Feb. 20, 1837; Joseph A. McGowan, *History of the Sacramento Valley* (New York: Lewis Historical Publishing, 1961), 1:250; Smith, "California: The Wheat Decades," 112–24, 174–79; F. Hal Higgins, "John M. Horner and the Development of the

Combined Harvester," *Agricultural History* 32 (Jan. 1958): 14–24; John T. Schlebecker, "The Combine Made in Stockton," *Pacific Historian* 10 (Autumn 1966): 15–20.

10. Pierce journal, Feb. 1, 1886; Feb. 9, 1886; Mar. 1, 1886; Mar. 4, 1886; July 5, 1886; May 5, 1888; May 7, 1888; June 8, 1888; July 25, 1888; Mar. 19, 1889; May 10, 1889; Pierce Jr. journal, Mar. 19, 1889; Apr. 10, 1889; Apr. 25, 1889; May 4, 1889; May 10, 1889; May 13, 1889; June 8, 1889; Dec. 18, 1889; Feb. 28, 1890; Mar. 20, 1890; Apr. 10, 1890; Apr. 17, 1890; Apr. 26, 1890; May 12, 1890; Aug. 21, 1890; Sept. 19; 1890; *Dixon Tribune*, Apr. 3, 1886; June 2, 1886; May 28, 1887; May 12, 1888; June 2, 1888; June 23, 1888; July 7, 1888; Apr. 13, 1889; May 18, 1889 (quote); June 15, 1889; June 7, 1890; *Pacific Rural Press*, Feb. 20, 1937; Smith, "California: The Wheat Decades," 174.

11. Pierce's accounts with several of these merchants are in box 1, Pierce Family Papers. See also, *Dixon Tribune*, Apr. 12, 1884; May 30, 1885; Mar. 5, 1887 (quote); Nov. 15, 1887; June 30, 1888; July 21, 1888; July 13, 1889; July 18, 1891; Frank T. Gilbert, *The Illustrated Atlas and History of Yolo County* (San Francisco: De Pue & Co., 1879), 83; Joann Leach Larkey, *Davisville '68: The History and Heritage of the City of Davis, Yolo County, California* (Davis: Davis Historical and Landmarks Commission, 1969), 169.

12. *Pacific Rural Press*, Sept. 20, 1884; *Wheat: An Illustrated Description*, 17–21; Hellmann, "Port Costa, California Wheat Center," 65; Margery Holburne Saunders, "California Wheat, 1867–1910: Influences of Transportation on the Export Trade and the Location of Producing Areas" (M.A. thesis, University of California, Berkeley, 1960), 76–89; Doug Urbick, "Port Costa," *Pacific Historian* 22 (1978): 361–62; Morton Rothstein, *The California Wheat Kings* (Davis: University of California, Davis, 1987), 9–10.

13. *Wheat: An Illustrated Description*, 17 (quote); *Pacific Rural Press*, June 16, 1883; Saunders, "California Wheat," 77.

14. *Wheat: An Illustrated Description*, 17–21; Edwin S. Holmes Jr., "Wheat Ports of the Pacific Coast," in U.S. Department of Agriculture *Yearbook, 1901* (Washington, DC: Government Printing Office, 1901), 569; Hellmann, "Port Costa, California Wheat Center," 63–65; Saunders, "California Wheat," 76–89; Urbick, "Port Costa," 361–70; J. D. Keith, "The Story of Crockett," unpublished MS (1930), 12–16, Bancroft Library.

15. *Pacific Rural Press*, Jan. 29, 1881 (quote); Oct. 13, 1888 (quote); *Yolo Weekly Mail*, Sept. 9, 1880 (quote); *Dixon Tribune*, May 12, 1883 (quote); July 7, 1883; Bannister, "California and Her Wheat Culture," 69 (quote).

16. Davis, "California Breadstuffs," 517, 534 (quotes); Smith, "California: The Wheat Decades," 202–4, 284–85; *Dixon Tribune*, Sept. 7, 1894.

17. *San Francisco Chronicle*, Aug. 4, 1887; Aug. 5, 1887 (quote); Aug. 28, 1887; June 29, 1901; *Dixon Tribune*, Sept. 3, 1887; Davis, "Wheat in California," 63; Rothstein, *California Wheat Kings*, 12–13; Hugh Myron Hoyt Jr., "The Wheat Industry in California, 1850–1910" (M.A. thesis, Sacramento State College, 1953), 117–20; Smith, "California: The Wheat Decades," 142–44; Michael Frederick Magliari, "California Populism, a Case Study: The Farmers' Alliance and People's Party in San Luis Obispo County, 1885–1903" (Ph.D. diss., University of California, Davis, 1992), 134–36.

18. *San Francisco Chronicle*, Aug. 5, 1887 (quote); *Dixon Tribune*, Mar. 5, 1887 (quotes); Sept. 3, 1887; Sept. 17, 1887; Feb. 25, 1888; *Pacific Rural Press*, Sept. 24, 1887; Pierce journal, May 10, 1887; July 4, 1887; July 7, 1887; Pierce Jr. journal, Sept. 30, 1895; *In the Matter*

of W. G. Bullard, An Insolvent Debtor (1887), Yolo County, Superior Court Case Files, no. 533, YCA; *In the Matter of B. F. Ligget, An Insolvent Debtor* (1895), Yolo County, Superior Court Case Files, no. 1938, YCA; *In the Matter of J. W. Gafford, An Insolvent Debtor* (1888), Yolo County, Superior Court Case Files, no. 1025, YCA; *Isaac Quinn v. William Dresbach* (1889), Yolo County, Superior Court Case Files, no. 1044, YCA; *Henry Stelling v. Peter Brannigan* (1894), Yolo County, Superior Court Case Files, no. 1749, YCA; *In the Matter of Frederick Knuppe, An Insolvent Debtor* (1894), Yolo County, Superior Court Case Files, no. 1767, YCA; Yolo County, "Mortgages," Book 31, 61, 87, 211, 279, 302, 424, YCA.

19. *Sacramento Daily Record–Union*, Jan. 27, 1894; Oct. 24, 1894; *Pacific Rural Press*, June 16, 1882; Aug. 22, 1895 (quote); *San Francisco Morning Call*, May 28, 1893; Davis, "Wheat in California," 63; N. P. Chipman, "Wheat and Fruit Growing in California," in *Official Report of the Eighteenth Fruit Growers' Convention of the State of California*, Nov. 20–23, 1894 (Sacramento: State Printing Office, 1895), 125 (quote); Smith, "California: The Wheat Decades," 218–24; Saunders, "California Wheat," 108–11, Rodman W. Paul, *The Far West and the Great Plains in Transition, 1859–1900* (New York: Harper & Row, 1988), 220–51. The general price deflation of the late nineteenth century accounted for much of the fall in wheat prices, but the rise in international competition was the cause of the greater fall relative to falling production and shipping costs.

20. Pierce Jr. journal, Nov. 6, 1893 (quote); Yolo County, "Assessment Lists," 1890, 1900, YCA.

21. *Dixon Tribune*, Feb. 22, 1890; *Davisville Enterprise*, Mar. 9, 1900 (quote); George Robertson, "Statistical Summary of the Production and Resources of California" (1850–1910), in California State Board of Agriculture, *Fifty-eighth Annual Report for 1911* (Sacramento: State Printing Office, 1912), 119–21, 400–401; Paul Rhode, "Learning, Capital Accumulation, and the Transformation of California Agriculture," *Journal of Economic History* 55 (Dec. 1995): 772.

22. *Sacramento Daily Union*, July 14, 1868; Jan. 9, 1869; Jan. 28, 1870; May 15, 1872; *California Farmer*, May 23, 1872; Yolo County, "Deeds," Book 1, 155; Book Y, 355, YCA; *William E. Brown v. California Silk Culture Company* (1875), Yolo County, District Court Case Files, 2nd ser., no. 1166, YCA; C. P. Sprague and H. W. Atwell, *The Western Shore Gazetteer and Commercial Directory, for the State of California . . . Yolo County* (San Francisco: Press of Bancroft, 1870), 106–9 (quote at 107); Gilbert, *Illustrated Atlas and History of Yolo County*, 44–45 (quote); Allan R. Ottley, "Some Notes on Early Yolo County and Davisville," speech given at the annual meeting of the Friends of the Davis Public Library, Feb. 5, 1960, 8, Department of Special Collections, University of California Library, Davis; Larkey, *Davisville '68*, 61.

23. Yolo County, "Mortgages," Book N, 66, YCA; Yolo County, "Deeds," Book T, 389; Book U, 59; Book 27, 615, YCA; Yolo County, "Assessment Lists," 1875, YCA; Yolo County, "Articles of Incorporation," Oak Shade Fruit Company, June 7, 1876, YCA; *Dixon Tribune*, Jan. 22, 1887 (quote); *Sacramento Bee*, Dec. 24, 1880; Gilbert, *Illustrated Atlas and History of Yolo County*, 45; Larkey, *Davisville '68*, 61.

24. *Sacramento Daily Union*, Jan. 20, 1869 (quote); *Dixon Tribune*, Dec. 11, 1875; Nov. 2, 1878; Jan. 25, 1879; Sept. 6, 1879; Oct. 25, 1879; Jan. 10, 1885 (quote); Dec. 25, 1886; Feb. 18, 1888; Mar. 3, 1888; *Yolo Weekly Mail*, Nov. 22, 1877 (quote) Jan. 29, 1880 June 10, 1880;

July 12, 1890; *Sacramento Bee*, Dec. 24, 1880; *Pacific Rural Press*, Jan. 28, 1882; Feb. 25, 1888; "Sub-Irrigation as Practiced on Mr. Briggs' Vineyard and Orchard Near Davisville," Miscellaneous and Working Papers, box 6, William Hammond Hall Papers, California State Archives, Sacramento; *R. W. Biggerstaff v. G. G. Briggs* (1884), California State Supreme Court, no. 9421, "Transcript on Appeal," 1–2, 18–19, California State Archives; "Abstract of Title . . . Briggs Orchard and Vineyard," D-344, box 2, City of Davis Collection, University of California Library, Davis; McGowan, *History of the Sacramento Valley*, 1:275; Larkey, *Davisville '68*, 61.

25. *Dixon Tribune*, Aug. 2, 1884; Sept. 5, 1885 (quote); Oct. 31, 1885; Sept. 4, 1886; Pierce journal, Nov. 17, 1880; *A Memorial and Biographical History of Northern California* (Chicago: Lewis Publishing Co., 1891), 496–97; J. M. Guinn, *History of the State of California and Biographical Record of the Sacramento Valley, California* (Chicago: Chapman Publishing Co., 1906), 385–87; Tom Gregory, *History of Yolo County* (Los Angeles: Historic Record Co., 1913), 664–65; *Davis Enterprise*, June 3, 1971; Larkey, *Davisville '68*, 185.

26. Pierce journal, July 4, 1879; Jan. 27, 1883; May 13, 1884; *Dixon Tribune*, Oct. 31, 1885; Sept. 4, 1886; Mar. 24, 1888; Apr. 25, 1888; May 12, 1888; May 11, 1889; July 19, 1890; July 4, 1891; Sept. 23, 1892 (quote); *Yolo Weekly Mail*, Dec. 25, 1886; Oct. 15, 1887; *Davis Enterprise*, May 27, 1971; June 10, 1971; Nov. 25, 1971; Larkey, *Davisville '68*, 185.

27. Pierce journal, Jan. 21, 1884 (quote); Feb. 26, 1884; Feb. 27, 1884; Feb. 29, 1884; Mar. 3, 1884; Mar. 13, 1884 (quote); Mar. 18, 1884; Aug. 15, 1888; Pierce Jr. journal, Sept. 18, 1888; Oct. 7, 1888, notes at end of volume; Yolo County, "Deeds," Book 44, 18, 28, YCA; *Dixon Tribune*, Aug. 25, 1888 (quote); Sept. 1, 1888; *Mail of Woodland*, Oct. 2, 1918; Larkey, *Davisville '68*, 200–201.

28. *Dixon Tribune*, Sept. 19, 1885; Dec. 19, 1885 (quote); Feb. 19, 1887; Sept. 17, 1887; Feb. 25, 1888; Feb. 16, 1889 (quotes); Feb. 23, 1889; June 15, 1889; June 22, 1889; Sept. 28, 1889 (quote); Feb. 22, 1890; July 19, 1890; *Yolo Weekly Mail*, May 21, 1887; Oct. 1, 1887; *Pacific Rural Press*, July 3, 1886; Yolo County, "Assessment Lists," 1890, YCA.

29. *Dixon Tribune*, Jan. 7, 1888 (quote); Aug. 30, 1890; *Yolo Weekly Mail*, Nov. 13, 1886; Dec. 18, 1886 (quotes); Dec. 25, 1886 (quote); July 16, 1887; July 12, 1890; Pierce journal, Dec. 13–17, 1886; David Vaught, *Cultivating California: Growers, Specialty Crops, and Labor, 1875–1920* (Baltimore: Johns Hopkins Univ. Press, 1999), 11–53.

30. Yolo County, "Articles of Incorporation," Putah Creek Water Company, Dec. 23, 1882, YCA; Yolo County, "Miscellaneous Records," Book A, 257, YCA; "Minutes of Meetings," "Account Book," and "By-Laws," Putah Creek Water Company, 1882–83, box 3, Pierce Family Papers; *Davisville Signal*, Apr. 27, 1883 (reprinted in *Davisville Enterprise*, May 1, 1902); *Dixon Tribune*, Apr. 28, 1883 (quote); *Davisville Enterprise*, Mar. 13, 1902; *Davis Enterprise*, June 3, 1971.

31. W. H. Fraser, "Rainfall and Wheat in California," *Overland Monthly* 33 (Jan. 1899): 523; Joshua Hendy Machine Works to George W. Pierce Jr., Feb. 20, 1884, box 4, Pierce Family Papers; *Dixon Tribune*, Apr. 12, 1884; June 28, 1884; Oct. 31, 1885; Jan. 16, 1886; Oct. 30, 1886; Jan. 15, 1887; Oct. 15, 1887; May 26, 1888; Feb. 23, 1889; Mar. 16, 1889; July 13, 1889; Aug. 3, 1889 (quote); Aug. 10, 1889; Sept. 7, 1889; Sept. 28, 1889; Oct. 5, 1889; *E. W. Brown v Sinclair Manufacturing Co.* (1894), Yolo County, Superior Court Case Files, no. 1780, YCA.

32. *Yolo Weekly Mail,* July 23, 1887; *Dixon Tribune,* June 25, 1887; July 2, 1887; Sept. 10, 1887; Nov. 26, 1887; Donald J. Pisani, *From the Family Farm to Agribusiness: The Irrigation Crusade in California and the West, 1850–1931* (Berkeley: Univ. of California Press, 1984), 130–31, 250–56.

33. *R. S. Carey v. Webster Treat* (1889), Yolo County, Superior Court Case Files, no. 963 (quotes), YCA; *R. S. Carey v. Webster Treat* (1889), Yolo County, "Register of Actions," YCA; *William W. Montgomery v. Webster Treat* (1889), Yolo County, Superior Court Case Files, no. 966, YCA; Yolo County, "Miscellaneous Records," Book A, 317, YCA; *Dixon Tribune,* May 28, 1888; Aug. 4, 1888; Aug. 11, 1888; Feb. 16, 1889; Mar. 16, 1889; July 27, 1889; Oct. 26, 1889; Pisani, *From the Family Farm to Agribusiness,* 245–47; Rice, Bullough, and Orsi, *The Elusive Eden,* 288.

34. *Biggerstaff v. Briggs,* "Transcript on Appeal," 23–32 (quote at 26); *Ah Hai v. Emma H. Briggs* (1895), Yolo County, Superior Court Case Files, no. 1832, YCA; *Dixon Tribune,* Apr. 5, 1879.

35. George W. Pierce, "Monthly Time Book for Employers and Workmen," 1868–82, no pagination, box 3, Pierce Family Papers; *Dixon Tribune,* June 27, 1885; Sept. 5, 1885 (quote); Sept. 25, 1886 (quote); May 5, 1888; July 7, 1888 (quote); Vaught, *Cultivating California,* 69.

36. *Yolo Weekly Mail,* Oct. 30, 1886; Oct. 1, 1887; Oct. 15, 1887 (quote); *Dixon Tribune,* Jan. 30, 1886 (quotes); Feb. 20, 1886; Oct. 16, 1886; Jan. 22, 1887; Jan. 12, 1889 (quote); Sept. 14, 1889; Oct. 12, 1889 (quote); Nov. 8, 1890; Nov. 14, 1891; McGowan, *History of the Sacramento Valley,* 1:327–29; Vaught, *Cultivating California,* 54–94; Vaught, "'An Orchardist's Point of View': Harvest Labor Relations on a California Almond Ranch, 1892–1921," *Agricultural History* 69 (Fall 1995): 563–91.

37. *Dixon Tribune,* May 16, 1885; Sept. 5, 1885; Oct. 3, 1885; Sept. 4, 1886 (quote); Nov. 8, 1890; Jan. 3, 1891 (quotes); Apr. 11, 1891; Jan. 23, 1892; July 28, 1893; Sept. 7, 1894; Mar. 22, 1895; June 7, 1895; Rhode, "Learning, Capital Accumulation, and the Transformation of California Agriculture," 780–81, 786; Vaught, *Cultivating California,* 11, 23–24, 33–35, 38.

38. *Bank of Woodland v. Andrew McClory* (1893), Yolo County, Superior Court Case Files, no. 1530, YCA; *E. W. Brown v. Sinclair Manufacturing Company* (1894), Yolo County, Superior Court Case Files, no. 1780, YCA; *Union Building and Loan Association v. Emma H. Briggs* (1895), Yolo County, Superior Court Case Files, no. 1599, YCA; *Bank of Woodland v. M. H. Briggs and J. R. Briggs* (1895), Yolo County, Superior Court Case Files, no. 1613, YCA; *West Valley Lumber Company v. Emma H. Briggs* (1895), Yolo County, Superior Court Case Files, no. 1822, YCA; *K. B. Soule v. Emma H. Briggs* (1895), Yolo County, Superior Court Case Files, no. 1847, YCA; *A. C. Hillman v. G. W. Griffin* (1895), Yolo County, Superior Court Case Files, no. 1871, YCA; *F. S. Redfield v. Emma H. Briggs* (1900), Yolo County, Superior Court Case Files, no. 2403, YCA; *Susan Maria Soule v. Emma H. Briggs* (1900), Yolo County, Superior Court Case Files, no. 2611, YCA; *Hai v. Briggs;* Yolo County, "Mortgages," Book 31, 325; Book 32, 76; Book 37, 626. YCA; *Dixon Tribune,* Mar. 5, 1892; July 14, 1893; July 28, 1893; Dec. 21, 1894; Dec. 28, 1894; Mar. 1, 1895; Mar. 22, 1895; June 7, 1895; June 28, 1895; Nov. 29, 1895; Dec. 27, 1895 (quotes); Feb. 19, 1897 (quote).

39. *Dixon Tribune,* Feb. 14, 1891; Mar. 7, 1891; Mar. 14, 1891; Mar. 28, 1891 (quote); June 22, 1894; Nov. 16, 1894; Nov. 15, 1895; Nov. 29, 1895; July 22, 1898; *Davisville Enterprise,*

Sept. 21, 1898; Yolo County, "Board of Supervisors Minutes," Book H, Nov. 10, 1896, YCA; Richard J. Orsi, "*The Octopus* Reconsidered: The Southern Pacific and Agricultural Modernization in California, 1865–1915," *California Historical Quarterly* 54 (Fall 1975): 196–220; Michael Magliari, "Populism, Steamboats, and the Octopus: Transportation Rates and Monopoly in California's Wheat Regions, 1890–1896," *Pacific Historical Review* 58 (Nov. 1989): 449–50; Donald Edgar Walters, "Populism in California, 1889–1900" (Ph.D. diss., University of California, Berkeley, 1952), 75; Lawrence Goodwyn, *The Populist Moment: A Short History of the Agrarian Revolt in America* (Oxford: Oxford Univ. Press, 1978), xxiv (quote); James Turner, "Understanding the Populists," *Journal of American History* 67 (Sept. 1980): 354–73; Vaught, *Cultivating California,* 48. Small wheat growers in isolated rural regions made up the bulk of California's relatively weak Populist movement; Magliari, "California Populism."

40. *Dixon Tribune,* Nov. 29, 1895.

41. Ibid., Oct. 3, 1885; Feb. 19, 1887; Mar. 19, 1887; Mar. 26, 1887; Nov. 26, 1887; Dec. 3, 1887; Feb. 4, 1888; Feb. 25, 1888; Apr. 28, 1888; May 26, 1888; June 7, 1890; Dec. 13, 1890; Oct. 10, 1891; Sept. 9, 1892; Nov. 25, 1892; Mar. 16, 1894; *Woodland Daily Democrat,* Jan. 24, 1893; *Pacific Rural Press,* Oct. 17, 1885; Nov. 12, 1887 (quote); Aug. 27, 1892; Jan. 21, 1893; *California Fruit Grower,* Oct. 11, 1890; Webster Treat, "Almond Culture," in "Proceedings of the Thirteenth State Fruit Growers' Convention," Mar. 11–14, 1890, in State Board of Horticulture of the State of California, *Annual Report for 1890* (Sacramento: State Printing Office, 1890), 72–75; Treat, "Profit in Almonds," *California: A Journal of Rural Industry* 1 (May 1890): 16; State Board of Horticulture of the State of California, *Annual Report for 1892* (Sacramento: State Printing Office, 1892), 317–18; Pierce Jr. journal, Jan. 27, 1892; Feb. 22, 1892; July 29, 1892; Dec. 27, 1892.

42. *Pacific Rural Press,* Jan. 21, 1893 (quote); Treat, "Almond Culture," 72–73; Treat, "Profit in Almonds," 16; Pierce Jr. journal, Sept. 9, 1896; *California Fruit Grower,* Oct.13, 1900 (quote); George W. Pierce, "The Almond Growers Exchange," in "Proceedings of the Forty-ninth California State Fruit Growers' Convention," Nov. 15–17, 1917, in California State Commission of Horticulture, *Monthly Bulletin* 6 (May 1917): 180 (quote); Vaught, *Cultivating California,* 38, 92–94, 116–18.

43. Pierce, "The Almond Growers Exchange," 181 (quote); Davisville Almond Growers' Association, Constitution and Minute Book, entries for Jan. 23 and 30, 1897, Board of Directors File, Predecessor and Concurrent Organizations, box 1, California Almond Growers' Exchange Records, Sacramento Archives and Museum Center, Sacramento (hereafter DAGA minutes); *California Fruit Grower,* Mar. 6, 1897; *Dixon Tribune,* Feb. 19, 1897; May 14, 1897; Aug. 6, 1897; Dec. 10, 1897; Elizabeth Margaret Riley, "The History of the Almond Industry in California, 1850–1934" (M.A. thesis, University of California, Berkeley, 1948), 28–29.

44. DAGA minutes, May 8, 1897 (quote); July 3, 1897; May 15, 1899; July 8, 1899; July 15, 1899; July 4, 1900; July 20, 1901; Aug. 9, 1902; *Davisville Enterprise,* May 19, 1899; July 14, 1899; Dec. 8, 1899; July 31, 1902; Aug. 14, 1902; Dec. 25, 1902; *Dixon Tribune,* Sept. 17, 1897; *Pacific Rural Press,* July 22, 1899; July 7, 1900; Aug. 11, 1900 (quote); Riley, "History of the Almond Industry in California," 29–34.

45. Pierce, "The Almond Growers' Exchange," 181 (quote); Caroline M. Olney, "Orchards, Vineyards, and Farms of Yolo County," *Overland Monthly* 40 (May 1902): 181–85 (quotes at 182); *Dixon Tribune*, July 20, 1900; H. E. Erdman and Grace H. Larsen, "The Development of Agricultural Cooperatives in California," California Agricultural Experiment Station, Giannini Foundation of Agricultural Economics, Feb. 20, 1964, filed under Henry E. Erdman, Miscellaneous Publications, Giannini Foundation of Agricultural Economics Library, University of California, Berkeley.

46. George W. Pierce to "Sirs," Dec. 12, 1901, box 4 (quote); George W. Pierce to "The Farmers of California," ca. Dec. 1901, box 4 (quote); Resolution (signed) organizing the Grain Growers' Association, Sept. 25, 1901, box 1, Pierce Family Papers; *San Francisco Bulletin*, Jan. 22, 1902 (quotes); Jan. 23, 1902; Jan. 24, 1902; *Davisville Enterprise*, Sept. 26, 1901; Jan. 23, 1902; Jan. 30, 1902; Mar. 20, 1902; *Dixon Tribune*, July 23, 1897; *Sacramento Daily Record–Union*, Aug. 2, 1902; *Pacific Rural Press*, Feb. 8, 1902.

47. George W. Pierce Jr., Account Book, 1897–1910, 119, 121, 141–48, box 2, Pierce Family Papers; Saunders, "California Wheat," 112–13; Rhode, "Learning, Capital Accumulation, and the Transformation of California Agriculture," 775–77.

48. DAGA minutes, Nov. 30, 1901; Aug. 3, 1903; May 5, 1905, May 27, 1905; "Manager's Report," Apr. 10, 1914; May 10, 1917, Board of Directors Files, Minutes, box 1, California Almond Growers' Exchange Records; Pierce Jr. journal, June 20, 1903; Sept. 14, 1907; George W. Pierce, "The Status of the Almond Industry of the Pacific Coast," in *Proceedings of the Thirty-fourth Biennial Meeting of the American Pomological Society*, Sept. 1–3, 1915 (n.p.: The Society, 1916), 80, 82 (quote); *Davisville Enterprise*, Aug. 5, 1903; Aug. 20, 1904 (quote); *Davis Enterprise*, May 14, 1910; June 17, 1911; Sept. 12, 1914; *Pacific Rural Press*, Sept. 16, 1905; July 3, 1909; *California Fruit Grower*, May 14, 1910 (quote); R. H. Taylor, "Marketing California Almonds," *University of California Journal of Agriculture* 4 (Oct. 1916): 44; H. E. Erdman, "The Development and Significance of California Cooperatives, 1900–1915," *Agricultural History* 32 (July 1958): 182–83; Carl August Scholl, "An Economic Study of the California Almond Growers' Exchange" (Ph.D. diss., University of California, Berkeley, 1927), 116, 259; Vaught, *Cultivating California*, 110–13.

49. George W. Pierce, "The Almond," address delivered at the Forty-fourth California State Fruit Growers' Convention, June 5, 1914, in California State Commission of Horticulture, *Monthly Bulletin* 3 (Nov. 1914): 456 (quote); Pierce, "The Status of the Almond Industry of the Pacific Coast," 75 (quote); R. Douglas Hurt, *American Agriculture: A Brief History* (Ames: Iowa State Univ. Press, 1994), 221.

Chapter Twelve. Legacies

1. Kevin Starr, *Americans and the California Dream, 1850–1915* (New York: Oxford Univ. Press, 1973), 63–68 (Mulford quote at 63); Joyce Oldham Appleby, "The Vexed Story of American Capitalism Told by American Historians," *Journal of the Early Republic* 21 (Spring 2001): 1–18; David Vaught, "After the Gold Rush: Replicating the Rural Midwest in the Sacramento Valley," *Western Historical Quarterly* 34 (Winter 2003): 447–67.

2. *Dixon Tribune*, Dec. 5, 1885; Nov. 5, 1887; Oct. 26, 1889; Dec. 14, 1889; Dec. 21, 1889;

Feb. 1, 1890; Mar. 1, 1890; Jan. 11, 1895 (quotes); Jan. 31, 1896; *Davis Enterprise,* Jan. 9, 1920; Feb. 12, 1970; W. H. Fraser, "Rainfall and Wheat in California," *Overland Monthly* 33 (Jan. 1899): 523.

3. *Dixon Tribune,* Dec. 5, 1885; Nov. 5, 1887; Feb. 1, 1890; Jan. 19, 1894; Feb. 2, 1894; Feb. 23, 1894; Jan. 11, 1895; Feb. 1, 1895; Sept. 13, 1895; Oct. 4, 1895; Oct. 11, 1895; Dec. 20, 1895; Jan. 24, 1896; Jan. 31, 1896; May 15, 1896; Jan. 8, 1897; *Yolo Semi-Weekly Mail,* Jan. 14, 1896 (quote).

4. *S. H. Cowell v. Lydia T. Armstrong* (1930), California State Supreme Court, no. 4341 (SAC), "Transcript on Appeal," 73–75, 298 (quote), 312, California State Archives, Sacramento; *Dixon Tribune,* Apr. 21, 1888; Nov. 3, 1888; Feb. 8, 1892; Dec. 30, 1892; Jan. 11, 1895; Feb. 1, 1895; Feb. 8, 1895 (quotes); July 5, 1895 (quote); Oct. 11, 1895.

5. *Henry Cowell v. R. S. Carey* (1895), Yolo County, Superior Court Case Files, no. 1531, Yolo County Archives, Woodland, CA (hereafter YCA); Yolo County, "Mortgages," Book 28, 327, YCA; Yolo County, "Deeds," Book 54, 383, YCA; *S. H. Cowell v. Lydia T. Armstrong,* "Transcript on Appeal," 142, 312; *Sacramento Daily Record–Union,* June 19, 1895; *Dixon Tribune,* Nov. 2, 1889; June 28, 1895.

6. *Sacramento Daily Record–Union,* June 19, 1895 (quote); *Dixon Tribune,* June 28, 1895 (quote); July 19, 1895 (quote).

7. George W. Pierce Jr., Daily Journals, 1888–1930, entries for Feb. 24, 1890; Mar. 8, 1890; Feb. 11, 1895; Feb. 16, 1895, Pierce Family Papers, Department of Special Collections, University of California Library, Davis (hereafter Pierce Jr. journal) *Dixon Tribune,* Mar. 1, 1890; Mar. 15, 1890; *Yolo Weekly Mail,* Mar. 1, 1890; *Mail of Woodland,* Oct. 27, 1908; Oct. 2, 1918; *Davis Enterprise,* Mar. 14, 1930; J. M. Guinn, *History of the State of California and Biographical Record of the Sacramento Valley, California* (Chicago: Chapman Publishing Co., 1906), 555 (quote).

8. *Davisville Enterprise,* Sept. 21, 1898; Oct. 8, 1898 (quote); Mar. 9, 1900; *Dixon Tribune,* Jan. 31, 1896; Oct. 16, 1896 (quote); *Davis Enterprise,* Mar. 14, 1930; Guinn, *History of the State of California,* 555–56.

9. Pierce Jr. journal, Sept. 12–15, 1892 (quote, Sept. 12); Jan. 14, 1911; Aug. 25, 1911; Feb. 12, 1912; *Dixon Tribune,* June 23, 1893; *Davisville Enterprise,* Mar. 13, 1902 (quote); Jan. 23, 1904; Jan. 30, 1904; Apr. 23, 1904; *Davis Enterprise,* Nov. 14, 1908 (quote); Dec. 26, 1908; Nov. 5, 1910; July 29, 1911; Aug. 5, 1911; Mar. 14, 1930; Guinn, *History of the State of California,* 555–56; Joann Leach Larkey, *Davisville '68: The History and Heritage of the City of Davis, Yolo County, California* (Davis: Davis Historical and Landmarks Commission, 1969), 38–39, 201.

10. George W. Pierce to State Farm Commission, Apr. 27, 1905, box 4, Pierce Family Papers; *Sacramento Daily Record–Union,* Mar. 27, 1905; *Davisville Enterprise,* Apr. 1, 1905; May 20, 1905; May 27, 1905; Dec. 2, 1905; Apr. 7, 1906; Pierce Jr. journal, Mar. 24–28, 1905; May 17, 1905; May 20, 1905; Aug. 25, 1905; Nov. 24, 1905; Feb. 16, 1906; Feb. 17, 1906; July 21, 1906; July 28, 1906; Aug. 11, 1906; Larkey, *Davisville '68,* 91–94; Ann F. Scheuring, *Abundant Harvest: The History of the University of California, Davis* (Davis: UC Davis History Project, 2001), 15–20.

11. *Davis Enterprise,* Oct. 17, 1908 (quote).

12. *Mail of Woodland,* Apr. 14, 1906 (quote); *Dixon Tribune,* May 15, 1886 (quote); Aug.

20, 1887; Apr. 14, 1888; Nov. 23, 1894; Nov. 15, 1895; Yolo County, "Board of Supervisors Minutes," Book F, May 3, 1887, YCA; Larkey, *Davisville '68*, 193–94.

13. *Dixon Tribune*, Jan. 22, 1887 (quote); June 15, 1889 (quote); Oct. 26, 1889 (quote).

14. Ibid., June 9, 1887; May 5, 1888; Apr. 27, 1889; June 8, 1894; *Yolo Weekly Mail*, July 16, 1887; Jan. 24, 1896; California State Fair and Exposition, *Premium List, Annual Fair of the California State Agricultural Society, 1863–1921*, Bancroft Library, University of California, Berkeley; *Sam N. Chantry v. William W. Montgomery* (1885), Yolo County, Superior Court Case Files, no. 463, YCA; Joann L. Larkey and Shipley Walters, *Yolo County: Land of Changing Patterns* (Northridge, CA: Windsor Publications, 1987), 37–38; Joseph A. McGowan, *History of the Sacramento Valley* (New York: Lewis Historical Publishing, 1961), 1:164–65, 263–74, 279.

15. *Davis Enterprise*, Apr. 14, 1906 (quote); Sept. 12, 1914 (quote); William O. Russell, ed., *History of Yolo County, California: Its Resources and Its People* (Woodland: n.p., 1940), 131–38; Larkey, *Davisville '68*, 23, 192, 194.

16. *Davis Enterprise*, Oct. 8, 1970 (all quotes).

Epilogue. Remnants

1. Yolo County, "Board of Supervisors—Roads and Highways," Book C, 284, Yolo County Archives, Woodland, CA (hereafter YCA); Yolo County, "Miscellaneous Records," Book A, 172, YCA; Joann Leach Larkey, *Davisville '68: The History and Heritage of the City of Davis, Yolo County, California* (Davis: Davis Historical and Landmarks Commission, 1969), 201; Joann Leach Larkey, *Winters: A Heritage of Horticulture, a Harmony of Purpose* (Woodland: Yolo County Historical Society, 1991), 20, 32; Joann L. Larkey and Shipley Walters, *Yolo County: Land of Changing Patterns* (Northridge, CA: Windsor Publications, 1897), 23.

2. Larkey and Walters, *Yolo County*, 23.

3. Margery Holburne Saunders, "California Wheat, 1867–1910: Influences of Transportation on the Export Trade and the Location of Producing Areas" (M.A. thesis, University of California, Berkeley, 1960), 116.

4. Robert Kelley, *Battling the Inland Sea: American Political Culture, Public Policy, and the Sacramento Valley, 1850–1986* (Berkeley: Univ. of California Press, 1989), 297–316.

5. *Davis Enterprise*, Feb. 12, 1970; Sue Coggins, *Puta-To to North Fork of Putah Creek* (n.p., 1970), 4, Department of Special Collections, University of California Library, Davis; Michael Marchetti and Peter B. Moyle, "The Case of Putah Creek . . . Conflicting Values Complicate Stream Protection," *California Agriculture* 49 (Nov.–Dec. 1995): 75–76; Larkey, *Winters*, 80–81, 84–86; Larkey, *Davisville '68*, 146.

After the Gold Rush is grounded in a wide range of primary sources and an expansive, if uneven, body of secondary literature. This short essay highlights the evidence and interpretations that were most crucial to the making of this narrative. For additional bibliographical information and complete citations, readers should consult the chapter notes.

More than three decades ago, W. N. Davis Jr., of the California State Archives, published a lengthy, two-part article in the *California Historical Quarterly* with the rather unassuming title "Research Uses of County Court Records, 1850–1879, and Incidental Intimate Glimpses of California Life and Society," vol. 52 (Fall/Winter 1973): 241–66, 338–65. "County Court records," he began, "are a rich and virtually untapped resource for historical research." They are "valuable sources for social, economic, biographical, genealogical, and legal history" that often "reveal the people candidly and factually in their vernacular, colloquial, and earthy dress" (241, 244). While genealogists have flocked to county archives in subsequent years to exploit these records, historians have by and large steered clear of them. These small and often isolated facilities are not nearly as glamorous as the Bancroft or the Huntington libraries and are often much more difficult to access, but they hold materials every bit as rich—not only civil, criminal, and probate court case files but also land records (deeds, mortgages, leases), assessment rolls, church, school, and marriage records, obituaries, directories, board of supervisors minutes, newspapers, photographs, and a whole host of other documents that offer researchers much more than "incidental intimate glimpses of life and society," Davis's modest subtitle notwithstanding. Indeed, county records (primarily Yolo, but also Sacramento, Solano, and Placer) are the foundation of this book.

State and federal court records proved invaluable as well. Researchers will find themselves rooting for county cases to be appealed to the California Supreme Court, where the documents—full transcripts of testimony, in particular—are often even richer (and more legible). *Pierce v. Robinson* (1859), *Beatty v. Clark* (1861), *Dresbach v. His Creditors* (1881), and *Brown v. Greene* (1884), for example, yield an almost inexhaustible amount of material on the economic and social development of Putah Creek/Davisville, much of which exists nowhere else. The case files of the California Land Commission, located at the Bancroft Library, University of California, Berkeley, not only document the specific legal issues concerning the 813 Mexican and Spanish land grants but also provide insights into each grant's complicated history, the particular region's environment, and the personalities of the litigants and their lawyers. The land case "dockets" kept by the U.S. General Land Office, also at the Bancroft Library on microfilm, contain appeals, affidavits, correspondence, and other materials pertaining to controversies that arose after the federal government had issued patents. The Rancho Los Putos docket, for example, proved just as valuable for this study as the land case itself.

Other archival sources supplement the case files and dockets. At the National Archives, the Records of the Department of the Interior (RG 48) and the Department of Justice (RG 60) contain extensive correspondence between federal and state officials on California land grants, while the Records of the General Land Office (RG 49) have township tract books, land-entry files, maps, and more correspondence. Federal, state, and county surveyor records (field notes, maps, and still more correspondence) can be found, respectively, at the U.S. Bureau of Land Management, California State Office, and the California State Archives, both in Sacramento, and the Yolo County Surveyor's Office, Woodland. Indispensable for the study of Rancho Laguna de Santos Callé is the thick folder of documents in box 816, U.S. Land Office, Sacramento, Records, California State Library, Sacramento. Attorney John Curry's recollections, "History of the Spanish Grants of Solano County" (1907), Law Library, University of California, Berkeley, are illuminating as well.

Individual experiences such as Curry's are the driving force of this narrative. In this regard, no one source proved more revealing than the Pierce Family Papers, Department of Special Collections, University of California Library, Davis. Account books, employee time logs, promissory and bank notes, receipts, correspondence, photographs, and especially the daily journals of George and George Jr. constitute, in my judgment, the single most valuable archival collection for California rural history. A close second might be the Jerome C. Davis Papers, California State Library, especially the five large ranch ledgers that document in minute detail the dramatic rise and fall of this key figure's prize-winning stock farm. Schedules from both the population and agricultural censuses for Putah and Tremont townships, assessment rolls and lists, and several county histories and maps from both California and a number of midwestern states (cited in the notes) allowed me to track individual removal patterns, persistence rates, squatter-landowner relations, and the development of the region's farm lands. Though Putah Creek/Davisville did not sustain its own newspaper for more than a few months at a time until 1898, residents could read about themselves, their neighbors, and their community in the *Sacramento Daily Union* and *Daily Alta California* (especially before the Civil War), *Knights Landing News, Yolo County Democrat, Yolo Weekly Mail, Solano Press, Weekly Solano Republican,* and *Dixon Tribune.* The *California Farmer* and *Pacific Rural Press* are also very informative.

Putah Creek itself plays a central role in this historical drama. Descriptions of its volatile behavior can be gleaned from newspapers, Land Commission records, and the Pierce daily journals, among numerous other sources. Various reclamation projects, including the several abortive attempts to construct the Putah canal, are documented in Swampland District No. 18 records, Yolo County Archives; state supreme court case *Cowell v. Armstrong* (1930); and "Why Putah Creek Changed Its Course," an undated clipping (ca. 1968) from the *Dixon Tribune,* on file at the Dixon Public Library. On early irrigation efforts and the controversies that ensued, see especially: "Sub-Irrigation as Practiced on Mr. Briggs' Vineyard and Orchard Near Davisville," William Hammond Hall Papers, California State Archives;

various records of the Putah Creek Water Company in the Yolo County Archives and the Pierce Family Papers; and state supreme court cases *Carey v. Treat* (1889) and *Cowell v. Carey* (1895). On weather in the Sacramento Valley, see W. H. Fraser, "Rainfall and Wheat in California," *Overland Monthly* 33 (Jan. 1899): 521–33.

Wheat is another main "character." Here again, the Pierce Papers provide unparalleled, on-the-ground insights into production, labor, technology, and marketing. Other useful information can be found in several contemporary articles, including three written by Horace Davis (one at the beginning of the wheat boom in 1868 and two at the end, in 1894 and 1898), Joseph Hutchinson's essay in the *Overland Monthly* in 1883, Alfred Bannister's in 1888, and the long, detailed report distributed by the San Francisco Produce Exchange in 1887 entitled "Wheat: An Illustrated Description of California's Leading Industry," copy in the Bancroft Library. The rise and fall of the "Grain King" and his Davisville protégé are documented in William Dresbach's bankruptcy trial and several other court cases; his store ledgers for the late 1860s and crop mortgages for the 1870s, both at the Yolo County Archives; and numerous newspaper clippings on Isaac Friedlander in the Mrs. Amelia Ransome Neville Scrapbooks at the California Historical Society in San Francisco. On the Grange, see especially *Greene v. Meyer* (1877), Frank T. Gilbert, *The Illustrated Atlas and History of Yolo County* (San Francisco: De Pue & Co., 1879), Ezra S. Carr, *The Patrons of Husbandry on the Pacific Coast* (San Francisco: A. L. Bancroft & Co., 1875), and the many newspapers already noted.

The next generation and the shift from wheat to fruit are documented in rich detail in the daily journals and ranch records of George W. Pierce Jr. Also valuable are the incorporation papers of the California Silk Company and the Oak Shade Fruit Company; the many bankruptcy trials in Yolo County during the 1890s, especially that of Davisville merchant B. F. Ligget; and the many lawsuits filed against Emma Briggs that same decade—all at the Yolo County Archives. The *Dixon Tribune* and the *Davisville Enterprise* proved particularly useful for this period. On almonds, see the several essays published by Webster Treat, of the Oak Shade Fruit Company, and Pierce Jr. cited in the notes; the Constitution and Minute Book of the Davisville Almond Growers' Association and other marketing records at the Sacramento Archives and Museum Center; numerous articles in the *California Fruit Grower;* and Caroline M. Olney, "Orchards, Vineyards, and Farms in Yolo County," *Overland Monthly* 40 (May 1902): 171–94. For a contemporary fruit enthusiast's observations, see N. P. Chipman's series of "Wheat v. Fruit" articles published in the *Pacific Rural Press* (among other places) in the late 1880s and early 1890s.

Despite the prominence of the wheat crop, there is only a fragmented history of wheat farming in California in the secondary literature. Historians have examined in considerable detail the development of the wheat belt on the western edge of the Midwest, from the Dakotas down to Kansas and into northern Texas, particularly in the 1880s. But for much of that decade, no state produced more wheat than California. Nearly all the state's famous valleys—San Joaquin, Napa, Sonoma, Santa Clara (now "Silicon"), Salinas, and San Fernando, as well as Sacramento—were planted in wall-to-wall wheat at the time. Moreover, California began establishing its reputation as the "granary of the world" as early as the late 1850s, a full generation before wheat gained prominence on the Great Plains. Yet the two best books covering California's wheat era—Michael J. Gillis and Michael F. Magliari, *John*

Bidwell and California: The Life and Writings of a Pioneer, 1841–1900 (Spokane, Wash.: Arthur H. Clark Co., 2003), and Donald J. Pisani, *From the Family Farm to Agribusiness: The Irrigation Crusade in California and the West, 1850–1891* (Berkeley: Univ. of California Press, 1984)—address the subject in considerable depth, but only as a secondary issue.

Part of my research strategy has been to draw from the traditional themes of agricultural history—production, distribution, technology, and government policy. In this regard, there is no shortage of secondary sources. The three classic articles published by Rodman Paul (two in 1958, the other in 1973) and the four less well known but equally valuable by Morton Rothstein (1963, 1969, 1975, 1987), all cited in the notes many times, provide an abundance of sources, information, and interpretations. Rothstein's short study, *The California Wheat Kings* (Davis: Univ. of California, Davis, 1987); Gilbert C. Fite, *The Farmers' Frontier, 1865–1900* (New York: Holt, Rinehart & Winston, 1966), chap. 9; Kenneth A. Smith, "California: The Wheat Decades" (Ph.D. diss., University of Southern California, 1969); Hugh M. Hoyt Jr., "The Wheat Industry in California, 1850–1910" (M.A. thesis, Sacramento State College, 1953); and Margery Holburne Saunders, "California Wheat, 1867–1910: Influences of Transportation on the Export Trade and the Location of Producing Areas" (M.A. thesis, University of California, Berkeley, 1960), should be consulted as well. Rarely cited but very informative is Forest G. Hill, "Place of the Grain Trade in California Economic Development, 1870–1900," Social Science Research Council, Western Committee on Regional Economic Analysis, Proceedings, 1954, manuscript copy in the Bancroft Library. On labor, see Richard Steven Street, "Tattered Shirts and Ragged Pants: Accommodation, Protest, and the Coarse Culture of California Wheat Harvesters and Threshers, 1866–1900," *Pacific Historical Review* 67 (Nov. 1998): 573–608.

Land policy in particular has drawn considerable scholarly attention. No one has understood California's highly complex land system better than Paul Wallace Gates, whose many penetrating essays on the subject have been collected in one volume, *Land and Law in California: Essays on Land Policy* (Ames: Iowa State Univ. Press, 1991). Gates's *California Ranchos and Farms, 1846–1862* (Madison: State Historical Society of Wisconsin, 1967) is also very useful. Donald J. Pisani has deepened our understanding of several of Gates's main themes in two pathbreaking articles of his own: "Squatter Law in California, 1850–1858" and "Land Monopoly in Nineteenth-Century California," both in his *Water, Land, and Law in the West: The Limits of Public Policy, 1850–1920* (Lawrence: Univ. Press of Kansas, 1996), 57–85, 86–101. Also valuable are Christian G. Fritz, *Federal Justice in California: The Court of Ogden Hoffman, 1851–1891* (Lincoln: Univ. of Nebraska Press, 1991), and Richard H. Peterson, "The Failure to Reclaim: California State Swamp Land Policy and the Sacramento Valley, 1850–1866," *Southern California Quarterly* 56 (Spring 1974): 45–60.

My primary objective, however, has been to write a "new" rural history—that is, a book that examines wheat farmers in their social and cultural contexts. Much of what we know about farm life in California during this period comes from contemporary critics, most notably land reformer Henry George (of "single tax" fame) and muckraking novelist Frank Norris (*The Octopus*). That approach has focused scholarly attention on the largest farmers, especially Hugh Glenn, whose empire of 66,000 acres in the northern Sacramento Valley seduced, among many others, William Dresbach. Many things about nineteenth-century California seem larger than life, but Glenn was hardly representative of the state's thousands of much smaller wheat farmers, who have all but disappeared from view in the literature. The most insightful treatment, though it is concerned primarily with the tail end of the state's wheat era, is Michael F. Magliari, "California Populism, a Case Study: The Farmers' Alliance and People's Party in San Luis Obispo County, 1885–1903" (Ph.D. diss., University of California Davis, 1992). And Gerald L. Prescott analyzes small grain farmers in "Farm Gentry vs. the Grangers: Conflict in Rural America," *California Historical Quarterly* 56 (Winter 1977/78): 328–45. Other social histories of rural California in the latter half of the nineteenth century, however, remain few and far between. For that matter, even Glenn has received minimal attention, the only full-length treatment being Jimmy V. Allen, "Hugh Glenn" (M.A. thesis, Sacramento State College, 1970).

For useful models, therefore, I had to look elsewhere—the Midwest, primarily, where the new rural history has flourished. Six books in particular have greatly influenced my thinking: John Mack Faragher, *Sugar Creek: Life on the Illinois Prairie* (New Haven: Yale Univ. Press, 1986), Jon Gjerde, *The Minds of the West: Ethnocultural Evolution in the Rural Middle West, 1830–1917* (Chapel Hill: Univ. of North Carolina Press, 1997), Susan E. Gray, *The Yankee West: Community Life on the Michigan Frontier* (Chapel Hill: Univ. of North Carolina Press, 1996), R. Douglas Hurt, *Agriculture and Slavery in Missouri's Little Dixie* (Columbia: Univ. of Missouri Press, 1992), Hurt, *The Ohio Frontier: Crucible of the Old Northwest, 1720–1830* (Bloomington: Indiana Univ. Press, 1996), and Susan Sessions Rugh, *Our Common Country: Family Farming, Culture, and Community in the Nineteenth-Century Midwest* (Bloomington: Indiana Univ. Press, 2001). Since most of the historical actors in *After the Gold Rush* migrated from the Midwest, these books also provide invaluable source material. For an explanation of why rural social history has flourished in the Midwest but not in California, see my "State of the Art—Rural History, or Why Is There No Rural History of California?" *Agricultural History* 74 (Fall 2000): 759–74.

We know much more, therefore, about farmers before they migrated to California than afterward. To put it another way, farmers who have been so closely studied in the Midwest are, essentially, the same people whom we know so little about in California. This historiographical disjuncture is all the more jarring when we factor in how much we know about farmers' experiences in the interim—the few months, on average, that they spent mining for gold in the Sierra Nevada foothills. Of the literally hundreds of books and articles written on the gold rush, three studies in particular have expanded our knowledge of miner culture well beyond the prevailing get-rich-quick emphasis: H. W. Brands, *The Age of Gold: The California Gold Rush and the New American Dream* (New York: Doubleday, 2002), Malcolm J. Rohrbough, *Days of Gold: The California Gold Rush and the American Nation* (Berkeley: Univ. of California Press, 1997), and Kevin Starr, *Americans and the California Dream, 1850–1915* (New York: Oxford Univ. Press, 1973), chap. 2. Though the conventional wisdom does not reflect it, wheat culture in subsequent decades was equally nuanced and complex.

There was more to agriculture along Putah Creek than wheat, of course. On cattle ranching, particularly during the 1850s and 1860s, the essential study is Hazel Adele Pulling, "A History of California's Range-Cattle Industry, 1770–1912" (Ph.D. diss., University of Southern California, 1944). Three sources that supplement Pulling nicely are Terry G. Jordan, *North American Cattle-Ranching Frontiers: Origins, Diffusion, and Differentiation* (Albuquerque: Univ. of New Mexico Press, 1993), Ray August, "Cowboys v. Ranchers: The Origins of Western American Law," *Southwestern Historical Quarterly* 96 (Apr. 1993): 457–88, and Gates, *California Ranchos and Farms*, chap. 2. On the transition to specialty crops, Paul Rhode, "Learning, Capital Accumulation, and the Transformation of California Agriculture," *Journal of Economic History* 55 (Dec. 1995): 773–800, provides the most sophisticated analysis. See also the appropriate chapters in Rodman Paul, *The Far West and the Great Plains in Transition, 1859–1900* (New York: Harper & Row, 1988), and my *Cultivating California: Growers, Specialty Crops, and Labor, 1875–1920* (Baltimore: Johns Hopkins Univ. Press, 1999).

I have also benefited from many fine environmental histories of the Sacramento Valley. Two pioneer studies by Kenneth Thompson—"Riparian Forests of the Sacramento Valley, California," *Annals of the Association of American Geographers* 51 (Sept. 1961): 294–314, and "Historic Flooding of the Sacramento Valley," *Pacific Historical Review* 29 (Sept. 1960): 349–60—are still immensely helpful, as are several chapters in Elna Bakker, *An Island Called California: An Ecological Introduction to Its Natural Communities* (Berkeley: Univ. of California Press, 1971). Jeffrey F. Mount, *California Rivers and Streams: The Conflict between Fluvial Process and Land Use* (Berkeley: Univ. of California Press, 1995) helped me understand Putah Creek's ever-changing behavior. Robert Kelley, *Battling the Inland Sea: American Political Culture, Public Policy, and the Sacramento Valley, 1850–1986* (Berkeley: Univ. of California Press, 1989), was an instant classic on the subject. Stephen Johnson, Gerald Haslam, and Robert Dawson, *The Great Central Valley: California's Heartland* (Berkeley: Univ. of California Press, 1993), document their observations with beautiful photographs, and Mike Madison, *A Sense of Order: The Rural Landscape of Lower Putah Creek* (Winters: Yolo Press, 2002), offers a provocative modern-day perspective.

Finally, local, county, and regional histories, though often discounted, provide valuable biographical, geographical, and community information. No one secondary source proved more beneficial to me than Joann Leach Larkey, *Davisville '68: The History and Heritage of the City of Davis, Yolo County, California* (Davis: Davis Historical and Landmarks Commission, 1969), whose scope of analysis is much broader than the title suggests. Joann L. Larkey and Shipley Walters, *Yolo County: Land of Changing Patterns* (Northridge, CA: Windsor Publications, 1987), Larkey, *Winters: A Heritage of Horticulture, A Harmony of Purpose* (Woodland: Yolo County Historical Society, 1991), Walters, *Knights Landing: The River, the Land, and the People* (Woodland: Yolo County Archives, 1992), Walters, *Woodland, City of Trees: A History* (Woodland: Yolo County Historical Society, 1995), and John Lofland, *Davis: Radical Changes, Deep Constants* (Charleston, S.C.: Arcadia Publishing, 2004) were also quite useful. Wood Young, *Vaca-Peña Los Putos Rancho and the Peña Adobe* (Vallejo: Wheeler Printing and Publishing, 1971), describes the two Solano County land grants in my study in some detail. Joseph A. McGowan, *History of the Sacramento Valley*, 3 vols. (New York: Lewis Historical Publishing Co., 1961) remains the best survey of the region.

References to illustrations are in italics